FROM RUPERT'S LAND TO CANADA

Essays in Honour of
JOHN E. FOSTER

From RUPERT'S LAND *to* CANADA

THEODORE BINNEMA,
GERHARD J. ENS &
R.C. MACLEOD, *editors*

THE UNIVERSITY OF ALBERTA PRESS

Published by

The University of Alberta Press
Ring House 2
Edmonton, Alberta, Canada T6G 2E1

NATIONAL LIBRARY OF CANADA CATALOGUING IN PUBLICATION DATA

Main entry under title:

From Rupert's Land to Canada
Includes bibliographical references.
ISBN 0–88864–363–2

1. Native peoples—Canada, Western—History.* 2. Fur trade—Canada, Western—History.
3. Canada, Western—History. I. Foster, John Elgin. II. Binnema, Theodore, 1963– III. Ens, Gerhard
John, 1954– IV. Macleod, R. C., 1940–.
E78.C2F76 2001   971.2'00497   C2001–910612–2

First edition, third printing, 2010.
Printed and bound in Canada by Blitzprint, Calgary, Alberta.

The University of Alberta Press gratefully acknowledges the support received for its publishing
program from The Canada Council for the Arts. In addition, we also gratefully acknowledge the
financial support of the Government of Canada through the Book Publishing Industry Development
Program for our publishing activities.

Contents

Foreword

LEWIS G. THOMAS

IN SEVENTY-ODD YEARS of association
with the University of Alberta's Department of History, I do not think that
I ever met a student, colleague or friend more determined to pursue the
study of history than John Elgin Foster. After finishing high school, a year at
Royal Roads Military College sharpened that resolve and set him firmly on
a path from which he never diverged. After leaving Royal Roads, John
returned to Alberta and enrolled at the University of Alberta, at a significant
time in the University's and the History Department's development.

In the late 1950s, the Department of History at the University of Alberta
had emerged from the understaffed and underfunded years immediately
following the war. It had become apparent, even to the worst pessimists,
that the feared post-war recession had been indefinitely postponed. The
country at large enjoyed continuing prosperity, while in Alberta, prospects
were considerably enhanced by the on-going development of energy resources.

The University and the Department of History shared in this steady
growth. The Department had maintained an Honours programme through
the immediate post-war years, and now could extend its graduate offerings
to include a doctorate. New staff appointments gave a breadth of teaching
and research expertise to a previously small department. This new staff and
an enhanced graduate programme also made an enrichment of course offerings possible and gave faculty a chance to concentrate their teaching in areas
of their main research interests. I was one beneficiary of this change. A.L.
Burt and M.H. Long both encouraged students and their colleagues to take
an interest in western Canadian history, and Morden Long gave me invalu-
able support in establishing the first undergraduate course offered in the
history of the Canadian West.

John Foster's arrival at the University of Alberta corresponded with these
changes, and he was, as both an undergraduate and graduate student, very
much a part of the evolving History Department. As an undergraduate he
was one of a lively group of students with a serious interest in history. He
was, moreover, one of a select group of those students with a strong interest

in Canadian history and a sense of the possibilities of the Canadian West as an area of academic specialization. After he graduated from the University of Alberta in 1959, he found work as a high school teacher in Edmonton. Through these years he kept in contact with his professors, and when he returned to the university to pursue his own graduate studies, it was with a desire to contribute to the reappraisal of the history of the Canadian West.

I was pleased to act as supervisor of his Master's thesis and Ph.D. dissertation. Both studies took advantage of the increased availability of Hudson's Bay Company and British missionary records on western Canada, and built on our shared interest in an often ignored segment of fur trade society. Growing up in southern Alberta, I had had neighbours and friends who traced their family histories back to the fur trade. They did not fit, however, into what was then seen as a Metis identity. They were emphatically Protestant and English-speaking, but they were well aware of their Aboriginal forbearers as well. John Foster took up the study of this group of people whom he termed the "country-born." In doing so, he played a critical role in showing that early western Canadian history was far richer and more complex than most Canadian historians at the time suspected.

Indeed John Foster played an integral part as a student, teacher and researcher in the development of western Canadian history as a field of historical enquiry: not just in Alberta, but also across Canada and in the wider historical community abroad. He was an inspired teacher, who was as effective with high school students as he later was with undergraduate and graduate students. He never needed to be convinced that teaching, research and writing were inseparable parts of the scholarly whole. He was also a singularly rewarding student, who gave as much to his teachers as they ever gave to him.

John Elgin Foster

Western Canadian Historian

THEODORE BINNEMA, GERHARD J. ENS
& R.C. MACLEOD

JOHN ELGIN FOSTER was working on three major projects—a guide to Metis Historical Studies, A History of the Wintering Village at Buffalo Lake, and a general history of the Metis in North America—when he passed away in 1996. These projects promised to bring into print what Jennifer Brown calls the "headnotes"[1] of 20 years of researching and interpreting the Metis in the Western Interior. John continually re-examined his own thinking about the fur trade and the West trying to find new lines of inquiry across disciplinary boundaries, and, most of all, played with ideas. Through his writing, and especially his teaching, he played a major role, as Gerald Friesen has noted, in the re-imagining of Western Canada that took place between the 1960s and 1990s. In particular, John was one of a handful of scholars who reinvigorated the field of fur trade and Native history in Canada. His work on Metis ethnogenesis inspired his students and introduced new perspectives and questions to the field.

From Rupert's Land to Canada, a collection of essays by John Foster's colleagues, students, and friends, is intended to honour his contributions to and influence on Western Canadian History. Given John's dedication to teaching, these essays have also been chosen and organized to make the book useful as a source for undergraduate courses on the Canadian West. This introduction, his essay on ethnogenesis of the Metis, and the bibliography of John's writings will introduce his work to younger students of the Canadian West.

Although John Foster seemed the quintessential Albertan (he disliked leaving the province even for vacations) he was born in London, Ontario on 19 October 1938. His parents moved west when John was 15 years old, joining his maternal grandparents who lived in Calgary. His grandfather was a Baptist minister and his grandmother ran three boarding houses in Calgary. John graduated from high school when he was 16 and moved further west to

꒜ *John Foster in 1995 realizing the joy of Archaeology.* Photo courtesy of Marie Foster.

attend Royal Roads Military College in Victoria with the intention of becoming an engineer. By his second year he realized he had chosen the wrong career and he left Royal Roads by mutual agreement after an incident in which he put his foot through a portrait of Queen Elizabeth.

John returned to Alberta and enrolled in the University of Alberta, completing his B.A. in History in 1959. After graduating he went back to get a degree in Education and began teaching high school in Edmonton. In the mean time he had also met and married Marie Ann Fedoruk. While he was teaching high school he continued his history studies completing a M.A. in History in 1966.

As a graduate student at the University of Alberta John came under the influence and guidance of Lewis G. Thomas. Thomas, whose research interests included the history of provincial politics, the western fur trade, exploration, and missionary activity in the west, sparked John's interest in western Canadian history and fur trade studies. John would later write, echoing W.L. Morton's observations about the distorting aspects of Canadian history written from a metropolitan perspective,[2] that the

> explanations offered in official histories did not seem to match the social reality I perceived in the surrounding community. The school yards of post World War II western Canada reflected ethnocultural groups not evident in Canadian history texts. More frequently, where I expected historical explanation the official texts simply chose to ignore the subject. ...Inevitably my quest for explanations of the nature of my community led to an interest in "beginnings." This interest breached the barrier of the Transfer and settlement to the pre-1870 world of peoples who were ancestral to a significant number of westerners today.[3]

Thomas was not only John's Ph.D. supervisor, but also became a close friend and mentor. In the 1950s, L.G. Thomas avidly pursued the history of missions in the Canadian west and visited the archives of the various missionary societies in London bringing a microfilm copy of the Church Missionary Society records back to the University of Alberta. These records became the basis of John's M.A. thesis which examined the Anglican Clergy in the Red River Settlement from 1820–1826.[4] Examining the efforts of three Evangelical Anglican clergymen (John West, David Jones, and William Cockran) John detailed how the Anglican Church laid a secure foundation for its mission in the Red River Settlement by adapting its mission to suit the particular circumstances of Rupert's Land. In particular, he explained how David Jones and William Cockran established working relationships with the members of the different communities in Red River (Hudson's Bay Company, Roman Catholic Missionaries, Principal Settlers, Metis, Scots, Demeurons, and the Indians), established themselves as leaders in the community, and became a force for British civilization in Red River.

His experience with the Anglican church records of the fur trade began to change John's perspective of both the fur trade and western Canadian history. Up until the 1960s the fur trade had been examined almost solely within the Metropolitan context. This one-dimensional approach conceptualized the fur trade as "the domination of European metropolitan centres over an ever-expanding and increasingly distant hinterland."[5] It was a strictly economic perspective that saw a distant metropolis exploiting the staple products that the hinterland was capable of producing in surplus, and this economic domination was the vehicle through which the metropolis extended its social, political, and cultural influence over the hinterland. While John never advocated abandoning the Metropolitan perspective completely, his immersion in missionary letters and reports from Rupert's Land convinced him that developments arising in the hinterland that established indigenous traditions were obscured when viewed through this unifocal lens. For John,

> additional insight into various socio-cultural aspects of the fur trade may be garnered by seeking restricted metropolitan perspectives. The view from York Factory or Red River Settlement will differ from that of London or Montreal. Likewise he [the historian] may profitably alter his perspective by viewing occurrences through the eyes of those who were not fur traders.[6]

These new eyes or lenses were those of the missionaries in the field. While these insights may seem commonplace to us today, in the early 1970s they heralded a new approach to fur trade history that saw the fur trade as a socio-cultural complex in which Indians, mixed-bloods, and whites were intertwined. In this perspective new facts and questions emerged and it became "readily apparent that the fur trade was as much an Indian creation as it was European."[7] One of the striking features of the history of Rupert's Land that caught John's imagination was the emergence of communities of mixed Indian and European ancestry. This topic would become the subject of his doctoral dissertation, which he completed in 1973.[8]

Taking his cue from Marcel Giraud's *Le Métis Canadien,* which noted distinct cultural differences between mixed-bloods originating in the posts of the Hudson's Bay Company and those originating in the posts of those trading concerns based in Montreal, John set out to study those mixed-bloods who had originated in the Hudson's Bay Company tradition. Most historians who had studied the Metis after Giraud had been attracted to those French-speaking mixed-bloods who followed the buffalo hunt and, in the nineteenth century, came to be known as *métis.* There were, however, a significant number of mixed-bloods in Rupert's Land who were not *métis.* These mixed-bloods lived in and around the posts of the Hudson's Bay Company, pursued activities familiar to the "homeguard" Indians and served with varying frequency as employees of the Company. This group, sometimes referred to as "English-speaking half-breeds," had proved to be an elusive people for historians.[9]

He traced the origins of this group in the Hudson Bay fur trade tradition by examining the interaction of English, Highland Scottish, and Orkney traders with the surrounding Homeguard Indians, and their adaptation to the circumstances of their new environment. This century-and-a-half experience in the fur trade produced a "new people" who were not only biologically but culturally distinct from both European and Indian peoples. The hallmark of these mixed-bloods, whom John called the "country-born," was the ethos of the "Indian-Trader" that internalized aspects of both English domestic structure and Cree social organization. Combining the idealization of the privileges, tasks, and duties of the HBC trader with familial and kinship connections to native bands, there emerged a distinct group and way of life that was Britannic but not British.[10]

After 1820, when many of these "country-born" moved to the Red River Settlement, they absorbed new influences primarily from the Anglican missionaries in the Settlement. It was the Hudson's Bay Company and the Anglican missionaries, the primary agents of British civilization in the western interior, that had the greatest impact upon the country-born. As a result their community, making up nearly half of the Settlement's population, constituted the largest bastion of support for local institutions derived from British practices. Their response reflected an adaptation of the trading-post ways to Red River. This adaptation, however, showed a great deal of diversity. Some moved comfortably among the *métis*, others were at home with the Indians at St. Peter's, and still others served a leadership role among Kildonan Scots.

Examining the various aspects of family and community life among the country-born in Red River, John came to the conclusion that this mixed-blood community had played a decisive role in shaping the development of the settlement prior to Confederation. Having close relations with persons belonging to other communities in Red River they served as cultural bridges explaining one to the other. This feature, combined with their support of British institutions and practices, made the country-born the amalgam that made the Red River experience possible.

Although John's study became required reading for anyone doing Red River or Metis history it was never published as a book.[11] Almost immediately after he defended his dissertation, the Department of History at the University of Alberta hired John and the stress of preparing new courses, being one of the youngest faculty members in a department where he had himself been a student, and the birth of his first child gave him little time to revise the manuscript as he might have liked to. He preferred moving on to the next project and developing new research ideas.

Though his dissertation examined a mixed-blood community that historians had all but overlooked, his approach was not all that dissimilar from Giraud's in that he chose a full-blown Metis community and most of his analysis was geared to explaining their major behavioural tradition. He dealt with the origins of this community, but only in the first chapter was this process of ethnogenesis examined in any detail. It was this subject that would occupy the next 20 years of his research and writing. To do so, John used an increasingly wide range of sources (census records, scrip applications, parish records and Metis folk history), and he shifted from the particular (country-born) to the general (Metis). He also began to read more anthropological theory.

By the mid 1970s he was much influenced by the writings of Fredrik Barth, Lionel Tiger, and Robin Fox.[12] From Barth he adopted a theory of cultural formation that focussed on the intersection of individual behaviour and collective institutions. Both Barth and Foster believed that shared individual experiences were critical in delimiting social or ethnic groups. These shared understandings, arising out of the different fur-trade experiences, were expressed as behaviour that distinguished the Metis from others.[13] His favourite quotation from Barth provided him with a methodology and approach to make sense of the available evidence on shared Metis experiences.

> To depict the connection between individual behaviour and collective institutions, it is necessary that one construct models with clearly differentiated micro- and macro-levels. I find it reasonable to see social institutions and customs as the outcome of a complex aggregation of numerous micro-events of behaviour, based on individual decisions in each person's attempts to cope with life. This is not to deny the existence of culture as a pre-established framework for choosing behaviour and interpreting experience—on the contrary, it is precisely to depict the interconnection of culture and behaviour that we need the models. Though every actor is dependent on his knowledge and codification, and hampered by conventional blinkers, there must none the less be a dynamic relationship between individual experience and learning, and the socially recognized collective facts which we call culture and institutions. The simplest form of this interconnection would seem to depend on sharing: individual behaviour produces experience, a confrontation with reality which may or may not seem consistent with preexisting conceptualizations and thus sometimes tend to confirm, sometimes to falsify them. If a number of persons in communication share a similar opportunity situation, experience the same confrontation with reality, have the same conceptualizations falsified, one would expect them to develop shared understandings and modify their collective culture and expectations in accordance with this.[14]

Barth's emphasis on ethnic groups and boundaries, rather than cultural groups, and the importance he placed on ascription in determining who is or is not a member of a particular people made sense to John because he studied mixed-blood individuals who might have similar cultural traits but who might variously identify themselves as Indian, Metis, or Euro-Canadian.

In investigating Metis origins John identified three distinct worlds of experience that were crucial to understanding Metis ethnogenesis: 1) the world of adult males; 2) the world of adult females; 3) and family life. All needed to be investigated to discover the constellation of events and circumstances that led the various mixed-blood communities to alter their view of themselves in relation to other communities. This perspective and program of research came not only from Barth, but also from the writings of Tiger and Fox whose particular formulation of a socio-biological theory John found particularly intriguing. It was another approach to analysing the adaptive history of social behaviour and he took seriously Tiger's claim that human communities were "fundamentally concerned with the same things as other primate communities—surviving, perpetuating the group, defending it, keeping some social order, using the environment reasonably constructively, and just generally muddling through."[15] John's three worlds of experience, in fact, very closely paralleled Fox's and Tiger's characterizations of social acts as patterned and predictable bonding issues: the world of adult males = male bonding; the world of adult women = female bonding; and family life = male/female bonding and mother/child bonding. Barth's differentiation between micro- and macro- levels of analysis and his call to construct models connecting individual behaviour to collective institutions also had a parallel to Fox's and Tiger's formulation of micro- and macro-structures. For Tiger macro-structure involved war, politics, and inter-group relations and was closely connected to male bonding. Micro-structure involved childbearing and nurturing the young, and was connected to female bonding. Although John was adamant that all these different levels or worlds needed to be investigated in order to unravel the different Metis origins, and he encouraged his students to undertake different kinds of analysis, he was most concerned with the world of adult males. This emphasis came not only from his intuitive grasp of male bonding issues, but also his belief that the world of adult males in the fur trade was the key to understanding the other worlds of Metis experience and explaining Metis ethnogenesis in different locations and contexts.

It would be a mistake, however, to read John's work in this period as theory driven. Explicit theorizing never intruded in his writings and he was very much an historian. In one of the first articles he wrote in the early 1980s, synthesizing his reading and research over the last decade, he made his disciplinary context explicit. His approach to Metis ethnogenesis was historical rather than anthropological. The objective of historical study, he said, was \

> an understanding of how historical actors, in this instance the Plains Métis and their neighbours, perceive, understood, and acted upon their experiences. To obtain this understanding, the historian identifies relevant sequences of events in the context of particular circum-

stances. The patterns of behaviour that emerge are analyzed in term of the logical associations that constitute explanation....

The historian's sources of data are surviving documents. His analysis emphasizes the consistencies and inconsistencies found within a document and among related documents and evaluated in terms of the historian's other experiences. The historian in his analysis is not necessarily tied to a methodology that could be identified as belonging to a social science discipline. In his analysis, empathy for the protagonists as much as rigorous logic should be reflected in sensitive and mature judgements that constitute historical explanations.[16]

Regarding his own borrowings from anthropological literature, John was careful not to abandon the strengths of his own disciplinary approach. Rather anthropological ideas were useful to him to provide a new perspective "from which the contents of familiar documents can be analyzed to give forth understandings not apparent previously in historical analysis."[17]

The article in which these observations appeared, presented a tentative reformulation of the process of Metis ethnogenesis. Drawing on the work of Jacqueline Peterson on the Great Lakes Metis, Jennifer Brown's work on fur trade company families, Sylvia Van Kirk's work on women in the fur trade, and his own researches over the previous decade John argued that Metis groups emerged as a result of a few "immigrant" adult males responding successfully to opportunities offered by particular niches in various fur trading systems. In the process of adapting to these opportunities, these males established households that successfully enculturated children to further exploit the household's particular trading niche. In time, the historical actors in the region came to view these households as communities distinct from that of the trading post and indigenous bands yet tied to each through kinship. On the Great Plains this occurred in the last decades of the eighteenth century when the provisioning niche in the *en derouine* fur trade opened the door for the development of freeman bands composed of former servants of the various fur trading companies in the St. Lawrence/Great Lakes tradition. These freemen, who had married into the surrounding Indian bands, ended their Company contracts in the North West and formed separate households that formed the basis for a distinct community. Organized as buffalo hunting and trapping bands these freemen bands were sufficiently stable in membership to permit the adult males and their cohorts to influence male children to emulate their fathers in exploiting this provisioning and trapping niche.[18]

Having argued that Metis as communities were an infrequent, if not unique, sociocultural product of particular events and circumstances, John was also very interested in those instances when the children of fur-trade unions did not establish a Metis identity and the processes that were involved in these cases. Examining the life and legend of Paulet Paul, a "mixed-blood" tripman on York Boat brigades, he found that Paulet's heroic achievements had been enshrined in Metis folklore; his feats of physical prowess, including guiding York Boats through rapids and his fighting abilities, established him as a "man of consequence" among both tripmen and Metis. The more mundane aspects of Paulet's life, however, suggested an identity other than that associated with the Plains Metis. From genealogical sources John was able to ascertain that Paulet had served as a husband and father in numerous households for relatively brief periods of time differentiating him from those freemen who established more permanent households. Indeed, Paulet Paul's domestic experience fit other fur trade patterns where traders did not leave their employment, but established serial households among neighbouring Indian bands as they were posted in different locales. These "House Indian" bands were features of the fur trade through its history, and the households of servants in these bands were marked by frequent changes in personnel. In this situation fur traders did not play a role in the enculturation of their children. That role then fell to the mother's male relatives who provided the appropriate role models for male children. That the legend of Paulet Paul, a House Indian, survived in Metis lore, John attributed to the fact that after 1820 many House Indian families drifted into the Red River Settlement where they sometimes made the transition to a Metis identity.[19]

John's last attempt to pull his ideas about Metis origins into a conceptual model was his article "Wintering, the Outsider Adult Male and Ethnogenesis of the Western Plains Metis."[20] (Because of the centrality of this article to John's later ideas, it has been reprinted here in this collection.) Here he clearly laid out the ideas he had been thinking about for two decades. Metis ethnogenesis in the fur trade, whether in the Great Lakes or on the Great Plains, occurred in a two-step process. The first step was the wintering of an outsider male with an Indian band in fur-trade country. This first step produced three relationships critical to Metis ethnogenesis: a country marriage to a prominent women in the Indian band; a male bond with the adult males of this Indian band; and a male bond with other servants also wintering in fur-trade country. "The shared experiences of these relationships gave expression to the Metis when the outsider with his country wife and family chose to live apart from the trading post and the Indian band."[21] The second step was the process of leaving fur trade employment ("going free") and establishing freeman bands with other former servants and their native families. Their kinship connection to the neighbouring Indian bands and the bonds established with the males in these bands permitted these freeman communities to survive, and their assiduous pursuit of provisions

⃠ *John Foster in 1995 with a colleague.* Photo courtesy of Marie Foster.

and furs in surplus amounts set them apart from neighbouring Indian bands. These freeman bands, exploiting economic niches in the fur trade, were stable communities in which the children were enculturated in circumstances distinct from that of the Indian band or trading post and constituted the social milieu in which the succeeding generation chose marriage partners.

Both his study of Paulet Paul and his more conceptual work were part of an conscious attempt by John to construct a model of Metis ethnogenesis. His research and writing in the 1980s and 1990s focussed on both elucidating this model and demonstrating how it operated both in the lives of specific individuals and communities. Along with Bob Beal and Louise Zuk he undertook a comprehensive study of the Metis wintering community of Buffalo Lake which flourished in central Alberta in the early 1870s. Using archaeological evidence, parish records, oral histories, and other documentary sources, John tried to reconstruct the history of this community in accordance with his model of Metis origins. While a preliminary report was completed in 1987,[22] he was still working on this larger project when he died.

This brief summary of John Foster's work and ideas does not do justice to the influence that he had on his students and colleagues. John was an inspirational teacher whose influence can be seen in the work of his students (including articles by Heather Devine, Heather Rollason Driscoll, Ted Binnema, and Gerhard Ens in this volume). He not only altered the way we

cx) *John Foster and Dick Harrison in 1990 with the first three isssues of* Alberta: Studies in the Arts and Sciences. *Photo courtesy of New Trail.*

understand Metis ethnogenesis, but helped open new avenues of exploring fur trade and native studies. John came to the university as a well-trained and experienced high school teacher, and he took his passion for teaching into the university. Year after year, students crowded into his early morning lectures on the history of the Canadian plains. Members of the History Department at the time, remember how his loud, lilting voice, and his students' occasional laughter, flooded into the hallway that housed faculty offices.

John Foster was a gifted mentor. Many remember John, half-hidden behind his cluttered desk, in animated conversation with his students. Sometimes, we were those students. Undoubtedly, the many hours he spent advising his students, undergraduate or graduate, interfered with scholarly output, but he seemed to get his greatest pleasure from those sessions, and few of the students who visited him regularly can forget John Foster leaning back in his chair, mischievous glint in his eye, after throwing out yet another of those questions that defied simple answers. As opinionated as he was, his students will remember his questions as much as his answers. His infectious love of history, and his certainty of its relevance escaped few of his students and inspired most of them.

John was also a valued colleague and friend to almost all members of the Department and many other members of the university community. His goal in everything he did from classroom teaching to committee work was to advance the course of scholarship and learning. The degree to which he worked behind the scenes to help get the School of Native Studies exemplifies this commitment to multi-disciplinary scholarship. Thanks to the countless hours put in by John and some of his colleagues the School of Native Studies was established on a solid footing in the fall of 1988, and John served as Academic Program Coordinator beginning in 1989, and stepped in temporarily to serve as interim Director in 1991–92. To honour John's contributions, the School of Native Studies has established the Dr. John E. Foster Memorial Award in Native Studies.

From 1988 to 1993, John Foster was also founding co-editor, along with Dick Harrison, of the multi-disciplinary scholarly journal, *Alberta: Studies in the Arts and Sciences*, published by the University of Alberta Press. In 1992 he was lead editor of an issue focusing on the buffalo. When delicate negotiations with contributors as diverse as artists and paleontologists gradually used up the time and space allotted to that issue, his co-editor urged cutting off the process and going to press, but John proposed, instead, making a virtue of their necessity by extending the deadlines and expanding the issue to more than 250 pages. His wisdom was confirmed when *Alberta* 3, no. 1, (1992) was simultaneously issued as a book, *Buffalo*, that won the Alberta Book Publishers Association award as the best book published in Alberta. The editors of the book, John Foster, Dick Harrison and Ian MacLaren, proudly picked up the award.

In addition to his work on the *Alberta* journal, John had a long relationship with the University of Alberta Press in many other ways. He published *The Developing West: Essays on Canadian History in Honor of Lewis H. Thomas* in 1982 with the Press. From 1983 until 1988 he served on the Press Committee, including a term as chair of the Committee from fall 1984 until spring 1986. During those years, John was very involved with the Riel Project, acting as a liason between the volume editors, the University and the Press and with the translation of *Le Métis Canadien* by George Woodcock. He also championed the Press's involvement with the "Missionary Oblates of Mary Immaculate in the West and North" series with Western Canada Publishers. One of his last favours to the Press was to write a Foreword to Ray Huel's *Proclaiming the Gospel to the Indians and the Métis,* which was published shortly after his death. John's influence on the University of Alberta Press to develop its list in Western Canadian History can still be seen today.

John was as eager outside the classroom as he was in it to discuss ideas, whether it was something he had read or something that one of his colleagues had encountered. When his office was not occupied by students, there was usually a group of faculty members present. On reflection, it seems likely that the professors were there for many of the same reasons the students were. They could be assured of an intelligent and good-humoured hearing for their ideas. Even the most informal session with John Foster was like a seminar in which ideas from history, anthropology and sociology were debated in the context of the news of the day. John was a life-long political junkie who worked actively in election campaigns but who loved above all to talk politics. Whether it was a national or a local issue he could always relate it to his historical research.

Finally, John Foster was helpful to his co-workers. If his younger colleagues in particular needed advice about such matters as textbooks or teaching strategies or the handling of difficult students, he was the one to approach. Those who did so knew that the response would be nonjudgmental and intellectually honest. His advice was sought because it was always worth having. John will be missed and remembered by all that knew him and even those who did not will benefit from the legacy he left behind.

Notes

1.   See Chapter 3, Jennifer Brown, "Partial Truths: A Closer Look at Fur Trade Marriage," 59–80.
2.   W.L. Morton, "Clio in Canada: The Interpretation of Canadian History," *University of Toronto Quarterly* XV (April 1946): 227–34.
3.   John E. Foster, "The Plains Métis," in R. Bruce Morrison and C. Roderick Wilson, editors, *Native Peoples: The Canadian Experience* (Toronto: McClelland and Stewart, 1986), 378–79.
4.   John E. Foster, "The Anglican Clergy in the Red River Settlement: 1820–1826" (MA Thesis, University of Alberta, 1966).
5.   See John Foster's discussion of this problem in "Rupert's Land and the Red River Settlement, 1820-70," in Lewis G. Thomas, ed., *The Prairie West to 1905. A Canadian Sourcebook* (Toronto: Oxford University Press, 1975), 20–21.
6.   John E. Foster, "Missionaries, Mixed-Bloods and the Fur Trade: Four Letters of the Rev. William Cockran, Red River Settlement, 1830–33," *Western Canadian Journal of Anthropology* 3, no. 1 (1972): 94.
7.   John E. Foster, "Rupert's Land and the Red River Settlement, 1820–70," 20.
8.   John Elgin Foster, "The Country-born in the Red River Settlement: 1820–1850," (Ph.D. Dissertation, University of Alberta, 1973).
9.   Ibid., 256–66.
10. As Michael Payne notes in his article in this collection, Foster was one of the first to marry fur trade social history to social history theory generated in other historiographical traditions. Foster's argument, summarized above, was based on the notion that Hudson's Bay Company trading posts operated on a model of a household economy and social structure—an idea he borrowed from Peter Laslett's *The World We Have Lost* (New York: Charles Scribner's Sons, 1965).

11. A number of articles were published out of his dissertation. These included: "The Homeguard Cree and the Hudson's Bay Company: The First Hundred Years," in D.A. Muise, ed., *Approaches to Native History in Canada*, History Division Paper #25 (Ottawa: National Museum of Man, 1979), reprinted in Bruce A. Cox, ed., *Native People Native Lands: Canadian Indians, Inuits and Métis* (Ottawa: Carleton University Press, 1987); "The Métis: The People and the Term," *Prairie Forum* 3, no. 1 (1978); "The Origins of the Mixed-Bloods in the Canadian West," in L.H. Thomas, ed., *Essays on Western History* (Edmonton: University of Alberta Press, 1976). Reprinted in R. Douglas Francis and Howard Palmer, eds., *The Prairie West: Historical Readings* (Edmonton: The University of Alberta Press, 1985; "The Indian Trader in the Hudson Bay Fur Trade Tradition," in Jim Freedman and J.H. Barkow, eds., *Proceedings of the Second Congress Canadian Ethnology Society*. Ethnology Division Paper #28 (Ottawa: National Museum of Man, 1976).

12. Ibid. Foster's course outlines for his seminar on Metis Origins, which he taught from the late 1970s through the 1980s, stressed the ideas of Barth and Tiger. See Fredrik Barth, ed., *Ethnic Groups and Boundaries: The Social Organization of Cultural Difference* (Boston: Little, Brown and Co., 1969); Lionel Tiger, *Men in Groups* (New York: Random House, 1969); Lionel Tiger and Robin Fox, *The Imperial Animal* (New York: Holt, Rinehart, and Winston, 1971).

13. For Foster's own formulation of these ideas see his "Some questions and perspectives on the problem of métis roots," in Jennifer S.H. Brown and Jacqueline Peterson, eds., *The New Peoples: Being and Becoming Métis in North America* (Winnipeg: University of Manitoba Press, 1985), 73–91.

14. Fredrik Barth, "Descent and Marriage Reconsidered," in Jack Goody, ed., *The Character of Kinship* (London: Cambridge University Press, 1973), 5.

15. Lionel Tiger and Robin Fox, *The Imperial Animal,* revised edition (New Brunswick: Transaction Publishers, 1991), 32.

16. John E. Foster, "The Plains Métis," 377.

17. Ibid., 378.

18. Ibid., 382–85.

19. "Paulet Paul: Métis or House Indian Folk-Hero?" *Manitoba History* 9 (Spring 1985). Though published prior to his article "The Plains Métis," it is clear from Foster's footnotes that the Paulet Paul piece was written after "The Plains Métis."

20. *Prairie Forum* 19, no. 1 (Spring 1994). Reproduced in this volume as Chapter 8.

21. Ibid., 2.

22. *Report on the History of Métis Hivernement Settlement at Buffalo Lake, 1872–77,* Historic Sites and Provincial Museum, Divisions of Alberta Government, Department of Culture, 1987.

Editorial Note

Throughout the text, the accenting of Metis/Métis is deliberately not consistent from chapter to chapter, as individual authors have their own preferred spelling.

Writings of John Elgin Foster

Books/Monographs

With Bob Beal and Louise Zuk, *Report on the History of Métis Hivernement Settlement at Buffalo Lake, 1872–77*. Historic Sites and Provincial Museum, Divisions of Alberta Government, Department of Culture, 1987.

Books Edited

With Dick Harrison, and I.S. MacLaren, eds., *Buffalo*. Alberta Nature and Culture Series. Edmonton: University of Alberta Press, 1992.

With Brigham Y. Card, Herbert C. Northcott, Howard Palmer and George Jarvis, eds., *The Mormon Presence in Canada*. Edmonton: University of Alberta Press, 1990.

The Developing West: Essays on Canadian History in Honor of Lewis H. Thomas. Edmonton: University of Alberta Press, 1983.

Contribution to Books

Foreword to Raymond J.A. Huel, *Proclaiming the Gospel to the Indian and Métis*. Edmonton: University of Alberta Press, 1996.

Introduction (French/English) to the reissue of Marcel Giraud's *Le Metis Canadien*. Saint Boniface: Les Éditions du Blé, 1984.

Theses

"The Anglican Clergy in the Red River Settlement: 1820–1826," M.A. Thesis, University of Alberta, 1966.

"The Country-Born in the Red River Settlement, 1820–1850," Ph.D. Dissertation, University of Alberta, 1973.

Articles

"James Bird, Fur Trader," in Bob Hesketh and Frances Swyripa, eds., *Edmonton: The Life of a City*. Edmonton: NeWest Press, 1995.

"Wintering, the Outsider Adult Male and Ethnogenesis of the Western Plains Métis," *Prairie Forum* 19, no. 1 (Spring 1994).

"The Métis and the End of the Plains Buffalo," *Alberta* 3, no. 1 (1992).

"Métis," *Encyclopaedia of World Cultures. Volume 1—North America*, edited by Timothy J. O'Leary and David Levinson. Boston: G.K. Hall & Co., 1991.

"Le Missionnaire and Le Chef Métis," *Etudes oblates de l'Ouest/Western Oblate Studies* 1 (1990).

"William Auld," *Dictionary of Canadian Biography VI.* Toronto: University of Toronto Press, 1987.

"Some Questions and Perspectives on the Problem of Métis Roots," in Jacqueline Peterson and Jennifer S.H. Brown, eds., *The New Peoples: Being and Becoming Métis in North America.* Winnipeg: University of Manitoba Press, 1986.

"The Plains Métis," in Bruce Morrison and C.R. Wilson, eds., *Native Peoples: The Canadian Experience.* Toronto: McClelland and Stewart, 1986.

"The Fur Trade to 1787," *Canada's Visual History.* Ottawa: National Museum of Man, 1986. (Text for Slide Series)

"The Fur Trade since 1787," *Canada's Visual History.* Ottawa: National Museum of Man, 1986. (Text for Slide Series)

"Paulet Paul: Métis or House Indian Folk-Hero?" *Manitoba History* 9 (Spring 1985).

"Buffalo Hunt," *Canadian Encyclopedia.* Edmonton: Hurtig Publishers, 1985.

"Fur Trade after 1760," *Canadian Encyclopedia.* Edmonton: Hurtig Publishers, 1985.

"Pemmican," *Canadian Encyclopedia.* Edmonton: Hurtig Publishers, 1985.

"Voyageur," *Canadian Encyclopedia.* Edmonton: Hurtig Publishers, 1985.

"Yorkboat," *Canadian Encyclopedia.* Edmonton: Hurtig Publishers, 1985.

"The Fur Trade Post," *Canadian Encyclopedia.* Edmonton: Hurtig Publishers, 1985.

"The Sayer Trial," *Canadian Encyclopedia.* Edmonton: Hurtig Publishers, 1985.

"The Pemmican Proclamation," *Canadian Encyclopedia.* Edmonton: Hurtig Publishers, 1985.

"James Bird," *Dictionary of Canadian Biography VIII.* Toronto: University of Toronto Press, 1985

"The Saulteaux and the Numbered Treaties—An Aboriginal Rights Position," in Richard Price, ed., *The Spirit of Alberta Indian Treaties.* Toronto: Institute for Public Policy, 1979. Reissued by the University of Alberta Press, 1987; 2nd edition 1999.

"Indian-White Relations in the Prairie West During the Fur Trade Period—A Compact?" in Richard Price, ed., *The Spirit of Alberta Indian Treaties*. Toronto: Institute for Public Policy, 1979. Reissued by the University of Alberta Press, 1987; 2nd edition 1999.

"The Homeguard Cree and the Hudson's Bay Company: The First Hundred Years," in D.A. Muise, ed., *Approaches to Native History in Canada*, History Division Paper #25, Ottawa: National Museum of Man, 1979. Reprinted in Bruce A. Cox, ed., *Native People Native Lands: Canadian Indians, Inuits and Métis*. Ottawa: Carleton University Press, 1987.

"The Métis: The People and the Term," *Prairie Forum* 3, no. 1 (1978).

"The Origins of the Mixed-Bloods in the Canadian West," in L.H. Thomas, ed., *Essays on Western History*. Edmonton: University of Alberta Press, 1976. Reprinted in R. Douglas Francis and Howard Palmer, eds., *The Prairie West: Historical Readings*. Edmonton: University of Alberta Press, 1985.

"The Indian Trader in the Hudson Bay Fur Trade Tradition," in Jim Freedman and J.H. Barkow, eds., *Proceedings of the Second Congress Canadian Ethnology Society*. Ethnology Division Paper #28. Ottawa: National Museum of Man, 1976.

"The Fur Trade," *World Book Encyclopedia* (1976).

"Archdeacon William Cockran," *Dictionary of Canadian Biography IX*. Toronto: University of Toronto Press, 1976.

"Rupert's Land and the Red River Settlement, 1820–1870," in L.G. Thomas, ed., *The Prairie West to 1905*. Toronto: Oxford University Press, 1976.

"Missionaries, Mixed-Bloods and the Fur Trade: Four Letters of the Rev. William Cockran, The Red River Settlement, 1830–33," *Western Canadian Journal of Anthropology* 3, no. 1 (1972).

"Programme for the Red River Mission: The Anglican Clergy, 1820–26," *Histoire sociale/Social History* IV (November 1969).

Acknowledgements

THE PUBLICATION OF THIS BOOK was made possible by the generosity and hard work of a large number of people. The family of John Foster—his wife, Marie, and their children, Bill and Hanya—were very supportive of the project, generously sharing their memories and insights of their husband and father.

The editors would also like to thank the contributors to the volume who waited patiently for the project to come together and then willingly met all of our urgent deadlines. We especially appreciate the contribution of L.G. Thomas and Michael Payne's assistance.

No project of this kind can succeed without the active support of a publisher. Mary Mahoney-Robson, Editor at the University of Alberta Press, shepherded this book from its inception to publication, and her enthusiastic support and tireless work were crucial to its success. Having worked for many years with John Foster on a variety of publishing projects at the Press, her commitment to this particular project went very deeply. We would also like to thank Janine Andrews, Acting Director of the University of Alberta Press, Alan Brownoff, who designed the book, and Michael Fisher, for the map of Rupert's Land.

The University of Alberta's Office of Vice President, Research, the Faculty of Arts, and the Department of History and Classics provided funding for this festschrift in honour of John E. Foster.

Publication of this work also has been supported by the University of Northern British Columbia through a publication grant program administered by the Office of the Vice President, Research.

Contributors

THEODORE BINNEMA is Assistant Professor of History at the University of Northern British Columbia in Prince George. John Foster supervised his M.A. thesis, a study of Siksika history. Foster also supervised his Ph.D. research until his death. Dr. Binnema's first book, *The Common and Contested Ground: A Human and Environmental History of the Northwestern Plains* is in press at the University of Oklahoma Press.

JENNIFER S.H. BROWN is Professor of History, and Director, Centre for Rupert's Land Studies at the University of Winnipeg. For over two decades, John Foster was a valued colleague and friend with whom shared many interests in fur trade and Métis history. He brought fresh vigour to these fields through his ideas, conference talks and papers, conversation, and teaching, and a fine legacy lives on in his students, two of whom have continued their studies with her. Brown's recent publications include *Reading Beyond Words: Contexts for Native History*, edited with Elizabeth Vibert (Peterborough: Broadview Press, 1996) and a number of articles on Northern Algonquian and Métis history and people.

GLEN CAMPBELL is Professor of French at the University of Calgary. He collaborated on the Louis Riel Project with John Foster. Dr. Campbell's recent publications include "Le christianisme poétisé de Georges Boileau (1885–1946)" in *Western Oblate Studies* 5, (2000), and "Alberta's Oblate Community: Poetic Vignettes" (Athabasca: Athabasca University, forthcoming).

HEATHER DEVINE is a Ph.D. candidate in the Department of History and Classics at the University of Alberta. Dr. Foster was her doctoral thesis supervisor prior to his death. She is currently co-editing an anthology of essays devoted to the life and work of Montana writer Joseph Kinsey Howard for the University of Calgary Press.

HEATHER ROLLASON DRISCOLL is a Ph.D. Candidate at the Department of History and Classics, University of Alberta. John Foster taught the graduate seminar that inspired this paper and he was Ms. Rollason Driscoll's initial doctoral supervisor. Ms. Rollason Driscoll's recent publications include (as Heather Rollason)"Some Comments Upon the Marked Differences in the Representations of Chipewyan Women in Samuel Hearne's Fieldnotes and the Published Journal" in *Earth, Water, Air and Fire: Studies in Canadian Ethnohistory* (1998); (as Rollason with R.C. Macleod) "Restrain the Lawless Savages : Native Defendants in the Criminal Courts of the North West Territories, 1878-1885" in the *Journal of Historical Sociology* (1997), and (as Rollason with R.C. Macleod) "Adaptation and Retention: The Meeting of Native and Canadian Legal Systems in the North West Territories in the Late Nineteenth Century" in the forthcoming collection titled *Canada: Confederation to Present.*

GERHARD J. ENS is Associate Professor of History and Classics at the University of Alberta. John Foster was his Ph.D. dissertation supervisor. Dr. Ens's recent publications include "Taking Treaty 8 Scrip, 1899–1900: A Quantitative Portrait of Northern Alberta Metis Communities," in *Lobstick: An Interdisciplinary Journal*; "After the Buffalo: The Reformation of the Turtle Mountain Metis Community," in *New Faces of the Fur Trade: Selected Papers of the Seventh North American Fur Trade Conference*, 1995; and *Homeland to Hinterland: The Changing Worlds of the Red River Metis in the Nineteenth Century* (Toronto: University of Toronto Press, 1996).

GERALD FRIESEN is Professor of History at the University of Manitoba. He benefited from John Foster's advice on many occasions, including John's careful reading of the fur trade chapters of *The Canadian Prairies: A History*. He is also the author of *Citizens and Nation: An Essay on History, Communication and Canada* (Toronto: University of Toronto Press, 2000).

JAN GRABOWSKI is Associate Professor of History at the University of Ottawa. His publications include a survey of Canadian history in Polish, *Historia Kanady* (Warsaw, 2001) and articles in *Annales de demographie historique* (Paris); *Ethnohistory, Revue d'histoire de l'Amerique francaise,* and *Recherches amerindiennes au Quebec.*

I.S. MACLAREN teaches Canadian Studies and Canadian Literature at the University of Alberta. With John Foster, he and Dick Harrison edited *Buffalo* (1992). Professor MacLaren's research and publication, both of which John Foster went out of his way to encourage, concentrate on the writing and painting of explorers and travellers in the Arctic and the West. With Lisa LaFramboise, he edited *The Ladies, the Gwich 'in, and the Rat: Travels on the Athabasca, Mackenzie, Rat, Porcupine, and Yukon Rivers in 1926* (Edmonton: University of Alberta Press, 1998). "Cultured Wilderness in Jasper National Park" appeared in *The Journal of Canadian Studies* in 1999.

ROD MACLEOD is Professor of History and Classics at the University of Alberta. John Foster was his colleague and friend for many years. Dr. Macleod's recent publications include "Canada's Mounties: Myth and Reality," *History Today*, February 2000; and R.C. Macleod and Heather [Driscoll], "'Restrain the Lawless Savages': Native Defendants in the Criminal Courts of the North West Territories, 1878–1885," *Journal of Historical Sociology* (June 1997).

FRITS PANNEKOEK is Director of Information Resources and Associate Professor at the University of Calgary. John Foster was a colleague and mentor for over thirty years providing inspiration and support for numerous public history projects. Frits Pannekoek's recent publications include: "The Rise of a Heritage Priesthood," in Michael A. Tomlan, ed., *Preservation of What, For Whom?* (Ithaca: The National Council for Preservation Education, 1999), 29–36; *A Snug Little Flock — The Social Origins of the Riel Resistance of 1869–70* (Winnipeg: Watson and Dwyer, 1991); and "The Commodification of Information and the Marginalization of Regional Culture" in *Proceedings of the TEND Conference* (United Arab Emirates: Higher Colleges of Education, 2000 CD format).

MICHAEL PAYNE is Head of the Research and Publications Program for the Cultural Facilities and Historic Sites Branch of Alberta Community Development. He worked with John Foster on several projects and committees including the Alberta 2005 Centennial history project and publication of the journal *Alberta Studies in the Arts and Sciences*. In addition, they shared an interest in fur trade social history and the history of Alberta that John encouraged as a friend and a colleague.

NICOLE ST-ONGE is Associate Professor of History at the University of Ottawa. John Foster gave her valuable insights and support during the writing of both her M.A. and Ph.D. theses. Dr. St-Onge has published extensively on the Métis population of Manitoba and is now involved in a project dealing with the Montreal fur trade labour force in the Northwest. Her second book (together with Dr. Grabowski) is forthcoming from the University of Oklahoma Press.

LEWIS G. THOMAS is Professor Emeritus of History at the University of Alberta. Professor Thomas first met John Foster when John enrolled as an undergraduate student in History at the University of Alberta. Later Professor Thomas taught John as a graduate student and supervised both John's M.A. thesis and Ph.D. dissertation. In addition to their shared research interests, Professor Thomas was a lifelong friend and colleague of Professor Foster.

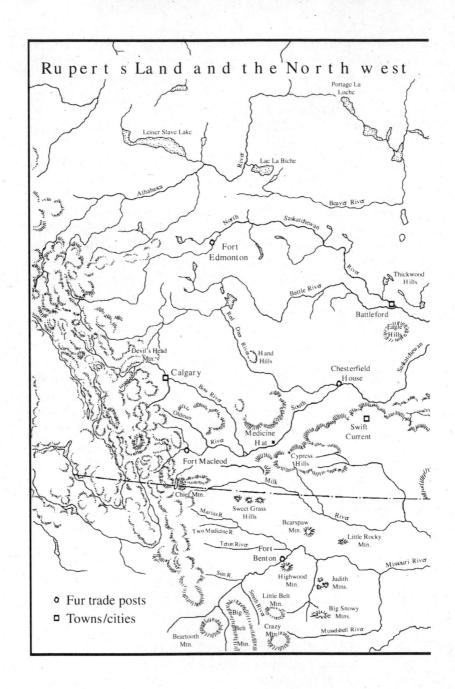

Rupert s Land and the North west

Portage La Loche

Lesser Slave Lake

Lac La Biche

River

Athabasca

Beaver River

North Saskatchewan

Fort Edmonton

River

Thickwood Hills

Battle River

Battleford

Saskatchewan

Eagle Hills

Red Deer River

Devil's Head Mtn.

Hand Hills

Chesterfield House

Calgary

Bow River

South

Swift Current

Oldman

Medicine Hat

River

Cypress Hills

Fort Macleod

Milk

Chief Mtn.

Sweet Grass Hills

Marias R.

River

Bearspaw Mtn.

Little Rocky Mtn.

Two Medicine R.

Teton River

Fort Benton

Missouri River

Sun R.

Highwood Mtn.

Judith Mtns.

Little Belt Mtn.

Smith River

Big Snowy Mtns.

Big Belt Mtn.

Crazy Mtn.

Musselshell River

Beartooth Mtn.

○ Fur trade posts
□ Towns/cities

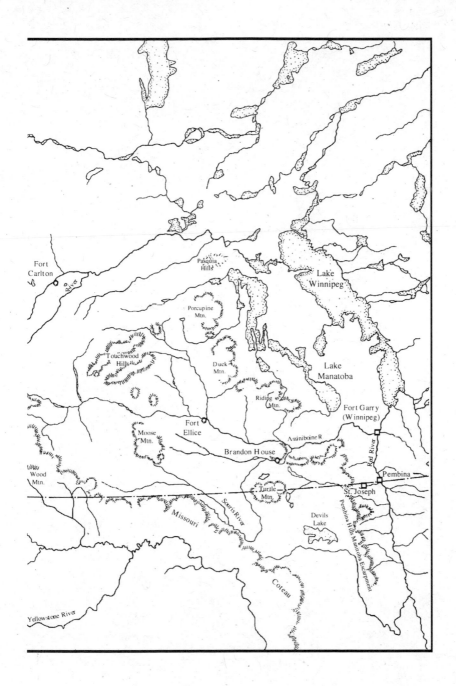

I

NATIVE HISTORY
AND THE FUR TRADE
IN WESTERN CANADA

1

Fur Trade Historiography

Past Conditions, Present Circumstances and a Hint of Future Prospects

MICHAEL PAYNE

IN 1973, L.G. Thomas published one of the first serious attempts to outline the historiography of what he termed the "fur trade era."[1] Thomas, like many other historians to this day, treated fur trade history as largely synonymous with the history of northern and western Canada up to the entry of these regions into Canada in 1870. This close association between the history of a region, or rather multiple regions comprising something between a third and a half of the area of modern Canada, and the history of a commercial enterprise is remarkable.[2] It has had a significant impact on the parameters of what is termed "fur trade" history.

As Thomas's article points out, much of this history is not particularly focused on furs or trade, but ranges broadly across the fields of imperial and colonial history, exploration and discovery literature, the history of missions, immigration and settlement, corporate history and biography. In recent years these topics have expanded to include a fair cross-section of social history concerns: everything from studies of social structure and social relations to gender and labour history. In 1973 Thomas remarked that historians had written "pitifully little" about Aboriginal people.[3] In some respects this is still a fair comment, but major advances have been made here as well.[4] Any discussion of fur trade historiography must start with the major caveat that the term "fur trade" history is often used more as a convenient designation for a range of historical interests than to define a coherent field of study. Jennifer Brown has likened fur trade history to the parable of the blind men and the elephant. There are lots of blind men and women examining the beast but limited agreement on its overall shape or meaning.[5] Some historians still accept the title of "fur trade" historian, but many would probably be happier to be defined as a labour, medical, economic, ethno or some other variety of historian who uses fur trade records.

Thomas's article is a good place to begin any consideration of fur trade historiography because it represents both a summation of over a century of historical writing while anticipating a watershed in that tradition.[6] First of all, the books Thomas suggests as the most significant contributions to this historiographical tradition were published, almost without exception, before 1945, the "golden" age of fur trade historical writing.[7] His survey of these books also suggests a substantial level of agreement among historians in the period up to the 1960s about the nature of the fur trade in western Canada and the main personalities and events in fur trade history. This does not mean that these historians all had the same concerns or even focused equal attention on the actual trade in furs. Some in fact barely refer to the fur trade and really are interested in agricultural settlement at Red River, the politics of Red River, or mission history. Nonetheless, historians such as J.B. Tyrrell, W.S. Wallace, L.J. Burpee, A.S. Morton and H.A. Innis saw the fur trade as a motive for exploration, as a integral part of the protracted struggle for control of the interior of North America between rival corporate and imperial interests, and a critical stage in the evolution of the Canadian nation. Perhaps the classic statement of the latter view can be found in the conclusion to Harold Innis's *The Fur Trade in Canada*:

> Canada emerged as a political entity with boundaries largely determined by the fur trade....The present Dominion emerged not in spite of geography but because of it. The significance of the fur trade consisted in its determination of the geographic framework.[8]

These historians also had a great interest in the business organization and practices of the different fur trade companies, and a taste for writing biographies of explorers and senior company officials.[9] The early volumes in the Champlain and Hudson's Bay Record Society series are excellent examples of the approaches to fur trade history described by Thomas. As Adrian Tanner has remarked, Aboriginal people were "well offstage left" in these works, and less distinguished fur trade employees along with their wives and families were "offstage right."[10] Nevertheless, many of these studies reflect the highest standards of traditional archival research and the editing of primary documents for publication. Histories of the fur trade also appeared in quantity. The bibliography for the revised edition of Innis's *The Fur Trade in Canada* is 21 pages long and includes about 400 citations of books, articles and published primary materials that were available by 1956.[11]

What Thomas describes is a tradition of historical writing in which Brown's blind men, and the occasional blind woman,[12] might differ on specifics, but they basically agreed on the nature of the beast they were describing. And they described it and speculated about its characteristics in great detail. However, many Canadian historians in the early 1970s thought that there was little new to say about fur trade history. As W.J. Eccles noted, the uncritical acceptance of the work of Innis, A.S. Morton and their contemporaries sometimes led "to the establishment of myth as conventional wisdom."[13]

Ironically it was three students who studied with L.G. Thomas: John Foster, Frits Pannekoek and Sylvia Van Kirk, who, along with Jennifer Brown, helped push fur trade history out of old trails and into new directions.[14] In their own ways and often looking at quite different issues, these scholars made a case that the fur trade could not be understood simply as a business or as a case study in economic relations between metropolis and hinterland.[15] Rather, as John Foster argued, the fur trade was also "a socio-cultural complex in which Indians, mixed-bloods, and whites were intertwined."[16]

It is easy to over emphasize the parallels between the work of these historians. However, all initially shared an interest in exploring the degree to which the fur trade produced an indigenous society in early western Canada that was neither exclusively European nor Aboriginal, but which was resilient and coherent enough to survive for over two centuries. Indeed, Frits Pannekoek has argued that the society engendered by the fur trade in western Canada continues "to affect politics, society, and ideas in Western Canada even now."[17]

This idea that western Canada had evolved a distinctive society prior to 1870 suggests interesting parallels with Quebecois historiography. Although Pannekoek and other historians working in western Canada have never made this an explicitly political issue,[18] it is worth noting that the idea of what Sylvia Van Kirk, echoing Peter Laslett, called "a world we have lost" puts a different spin on subsequent history in western Canada.[19] Under this scenario the great historical narrative of the opening of the West (and all the mythology that goes with it, including homesteaders, immigrants and Mounties) is actually the closing of the North West for its fur trade, Métis and Indian residents. Much like those Quebecois historians who treat the conquest of Quebec as an irretrievable rupture in the normal social, economic and political evolution of New France, Pannekoek and Van Kirk, in particular, depict the unraveling and overthrow of fur trade society. Van Kirk treats this as a truly lamentable loss. In her analysis, it was "...a society which recognized the importance of family and kin and in which native women had a vital contribution to make." This society was "...based on a close economic partnership between Indian and white and extensive intermarriage," and its decline "...is to be regretted, for the blending of European and Indian culture could have been an enriching human experience."[20]

This emphasis on cultural exchange and partnership also found expression in Van Kirk's studies of marriage patterns, and Jennifer Brown's studies of fur trade family structures and relations.[21] John Foster saw the experience of the Métis and the people he called the "country born" or Mixed Bloods[22] as a living embodiment of this cultural blending. He was quite adamant that the historical significance of these people went far beyond the simple fact of their parentage. Instead he argued that their social attitudes and values, patterns of enculturation, material culture, even their definitions of what constituted the "good life" were all worthy of serious examination.[23]

Foster also was very interested in exploring the historical experience of individuals and specific communities. His work on Paulet Paul, the Métis community at Buffalo Lake, and his interest in what made some people identify themselves as Métis, others as Indian, and still others as Euro-Canadian in the mid-nineteenth century, suggest some of the diversity of the "sociocultural complex" he initially proposed in 1973.[24] This interest in individual and group experience is also reflected in the work of Pannekoek, Van Kirk, Brown and other historians for projects such as the multi-volume *Dictionary of Canadian Biography*.[25] In recent years, this urge to particularize fur trade experience has lead to the proliferation of genealogical, particularly of Métis families, and demographic studies. These studies suggest peoples' choices of identity are rarely simple or obvious; instead they can arise through the interaction of multiple factors including geography, historical experience, other peoples' perceptions, as well as self identification. Genealogically based studies can also shed light on the social relations in fur trade communities and the role of personal connections in the operation of fur trade enterprises, especially in areas such as the recruitment and promotion of company employees. Studies focusing on the Métis have also shown that Métis identities and experiences do not all arise from Red River.[26]

Brown's and Van Kirk's studies of the experience of women and families in the fur trade have been enormously influential, not just in fur trade history but in pre-Confederation Canadian history generally. This stems in part from the skillful way these scholars have blended individual stories, such as the experience of the Chipewyan woman Thanadelthur (who now seems to appear alongside John A. Macdonald and Jacques Cartier in every Canadian textbook) or Letitia Hargrave, with the experience of extended family and other groupings to reveal broad social trends. As Jennifer Brown has noted, however, the success of their work has come to depend not just of the virtues of their research, but their choices of subject matter as well. In textbooks and survey courses, and in museum exhibits and historic site presentations, the combination of women and the fur trade or Indians and the fur trade accommodates "...two constituencies at once, killing two birds with one stone, as it were."[27]

The connection between their work and what Maurice Careless has defined as the idea of "limited identities," organizing history around gender, ethnicity, class, and/or region,[28] is clear. However, this interest in history from other perspectives than the national and political is scarcely unique to fur trade or even Canadian history.[29] Throughout the 1970s and into the early 1980s, historians made a concerted effort to bring fur trade historiography into closer connection with the kinds of historical issues being debated by other Canadian and international historians. In particular, there was a strong interest in reappraising the fur trade in terms of what the journal *Social History/Histoire sociale* and others have called "history from the bottom up," thus changing perspective and moving history away from a primary focus on elites. Some historians, such as Arthur Ray, also argued for the use of quantitative methods and statistical records as another way of altering the focus of fur trade studies.

Ray's book *Indians in the Fur Trade: Their Role as Hunters, Trappers and Middlemen in the Lands Southwest of Hudson Bay, 1660–1870*[30] was, in its own way, just as influential as the work of Foster, Van Kirk, Pannekoek and Brown. Like Jennifer Brown, whose interest in social structure and social relations is informed as much by her anthropological as her historical training, Arthur Ray did not begin his academic career as a historian. Ray began writing about fur trade history through his training as a historical geographer. As a result, both brought an interdisciplinary, and often critical, view of the tradition of fur trade writing described by L.G. Thomas to their early books and articles. Ray has been particularly critical of the tendency of many fur trade scholars to ignore account books and other quantitative trade records in favour of fur trade memoirs, correspondence and other qualitative, nonstatistical materials.[31]

Although reasserting the centrality of economics in fur trade studies, he has described his interest in the fur trade in much broader terms. In his books and articles Ray has defined the fur trade "...as an economic system having geographical expression as well as historical and anthropological ramifications." This led Ray to concentrate much of his early research on studying aspects of Indian-European exchange and trying to understand "...the Indians' role in the economics of the trade."[32] Far from being the passive dupes of sharp-trading Europeans, Ray has used the fur traders' own records to argue that Aboriginal people were canny consumers with a strong sense of self-interest in their dealings with fur trade companies. Moreover, they exerted considerable control over trade relations, prices and the quality of trade goods, and many found the fur trade opened new economic opportunities, which they willingly embraced. His study of Hudson's Bay Company records suggests that Indians rarely traded for goods that had no practical or social value, that they refused sub-standard or defective products, and that they resisted changes in price or the terms of trade that favoured fur trade companies. He suggests that their demands for trade goods were, at least initially, limited or "inelastic," and that most could chose to participate in trade or not as they saw fit.

Similarly, Ray outlines how some Aboriginal peoples responded to the new economic possibilities opened up by the fur trade by becoming traders themselves. Many exchanged trade goods for furs with more remote bands or began supplying posts with food and other products. They also adjusted their subsistence patterns to produce more furs for trade. The results of these changes were not always beneficial, and advantages changed over time, but as Ray has argued it is important to recognize that Indians were active participants in the fur trade with their own motives and goals. In fact, Ray has proposed a fundamental shift in how historians look at the fur trade in an influential 1978 article entitled "Fur Trade History as an Aspect of Native History." [33] In this article Ray suggests standing fur trade historiography on its head. Instead of treating Aboriginal involvement as a subset of fur trade history, perhaps fur trade history is best seen as a small, but significant, part of a broader history of Canada's First Nations.[34] This approach also suggests the possibility of seeing how Aboriginal people and cultures affected the fur trade and fur traders rather than always concentrating on the reverse.[35]

Although by no means a full listing of all of the significant studies or scholars working in the area of fur trade history in the 1970s and early 1980s,[36] Brown, Ray, Pannekoek, Foster and Van Kirk exemplify the revisionist tenor and many of the key historiographical issues of the period. They were interested in changing the perspective of history from the top down to the bottom up, in introducing questions of gender and ethnicity, in recognizing the agency and trying to understand the motivations of people who had often been treated as passive victims or totally ignored in other histories. They were also very interested in exploring other types of historical evidence beyond conventional written archival sources. Ray used trade records and account books, Pannekoek census records, and Brown and Van Kirk oral histories, all with a view to reaching a deeper and more inclusive understanding of Thomas's "fur trade era."

Most of the work of these and other scholars in the period up to the mid 1980s, however, did not substantially alter the chronological and geographic focus outlined by Thomas. Studies of the fur trade up to the mid-1980s also accepted the idea that the arrival of Europeans and the start of the fur trade represented the central dynamic in the history of this vast region from the mid-seventeenth century to the late nineteenth century. The fur trade explained population movements, cultural change and adaptation, and political and economic conditions of First Nations. The fur trade integrated western and northern Canada into both a national and the international economy. The demands of the fur trade drove exploration, technology, business organization, immigration, resource management, attitudes towards the environment, scientific discovery, even who people married and how their children were educated.

Since the mid-1980s the fur trade "centricness" of this historiographical tradition has been increasingly questioned by historians, archaeologists and anthropologists. Instead of being treated as the main engine of historical change in the North West between 1670 and 1870, the fur trade is now often treated as one of many influences on the history of the region which may not have changed as dramatically as earlier histories implied. Recent works on the fur trade often mix a degree of skepticism with their revisionism.

Much of the research and writing undertaken by Jennifer Brown since the publication of *Strangers in Blood* reflects these urges. For example, she has expressed considerable concern over the somewhat simplistic way many researchers have used the idea of a "fur trade society." Instead she suggests the existence of multiple fur trade societies, or alternatively no society at all but rather sets of social ties and exchanges that give the fur trade a socio-cultural dimension but stop well short of any sociological definition of society. She has been equally skeptical about histories that make the fur trade central in the experience of Aboriginal people in the Canadian Northwest. Such a view ignores the fact that "...Native people often had many other priorities and activities on their minds besides the fur trade."[37] Indeed many chose to participate intermittently, or not at all, in the fur trade and visited posts or stayed away according to their understanding of their best interests. Brown has also expressed concern that viewing Aboriginal history from a fur trade perspective results in a rather narrow focus on white-native relations; as if the only things that mattered in the lives of the Cree or Chipewyan were how they were treated at posts and what they were offered for their furs. In fact, in many ways the fur trade was grafted onto long-standing trade and diplomatic ties among different Aboriginal groups, and formed a economic subset of these larger and more significant relations.[38]

Other researchers have also explored some of these issues. Dale Russell has argued—somewhat controversially—that comparatively few Cree or Assinboin were active participants in the early fur trade before large numbers of posts were built in the interior. This suggests that ideas of early or rapid cultural change and the development of dependency of European goods are improbable and badly over-estimate the significance of the fur trade for Aboriginal people living in the interior of western Canada in the eighteenth century. Russell also suggests that the belief that the fur trade armed the Cree and Assiniboin and enabled them to expand their territories north and west—an idea which he traces back to a few unsubstantiated speculations made by Sir Alexander Mackenzie in 1801 — is equally unlikely.[39] Russell's book suggests that for about the first century the fur trade had relatively little impact outside of the palisades of the posts themselves.[40]

Paul Thistle is equally skeptical about the nature and scope of the changes engendered by the fur trade. He has suggested that historians interested in exploring cultural change and adaptation among Aboriginal people need to draw a distinction between "core" cultural institutions or values and material culture. People can change how they hunt and prepare their food without changing their belief systems, how they raise their children, or how they structure their communities. According to Thistle, and others, Aboriginal people were quite capable of integrating European technology into their lives without being transformed by that technology.[41] Overall it has become increasingly common to suggest that Aboriginal cultures were remarkably resilient and that understanding cultural persistence among Aboriginal people is as important and perhaps more important than explaining change in their ways of life.[42]

In similar fashion, other historians have tried to understand what impact living and working in the fur trade had on fur trade employees of Indian, Métis, Mixed Blood, Scottish, Orcadian, *Canadien*, English and even Norwegian backgrounds. Philip Goldring and Carol Judd have looked at career prospects and recruitment patterns in the fur trade, as well as some of the social implications of such a diverse workforce.[43] Michael Payne has looked at social structure and relations, work and leisure patterns and material culture at individual posts. In some aspects of their lives fur traders were very reluctant to adapt their behaviour to new conditions in the North West, while in other areas — particularly material culture — they were very willing to borrow from their Aboriginal trading partners.[44] Arguably just as cross-cultural trade may have affected, without transforming, Aboriginal cultures, so too did it shape, but far from revolutionize, the behaviour and lifestyle of the traders themselves.

Many of these studies bring a revisionist slant to the fur trade because they look at the trade not just from the bottom up but also from the individual fur trade post or fur trade district out. The idea of studying individual fur trade posts or specific regions is not entirely new. Both A.S. Morton and Harold Innis took a great interest in identifying the locations of posts[45] and many published collections of primary documents focused on journals and other materials from individual posts. However James Parker's study of Fort Chipewyan and Elaine Allen Mitchell's study of Fort Timiskaming really began a strong trend towards researching the fur trade from a regional or an individual post perspective.[46] Such studies have several advantages. One is simply practical. A local or regional perspective places some logical limits on the sheer volume of primary material facing researchers.[47] Case studies also offer an excellent way to test claims made by other historians based on broader samples of fur trade documents. This is certainly true for studies such as Daniel Francis and Toby Morantz's *Partners In Furs*. It examines the history of several posts on eastern James Bay and finds that the fur trade was no "...monolithic enterprise, uniform at all times in all parts of the country."[48] Quite the contrary, Francis, Morantz and others have detailed many ways in which the fur trade and fur traders adjusted themselves to local conditions and needs. These consisted of trading different products, offering different standards of trade, eating different foods, speaking different languages, or just recognizing that trading with the Blackfoot or Peigan was very different from trading with the Ojibwa or Woods Cree.[49] These studies have also shown that posts varied by function. Some were more administrative and transportation centres than trade centres, others were responsible for the production of trade goods or supplies, and at most posts trade itself occupied very little time.[50]

Just as the fur trade has been forced to share centre stage in historical narratives, other historians have been suggesting that its former geographical and chronological boundaries need revision as well. Perhaps most notably, Arthur Ray has pointed out that the fur trade survived long past 1870 and is far from a spent economic force even today.[51] In similar fashion, Ray and others have noted that the fur trade retreated from the Prairie West in the period after 1870, but did not disappear in northern communities. Some aspects of the trade, including fur farming, actually expanded in the twentieth century.

This interest in the post-1870 fur trade along with a regional approach shapes Frank Tough's recent study entitled *As Their Natural Resources Fail: Native Peoples and the Economic History of Northern Manitoba, 1870–1930*.[52] Tough is very critical of approaches to fur trade history that apply notions of partnership and the autonomy of Aboriginal producers of furs uncritically and without regard to period or regional economic circumstances. He suggests that by the later nineteenth century—if not earlier—the Aboriginal population of northern Manitoba had developed a well-integrated "post and bush" economy that balanced seasonal labour, and the production of furs and other goods for the HBC and other traders, with subsistence hunting, fishing, trapping and other activities. Resource depletion and changes in the market for furs and other local products after 1870 had a major impact on this regional economy and the people it supported. With the post half of this economy in disarray, life became very difficult indeed. By refocusing attention on the political and economic history of the fur trade, Tough suggests a much less benign legacy of three centuries of trade than many other historians allow.

An interest in the broad geographic extent of the fur trade can also be seen in the growing number of studies of the fur trade in the United States,

Russian Alaska, and the Arctic.[53] Other scholars have taken a renewed interest in the ultimate markets for furs in the eighteenth and nineteenth centuries—London, Paris and Amsterdam—and in particular how furs were sold, who bought them, and how the trade was organized and financed.[54] Overall, the chronological and geographic assumptions that lay behind L.G. Thomas's idea of a historiography of the "fur trade era" have limited relevance, at best, for recent writers.[55]

A recent book that extends both the time period and the kind of evidence used in fur trade and aboriginal history is *Voices From Hudson Bay: Cree Stories From York Factory*. This book looks at York Factory as a trade centre and community in the twentieth century based on interviews done with Cree elders who lived at York Factory before the post closed in 1957. In this case, oral histories bring a different perspective and create a parallel set of records to the Hudson's Bay Company's post records for the period.[56] As well as using oral histories, some researchers have begun to use photographs and film, both as a supplement to and as a corrective of more conventional archival manuscript and government records.[57]

·Perhaps the most significant change in this aspect of fur trade history, however, has been a growing skepticism about the uncritical use of archival and published primary documents by historians. This tendency is not entirely new, but it has become increasingly important in recent years. Fur trade records often refer to "starving" Indians, and many Indians themselves claimed to be starving upon arrival at posts, but is this proof that accommodating the fur trade in their seasonal round put Aboriginal people at risk of famine? According to an influential article by Mary Black-Rodgers, these sorts of statements need to be carefully considered and perhaps reappraised in terms of the rhetoric of trade and the preconceptions of fur traders.[58] The kind of attention to semantics and the ability to read the sub-text along with the literal text of documents that Black-Rodgers suggests has become something more than just accounting for the structural biases of gender, class, and ethnicity in fur trade documentation. A good recent selection of research that attempts to "read beyond words" is a collection of articles with that title edited by Jennifer Brown and Elizabeth Vibert.[59] In similar fashion, a recent dissertation by Laura Peers looks at how historic sites, and to a lesser extent museums, depict Aboriginal people in fur trade contexts. Peers suggests that these depictions convey much more than just the words spoken by interpretive guides. Instead they too have a sub-text that needs to be "read" and understood by both visitors to sites and the people who work in these heritage institutions.[60]

Other scholars, perhaps most notably Ian MacLaren, have pointed to the need for researchers to consult the original manuscript versions of fur trade journals and diaries rather than simply relying on the published versions of these documents. As MacLaren has shown in a series of studies, editors and ghost writers made substantial changes in preparing the work of Paul Kane, Samuel Hearne and other often cited fur traders and explorers for publication. Paul Kane's published journal bears little resemblance to his field notes. His descriptions of life at Fort Edmonton, which have been used in many fur trade histories, are not necessarily the product of his direct observations. Instead his published journal may well represent his editor's or ghost writer's ideas of what post life ought to be like.[61] Interestingly, MacLaren has increasingly turned his attention to the similar process by which the sketches of various artists, including Kane and George Back, were also reinterpreted for publication or sale to collectors. Once again, many of these reworked and often substantially altered paintings and engravings have been used uncritically as authentic depictions of fur trade and Aboriginal subjects, which they are anything but.[62]

One final feature of recent fur trade historiography is also worth noting. Fur trade posts are among the best documented communities in Canada between the mid-seventeenth and late nineteenth centuries.[63] Archival records allow us to know how James and Letitia Hargrave furnished their quarters at York Factory, and what post employees were working at on 26 May 1740 at Prince of Wales' Fort.[64] The range and quantity of these records means that researchers can study virtually any subject from recreation and leisure patterns to work and class relations or medical history. Increasingly historians with a limited interest in the fur trade as either a business or a "socio-economic complex," but a strong interest in sports history, or environmental history, or the history of education are finding fur trade records valuable resources for their studies. Good examples of this are the use of fur trade records for the study of labour history,[65] the history of medicine,[66] and the history of climate and climate change.[67]

This growth of interest in fur trade records as source material for work across a broad range of disciplines and by scholars with research interests that range far beyond cross cultural trade or Aboriginal history is not likely to decline. Similarly the kind of assurance that we know the main outlines and significance of the fur trade and that led W.J. Eccles to suggest myth had hardened into conventional wisdom is unlikely to return. Nor are we likely ever to be comfortable with defining the history of the Canadian north or west as "fur trade" history again. In losing its central place, however, fur trade history has been enriched, not impoverished. The fur trade seems much more interesting and complex and nuanced now that it does not have to support the entire history of the North West.[68]

Notes

1. L.G. Thomas, "Historiography of the Fur Trade Era," in Richard Allen, ed., *A Region of the Mind* (Regina: Canadian Plains Research Centre, 1973), 73–85. This article is a revised version of a paper he first delivered at the Centennial Conference on the History of the Canadian West held in Banff, Alberta in 1967.

2. For example, historians of Canada's early maritime colonies are not labeled fish trade historians or timber trade historians unless they are specifically interested in and writing about the cod fishery or the square timber trade.

3. Ibid., 83.

4. The relationship between Aboriginal history and "fur trade" historiography has been explored in two excellent historiographical essays written by Jacqueline Peterson and John Anfinson in the early 1980s. Unfortunately there is no equivalent review that covers the literature on this important topic over the last decade and a half. See Jacqueline Peterson and John Anfinison, "The Indian and the Fur Trade: a Review of Recent Literature" in W.R. Swagerty, ed., *Scholars and the Indian Experience: Critical Reviews of Recent Writing in the Social Sciences* (Bloomington: Indiana University Press, 1984), 223–57. A revised version of this essay that focuses more closely on Canadian research in this area was published the following year as "The Indian and the Fur Trade: A Review of Recent Literature," *Manitoba History* 10 (Autumn 1985): 10–18.

5. See Jennifer Brown, "The Blind Men and the Elephant: Fur Trade History Revisited" in Patricia A. McCormack and R. Geoffrey Ironsides, eds., *The Uncovered Past: Roots of Northern Alberta Societies* (Edmonton: Canadian Circumpolar Institute, University of Alberta, 1993), 15–19.

6. There are several reasons why the early 1970s mark a major change in fur trade historiography. One practical reason was the moving of the Hudson's Bay Company Archives from London to Winnipeg in 1974. This made these remarkable records much more accessible to Canadian scholars.

7. The 1930s probably represent the height of interest in fur trade history. The decade is neatly bracketed by Harold A. Innis's *The Fur Trade in Canada: An Introduction to Canadian Economic History* (Princeton: Yale University Press, 1930) and A.S. Morton's less analytical, but massive chronological narrative, *A History of the Canadian West to 1870–71* (London: T. Nelson and Sons, 1939). Both these books have subsequently been republished in new editions. The most recent republication of *The Fur Trade in Canada* is of particular interest because in includes a new introductory essay by Arthur Ray. See Harold A. Innis, *The Fur Trade in Canada: an Introduction to Canadian Economic History* (Toronto: University of Toronto Press, 1999).

8. Harold Innis, *The Fur Trade in Canada* (Toronto: University of Toronto Press, 1956) revised edition, 393. Innis's "staples theory" cast the fur trade in a central role in a grand paradigm explaining much of Canada's social, economic and political history. This helped to confirm the fur trade's place in national historical narratives "as a critical social-evolutionary stage…a great height of land, a Portage La Loche, between ancient and modern Canada." Brown, "Blind Men," 15.

9. These subjects still attract attention. A good example of a recent biography of an explorer and fur trade company officer is Barry Gough's *First Across the Continent: Sir Alexander Mackenzie* (Toronto: McClelland and Stewart, 1997). Published primary fur trade and exploration materials also continue to appear on a regular basis. A recent example of new editorial approaches to well-known primary journals can be found in

David Thompson, *Columbia Journals,* edited by Barbara Belyea (Montreal: McGill-Queen's University Press, 1994).

10. Adrian Tanner, "The End of Fur Trade History," *Queen's Quarterly* 90, no. 1 (Spring 1983): 189.

11. See Innis, *Fur Trade,* 421–41.

12. The major exceptions to the male domination of fur trade history in the period up to the 1960s were Agnes Laut, Grace Lee Nute, Margaret Arnett MacLeod and Alice Johnson. The work of Laut, Nute and Johnson fits comfortably within the general trends of fur trade historiography in that time period. By contrast, MacLeod's work on the letters of Letitia Hargrave, which remain one of the great primary sources for any analysis of fur trade social mores, anticipates more recent interest in fur trade social history. See for examples, Agnes C. Laut, *Pathfinders of the West, being the thrilling story of the adventures of the men who discovered the great Northwest, Radisson, La Verendrye, Lewis and Clark* (Toronto: William Briggs, 1904); Grace Lee Nute, *Caesars of the Wilderness: Medard Chouart, Sieur des Groseilliers and Pierre Esprit Radisson, 1618 to 1710* (St. Paul: Minnesota State Historical Society, 1978), first published 1943; Alice M. Johnson, ed., *Saskatchewan Journals and Correspondence; Edmonton House, 1795–1800, Chesterfield House, 1800–1802* (London: Hudson's Bay Record Society, 1967), and Margaret Arnett MacLeod, ed., *The Letters of Letitia Hargrave* (Toronto: The Champlain Society, 1947).

13. See W.J. Eccles, "A Belated Review of Harold Adams Innis, *The Fur Trade in Canada*" *The Canadian Historical Review* 60, no. 4 (December 1979): 419–41.

14. This is the title of a very influential collection of papers presented at the Third North American Fur Trade Conference in Winnipeg in 1978. See Carol M. Judd and Arthur J. Ray, eds., *Old Trails and New Directions: Papers of the Third North American Fur Trade Conference* (Toronto: University of Toronto Press, 1980).

15. The four dissertations are John Elgin Foster, "The Country-born in the Red River Settlement, 1820–1850" (Ph.D. dissertation, University of Alberta, 1973); Frits Pannekoek, "The Churches and the Social Structure in the Red River Area, 1818–70" (Ph.D. dissertation, Queen's University, 1973); Sylvia Van Kirk, "The Role of Women in the Fur Trade Society of the Canadian West, 1700–1850" (Ph.D. dissertation, University of London, 1975), and Jennifer S.H. Brown, "Company Men and Native Families: Fur Trade Social and Domestic Relations in Canada's Old Northwest" (Ph.D. dissertation, University of Chicago, 1976). For an excellent summary of their main findings see, Sylvia Van Kirk, "Fur Trade Social History: Some Recent Trends" in Judd and Ray, eds., *Old Trails,* 160–73.

16. John Foster, "Introduction" in Lewis G. Thomas, ed., *The Prairie West to 1905: A Canadian Sourcebook* (Toronto: Oxford University Press, 1975), 20.

17. Frits Pannekoek, *The Fur Trade and Western Canadian Society 1670–1870* (Ottawa: Canadian Historical Association, 1987) Historical booklet no. 43, 23.

18. It is interesting that these studies appeared in the mid-1970s at a time when western Canadian "alienation" was a much-discussed phenomenon, and political battles over federal-provincial relations were common. Asserting a unique, and long-standing, western Canadian society with its own history and culture is not explicitly political, but it could be.

19. Sylvia Van Kirk, *"Many Tender Ties": Women in Fur Trade Society, 1670–1870* (Winnipeg: Watson & Dwyer, 1980). Van Kirk uses this phrase as the title for her concluding

chapter on the 1850s and 1860s when fur trade marriage and other social mores came under attack from missionaries and other new residents of the North West.

20. Ibid., 242.

21. Jennifer Brown, *Strangers in Blood: Fur Trade Company Families in Indian Country* (Vancouver: University of British Columbia Press, 1980).

22. Terminology used in fur trade studies is a source of both confusion and contention. The term Métis is particularly problematic. Today it is often used to describe anyone of mixed Aboriginal and European background, but historically it had a much narrower meaning. It was usually applied to people of mixed ancestry who were French-speaking and Catholic. People of Scots, English or Orkney and Aboriginal ancestry, who often spoke English and belonged to Protestant churches, were often called Halfbreeds—a term which now has strongly pejorative connotations. Foster tried to encourage the use of "country born" for these people, but most historians have opted for the term "Mixed Blood," though of course it was genes not blood that was mixed. Even these identities are fraught with difficulties. Many people of Scottish and Cree background identified themselves with the Métis community and cause in Red River, while others with French surnames did not. Jennifer Brown and Jacqueline Peterson discuss these issues and the problems with retrospective ethno-cultural identifications in their introduction to *The New Peoples: Being and Becoming Métis in North America* (Winnipeg: University of Manitoba Press, 1985), 3–7. John Foster also wrote on the subject, including a 1978 article entitled "The Métis: The People and the Term," which appeared in *Prairie Forum* 3, no. 1 (Spring 1978): 79–90.

23. See Foster, "Country-born." Unlike Pannekoek, Van Kirk and Brown, John Foster never did turn his dissertation into a book. However, he expanded upon many of the ideas in his dissertation in a series of articles published throughout the 1970s, 1980s and into the 1990s. Two of his first, and most influential, articles are "The Origins of the Mixed Bloods in the Canadian West" in Lewis H. Thomas, ed., *Essays on Western History* (Edmonton: University of Alberta Press, 1976), 71–80 and "The Indian-Trader in the Hudson Bay Fur Trade Tradition" in Proceedings of the 2nd Congress, Canadian Ethnology Service, Mercury Series no. 28 (Ottawa: National Museum of Man, 1975), 571–85. The latter introduced the idea, borrowed from Peter Laslett's studies of British social history, that fur trade posts operated on the model of a "household" economy and social structure. This was one of the first attempts to marry fur trade social history to social history theory generated in other historio-graphical traditions. In recent years this has become much more common, and historians working with fur trade records have made particular use of ideas borrowed from British, American and sometimes other Canadian social historians.

24. See for example, John Foster, "Paulet Paul: Métis or 'House Indian' Folk Hero?" *Manitoba History,* no. 9 (Spring 1985): 2–7 and "Some questions and perspectives on the problem of Métis roots" in Peterson and Brown, *The New Peoples*, 73–91. John Foster was working on a study of the Métis settlement of Buffalo Lake in central Alberta at the time of his death in 1996. Some preliminary findings on this commu-nity were included in a study he undertook with R.F. Beal and Louise Zuk for the Historic Sites Service and Provincial Museum of Alberta. R.F. Beal, J.E. Foster and Louise Zuk, *The Métis Hivernement Settlement at Buffalo Lake, 1872–1877* (unpublished ms., Department of Culture, Alberta, 1987). Métis history has become one of the most vibrant areas of historical research on the Canadian west with its own historio-graphical debates and interests. The work of historians such as Douglas Sprague,

Diane Payment, Thomas Flanagan, and Gerhard Ens are good examples of research in this area since John Foster's early work.

25. This massive collaborative effort contains many outstanding biographies of fur trade figures, including Aboriginal people who have rarely been treated as individuals by most Canadian historians up until now. One peculiarity of this reference source is that volumes are organized by the date of death of the individuals profiled. Fortunately excellent nominal indexes assist researchers in finding the appropriate volume for the person they are studying. See *Dictionary of Canadian Biography* (Toronto: University of Toronto Press, 1966–). Fourteen volumes have appeared to date covering the period from 1000 to 1920 AD.

26. The use of genealogy by historians interested in the fur trade to reveal the complexities of personal and family history, patronage relations, and issues of individual and group identity is well-reflected in several articles that appear in Peterson and Brown, eds., *The New Peoples*. See in particular the articles by Peterson, Spry, Long, Nicks and Morgan, and Brown. Demography is the particular focus of a valuable study by Trudy Nicks entitled "Demographic Anthropology of Native Populations in Western Canada, 1800–1975" (Ph.D. dissertation, University of Alberta, 1980).

27. Brown, "Blind Men," 15.

28. J.M.S. Careless, "'Limited Identities' in Canada," *Canadian Historical Review* 50, no. 1 (March 1969): 1–10.

29. In some respects, these studies reflect L.G. Thomas's hope for fur trade historiography: setting "…regional history in its proper place, not as an end in itself but as a means to an understanding, or at least a partial appreciation, of the nature of history." Thomas, "Historiography," 84.

30. Arthur Ray, *Indians in the Fur Trade: Their Role as Hunters, Trappers, and Middlemen in the Lands Southwest of Hudson Bay, 1660–1870* (Toronto: University of Toronto Press, 1974).

31. See Arthur Ray, "The Early Hudson's Bay Company Account Books as Sources for Historical Research: An Analysis and Assessment," *Archivaria*, no. 1 (1976): 3–38 and Arthur J. Ray and Donald Freeman, *"Give Us Good Measure": An economic analysis of relations between the Indians and the Hudson's Bay Company before 1763* (Toronto: University of Toronto Press, 1978), esp. chapters 9 and 10, 81–124.

32. Ibid., xv–xvi.

33. Arthur Ray, "Fur Trade History as an Aspect of Native History" in I.A.L. Getty and D.B. Smith, eds., *One Century Later* (Vancouver: University of British Columbia Press, 1978), 7–19.

34. This is certainly the direction Arthur Ray has taken in some of his more recent work such as *I Have Lived Here Since the World Began: an illustrated history of Canada's native people* (Toronto: Lester Publishing, 1996), which is a highly regarded survey of Aboriginal history in Canada.

35. An excellent example of how this approach can change traditional historical narratives is Gerald Friesen's survey history *The Canadian Prairies A History* (Toronto: University of Toronto Press, 1984). In this very influential book—it is still probably the most popular general text for western Canadian history courses—Friesen chose to write two parallel chapters on the "natives' fur trade" and the "Europeans' fur trade." The quality and quantity of new research prompted by a change in perspective that makes the "fur trade" an "Indian trade," as Peterson and Anfinson suggest, is reflected in their previously mentioned review articles.

36. There are several very useful summaries of fur trade historiography and bibliographical guides to sources that students may wish to consult. Shepard Krech III has produced an excellent bibliography covering publications up to 1991. The introduction to this bibliography also comments on general research trends in a number of areas of anthropology and history. Shepard Krech III, *Native Canadian Anthropology and History: A Selected Bibliography* (Winnipeg: Rupert's Land Research Centre, University of Winnipeg, 1994). Several articles, most notably those by Kerry Abel, Thomas Wien and Tina Loo, in M. Brook Taylor, ed., *Canadian History: A Reader's Guide volume 1: Beginnings to Confederation* (Toronto: University of Toronto Press, 1994) also cover fur trade historiography and sources.

37. Brown, "Blind Men," 17.

38. The direction of Brown's evolving research interests and the questions she feels fur trade studies need to address can be seen in the above article as well as "Fur Trade History as Text and Drama," and in her comments at a workshop on Fur Trade and Native History summarized in the Rupert's Land Research Centre Newsletter. See Michael Payne (compiler), "Summary Report Fur Trade and Native History Workshop," *Rupert's Land Research Centre Newsletter* 7 no. 1 (Spring 1991): esp. 16–17.

39. Dale R. Russell, *Eighteenth Century Western Cree and their Neighbours,* Mercury Series Paper 143 (Ottawa: Canadian Museum of Civilization, 1991) . Russell also argues that despite the claims of earlier historians and anthropologists some Cree had adapted to life as Plains buffalo hunters before the fur trade gave them access to guns and other trade goods. He suggests that the fur trade produced very little population movement—at least until after the great epidemics of the late eighteenth and nineteenth centuries. The issue of dependency in the fur trade is a complex one. The fur trade was long assumed to have created technological dependency among Aboriginal groups. Various authors have speculated that within a generation or two Aboriginal hunters needed guns because they no longer knew how to use more traditional methods. Russell and others dispute this conclusion pointing to the continued use of bows and arrows and other supposedly lost skills well into the nineteenth century. Moreover, if Russell is correct and the vast majority of plains dwellers had little contact with posts, rapid dependency is highly unlikely. See Russell, *Eighteenth Century Western Cree,* 11–13.

40. He is not alone in this view. John Milloy in *The Plains Cree: Warriors, Traders and Diplomats, 1790–1870* (Winnipeg: University of Manitoba Press, 1988), 47–58, suggests that the entire fur trade prior to the 1830s can be seen as a peripheral part of a much larger and more important trade among Plains and Woodlands peoples in horses, food, and other products centred on the Mandan-Hidatsa villages in the Dakotas. As he puts it, "Considering the fact that the British, French and Canadian merchants traded through it, it can be suggested in all seriousness that for a time the European outlets were a sub-system within the Mandan-Hidatsa trade organization." Recently, an archaeologist, Heinz Pyszczyk, has surveyed the findings from dozens of proto-Contact and early post-Contact archaeological sites and found almost no evidence of European goods. He suggests this means very few European trade goods were present in the interior prior to the widespread construction of inland posts. See Heinz Pyszczyk, "Use of Fur Trade Goods by Plains Indians in Central and Southern Alberta, Canada," *Canadian Journal of Archaeology* 21 (1997): 45–84. This in turn suggests the "fur trade era" was at best about a century, not two centuries, in length.

41.   Paul C. Thistle, *Indian-European Trade Relations in the Lower Saskatchewan River Region to 1840* (Winnipeg: University of Manitoba Press, 1986), 33–40. Similar ideas can be found in many other studies. One of the best reappraisals of ideas of rapid cultural change can be found in Daniel Francis and Toby Morantz, *Partners in Furs: A History of the Fur Trade in Eastern James Bay 1600–1870* (Montreal: McGill-Queen's University Press, 1983). The idea that Aboriginal peoples rapidly became dependent of European technology dates back to some of the writing of fur traders themselves. A good summation of this view can be found in E.E. Rich's article "Trade Habits and Economic Motivation Among the Indians of North America" *Canadian Journal of Economics and Political Science* 26 (1960): 35–53. Thistle, Francis and Morantz, and others have argued that "dependency" is an inaccurate and misleading way to look at a complex relationship marked by interdependence, or even the dependence of fur traders on Aboriginal people. Much of the debate in this area revolves around issues of definition—what exactly is meant by dependency and dependency on what—and questions of how and when this partnership in furs became distinctly unequal. Few would suggest that the initial benefits of trade did not decline by sometime in the nineteenth century.

42.   Cultural persistence, even in the face of outright repression, is also a major theme in Katherine Pettipas, *Severing the Ties that Bind: Government Repression of Indigenous Religious Ceremonies on the Prairies* (Winnipeg: University of Manitoba Press, 1994).

43.   See Philip Goldring, *Papers on the Labour System of the Hudson's Bay Company, 1821–1900: Volumes I, II and III* (Ottawa: Parks Canada, 1979, 1980 and 1982) and Carol M. Judd, "Native Labour and Social Stratification in the Hudson's Bay Company's Northern Department (1770–1870)," *Canadian Review of Sociology and Anthropology* 17 (1980): 305–14 and "Mixt Bands of Many Nations: 1821–70" in Judd and Ray, eds., *Old Trails*, 126–46. It should be noted that Goldring and Judd reach quite different conclusions about the career prospects of mixed-blood children of HBC employees.

44.   See Michael Payne, *"The Most Respectable Place in the Territory": Everyday Life in Hudson's Bay Company Service at York Factory, 1788–1870* (Ottawa: Environment Canada, Parks Canada, 1989) and "Fort Churchill, 1821–1900: an Outpost Community in the Fur Trade," *Manitoba History*, no. 20 (Autumn 1990): 2–15.

45.   Perhaps the best early example of this interest in identifying and listing posts is E. Voorhis, *Historic Forts and Trading Posts of the French Regime and of the English Fur Trading Companies* (Ottawa: Department of the Interior, 1930). This encyclopedic compilation has been substantially revised and updated in Terry Smythe, "Thematic Study of the Fur Trade in the Canadian West: 1670–1870," a manuscript prepared for the Canadian National Historic Sites Service of Parks Canada in 1968.

46.   See Elaine Allen Mitchell, *Fort Timiskaming and the Fur Trade* (Toronto: University of Toronto Press, 1977). James Parker completed his M.A. thesis on Fort Chipewyan in 1967. A revised version was published as *Emporium of the North: Fort Chipewyan and the Fur Trade to 1835* (Regina: Canadian Plains Research Centre/Alberta Culture and Multiculturalism, 1987).

47.   The quantity of fur trade archival records is staggering. When they were moved from London to Winnipeg in 1974, the Hudson's Bay Company Archives weighed some 68 tons. There are over 1200 account books for York Factory alone covering the period up to 1870. All studies of the fur trade therefore involve some sort of sampling of the primary record.

48. Francis and Morantz, *Partners in Furs*, 167.

49. An interesting case study of some of the complexities of trade even with a single "tribal" group such as the Blackfoot/Siksika can be found in Theodore Binnema, "Old Swan, Big Man, and the Siksika Bands, 1794–1815," *Canadian Historical Review* 77 (1996): 1–32.

50. Many of these local and regional studies have been undertaken in Canada by Parks Canada or provincial heritage agencies, and in the United States by the National Parks Service. Some of these studies are reviewed in Michael Payne, "Fur Trade Social History and the Public Historian: Some Other Recent Trends" in Jennifer Brown, W.J. Eccles, and Donald P. Heldman, eds., *The Fur Trade Revisited: Selected Papers of the Sixth North American Fur Trade Conference, Mackinac Island, Michigan, 1991* (East Lansing: Michigan State University Press, 1994), 481–99. Other examples of local or regional studies of the fur trade include Victor Lytwyn, *The Fur Trade of the Little North: Indians, Pedlars, and Englishmen East of Lake Winnipeg, 1760–1821* (Winnipeg: Rupert's Land Research Centre, University of Winnipeg, 1986); Daniel Francis and Michael Payne, *A Narrative History of Fort Dunvegan* (Winnipeg: Watson & Dwyer, 1994); Graham MacDonald, *A Good Solid Comfortable Establishment An Illustrated History of Lower Fort Garry* (Winnipeg: Watson & Dwyer, 1992); MacCormack and Ironside, eds., *The Uncovered Past* — a collection of papers about Fort Chipewyan and Fort Vermilion based on a 1988 conference — and various studies by Parks Canada in that agency's manuscript and microfiche report series on sites such as Lower Fort Garry, Fort Langley, Rocky Mountain House, Prince of Wales' Fort, Fort St. James and York Factory.

51. See Arthur J. Ray, *The Canadian Fur Trade in the Industrial Age* (Toronto: University of Toronto Press, 1990).

52. Frank Tough, *As Their Natural Resources Fail: Native Peoples and the Economic History of Northern Manitoba, 1870–1930* (Vancouver: University of British Columbia Press, 1996).

53. This broadened geographic scope appears to have encouraged greater interest in fur trade history among scholars outside of Canada. There has always been a certain interest in the history of the fur trade in the northern United States, particularly in states bordering the Great Lakes and western Canada. In recent years however, this interest has grown to the point where regular fur trade conferences are held at places such Fort Vancouver in Washington. The North American Fur Trade Conferences are often held in the United States and regularly attract scholars from Canada, the United States and Europe. These conferences have featured papers on the fur trade in Texas and Louisiana, New England, Russian Alaska, and other areas, not to mention the recruitment of employees in Hawaii. There is also a growing awareness in Canada of significant trade and other ties between the Canadian west and centres such as St. Louis and New Orleans on the Mississippi River, Fort Benton and other Missouri River posts, and posts around the Columbia River. In total there have been seven North American Fur Trade conferences held dating back to 1965. Collections of selected papers have been published for each of these conferences. Two of these collections are cited earlier in these notes. Other significant collections of papers from these conferences include Thomas C. Buckley, ed., *Rendezvous: Selected papers of the Fourth North American Fur Trade Conference* (St. Paul: North American Fur Trade Conference, 1981): Bruce Trigger, Toby Morantz and Louise Dechene, eds., *Le Castor Fait Tout: Selected papers of the Fifth North American Fur Trade Conference* (Montreal:

North American Fur Trade Conference, 1987) and Jo-Anne Fiske, Susan Sleeper-Smith and William Wicken, eds., *New Faces of the Fur Trade: Selected papers of the Seventh North American Fur Trade Conference* (East Lansing: Michigan State University Press, 1998).

54. See for example, Harry W. Duckworth, "British Capital in the Fur Trade: John Strettell and John Fraser" in Brown, Eccles and Heldman, eds., *The Fur Trade Revisited,* 39–56. Another example of this kind of study that examines how company owners and managers tried to organize the trade and balance supply with demand can be found in Elizabeth Mancke, *A Company of Businessmen: The Hudson's Bay Company and Long-Distance Trade, 1670-1730* (Winnipeg: Rupert's Land Research Centre, 1988).

55. For example, the Rupert's Land Research Centre organizes a biennial research collo-quium. The Centre has published two colloquium proceedings, and it offers copies of selected paper presentations. These papers are not limited to either the pre-1870 Rupert's Land period or to the geographic area of Rupert's Land—the Hudson Bay drainage basin. In fact, the Colloquium has met at least three times outside of Rupert's Land in Vancouver, Washington in 2000, Whitehorse in 1996 and in Stromness in Orkney in 1990. Like the proceedings of the various North American Fur Trade Conferences, the papers delivered at the Rupert's Land Colloquia give a good sense of trends in the area of fur trade studies. The two published proceedings are Ian MacLaren, Michael Payne, and Heather Rollason, eds., *Papers of the 1994 Rupert's Land Colloquium* (Winnipeg: Centre for Rupert's Land Studies, 1997) and David Malaher, ed., *Selected Papers of the Centre for Rupert's Land Studies Colloquium 2000* (Winnipeg: Centre for Rupert's Land Studies, 2000).

56. Flora Beardy and Robert Coutts, eds., *Voices From Hudson Bay: Cree Stories from York Factory* (Montreal; Kingston: McGill-Queen's University Press, 1996).

57. For example, see Peter Geller, "Creating Corporate Images of the Fur Trade: The Hudson's Bay Company and Public Relations in the 1930s" in Brown, Eccles and Heldman, eds., *Fur Trade Revisited,* 409–26 and "Northern Exposures: photographic and filmic representations of the Canadian North, 1920–1945" (Ph.D. dissertation, Carleton University, 1996).

58. See Mary Black-Rodgers, "Varieties of 'Starving': Semantics and Survival in the Sub-arctic Fur Trade, 1750–1850," *Ethnohistory* 33, no. 4 (1986): 353–83.

59. See Jennifer S.H. Brown and Elizabeth Vibert, eds., *Reading Beyond Words: Contexts for native history* (Peterborough: Broadview Press, 1996). This book includes numerous articles by young scholars that suggest some of the directions fur trade and native history may be going in the future.

60. Laura Lynn Peers, "Playing Ourselves: Native histories, native interpreters, and living history sites" (Ph.D. dissertation, McMaster University, 1996).

61. See for example, Ian MacLaren, "'I came to rite thare portraits': Paul Kane's Journal of his Western Travels, 1846–1848," *The American Art Journal* 21, no. 2 (Spring 1989): 6–88 and "Samuel Hearne's Accounts of the Massacre at Bloody Fall, 17 July 1771," *Ariel: A Review of International English Literature* 22, no. 1 (January 1991): 25–51. This interest in the difference between draft or field note and published primary source can also be seen in Glyndwr Williams, "The Puzzle of Anthony Henday's Journal, 1754–1755" *The Beaver*, Outfit 309, no. 3 (1978): 41–56.

62. See for example, I.S. MacLaren, "The Aesthetics of Back's Writing and Painting from the First Overland Expedition" in C. Stuart Houston, ed., *Arctic Artist: The*

Journal and Paintings of George Back, Midshipman with Franklin, 1819–1822 (Montreal: Kingston: McGill-Queen's University Press, 1994), 275–310.

63. The Hudson's Bay Company Archives in the Provincial Archives of Manitoba are reputed to be the second largest private, nongovernmental archival collection in the world after the archives of the Vatican.

64. The masons were building a stone house but they had to cover their work every evening with horse dung to keep the frost from damaging their work. Provincial Archives of Manitoba, Hudson's Bay Company Archives: B.42/a/20, fo.23.

65. The study of fur trade labour relations can be traced back to Clare H. Pentland, *Labour and Capital in Canada, 1650–1860* (Toronto: James Lorimer, 1981). Philip Goldring and Carol Judd both undertook studies of the recruitment and deployment of fur trade workforce in studies cited above. See also, Glen Makahonuk, "Wage-labour in the Northwest Fur Economy, 1760–1849," *Saskatchewan History* 41, no. 1 (1988): 1–17 and Edith Burley, *Servants of the Honourable Company: work, discipline, and conflict in the Hudson's Bay Company, 1770–1870* (Toronto: Oxford University Press, 1997). The latter, in particular, offers an intriguing analysis of work in the fur trade as "contested terrain."

66. The role of the fur trade in introducing various infectious diseases into the western interior of North America has generated numerous scholarly studies. An interesting study of how the operations of the fur trade helped to spread disease can be found in Arthur Ray, "Diffusion of Diseases in the Western Interior of Canada, 1830–1850," *The Geographical Review* 66, no. 2 (April 1976): 139–57. More recently Jody Decker, "Tracing Historical Diffusion Patterns: The Case of the 1780–82 Smallpox Epidemic among the Indians of Western Canada" *Native Studies Review* 4, nos. 1–2 (1988): 1–24 also looks at the diffusion of disease. In "The York Factory Medical Journals, 1846–52," *Canadian Bulletin of Medical History/Bulletin Canadien d'Histoire de la Medicine*14 (1997): 107–31 she looks at the training and medical practices of Hudson's Bay Company surgeons stationed at York Factory. Other researchers have looked at the spread and impact of specific diseases, the kinds of drugs and medical equipment available at fur trade posts, and the use of plants and other natural remedies by Aboriginal peoples. Calvin Martin's controversial *Keepers of the Game: Indian-Animal Relationships and the Fur Trade* (Berkeley: University of California Press, 1978) suggests that epidemic diseases transformed the Aboriginal world view and made the fur trade possible. His arguments are explored, and challenged, in Shepard Krech III, ed., *Indians, Animals and the Fur Trade: A Critique of "Keepers of the Game"* (Athens, Georgia: University of Georgia Press, 1981).

67. Many Hudson's Bay Company post journals include daily observations on winds, weather conditions and temperature readings. These records are used in Timothy F. Ball's "Climatic change in central Canada: a preliminary analysis of weather information from the Hudson's Bay Company Forts at York Factory and Churchill Factory, 1714–1850" (Ph.D. dissertation, University of London, 1983).

68. John Foster played a critical role in this change—not just through his own research and writing, but as a teacher and as a friend of many of the authors mentioned in this article.

2 Montreal Iroquois *engagés* in the Western Fur Trade, 1800–1821

JAN GRABOWSKI & NICOLE ST-ONGE

A more discordant, headstrong, ill-designing set of rascals than form this group God has never permitted together in the fur trade

ALEXANDER ROSS

THE ROLE OF AMERINDIANS in the fur trade has long fascinated researchers. However, most historians have focused on Natives as suppliers of furs and consumers of trade goods. With the exception of one pioneering work[1] it is striking how little has been done to assess the role of Natives involved in fur trade wage labour during the first half of the nineteenth century. Yet, between 1800 and 1821, large numbers of Iroquois from the Montreal area, known also as *domiciliés*, signed engagements with fur trading companies and became salaried employees.[2] Historical accounts note, in passing, the presence of Iroquois in the west,[3] however, studies of the fur trade have largely ignored the phenomenon of the Iroquois presence among the *engagés*. Drawing on thousands of voyageur contracts, and a variety of reports, letters and narratives, this research bridges a gap between the two historiographical traditions; one focusing on the dynamics of the fur trade in the interior, and the other studying the economy of Lower Canada. Our goals are twofold, first, to establish the background for the involvement of Canadian Iroquois *engagés* in the fur trade and to assess its influence on Iroquois' communities in the Laurentian Valley. This is of special interest since the historiography surrounding the Iroquois establishments in Canada has focused on the French régime,

TABLE 2-1
Notaries and Engagements, 1790–1821

Notary	Engagements	Amerindian Engagements
Louis Chaboillez	9,346	527
J.-G Beek	5,045	547
Jonathan Gray	1,340	19
Nicolas Doucet	415	35
Louis Raymond	30	—
Joseph-Edouard Faribault	21	—
TOTAL	16,197	1,128

leaving the later period largely unresearched.[4] Second, it is our intention to evaluate the economic, social and cultural adaptation of this St. Lawrence valley native population to the western frontier and its inhabitants. The Iroquois from the Laurentian valley entered the salaried workforce of the fur trade in response to the mounting demographic pressure exerted by the burgeoning French Canadian population and the depletion of their traditional resource base. Simultaneously, the fur trading concerns out of Montreal developed new strategies requiring a new breed of voyageurs specialized in hunting.

❧ Voyageurs in the Notarial Records

During the first two decades of the nineteenth century more than 1100 Amerindians (for the most part *domiciliés* Iroquois from Sault St-Louis [Caughnawaga, Kahnawake] and from Lac-des-Deux-Montagnes [Oka, Kanasetake]) signed engagements with fur trading companies, left their homes, and headed West.[5] The information derived from notarial records enables us to evaluate, for the first time, the Amerindian participation in the salaried workforce of the western fur trade.[6] An examination of notarial files from Montreal, Chateauguay, l'Assomption, Longueuil, St-Eustache, Laprairie, Ste-Scholastique and St-Benoit, reveals six notaries who made out contracts for the West. Only three among them had a substantial Amerindian clientele. Amerindian contracts come from the records of notaries Louis Chaboillez, J.-G Beek, and Nicolas Doucet. A number of non-native contracts for the West are to be found in the files of Louis Raymond, Joseph-Edouard Faribault, and Jonathan Gray.[7]

GRAPH 2–I

Amerindians and French Canadians in Fur Trade Engagements, 1800–1820

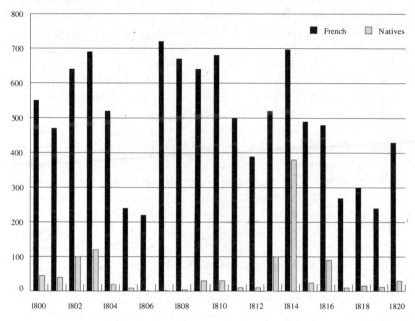

Owing to the nature of the studied documents, the numerical estimates are usually conservative. According to Allan Greer, who traced similar engagements to one-third of the adult male population of the French Canadian parish of Sorel "this is certainly an underestimate of the actual numbers involved since a great many *engagés* served without signing a notarized engagement for the benefit of future historians."[8] There is no reason why this statement should be any less true of Indian villagers. The number of Amerindians retained for this study has also been reduced by the removal from the list of all nonaboriginal names. At the turn of the nineteenth century some Amerindians acquired French or English names. At the same time, a considerable number of nonaboriginal farmers and artisans settled in Sault St-Louis and in other native villages. In order to avoid confusing the two groups, the individuals included in the "Native" group and retained for this study, come from one of the Amerindian communities, have Iroquois or Algonquian names or are described as "sauvages" in the contract.[9]

Amerindians who had settled in the Laurentian Valley had been active participants in the fur trade since the seventeenth century. At the end of the seventeenth century French authorities recognized that the Canadian

Iroquois not only supplied the furs to the local merchants, but also began to assume the role of intermediaries and traders.[10] This involvement was, however, relatively marginal to the official network of trade. During the entire French colonial period there are but a few known instances when the *domiciliés* Iroquois agreed to enter in contractual agreements with the fur trading companies. We can only speculate about the number of Iroquois who travelled to the West without formal contracts at the end of the eighteenth century. We know that the Great Lakes Ojibwa, some Ottawas and at least a few Iroquois were migrating westward before 1799, in conjunction with Montreal fur trading concerns.[11] Iroquois trapper-voyageurs were active in the "Petit Nord," the neck of land lying between Lake Superior and Hudson Bay and extending west to Lake Winnipeg, in the closing decades of the eighteenth century. In the 1780s, Montreal merchant Beaubien Desriviere based his Timiskaming fur trading venture in the Iroquois village of Lac-des-Deux-Montagnes, which furnished most of the men he needed as well as provisions. Rival trading concerns complained bitterly of the ruthless hunting methods of "Desriviere's Iroquois" who apparently, terrified the Timiskaming and Abitibi Indians.[12] Unfortunately if this employment had the benefit of formal written engagements they have not yet been located. It is only after 1799 that the Amerindian voyageurs became a discernible group among *engagés* contracts. Thereafter the notarial records begin to reveal growing numbers of Amerindians entering into the service of fur trading companies (see Graph 2–1). Between 1800 and 1821 Amerindian voyageurs constituted, on average, 8 percent of all *engagés* hired in Montreal. The size of this participation fluctuates from year to year for a variety of reasons. There are, however, two distinct periods, 1800–1803 and 1813–16, when Native *engagés* represent 15 and 34 percent of all hirings respectively.

❧ Engagements and Population Dynamics

An examination of the evidence reveals two interesting realities. First, the records show that a disproportionately large number of Iroquois from Sault St-Louis engaged in service in the fur trade, and a disproportionately large number of Iroquois who did engage, engaged only once. In general, French Canadian parishes deeply involved in the fur trade maintained a high rate of growth despite the fact that many men were *engagés*. It seems that their men generally stayed west temporarily, and a clear majority returned to their parishes of origin.[13] In the case of the *domiciliés* Iroquois, an opposite process seems to have taken place. The Iroquois chose to leave their villages permanently, rather than to return home at the end of their contract.

Although Native censuses and counts are of uncertain accuracy, they enable researchers to assess patterns of growth and decline over a period of time. Population estimates of Amerindian villages are based largely on

GRAPH 2-2

Sault St-Louis Population, 1740-1850

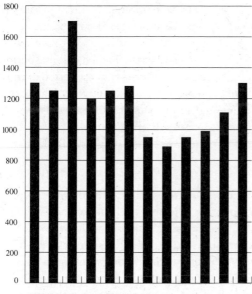

observations of contemporary observers. These estimates therefore must be based on numbers of warriors, huts, military contingents, and other general remarks (see Graph 2–2).[14]

The native villages located in the Laurentian valley were rare examples of numerically stable or even expanding aboriginal communities in colonial North America. Migrants and refugees often augmented their numbers in times of war. In the case of Sault St-Louis, the mission increased to more than 1000 people during the first decade of the eighteenth century.[15] The population then grew slowly but steadily during the period of relative tranquility, following the Treaty of Utrecht. At the height of the Seven Years' War the Native village might have grown to more than 1800 people.[16] Although information on the last decade of the eighteenth and the first of the nineteenth century is lacking, the census of 1808 shows that the population of Sault St-Louis had fallen below that of 1700. It would not recover to the level of 1780 until the 1850s.[17] The population decline correlates with an increase in Sault St–Louis engagements signed during the 1800–1803 period. During these four years at least 289 Iroquois signed contracts and left the village. In 1814 Joseph Bouchette noted that the village of Coghnawaga consists of a church, a house for the missionary, who resides with them, and about 140 others, principally built of stone, formed into two or three rows, something resembling streets, but not at all to be remarked either for interior or exterior cleanliness or regularity; their occupants may be altogether about 900.[18]

The mission that had grown steadily throughout the French colonial period and had successfully maintained its size in the post-Conquest period of transition underwent a period of turbulence between 1790 and 1820. The parish registers indicate, at the same time, a decline in number of baptisms.[19]

Contemporary observers noted the growth in the numbers of Canadian Iroquois in the "Grand Nord"[20] and their parallel disappearance from the Montreal area reserves:

> Their love of adventure, their physical strength and power of endurance, their skill as hunters and trappers, their dexterity in handling the paddle, made them valuable aids in the thriving commerce which was then spreading over the continent. Sometimes their engagements were of longer duration, lasting ten, fifteen or twenty years; sometimes they did not return at all. These long engagements became rarer after the amalgamation with the Hudson's Bay Company in 1821, but they were still prevalent for many years, and the long absences from Caughnawaga was the reason given in 1843 for the dwindling population of the village.[21]

Our research indicates that the hiring patterns between French Canadians and their Iroquois counterparts differed significantly. Unlike the French Canadians, a clear majority of native voyageurs hired themselves out only once. It is possible that they lost interest in salaried fur trade employment following their first experience. Contemporary testimonies and patterns of demographic decline indicate, however, that they chose to spend many years if not the balance of their lives, in the North West. Bruce M. Watson, who reconstructed the working histories of 119 Iroquois residing in the Columbia Department between 1810 and 1858, notes that at least 63 of these known Iroquois chose to remain west of the Rockies for ten or more years.[22] Only 18 of the 119 individuals are traced back to the Montreal pay lists (when they picked up the balance of their pay) after having fulfilled one or two engagements in the Columbia Department.

There were at least 921 engagements of Iroquois voyageurs from Sault St-Louis,[23] signed between 1800 and 1821 (Table 2–2). Only 134 natives signed engagements on more than one occasion, while 612 were parties to only one contract. The "frequent travellers" repaired to the west two, three or more

TABLE 2–2
Engagements Signed 1800–1821[26]

Parish	Number of Engagements 1800–1820	Total Population in 1790
Assomption	437	2,620
Berthier	505	2,415
Laprairie	539	1,704
Montreal	495	6,400
Yamaska	448	1,324
Sorel	798	1,208
Sault St–Louis	921	1,200

times during their careers. The 612 others (or 66%) signed only once and most probably never returned from the trip. The hirings in French Canadian parishes were different. In Berthier, out of 505 engagements signed during the same period, 199, or 39%, were made out to one-time travellers. In Sorel, only 219 out of 798 (27%) engagements were signed by one-time voyageurs.

Mounting evidence from the West suggests that large numbers of the Iroquois established themselves in different communities throughout western Rupert's Land, and as far as Oregon and California. They settled down and started families with local Chinook, Walla Walla, Snake or other local Native and Métis women. An exodus of that kind and extended duration could not fail to have had profound impact on those left behind. Commenting on the state of French Canadian parishes whose men were involved in the fur-trade, John Lambert wrote:

> The country people in the vicinity are mostly employed as voyageurs in the North-west fur-trade, and the cultivation of their farms is left to their wives and children. When they return home, they seldom bring more than enough to support them during the winter. The soil is thus neglected, and the town is badly supplied with provisions.[24]

These disturbing circumstances were prevalent in communities to which the voyageurs actually returned. The conditions in Sault St–Louis, whose young males were leaving the village never to return, could have only been more dramatic.[25]

In the 1800–1821 period Berthier, Sorel, Laprairie and Sault St-Louis, were the only four parishes responsible for more than five hundred engagements each. L'Assomption, Yamaska and Montreal were close contenders providing the fur trade with, respectively, 437, 448 and 495 engagements. In terms of its rate of participation, the Iroquois parish of Sault St-Louis was by far the most important among them, and further research can only revise upwards the numbers of Sault St-Louis *engagés*.[27] The proportion of Sault St-Louis population employed by the fur trade is startling. The parish with the smallest population provided the fur trade, during the discussed period, with the greatest number of *engagés*. Furthermore, since many of these fur trade employees never returned, their employment represents a significant westward migration of Iroquois. But why were these people leaving their communities?

❧ The Westward "Push" and "Pull"

Large scale Amerindian emigration from the Montreal area occurred at a time when native communities in Lower Canada were under growing pressure from a steadily increasing French Canadian population. At the same time, the fur trade offered attractive opportunities for the young men of these communities. The periods of increased native presence among the *engagés* coincide with the periods of heated competition between fur trading companies (see Graph 2-1). The initial hiring spree of 1800–1803 covers the period of bitter struggle between the "New" North West Company (XYC) and the North West Company (NWC). Similarly, the second peak of native involvement occurred during the period of open confrontation between the Hudson's Bay Company (HBC), and the NWC over the Athabasca trade.[28] Though the Iroquois served as canoemen and labourers, it appears that the primary reason for their hiring was their trapping skills. Armed with steel traps and "castoreum," they were sent by the Montreal traders into areas such as the Peace River district where the local populations were uninterested in trapping or demanded too high a price for their goods. For example, in 1802 over 250 Indians, a majority Iroquois but also Nipissings and Algonquins, came from the East with the NWC canoes to Fort Augustus [Edmonton]. By 1815, even the London based HBC began hiring Iroquois and Algonquians out of Montreal to help them challenge the NWC monopoly in the Athabasca trade. These Native voyageurs, trappers, and eventually freemen also made their way into what is now the American Northwest. By 1816 organized expeditions with large Iroquois and Hawaiian components were leaving Fort Flathead for the Snake River area with the express purpose of denuding the area of beaver before the Oregon district fell completely into American hands.[29] Yet, the new policies and confrontations would not have evolved beyond the planning stage, had it not been for apparent

Iroquois' willingness to participate in northwestern hunt and travel. In order to understand the Iroquois involvement, one has to focus on the reasons and motives that were invoked by the recruiters and nonaboriginal voyageurs.

Greer's study of the involvement of the Sorel population in the fur trade revealed that between 1790 and 1820 the parish became a major supplier of labour to the fur trade.

> Through most of the eighteenth century, comparatively few men from this area served as engagés, but by the end of the century, that is, from about the time the Northwest Company was formed, unusually large numbers of local men were departing with the western fur brigades.[30]

The men from Sault St-Louis appear to have rarely signed formal engagement contracts in the eighteenth century. They became active contractual participants of the fur trade only after 1800, a decade later than their French Canadian counterparts from Sorel.

Hirings in Sorel were linked to the high cost of labour in the parishes traditionally involved in the fur trade, such as Lachine and Montreal. According to officials at the NWC and the HBC, distant and rural parishes furnished a more reliable, obedient and cheaper workforce.[31] French Canadians targeted by the companies in the 1790s came from impoverished areas where agriculture, owing to poor soil, was less of a solution to the survival of the community.[32] Wealthier parishes proved to be more resistant to the lures of the fur trade.[33]

Information on *domiciliés'* crops at that time is lacking, but the increasing pressure of nonaboriginal presence might have contributed to the Iroquois' decision to explore the opportunities offered by the fur trade and to move West. The mission of Sault St-Louis found itself at its present location after three previous transfers orchestrated by the Jesuits in the late seventeenth and the early eighteenth centuries. Soil depletion was one factor noted but the missionaries also invoked proximity to the French settlements which resulted in increased liquor sales to the natives. The transfers enabled the Society of Jesus, at the same time, to grant the temporarily abandoned lands to French Canadian farmers. This process of Iroquois' dispossession was evident already in the early 1700s.[34] Further signs of impending expropriation came in 1736 and in 1750.[35] In the second half of the eighteenth century the territory of Sault St-Louis found itself under increasing scrutiny of the land-hungry French farmers. For the Jesuit seigneurs, rent-paying French farmers definitely seemed more attractive than the Iroquois. In 1762 the Iroquois from Sault St-Louis brought the Jesuits before the British military court in Montreal. They stated that the Jesuits had been for some time granting Iroquois territories to French habitants, depriving the Natives of their rights and livelihood. General Gage, having examined the titles and arguments of both sides, decided in favour of the Natives and ordered that all recent grants be cancelled.[36]

The land base of the Native village remained precarious, since in 1798 "26 chiefs and seigneurs" of the Sault sued the last living Canadian Jesuit in the court of King's Bench in an unsuccessful attempt to dislodge squatters from the territories they claimed as theirs.[37] The chiefs from the Sault accused the Jesuit, Jean Joseph Casot, and local French farmers of encroaching upon their lands, and this despite stern warnings given by General Gage in 1762. If these trials and protests can be interpreted as signs of growing Iroquois anger, discomfort and lack of economic opportunities in Sault St-Louis, the increasing involvement of Native voyageurs in the western fur trade becomes less of a surprise.[38] The erosion of Amerindian land base, the exhaustion of traditional hunting territories, and a new demand for Amerindian labour by Montreal-based companies appears to have encouraged the unique response of Lower Canadian Iroquois to opportunities in the western fur trade.

✺ Wages

It is clear that the men of Sault Sr. Louis had strong motivations to move west, but it is also apparent that the NWC was particularly interested in hiring these Iroquois men. Obviously, in this period, competition between Montreal-based fur interests increased the overall demand for manpower and certainly in the French Canadian hirings cost of labour was the decisive factor. Did Amerindians from Sault St-Louis and Lake of Two Mountains agree, as the French Canadians from Sorel before them, to work for less than the "mercenary" voyageurs from Montreal or Lachine? John Ewers argued that these Indians were hired because they accepted lower wages than French Canadians.[39] Were they another unused pool of highly-skilled labour tapped by the trading companies? Available financial data gives little support to this hypothesis.

The data in Table 2–3 reflects the wages of *engagés* on most frequented routes. A cursory analysis of the table points to the fact that the Iroquois' salary was roughly equal to that of French Canadians. Upon closer scrutiny, it becomes also evident that in some cases Native voyageurs were paid more.[40] The willingness of contracting agents to part company with these amounts of money indicated that the *domiciliés* Iroquois had more to offer than their competitors. The *domiciliés* had a well-earned, and ancient reputation of people able to drive hard deals. Already in the seventeenth century French sources reported that while the majority of Amerindians had little or no knowledge of money, those "living close to the French" knew it well

TABLE 2-3

Amerindian and French *Engagés* in the Fur Trade:
Destinations and Wages, 1799–1821[41]

Destination	Mean Wage (m) (Natives)	Median Wage (x) (Natives)	Mean Wage (m) (French)	Median Wage (x) (French)
Nord-Ouest [Nord; Dependances de Nord Ouest] 3 Years	750#	700#	724#	700#
Temiscamingue	99.5#	96#	98#	96#
Fort William or Fort Kaministiquia	352#	300#	343#	300#
Michilimackinac	275#	250#	241#	250#
Sault Ste Marie	238#	200#	232#	200#

and used it frequently.[42] In the beginning of the eighteenth century voices were raised that the Iroquois from the Sault were too "wily."[43] Once in the West, in the early nineteenth century, the *domiciliés* Iroquois still were known to be far less "docile" than other Amerindians and French Canadians employed by the trading companies.[44] One agent for the Hudson's Bay Company went as far as describing the Iroquois as "discordant headstrong ill-designing set of rascals." Although other accounts were less damning, few denied the Iroquois their independence and resourcefulness.[45]

The brief, pre-printed forms of contracts and laconic words that fill them do little to satisfy our curiosity. The reports from the West suggest, at the same time, that the Iroquois from Sault St-Louis and from other Laurentian Valley villages, traditionally regarded as expert hunters,[46] went to hunt rather than to trade and to ferry the goods.[47] Their principal objective was to stay in the West for extended periods of time, and to increase the beaver harvests in targeted areas where local Native Peoples were, apparently, either reluctant, unwilling, or unable to provide companies with the desired number of pelts.

Outfitters and sales agents for the NWC, [Simon] Mctavish, [Joseph] Frobisher and Co., were among the first to engage Iroquois as salaried personnel for the western trade. The NWC remained, throughout the studied period, the employers of the largest contingent of eastern native employees under formal contract sent westward.

Initially the NWC used the Iroquois as Voyageurs: "The Iroquois were efficient canoemen: they were, after generations of commercial and military excursions, familiar with the waters of the western Great Lakes, and unlike many tribes, they had no apparent aversion to venturing far from their homelands."[48] The number of Iroquois heading west and signing contracts prior to their departure increased substantially in the first year of the nineteenth century. In this period the Iroquois served not only as voyageurs but also as trappers and hunters. They would sign contracts of three years or more and in exchange for being outfitted, the Iroquois would trade the furs they trapped to the company hiring them.[49]

The first eastern Amerindians to be hired specifically to hunt were six Nipissings who signed contracts with the X Y Company (New North West Company), partners, Forsyth, Richardson & Co., on 27 March 1800, to go "dans le nord pour la chasse des bêtes sauvages."[50] The other Montreal fur trading concerns such as the NWC and the Michilimackinac Company soon followed suit.

Iroquois might have been interested in this arrangement for three reasons. First, it allowed them to trap far afield of their own long overhunted homeland giving them a new source of revenue no longer open to them near the missions. Second, some authors have argued, it gave restless young men of the tribes a chance to fulfill, on these far-ranging expeditions, the traditional role of hunter-warrior.[51] A third possibility exists. Since some of these Iroquois left accompanied by their wives, and many never came back, it is possible they viewed employment with the fur trading concerns as a form of subsidized relocation venture.

ꙮ Companies and Destinations[52]

To understand the different nature of French and Iroquois participation in the fur trade the companies involved and destination patterns need to be assessed. The difference between the two groups was the planned duration of the stay (which had little to do with the duration stated on the contract), and the activities to be performed in the West. French Canadians, for the most part, were expected to conduct the company's business, and return to Lower Canada, while the Iroquois were supposed to stay and to hunt.

Destinations and routes for which the French and the Indians were hired seem to have been similar. In both cases the largest single group repaired to Michilimackinac (see Table 2–4 and Table 2–5); 26 percent of Amerindians and 32 percent of the French voyageurs made the trek to the most popular meeting place of the western fur trade. Hundreds of voyageurs (of both races) hired by the government in 1814, at the time of war, to go to the area, have also added to the total. The war, as the passage below suggests, might

TABLE 2−4

Amerindians/Destinations, 1800–1821

Destination	Number of Engagements	Percentage
Fort William/Lac la Pluie	290	29%
Michilimackinac	257	26%
Temiscamingue/Abitibi	112	11%
Fort Moose	74	7%
Nord-Ouest	58	6%
Other	202	21%
TOTAL	993	100%

TABLE 2−5

French Canadian Voyageurs/Destinations, 1790–1821

Destination	Number of Engagements	Percentage
Michilimackinac	4,708	32%
Nord-Ouest	2,516	17%
Fort William	1,967	14%
Grand Portage	867	6%
Other	4,612	31%
TOTAL	14,670	100%

have had an overall salutary effect on fur-bearing animals and, by the same token, on Amerindians' commercial pursuits:

In 1815, a party of St. Regis Indians from Canada ascended the Oswegatchie river in the county of St. Lawrence, in pursuit of beaver. In consequence of the previous hostilities between this country and England, this district had not been hunted for some years, and the beaver had consequently been undisturbed. The party, after an absence of a few weeks, returned with three hundred beaver skins.[53]

TABLE 2-6
French Canadian Voyageurs by Company, 1790–1821

Company	Number of Engagements	Percentage
North West Company	8,185	55%
Cie de Michilimackinac	1,554	10%
XY Company	1,306	9%
Other	3,904	26%
TOTAL	14,949	100%

TABLE 2-7
Amerindian Voyageurs by Company, 1800–1821

Company	Number of Engagements	Percentage
North West Company	851	75%
Roderick McKenzie	88	8%
Cie de Michilimackinac	58	5%
Other	131	12%
TOTAL	1,128	100%

Not far behind were other popular destinations for Native and non-Native voyageurs: the vaguely described area of Nord-Ouest and Fort William\Lac de la Pluie accounted for, respectively 35 percent and 31 percent. Similar patterns are visible in the case of lesser destinations.

A quick review of companies hiring French Canadian and Native voyageurs reveals fewer parallels than the previously discussed destinations. Although in both cases the single, most important employer was the NWC, it hired 55 percent of French Canadians and a formidable 75 percent of the Natives. French Canadians were hired by a wide variety of companies (see Table 2–6 and Table 2–7). Their engagements were signed not only by powerful merchants like McGill, McTavish and McGillivray, but also by lesser participants like Pothier, Parker, Raymond, Grant, Laselle, Bouthillier and numerous others.

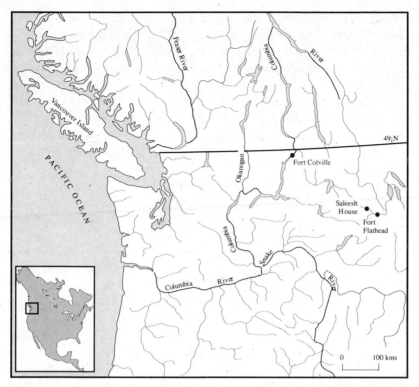

Map labels:
Fraser River
Columbia River
Vancouver Island
PACIFIC OCEAN
49¡N
Okanogan
Fort Colville
Saleesh House
Fort Flathead
Columbia
Snake
Columbia River
River
0   100 kms

ᕠ *FIGURE 2–1*

These smaller merchants accounted for 26 percent of all signed contracts. In the case of Amerindians their share fell to 12 percent. The Natives seem to have been shunned by the smaller companies, that had little interest in far North West trade. Either there were risks attached to these hirings, or, more probably, only large companies had long-term plans and strategies that required the expedition and settling of Native hunters in the "Grand Nord."[54]

ᕠ In the North West

Once in the North West, the Iroquois played a significant and unique role in the fur trade. The fragmented sources of trading post journals, explorers' reports, and trapping expedition journals and letters, allow us to describe the westward expansion of Iroquois voyageurs and trappers. As noted earlier, Iroquois trappers working for Montreal fur traders were a well established presence in the "Little North," the Temiskaming area, by the 1780s.

Rapidly they ranged further west. HBC trader James Slater from Great Fall House would complain bitterly, in 1804, of the ever diminishing returns in furs due to the presence of "Indians from Montreal" hired by the NWC and perhaps the XYC to trap furs in the East Winnipeg country. This was familiar territory for the Iroquois who had been ranging westward with the depletion of their hunting territories.[55] The difference, by 1800, was the Iroquois contractual obligation to large trading concerns. By the end of the eighteenth century, Iroquois, again in association with large fur trading concerns, found their way into the "Grand Nord." In 1794 Duncan McGillivray, a fur trader associated with the NWC who worked out of posts on the North Saskatchewan River most of his life, reported "3 Iroquois now engaged in the Company's service" near the present site of Prince Albert.[56] Peter Fidler, fur trader, mapmaker and explorer for the HBC gave an early record of this unusual migration. In 1797, while in charge of Buckingham House on the North Saskatchewan River, he noted the arrival of several Iroquois at the fort. The earliest arrivals are recorded in February but they continued to visit Buckingham house well into the month of May.[57] It is clear from fur trader journals that the Iroquois were being sent principally as trappers.[58] For the same region Alexander Mackenzie noted that "a small colony of Iroquois emigrated to the banks of the Saskatchewine [sic] in 1799, who had been brought up from their infancy under the Romish missionaries and instructed by them in a village within nine miles of Montreal."[59]

Young NWC clerk Daniel Harmon, while crossing Rainy Lake in the summer of 1800 wrote in his journal "Also came here three Canoes manned by Iroquois, who are going to hunt the beaver for the North West Company in the vicinity of the upper Red River."[60] NWC bourgeois Archibald McLeod noted the comings and going of both his Iroquois and those of the XYC at Fort Alexandria on the upper banks of the Assiniboine River in the winter of 1800–1801. It is clear from McLeod's diary, and his lament at their lack of returns [furs], that they are there principally as trappers.[61]

This influx of eastern native migrants continued to grow in the opening years of the nineteenth century. HBC trader William Tomison working in the Saskatchewan district in 1801–1802 lamented the impact of the Iroquois presence noting that in the summer of 1801 the NWC and XYC had brought in more than 300 "Eroquees or Mohawk Indians" on three-year contracts.[62] These Indians who left "Nothing wherever they Come" had swarmed over the Saskatchewan district. He went on to comment in his journal that this process of exhaustive fur trapping had begun several years back by "many Bungee Tawau Miscelamacana [and] Eroquee Indians" who came in the wake of the Montreal fur traders.[63]

This 1801 large scale migration of at least 300 eastern Natives incited comments by NWC fur trade, surveyor and mapmaker David Thompson in his journals' description of forks of the Peace and Smoke Rivers [present day northern Alberta]:

> ...but from Canada the trade was open to every adventurer, and some of these brought in a great number of Iroquois, Nepissings and Algonquins who with their steel traps had destroyed the Beaver on their own lands in Canada and New Brunswick; the two latter, the men were tall, manly, steady and good hunters, the few women they brought with them were good looking and well behaved. The Iroquois formed about half the number of these immigrants, they considered themselves superior to all other people, especially the white people of Canada. ...the few women they brought with them were any thing but beauty and their dress was careless with the shirt on the outside and petticoats to only a little below the knees, the toes and feet turned inward which made them walk like duck...Part of these went up the Red Deer River, and about 250 of them came up the Saskatchewan River, in company with the canoes of the Fur Traders to one of the upper posts called Fort Augustus [near present day Edmonton, Alberta].[64]

Thompson goes on to comment that there followed four years of extensive trapping with the use of steel traps and the Castoreum of the female beaver.

> For several years all these indians were rich, the Women and Children, as well as the Men, were covered in silver brooches, Ear Rings, Wampum, Beads and other trinkets. Their mantles were of fine scarlet cloth, and all was finery and dress. The canoes of Furr [sic] Traders were loaded with packs of Beaver, the abundance of the article lowered the London prices...[he goes on] Four years afterwards almost the whole of these extensive countries were denuded of beaver, the Natives became poor.[65]

The expansion continued, to the north, south, and further West. In 1802 Peter Fidler noted a small band of Iroquois, who had left Montreal the previous summer, headed for the South Saskatchewan and in the Cypress Hills area.[66] Soon they would reach the Athabasca District and in 1804 Fidler would again be reporting "a party of 110 Iroquois up the Peace River and near the Rocky Mountain." These last Iroquois were part of a contingent of 195 men employed as trappers by the NWC that had brought in 315 packs of furs of 85 lbs. each. Of these, 76 of these were brought in by the Peace River Iroquois. He goes on to comment that the XY Company had 93 men working the area as trappers but their ethnic composition is not noted.[67] The presence of Iroquois trappers continued along the Peace and Athabasca rivers in subsequent years. Harmon commented on his arrival to Fort Dunvegan in 1808 that "about the Fort are encamped a number of Iroquois trappers and Beaver Indians, who have been awaiting our arrival."[68] By 1810 the Iroquois were trapping in the Columbia River basin near Saleesh House where they assisted Thompson in his (unsuccessful) search for birch rind for the making of canoes.[69]

Iroquois numbers in the North West increased with the growing involvement of the HBC in the Athabasca trade prior to the fusion of 1821. Starting in 1815 the HBC mandated Colin Robertson to mount an extensive campaign to increase returns from the Athabasca region which, until then, had been the near exclusive domain of the NWC. On 17 May 1815, 16 canoes left Montreal heading for the Athabasca.[70] François-Benjamin Pillet, a former employee of J.J. Astor in the Columbia, residing at the Indian village of Lac-des-Deux-Montagnes, furnished provisions and engaged Indians for the venture. The following year the HBC central committee planned for an expedition comprised of 40 canoes, with the requisite numbers of engagés, carrying among other things 10,000 lbs. of tobacco.[71] In February 1818 Robertson requested reinforcements for the Athabasca venture; "I thought fifteen to twenty Canadians and about ten Iroquois sufficient."[72]

The HBC also used Iroquois, *engagés* or freemen, as mediators and go-betweens with local western tribes in their effort to break the NWC stranglehold on the region. In January 1820 Robertson sent a clerk named Ignace Giasson and six Iroquois from St Mary's Fort to winter in the New Caledonia district to "open an intercourse with the natives, and prepare them for the reception of our people."[73] They returned with 500 beaver skins.[74]

Though the Iroquois appear to have adapted quickly and remarkably well to the new terrains, be it great plains or the Rocky mountains, and its accompanying fauna (bison herds and grizzly bears), relationships with the local tribes were somewhat mixed. The large-scale influx of eastern Natives in 1801 met with some opposition from the Gros Ventres (Atsina) Indians.[75] David Thompson placed the blame for the hostilities squarely on the Iroquois who, unlike the Algonquins and Nipissings, did not follow NWC traders' advice. They apparently decided to strike southward in search of beaver despite the presence of "powerful indians of the plains":

> This advice had a very different effect on the Iroquois, who determined to send a large party to examine the country to the southward and see what the disposition of the Natives were to them, whom they appear to despise. Accordingly part hunted near the Fort while a party of about seventy-five men well armed went off, foolishly taking their

self conceit and arrogance with them...[arrived to] fourth [camp] which was a larger camp of Willow Indians [Fall or Atsina Indians] ...After smoking and feasting, they performed a dance; and then sitting down, by signs invited the Willow Indians to a gambling match, this soon brought on a quarrel, in which the arrogant gestures of the Iroquois made the other party seize their arms...lay dead about twenty-five of them; the others fled, leaving their blankets and a few other things to the Willow Indians, and returned to Fort Augustus in a sad state.[76]

More Iroquois, probably from this same contingent, lost their lives in the winter of 1801–1802. Peter Fidler while wintering at Chesterfield House situated on the junction of the Red Deer and South Saskatchewan River reported a harrowing tale of intrigue and murder. Two Canadians and a small band of Iroquois were heading towards Chesterfield House while searching for beaver. An advance party consisting of four Iroquois and two Canadians went ahead. They were intercepted by Gros Ventres, and the Iroquois were promptly killed. The main party would fare no better:

The next day when the Gros Ventres came to Fidler to trade, he reproved them for the slaughter of the Iroquois and exhorted them not to molest the remaining Iroquois who were due to arrive within a few days.[3 March 1802] "at 2 1/2 A.M. the watch gave the alarm that all the Fall Inds was coming to attack us when immediately all hands was under arms in the bastion" it turned out that they were merely going down to the river "to meet the Iroquois and 2 Canadians to kill them—it was absolutely not in our power to prevent it—at 3 P.M. to the number of 200 men and more returned, they kept on the opposite side of the river and did not come near us...Fall inds had killed the 10 Iroquois and 2 Canadians about 16 miles from the house and they told him that had we all been there belonging to both houses [Fidler's HBC post and the nearby NWC house] they would have served us the same.[77]

It is clear from some of the journals' descriptions that the local natives resented the Iroquois presence not merely for their trespassing but for the havoc their trapping practices were causing among the fur-bearing populations. Harmon notes in his 13 October 1818 entry from Stuart Lake (New Caladonia) that: "As they are rovers, they do not feel the same interest, as those who permanently reside here, in keeping the stock of animal good, and therefore they make great havoc among the game destroying alike the animals which are young and old."[78] Trudy Nicks notes that in 1814, W.F. Wenzel, a NWC bourgeois, wrote to Roderick Mackenzie that the Athabasca district was "dwindling down to nothing" and placed the blame squarely on the Iroquois trappers.[79] Other tribes that did not tolerate well the presence of migrant trappers were the Peigan or Blackfoot tribes. By 1810 seemingly well established eastern trappers were working in the area of present-day Montana. Thompson would encounter Iroquois trappers in the area of Saleesh House. Surprisingly in his journal entries for 1812 Thompson, while discussing work assigned to two men, Michel Bourdeaux and Michel Kinville, makes a seemingly offhand comment that "they were the sole survivors of about three hundred and fifty hunters almost all of them of french origin."[80]

Several fur traders remark in their journals on this "scorched earth" approach. Alexander Ross while describing the efforts of the NWC to increase its return from the Columbia basin commented on the discussions surrounding the creation of fur brigades in 1816:

> Trade on the Columbia in lieu of being confined to the northern branch and the seacoast, as had been the case since the North West had the trade, would be extended on the south and east towards California and the mountains, embracing a new and unexplored tract of country. To obviate the necessity establishing trading posts among so many warlike and refractory nations, formidable trading parties were, under chosen leaders, to range the country for furs, and the resources thus collected were annually to be conveyed to the mouth of the Columbia, there to be shipped to the Canton market...Another object connected with this new arrangement was the introduction of Iroquois from Montréal. These people being expert hunters and trappers might, by their example teach others.[81]

By 1810 Iroquois trappers were already to be found in the Columbia district in the area of Saleesh House. After the 1816, the NWC moved very quickly to assemble armed trapping expeditions. Ross Cox in his journal describes such a party leaving Fort George on 16 April 1817:

> Our party consisted of eighty-six souls, and was perhaps the largest and most mixed that ever ascended the Columbia. In it were five Scotchmen, two English, and one Irish; thirty-six Canadians, twenty Iroquois Indians, two Nipissings, One Cree, and three half-breeds; nine natives of the Sandwich Islands; with one boy, a servant, two women, and two children.[82]

The Iroquois appeared to have followed the NWC into the Columbia district in large numbers. For instance in the summer of 1818 a North West Company brigade under Alexander Ross and Donald McKenzie consisted of 25 Canadians, 32 Owhyhees [Hawaiians], and 38 Iroquois. By the time of the merger of the two companies in 1821 and the take over of the Columbia district by the revamped HBC these "Civilized Indians from the neighbourhood of Montreal, chiefly the Iroquois nation" formed nearly a third of the number of men employed by the Company on the Columbia.[83] These Iroquois continued to work as canoemen and trappers along with French Canadians, Hawaiians and a few Abenaki and Algonquins. They played a key role in the struggle for control by the HBC of the Snake River country against the American traders. Fearing the advances of American fur traders into the area, and the ever growing possibility that the Snake River area would eventually become U.S. Territory Sir George Simpson and the HBC after adopted a policy of trapping the district dry after 1821:

> If properly managed no questions exists that it would yield handsome profits as we have convincing proof that the country is a rich preserve of Beaver and which for political reasons we should endeavour to destroy as fast as possible.[84]

This policy would be in place for many years. As late as 1827, the Company wrote to Simpson: "it is extremely desirable to hunt as bare as possible all the country South of the Columbia and West of the Mountains."[85] As the manifestos for the fur trapping expeditions indicate, the Iroquois were often the largest ethnic group after the French Canadian/Métis used as hunters in the Columbia Basin generally and the Snake River in particular.

Events unfolding in the Columbia district illustrate the ambivalent attitudes of both the Fur Companies and the Iroquois towards the latter's socioeconomic role in the North West. As Karamanski points out, like most western bound trappers, the Iroquois were spurred by the profit motive. Working land that was not their own, they adopted trapping techniques that stripped the swamps and streams of beaver both of prime and worthless pelts alike.[86] They also showed no hesitation in exercising their rights as free trappers and joining other fur trading concerns at the termination of their contracts if the terms offered were more favourable. Often they simply reneged on their contract obligations if others offered more lucrative alternatives. Also, besides trapping, the Iroquois often engaged in illicit trading with local Indians much to the consternation of company officials: "The Iroquois, contrary to the established rules of trade and the general practice among the Natives trafficked privately with the Indians...the Iroquois have been repeatedly warned against such practices, but without effect: they still continued to act as before."[87]

Ross would say of his Iroquois trappers: "A more discordant headstrong, ill-designing set of rascals than form this group, God never permitted together in the fur-trade."[88] The Iroquois obviously accepted only with difficulty a system that kept them in perpetual debt. Outfitted at an inflated price, the freemen trappers returns were systematically underevaluated especially after the end of the period of intensive competition in 1821. The first known defections from the Columbia district came in 1822, when a group of trappers crossed the mountains and reached American posts much laden with furs.[89] For the next few years there was most likely a trickle of desertions across the mountains. The desire for profit was not the only reason the Iroquois reneged on their contractual obligations. The 1818 Snake River expedition under NWC trader Donald Mackenzie lost several of its Iroquois trappers for an extended period of time. It is only with the arrival of "the Iroquois Oskononton" to Fort Nez Perce several month later that Ross heard the full story:

> After crossing the Blue Mountain,...my comrades to the number of twenty-five teased Mr Mackenzie to allow us to hunt and trap in a small river which appeared well stocked with beaver...My comrades began to exchange their horses, their guns, and their traps to these people for women, and carrying the traffic to such an extent they had scarcely an article left.[90]

The major defection came during the HBC Snake Expedition of 1825 under the leadership of Peter Skene Ogden. This large and well equipped trapping expedition hunted in the interior for several months.[91] Pierre Tevanitagon and John Grey led 23 free trappers, nearly all of them Iroquois, out of Ogden camp and over to the Americans.[92] These Iroquois, among others, became the famed "mountain men" trading yearly with the highest bidder at the Rocky Mountain Rendezvous.

ᕍ Decline of the Fur Trade

When opportunities in the fur trade diminished after 1821, the Iroquois, opting to remain in the North West, pursued one of three adaptive strategies. One strategy, as exemplified by Michel's Band, shows a group of Iroquois extended families opting for treaty status and a reserve and retaining for several years an "Iroquois" status Indian group identity. The second option was for individuals or small groups to integrate into local tribes such as the Flatheads through marriage resulting in the complete assimilation of their descendants.[93] The third adaptive strategy pursued by the Iroquois, and seemingly the most popular, was their integration into the fast growing freemen component of the North West's population and thus their participation in a process of ethnogenesis, the formation of the western Métis. Examples of this can be seen in the Colville and Willamette valleys and in the area of Jasper House.[94]

By the second half of the nineteenth century the fur frontier was receding. The fate of the western Iroquois in these changing times was similar to that of the Métis and nonaboriginal free trappers. Some men became guides for government explorers, emigrant wagon trains, and foreign sportsmen. The Oblate Father Petitot would meet several of the expatriate Iroquois in the Great Bear Lake region.[95] Others followed the fur trade frontier farther and farther northwest and continued as trappers in the Mackenzie district. Finally, some Iroquois accepted the closing of the frontier and settled down, often on independent ranches or small farms.[96] The histories of three Iroquois bands in the North West can be followed past 1850. They illustrate well some of the different life strategies followed by these migrant eastern natives.

An example of an Iroquois band remaining in the West can be seen in the Jasper House district. According to Father Lacombe O.M.I., these Iroquois had become free traders after two or three years of service with the fur companies:

> they bought a large outfit of ammunition, traps, knives, axes, blankets, etc., and left Edmonton to go and hunt for themselves in the direction of the Rocky Mountains, at the head of the Athabasca River, where was established afterwards Jasper House, facing Mount Millet.
> These Iroquois were living together like brothers, sharing their good and bad luck. Being Catholics, they determined, though far from church and priest, not to neglect their religious duties.... Not having been married in their own country the young Iroquois took the Indian maidens as their wives.[97]

Members of this band of Iroquois were encountered by Father Jean Pierre de Smet on 16 April 1845:

> April 16th 1845. On the banks of Lake Jasper, we met an old Iroquois called Louis Kwaragkwanté, or Walking Sun, accompanied by his family, thirty-six in number. He had been forty years absent from his country...has dwelt for the last thirty-four years in the forest of the Athabaska and on Peace River and subsisted by hunting and fishing... The little Iroquois camp immediately set out to follow me to Fort Jasper. Most of them know their prayers in Iroquois.[98]

This Louis Kwaragkwante/Cahiheue/Calihoo from Sault St-Louis, signed a formal contract with McTavish, Frobisher and Co. to work "dans le nord" on 11 November 1800.[99] The party of Iroquois, all male, who went with Louis to Fort des Prairie [Edmonton] are said to have numbered forty.[100] Louis Cahiheue adapted well to life in the North West. He first married a Sekani woman in 1800 [probably 1801] and then he took as a second wife in 1803 a French *métisse*, Marie Patenaude. He had seven children from the first union and eight from the second.[101] They were visited by Father Lacombe in 1853 and by Father Remas in 1856. This last Oblate convinced them to relocate to the Lac Ste-Anne mission. Father Lacombe noted their presence in his first Ste-Anne mission report.[102] In the late 1860s the importance of the Ste-Anne mission declined and a majority of the population moved to the St-Albert mission a short distance to the southeast.[103] Two sons from his second marriage, Michel and Baptiste, along with their extended Iroquois-Cree-Métis families chose to adhere to Treaty Six in 1877–78. They were given 40-square miles of land near present day St. Albert, Alberta. In addition to farming, members of the band did freighting with their own horses for the Department of Indian Affairs and for the HBC. Many of the children were sent to the High River Industrial School to learn a trade. In 1903 Mr. Gibbon, Indian Agent at Edmonton, gave the following account:

> it is obvious that the Iroquois blood in this generation is attenuated to the vanishing point. They have lost their language, and, if they retain any tribal characteristics, they have become so feeble that the ordinary observer of Indian manners is unable to discern them. In appearance, habits and social status, they are indistinguishable from the half-breeds of the country.[104]

With time many of the band members took [Métis] scrip and left the band rolls. Finally on 31 March 1958, the remaining members of Michel's Band became enfranchised by Order in Council P.C. 1958–375.[105]

Not all the Iroquois chose to follow the priest to the Lac Ste-Anne area. Iroquois were noted residing near the HBC post of Jasper House by members of the Palliser expedition (1857–1860). Expedition member Dr. Hector comments in his 30 January 1859 journal entry:

> These Iroquois were originally trappers in the service of the NW Company, and on the junction of that company with the Hudson Bay Company, they turned "freemen," as those are termed in the country who are not in the service of the Company, and have since tented about like Indians, trading the skins and furs they procure at Jasper

House. There are only 30 tents of them, and they all talk the Cree language besides their own, and have latterly intermarried a good deal with Cree Half-breeds of Lac St. Ann's.[106]

He later commented on the fact that they lived in huts constructed of pine tree branches and that their hunters used dogs "which are beautifully trained to turn the [mountain] sheep as they rush up the mountain to reach the most inaccessible precipices."[107] Their existence would be noted again 20 years later in the following terms: "where the Saskatchewan issues from the Rocky mountains are a small number of Iroquois metis."[108] Victoria Calihoo, wife to the grandson of Louis Cahiheue (Calihoo), wrote of these people in 1948:

A few other Iroquois came west later and some of them went up the Athabasca river to Yellow Head Post, where they worked for the Hudson's Bay Company. Wianda and Gauthier are the only names I can remember now...Among us, we know them as the Rocky Mountain people.[109]

Frish argues it is from this band that the twentieth century Iroquois-Métis settlements at Grande Cache and Pocahontas developed.[110]

Less is known of the numerous Iroquois freemen trappers and their large families who roamed the Oregon district. They appear to have adapted quite well to life of the prairie and foothills. Mention of their love of horses and the bison chase, to the detriment of trapping, is often made by local post-masters.[111] They found wives locally either of Native or French Métis origin[112] and resisted attempts by the Company to have them retire in Red River much preferring to settle in the Willamette Valley [present day Oregon]. Brown writing in 1950 notes that this was the beginning of the settlement known locally as "French-Prairie" where French-speaking descendants of these first settlers were still to be found.[113] Henry B. Zenk in his study of the Grand Ronde reservation mentions French-Iroquois families arriving from French Prairie in the 1860s and 1870s. These families where quite important and politically active in both communities.[114] Others also congregated near Fort Colville. Cartographer Charles Wilson while mapping for the British Boundary Commission on 30 June 1860 wrote in his journal:

Descending into the valley we soon were among cornfields, cattle & houses & found ourselves quite the object of curiosity, being the first English soldiers that the people have ever seen; and such a curious medley of people these said people are, nearly all of them old servants of the HBC, the old trapper, the voyageur, the Canadian, French, Iroquois and half-breed...the hardy pioneer of civilization now quietly settled in the valley with their wives and families round them.[115]

He would add on the next day's entry that "the languages are as various as the races, the prominent one being Canadian French of the worst kind, which of all languages or dialects I ever heard offends my ears; it is murdering French with a vengeance."[116]

One last group of Iroquois, a band of 24, settled between 1812–1828 in the area of Western Montana, Northern Idaho and eastern Washington among the Flathead Indians who apparently received them with great hospitality.[117] They married into the tribe and their leader Ignace Lamousse appears to have become an important man or "chief" among the Flathead. He also was an Iroquois neophyte, teaching the Flathead the Lord's Prayer, the sign of the cross, and observing Sunday as a day of rest. He and his family were instrumental in bringing the famed Jesuit missionary, Father Pierre de Smet, to the area. In a letter dated 22 July 1840 Father de Smet recorded having said mass at Henry's Lake where the "praises of God were chanted in the Flathead, Nez Perce and Iroquois Languages."[118] Writing in 1871, the U.S. Indian Agent at the Flathead agency, Jocko Reserve, Montana would note the long-lasting religious influence of Iroquois Indians from Canada on the local population.[119]

The Christian Iroquois from Montreal area were known to have participated in the western fur trade during the French colonial period. At that time, however, they conducted their business independently of the mainstream trading companies. The opening years of the nineteenth century gave rise to a new phenomenon. The notarial files indicate unequivocally that the same Iroquois entered into formal contractual, long-term obligations with fur-trading concerns, and left their villages to travel westward.

The reasons for this apparent change were twofold: on the one hand the fur trading concerns readjusted their labour requirements in response to increased competition, while on the other, the economic viability of Laurentian reserves was put into question by their ever-shrinking land base and the depletion of their traditional hunting territories. The demographic and human repercussions of the absence of hundreds of young males from Native villages were profound.

Unlike French Canadian *engagés* from distant parishes, hired principally as poorly-paid voyageurs, the Iroquois served in more than one capacity. They were both canomen and skilled hunters and trappers. In the race for

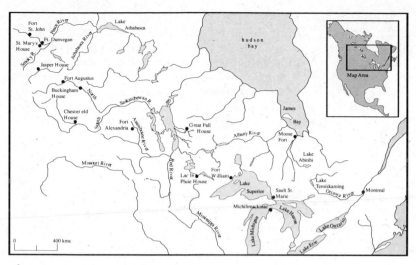

♲ *FIGURE 2-2*

furs all major trading concerns: the XYC, NWC, and HBC resorted to their services and paid them handsomely.

It should be noted that this Native Catholic migration westward did not end with the amalgamation of the HBC and the NWC in 1821. When one examines the biographies of 119 known Iroquois in the Columbia district [1810–1858] nearly two thirds arrived in the area after the union; many directly from Sault St-Louis.[120] This east-west Iroquois link is evident when the description and names of the voyageurs used for both the 1858 Palliser expedition and Wolseley's 1870 Red River Expeditionary Force are examined. Most are of Iroquois descent.[121]

By linking data extracted from Montreal notarial documents to information contained in western fur trade journals and letters it is possible to ascertain the existence, and begin to evaluate the impact, of a previously little known Native western migration through the aegis of fur trade employment. Further research is being done by the authors to evaluate the importance of the fur trade employment for other Laurentian Valley native communities and to flesh out the patterns of diffusion and adaptation of eastern Natives on the fur trade frontiers in the nineteenth century. The information presented clearly indicates that profound changes were occurring in the patterns of Native participation in the fur trade economy in the early years of the nineteenth century. These changes had a significant impact on both, the eastern Iroquois settlements, and the creation of the fur-trading communities in the West.

Acknowledgements

The authors would like to express their gratitude to Alfred Fortier, of the Société Historique de Saint-Boniface, who provided them with the initial list of more than 15,000 engagements. They would like also to thank Jacques Barbier, Paul Lachance, Philip Goldring and D. Peter MacLeod for their highly valuable comments on the earlier drafts of this article. The errors that remain are the sole responsibility of the authors. Thanks are due to research assistants Brian Locking and Gavin Kerr.

Notes

1.   Trudy Nicks, "The Iroquois and the Fur Trade in Western Canada," in Arthur J. Ray and Carol Judd, eds., *Old Trails and New Directions* (Toronto and Buffalo: University of Toronto Press, 1980), 88–101.

2.   The term *domiciliés* described not only the Iroquois but also several other Amerindian nations living in the vicinity of the French settlements. The Hurons had established themselves close to Québec, in Lorette. The Abenakis lived in two villages, not far from Trois-Rivières, and the Iroquois were concentrated in Sault St-Louis (Kahnawake) and in Lac-des-Deux-Montagnes (Oka, Kanasetaké). The latter settlement was also home to numerous Nipissings, Algonquins and some Hurons.

3.   Alexander F. Chamberlain, "Iroquois in Northwestern Canada," *American Anthropologist* 6, no. 4 (1904): 459–63; John C. Ewers, "Iroquois Indians in the Far West," *Montana the Magazine of Western History* (1963): 2–10; Jack A. Frisch, "Some Ethnological and Ethnohistoric Notes on the Iroquois in Alberta," *Man in the Northeast* 12 (1976): 51–64; James Gibbons, "Iroquois in the North West Territories," *Annual Archaeological Report* (1903): 125–26; Theodore Karamanski, "The Iroquoian Fur Trade of the Far West," *Beaver* (Spring 1992): 1–13; Glen Makahonuk, "Wage Labour in the Northwest Fur Trade Economy, 1760–1849," *Saskatchewan History* 41, no. 1 (Winter 1988): 1–18.

4.   In the absence of studies of Iroquois communities in the nineteenth century, following sources are useful in the related research: Denys Delâge, "Les Iroquois chretiens des 'reductions,' 1667–1770," *Recherches amérindiennes au Québec* 21, no. 3 (1991): 39–51; Jan Grabowski, "French Justice and Indians in Montreal, 1670–1760," *Ethnohistory* 43, no. 3 (1996): 405–29; Gretchen Lynn Green, "New People in an Age of War: The Kahnawake Iroquois, 1667–1760" (Ph.D. Thesis, The College of William and Mary, 1991); Peter D. MacLeod, "Microbes and Muskets; Smallpox and the Participation of the Amerindian Allies of New France in the Seven Years War," *Ethnohistory* 39, no. 1 (Winter 1992): 42–64.

5.   Although there exists several dozen contracts for Lac-des-Deux-Montagnes natives, this study will focus on the much more numerous Iroquois from Sault St-Louis.

6.   At the end of the eighteenth and in the beginning of the nineteenth centuries a typical, pre-printed, engagement contained the following information: names of the contracting parties, their parishes of origin, remuneration, destination and duration of the trip, equipment provided and the responsibilities of an *engagé* (i.e., location in the canoe, etc.).

7.   The authors do not claim to have examined, in detail, the files of all the notaries active in the Montreal district during the discussed period. There are still several

études that require further scrutiny. However, owing to the number of researched engagements, it is unlikely that the scale of the phenomenon of native participation in the salaried fur trade, could be called into question.

8. Allan Greer, "Fur-Trade Labour and Lower Canadian Agrarian Structures," *Historical Papers/Communications historiques* (1981): 201. It has to be noted that Greer's study discussed the late eighteenth century fur trade. After 1800 duly notarized engagements became a required element of each hiring for the West, and although exceptions were still possible, they were less frequent than during the preceding period.

9. Among French and English names found (and left out from the studied group) in Sault St-Louis and in Lac-des-Deux-Montagnes in the 1820s we find the following: Beauvais, Delisle, Jacob, Mailloux, Merry, Monique, Neau, Perthuis, Philippe, Picard, Simonette, Turgeon, Vincent. Many Amerindians had (and still have) these surnames today, but there were also numerous French Canadians of the same name. A genealogical inquiry would be necessary to separate the native and the nonnative groups. Such an undertaking would extend far beyond the frame of this article. It would change little, if anything, in the larger picture and, more importantly, the results of such a research would be highly dubious methodologically. How can one establish, in the absence of specific information contained in notarial or judicial documents, the ethnic identity of the inhabitants of the village?

10. Jan Grabowski, "Les Amérindiens domiciliés et la 'contrebande' des fourrures," *Recherches Amérindiennes au Québec* 24, no. 3 (1994): 45–52

11. See Laura Peers, *The Ojibwa of Western Canada, 1780 to 1870* (Winnipeg: The University of Manitoba Press, 1994), 14–21.

12. Elaine Allan Mitchell, *Fort Temiskaming and the Fur Trade* (Toronto: University of Toronto Press, 1977), 34–35.

13. Greer, "Fur-Trade Labour," 202

14. The Native censuses have serious flaws. Some of them were done in the winter, when a large part of the male population was away hunting. If the count was taken for the purpose of gift distribution, several Amerindians would have, most probably, been excluded on the grounds of their extended absence from the village. In the seventeenth and eighteenth centuries the counts were often based on the number of warriors or even huts (or cabins). The interpretation of these data can only be approximate. Nevertheless, taking into account all available information, spread over a longer period of time, one can hope that the results, although not as precise as in the case of French Canadians, will be good enough to indicate demographic patterns of growth and decline. Other sources, such as the parish registers, not preserved for the French régime, become available for the nineteenth century. They offer information on population dynamics (birth/death rates). They are less helpful in establishing the overall size of the extant population.

15. Gordon Day, *The Identity of the Saint Francis Indians* (Ottawa: National Museums of Canada, 1981), 34; P. Camille de Rochemonteix, S.J., *Rélations par lettres de l'Amérique septentrionale (années 1709–1710)* (Paris: Latouzey & Amé, 1904), 211.

16. In 1732 the mission counted 250 warriors, suggesting a total of about 1250 inhabitants (1:4, or 1:5 being the ratio accepted in historical literature). Archives du Séminaire de Saint-Sulpice (ASSSM), *Fonds Faillon*, C257, M. Hocquart, 10 octobre 1732. Two years later the sources report an additional 250 people, or 1500 Indians in residence. Rapport de l'Archiviste de la Province du Québec (*RAPQ*), (1926–1927): 268; Archives Nationales (AN), Colonies, C11A, 66: 181–219 and 75: 206. Documents

Relative to the Colonial History of the State of New York (*NYCD*), E.B. O'Callaghan, ed. (Albany, 1855), 9: 1052–1054. For a detailed account of missions' demographic profile see: John A. Dickinson and Jan Grabowski, "Les populations amérindiennes de la vallée laurentienne, 1608–1764," *Annales de la demographie historique*, France (1993): 51–65.

17.   We would like to express our gratitude to Hélène Bédard for her kind help in providing us with the Sault St-Louis population counts for 1808, 1822, and 1826. 1764: 200 warriors, Schoolcraft, 1856 (3): 553; 1768: 300 warriors (ca. 1200 people), ibid.; 1778: 1200 people, Schoolcraft, 6: 714; 1808: 816 [la liste des sauvages présents : liste faite pour la distribution des couvertes], ANC, RG 10, vol. 11, pp. 9945–46]; 1808: 866 , census: 1808, ANC, RG 10, vol. 11, p. 10008, 1822 : 937 ANC, RG 10, vol. 15, p. 12062; 1826 : 947 ANC, RG 10, vol. 18, p.13432 Return of Indians of Sault St-Louis for 1826; 1830: 990, ANC, RG 10, vol. 84, p. 33317; 1831: 1051, ANQM, Sault St-Louis census; 1835 : 932, I.I.A.D.H. 1985: 27 oct. 1836; 1858: 1342 The Year Book and Almanac of Canada for 1871: p. 12; 1868: 1601 The Year Book and Almanac of Canada for 1871: p. 12.

18.   Joseph Bouchette, *A Topographical Description of the Province of Lower Canada with Remarks upon Upper Canada and the relative Connexion of Both Provinces with the United States of America* (London, 1815), 124.

19.   Archives Nationales du Québec à Montréal (ANQM), Sault St-Louis, Registres paroisseaux. Between 1795–1799 and 1802–1805 the number of yearly baptisms drops from 40 to 30. However, parish registers have to be treated with caution. Most of the voyageurs leaving for the West would be young males, most of them still single. The declining or growing birthrate can have as much to do with their absence as it can with the changing patterns of women's behaviour.

20.   The "Grand Nord," as opposed to the "Petit Nord," encompassed those vaster lands that opened to the north and west of Lake Winnipeg. D. Wayne Moodie, "The trading post settlement of the Canadian Northwest, 1774–1821," *Journal of Historical Geography* 13, no. 4 (1987): 360–74.

21.   E.J. Devine, *Historic Caughnawaga* (Montreal: Messenger Press, 1922), 327.

22.   Bruce M. Watson, personal communication, 1995.

23.   Native voyageurs from other villages (i.e., St-Régis and Lac-des-Deux-Montagnes) have been excluded from this list.

24.   John Lambert, *Travels through Lower Canada and the United States of America in the Years 1806, 1807 and 1808*, 2 vols. (London, 1814), 509–10, cited in Greer, "Fur-Trade Labour," 207.

25.   Apparently some of the Iroquois voyageurs from Sault St-Louis returned to the village after a 20–30 year absence. Although this phenomenon raises some interesting questions for the later period, it changes little in the social and economic situation of Sault St-Louis during the 1800–1820 period.

26.   Includes only parishes with more than 400 engagements to their account.

27.   There is a disproportional number of Amerindian engagements that fail to mention the parish of origin of native voyageurs. After proportional distribution, Sault St-Louis accounts for 1043 engagements signed between 1800 and 1821.

28.   Ann M. Carlos, *The North American Fur Trade, 1804–1821: A Study in the Life-Cycle of a Duopoly* (New York and Toronto: Garland Publishing, 1986), 171–92.

29.   E.E. Rich, ed., *Peter Skene Ogden's Snake Country Journals 1824–1825 and 1825–1826* (London: The Hudson's Bay Record Society, 1950), 79.

30. Greer, "Fur-Trade Labour," 200.

31. Greer, "Fur-Trade Labour," 199.

32. The recruitment of rural French Canadians from Sorel was dictated, as well, by their familiarity with canoeing and with boat travel. The *domiciliés* were long known for their canoeing skills, and it would be surprising to assume that the fur trading companies became aware of this fact only at the very end of the eighteenth century.

33. Greer, "Fur-Trade Labour," 201.

34. For an excellent discussion of this phenomenon see: Louis Lavallée, *La Prairie en Nouvelle-France, 1647–1760: Etude d'histoire sociale* (Montreal: McGill-Queen's University Press, 1993), 56–60.

35. Archives nationales, colonies (A.N. Col). C11A, 65: 99–100 and 95: 188.

36. *Canada Indian Treaties and Surrenders*, App. G, 2: 293–304.

37. ANQM, Cour du Banc du Roi, Avril 1798-Juillet 1799, 218–01\01–01–01A, Juin 1798. "Les demandeurs [Iroquois chiefs] sont vraiment les Seigneurs et Propriétaires de la Seigneurie du Sault St-Louis, et parceque ladite Seigneurie su Sault St-Louis n'a jamais été legalement separée et bornée du coinsentement des propriétaires d'icelle, dans l'endroit ou existent actuellement certaines bornes, qui ont été déplacées de leur vraie position, les quelles bornes ne se trouvent point dans la vraie ligne de séparation, mais à une très grande distance, comme ont allegué les demandeurs..." In his reply the defendant, Jean Joseph Casot, maintained that not only were there no unauthorized re-zonings done, but that the chiefs were not Seigneurs, and had no right to use this title. See: Deposition of Casot, June 1798.

38. It is significant that during the same time Natives from Lac-des-Deux-Montagnes protest to the authorities the encroachments of French farmers in their seigneurie, and point to the fact that the Sulpicians were responsible for their land being given *en roture* to French Canadian farmers. See: ASSSM, *Fonds Oka*, Speech addressed to Sir John Johnson, 8 February 1788.

   Although we know of few engagements for the Lac-des-Deux-Montagnes area during this time, it was noted that, in 1788, Eustache Beaubien Desrivieres recruited a sizeable contingent of Iroquois, to form trading expeditions to the Temiscamingue. Mitchell, *Fort Timiskaming and the Fur Trade*, 34.

39. Ewers, "Iroquois Indians in the Far West," 5.

40. Amerindians were more often than French Canadians hired for the well-paying jobs of guides. They also received more money for *devant* and *gouvernail* positions in the canoe.

41. The table is based on financial statements included in all Amerindian contracts and in the random sample of 2500 French Canadian voyageurs.

42. Louis Lom d'Arce, Baron de Lahontan, *Dialogues Curieux entre l'auteur et un sauvage de bon sens qui a voyagé et Mémoires de l'Amérique septentrionale*, Gilbert Chinard, éd. (Baltimore: The John Hopkins University Press, 1931), 95.

43. The inhabitants complained that the *domiciliés* were all too well informed about the value of their furs, see ANQM, Archives judiciaires, pièces détachées (AJPD), 69, 24 octobre 1702, Procureur du Roy c. Joseph Trottier Desrusseaux, Interrogatoire du 24 août 1702, "...que les Iroquois sont trop futtés parce quilz nont Jamais offert pour une couverte plus de deux peaux."

44. Iroquois demanded salary increases and , when their demands were not satisfied, they were likely to desert to competing companies, or even become independent

trappers selling to the highest bidder. Robert Rumilly, *La Compagnie du Nord-Ouest: Une Épopée montréalaise* (Montreal: Fides, 1960), Vol. 2, 260.

45. Cited after: Daniel Francis, *Battle for the West: Fur Traders and the Birth of Western Canada* (Edmonton: Hurtig Publishers, 1982), 146.

46. See Innis, *The Fur Trade in Canada*, 264.

47. All accounts of the western fur trade are aware of this role performed by the Iroquois *engagés*, but they fail to recognize the statistical importance of this phenomenon. The Iroquois hunters are perceived and described as isolated individuals performing a largely irrelevant errand for the hiring companies. See Innis, *The Fur Trade in Canada*, 237; Rich, *The Fur Trade and the Northwest to 1857*, 227.

48. Karamanski, "The Iroquoian Fur Trade," 5.

49. Ibid.

50. Their destination may well have been the "Little North" [east of Lake Winnipeg] where, in the early 1800, Postmasters complained of diminished returns due to Iroquois trappers. Victor P. Lytwyn, *The Fur Trade of the Little North: Indian, Peddlars, and Englishmen East of Lake Winnipeg, 1760–1821* (Winnipeg: Rupert's Land Research Center, 1986), 108.

51. See for example Karamanski, "The Iroquoian Fur Trade," 5.

52. One should remember that informal hunting and trading (without the benefit of a formal signed contract) continued unabated during the whole period examined. This is certainly true in the "Little North" where Iroquois trappers either collaborated with the large trading concerns or, just as often, openly defied them. This would continue even after the amalgamation of 1821. As Lytwyn notes as early as 1804 in the area east of Lake Winnipeg, especially the Lake Sanderson district, HBC personnel were noting a decline in the fur returns due to "Indians from Montreal" who had been hired to trap furs in the East Winnipeg country by the NWC or possibly the XYC. In the Ottawa valley district the HBC would have to deal with vexing opposition well into the 1840s. As E.E. Rich notes "the district was studded with opposition posts, petty traders taking full advantage of their easy access to Montreal" and full of Iroquois and Algonguins taking advantage of the "extraordinary and oppressive license" which the governor had granted them, in 1830 to hunt at will regardless of tribal boundaries. Lytwyn, *The Fur Trade*, 108; Rich, *The History of the Hudson's Bay Company 1670–1870*, Vol. 2, 523.

53. James E. De Kay. *Zoology of New York or New York Fauna*; part I, Mammalia (Albany, N.Y.: W. & A. White and J. Visscher), 73 in: Natural History of New York State (Thurlow Weed, Albany, NY). We are indebted for this citation to Joel Cadbury from Cornell University.

54. In the case of Native hirings similar doubts can be raised about the absence of the Hudson's Bay Company among the major employers (see Tables 2–5 and 2–6). The conspicuous absence of the HBC hirings from the notarial records in Montreal can be linked to different trading policies pursued, in the beginning of the discussed period, by HBC and the North West Co. While the former preferred to have the furs delivered by Amerindians to its posts, the latter were known to rely on *engagés* bringing the trade to native villages. A possible "in-house" and informal hiring practices of the HBC might be additionally responsible for this phenomenon. Most of all, however, Hudson's Bay Company was not, before its Athabaska drive of 1814, a company with intermediate staging posts between Montreal and the Great Lakes.

55. Lytwyn, *The Fur Trade of the Little North*, 108.

56. Karamanski, "The Iroquoian Fur Trade," 6. Trudy Nicks reports that the first recorded Iroquois in the Northwest were in the employ of a former NWC man named Davis Grant in 1794. Three of these Iroquois were lured away by the NWC and may be the same individuals mentioned by McGillivray. Nicks, "The Iroquois...," 87.

57. J.G. MacGregor, *Peter Fidler: Canada's Forgotten Surveyor 1769–1822* (Toronto: McClelland and Stewart, 1966), 102.

58. These appear to be the previously mentioned Iroquois who had headed West without benefit of a formal contract. The extent to which they were tied to a particular company is unclear.

59. A. Mackenzie, *Voyages from Montreal on the River St. Laurence through the Continent of North America...* (London: R. Noble, 1801) cited by Frish, "Some Ethnological...," 53.

60. W.K. Lamb, ed., *Sixteen Years in the Indian Country, the Journals of Daniel William Harmon 1800–1816* (Toronto: MacMillan Co., 1957), 25. Chamberlain quotes another edition [1903] and adds a second sentence: "Some of them have their families with them" not found in the Lamb edition. Alexander F. Chamberlain, "Iroquois in Northwestern Canada," *American Anthropologist* 6 (1904): 460.

61. Charles M. Gates, ed., *Five Fur Traders of the Northwest* (St. Paul: Minnesota Historical Society, 1965), 125–85.

62. The data base notes approximately one hundred natives *engagés* leaving Montreal in the summer of 1800 and a second contingent also of about 100 leaving in 1801; a clear indication that notarial documents are, at best, a conservative estimate of Iroquois' participation in the western trade.

63. Alice M. Johnson, *Saskatchewan Journals and Correspondence: Edmonton House, 1795–1800, Chesterfield House 1800–1802* (London: Hudson's Bay Record Society, 1967), xci.

64. Trudy Nicks argues convincingly that Tyrrell, Thompson's original editor, made an error of interpretation when arguing for a 1798 date and the big influx of Iroquois to the Saskatchewan district did occur in 1801. The error was simply perpetuated in the Glover edition. Ewers in his article argues the influx occurred in 1789 but this is most likely a typographical error. Richard Glover, ed., *David Thompson's Narrative 1784–1812* (Toronto: The Champlain Society, 1962), 229; Nicks, "The Iroquois and the Fur Trade," 97 (ft 10); Ewers, "Iroquois Indians in the Far West," 2–10.

65. Glover, *David Thompson's Narrative*, 156.

66. MacGregor, *Peter Fiddler*, 138.

67. Ibid., 157.

68. Lamb, *Sixteen Years*, 118.

69. Glover, *David Thompson's Narrative*, 302.

70. E.E. Rich, ed., *Colin Robertson's Correspondence Book, September 1817 to September 1822* (London: Hudson's Bay Record Society, 1939), lviii.

71. Canoe personnel varied from a complement of four to one as high as eight. Meaning over 200 *engagés* probably left that summer manning the HBC fleet.

72. Rich, *Colin Robertson's Correspondence Book*, 41. It is difficult to know the exact numbers of Iroquois *engagés* involved in the HBC Athabasca enterprise. Only a handful of HBC pre 1820 Montreal contracts have been located to date. However Iroquois involvement is confirmed by Trudy Nicks analysis of the journals for Fort St. Mary's on the Peace River. Nicks, "The Iroquois and the Fur Trade," 98, ft.15.

73. Rich, *Colin Robertson's Correspondence Book*, 108.

74. Some of the tribes, such as the Carrier and Beaver tribes, would protest loudly the arrival of Iroquois as *trappers* sometimes to the point of resorting to murder. Nicks, "The Iroquois and the Fur Trade," 93.

75. The western nations' displeasure at the sight of the Canadian Iroquois might well have been linked to the previous sojourn of the Sault St-Louis warriors in the West. During the Second Fox War, in 1734–35 over two hundred Iroquois from the Sault took part in French punitive expedition against the Fox. They were involved in the bloody battle at Little Butte des Morts, earning long-lasting hate of the Sauks, Foxes and their allies.

76. Glover, *David Thompson's Narrative*, 230.

77. MacGregor, *Peter Fiddler*, 138.

78. Lamb, *Sixteen Years*, 191–93.

79. Louis Masson, ed., *Les Bourgeois de la Compagnie du Nord Ouest: recits de voyages, lettres et rapports inédits relatif au Nord Ouest Canadien* 1 (Québec: A. Coté et Cie, 1889–1890), 109 quoted in Nicks, "The Iroquois and the Fur Trade," 91.

80. Glover, *David Thompson's Narrative*, 392. Thompson's editors caution that this number must be taken as approximate, and applicable to free-hunters of either Algonguin, Iroquois, or mixed-blood that had been killed by Peigan or Blackfoot during Thompson's acquaintance with the tribe.

81. Milo Milton Quaiffe, ed., *The Fur Hunters of the Far West* (Chicago: The Lakeside Press, 1924), 61.

82. Ross Cox, *Adventures on the Columbia River Including...* (New York, 1832), 236–37 quoted by George I. Quimby, "Hawaiians in the Fur Trade of North-west America 1785–1820," *The Journal of Pacific History* 7 (1972): 102.

83. Quaiffe, *The Fur Hunters of the Far West*, 286.

84. Rich, *Peter Skene Ogden's Snake Country Journals 1824–1825*, xivi.

85. Ibid., lixx.

86. Karamanski, "The Iroquoian Fur Trade," 7.

87. Quaiffe, *Fur Hunters of the Far West*, 148.

88. Rich, *Peter Skene Ogden*, xli.

89. Ibid., 49. The Americans were not the only trading concerns interested in employing the French and Iroquois trappers. Ogden would note in his 22 May 1825 entry: "As we were on the eve of starting this morning one of our trappers arrived in company with two of our freemen [Joe Mcleod and Lazard Teycateyecowige] who deserted from the flat head post 1822. They belong to a party of 30 men who were fitted out by the Spaniards & Traders on the Missouri & have spent the winter in this quarter & have met with little Success of the 14 who deserted 6 are dead & the remainder with the Spaniards at St. Louis & Missouri...now 15 days march from the Spanish Village...outfitting centre for the fur trade of the Southern Rocky Mountain region." See *Oregon Historical Quarterly* 35, 109; Rich, *Peter Skene Ogden*, 49 (footnote 2); HBCA, B.208/e/1, fo 4d., "Spokane House Report 1822/23" by Alexander Kennedy lists the "Men who did not come out from the Snake Country last Fall" as follows: J. Gardepie, Jos. St. Amand Francois Wm. Hodgens, Ignace Solihonie, Pierre Cassawesa, Ignace Solihonies Stepson Francois Method, Louis St. Michel, J. McLeod, Francs. X Fenetoresue, Thos. Nakarsketa, Lazard Teycateyecowige, Patrick OConnor, Ignace Takekeurat.

90. Quaiffe, *Fur Hunters of the Far West*, 177.

91. Rich, *Peter Skene Ogden*, 209 [appendix A; William Kittson Journal of Snake Expedition, 1824–1825] — "Monday 20th December 1824, The party is now together consisting of 22 lodges which contain besides Mr Ogden and myself, Charles McKay an interpreter of the Piegan language 10 engages 53 Freemen and lads, 30 Women and 35 children, all well furnished in arms ammunition Horses and traps...the Flat Heads, Pendent Oreilles and Kootenai have their tents near us."

92. Ibid., 51–56.

93. A variant of the above mentioned strategies would be the Iroquois participation in the creation of a new, hybrid, "reservation" culture and language (Chinook Jargon) when they and members of several different tribes were forced to relocate on a single reservation called "Grand Ronde" (Oregon, U.S.A.). Zenk, "Chinook Jargon and Native Cultural Persistence," I–XX.

94. For a pertinent discussion of the theoretical debates surrounding the concept of ethnogenesis as applied to the Americas see Kevin Mulroy, "Ethnogenesis and Ethnohistory of the Seminole Maroons," *Journal of World History* 4 (1993): 287–305.

95. Chamberlain, "Iroquois in Western Canada," 460.

96. Karamanski, "The Iroquoian Fur Trade," 13.

97. A.O. MacRae, *History of the Province of Alberta* (n.p.: The Western Canada History Company, 1912), 63.

98. H.M. Chittenden and A.T. Richardson, eds., *Life, Letters and Travels of Father Pierre de Smet, s.j., 1801–1873: Missionary Labors and Adventures Among the Wild Tribes of North American Indians* (New York: F.P. Harper, 1905), 536.

99. Alfred Fortier, Liste des Voyageurs, SHSB, 1993.

100. Chamberlain, "The Iroquois in Western Canada," 461.

101. Frish, "Ethnological and Ethnohistorical Notes," 54.

102. A. Philippot, o.m.i., *Le Frere Alexis Reynard, o.m.i. (1828–1875)* (Lablachere [Ardeche]: Oeuvre Apostolique de M.I., 1931), 166.

103. Donat Levasseur, o.m.i., *Les Oblats de Marie Immaculee dans l'Ouest et le Nord du Canada, 1845–1967* (Edmonton: University of Alberta Press/ Western Canada Publishers, 1995), 56–57.

104. James Gibbons, "Iroquois in the North West Territories," *Annual Archaeological Report for 1903*, 125–26, quoted in Chamberlain, "Iroquois in Western Canada," 461–62.

105. Frish, "Some Ethnological and Ethnohistoric," 54.

106. Irene M. Spry, ed., *The Papers of the Palliser Expedition, 1857–1860* (Toronto: The Champlain Society, 1968), 367.

107. Ibid., 377.

108. V. Havard, "The French Halfbreeds of the Northwest," *Annual Report of the Smithsonian Institution, 1879* (Washington, 1880), 318, quoted in Chamberlain, "The Iroquois in Western Canada," 462.

109. Victoria Calihoo, "The Iroquois in Alberta," *Alberta Historical Review* 7 (1959): 18.

110. Frish, "Some Ethnological and Ethnohistoric," 58. For a discussion of the Grande Cache Iroquois-Metis community see Trudy Nicks and Kenneth Morgan, "Grande Cache: The historic development of an indigenous Alberta métis population," Jacqueline Peterson and Jennifer S.H. Brown, eds., *The New Peoples, Being and Becoming Métis in North America* (Winnipeg: University of Manitoba Press, 1985), 163–81.

111. Quaiffe, *Fur Hunters of the Far West*, 148.

112. Ibid., 177.

113. Rich, *Peter Skene Ogden,* xliv.

114. Henry B. Zenk, "Chinook Jargon and Native Cultural Persistence in the Grand Ronde Indian Community, 1856–1907: a Special Case in Creolization" (Ph.D. dissertation, University of Oregon, 1984), 30–38.

115. George F. G. Stanley, ed., *Mapping the Frontier Charles Wilson's Diary of the Survey of the 49th Parallel, 1858–1862* (Toronto: Macmillan of Canada, 1970), 110.

116. Ibid., 111.

117. Chittenden and Richardson, *Life, Letters and Travels of Father Pierre de Smet,* 19. It should be noted that no reference is made to this group of Iroquois working as trappers during their stay with the tribe.

118. Ibid.

119. Chamberlain, "Iroquois in Western Canada," 463.

120. Bruce M. Watson, personal communication, 1996.

121. William Francis Butler, *The Great Lone Land,* 19th edition, first published 1872 (Toronto: The Musson Book Co., 1924), 167.

3

Partial Truths

A Closer Look at Fur Trade Marriage

JENNIFER S.H. BROWN

I N 1 9 8 0 , Sylvia Van Kirk and I both examined fur trade social history in separate studies. Sylvia Van Kirk's *"Many Tender Ties": Women in Fur-Trade Society, 1670–1870* focused on the role of women in the fur trade, and mine, *Strangers in Blood: Fur Trade Company Families in Indian Country,* on the changing situations of the traders' Native families.[1] They seemed appreciated at the time, and were part of a broader turn towards the social history of Rupert's Land (the region that the Hudson's Bay Company held by charter for 200 years) and Red River, as exemplified also in the innovative work of John Elgin Foster and Frits Pannekoek.[2] But we could not have predicted the extent to which those topics have come of age. Within the last decade, hundreds, even thousands, of people have discovered their roots in fur trade family history; new information, oral histories, documents, links among these old families appear every day. Our books are still in print; but now they simply provide beginnings—clues, contexts, and connections for people who are recovering and telling their own family stories from all kinds of sources, written, oral, and pictorial. This article, written to honour the memory of John Foster, offers me an occasion to take another look at fur trade marriages and our ways of thinking about them.

Van Kirk and I studied these unions on one level by surveying many of the best documented examples and by tracing the patterns they followed. Another approach, which we have also taken in some instances, is to delve into individual lives in detail, as do many traders' biographers and family historians. This essay contributes to biography, specifically that of a relatively obscure clerk, George Nelson. Its main focus, however, is on the multiple, contested, and sometimes elusive meanings of his two successive fur trade marital "connexions" as he sometimes called them.

A close look at Nelson's experiences and writings generates questions as well as answers. Our understandings of "marriage according to the custom of the country" (*en façon du pays*), as these relations are commonly described, are partial in both senses of the word. The source materials are never as complete as we would wish for the distant, other worlds of the fur trade. And just as partiality in the sense of interest conditions our sources, so too it affects our outlooks in both constructive and limiting ways, as we look backwards from late twenty-first-century historiographic concerns with women's and Native history, and more broadly, with the uncovering of culture and social order in hidden places. In a recent critique of ethnographic writing, James Clifford wrote, "Even the best ethnographic texts — serious, true fictions — are systems, or economies, of truth. Power and history work through them, in ways their authors cannot fully control. Ethnographic truths are thus inherently *partial* — committed and incomplete."[3] Historians need to admit that such problems are also endemic in both their documentary sources and their own writings.

Similarly, Simon Ottenberg, a senior Africanist scholar, has urged scholars to be more reflexive and retrospective about their work. In an essay entitled, "Thirty Years of Fieldnotes: Changing Relationships to the Text," he ponders the fact that the anthropological fieldnotes that have underpinned his publishing and teaching never existed in a vacuum; they are also enmeshed in the intangible "headnotes" or recyclings that the notes have undergone in his mind in the years since he recorded them.[4] Scholars, silently or unawares, all accumulate mental headnotes that get entwined with the paper notes and files that fill their offices over time. These selective memories (and forgettings), impressions, constructs, and conclusions take root and grow in different directions as we teach, think, and tell stories about our work, and as we age and move through life's experiences.

Among my headnotes on fur trade "marriages" are thoughts not only about the range of diversity we see when we compare many exemplars across time and space, but also about the degree of internal complexity that these relationships exhibit when we examine just a few of them more closely. Anthropologist Marilyn Strathern has borrowed images from the new field of fractal graphics with regard to the mapping of irregular coastlines to illuminate problems of complexity and scale in ethnographic writing; and her metaphorical point is useful for this analysis. As she notes for coastlines, "Whether one looks at a large-scale map or investigates every inlet and rock on a beach, the scale changes make no difference to the amount of irregularity.... We may think of the amount of irregularity as an amount of detail...despite an increase in the magnitude of detail, the quantity of information an anthropologist derives from what s/he is observing may remain the same." In essence, she observes, "similar information is reproduced in different scales...[coastal corrugations] present the same involute appearance from near or far."[5]

Fur trader George Nelson's two "marriages according to the custom of the country" serve in this essay as the "inlet or rock[s] on a beach." Closely studied, their detail and complexity yield quantities of information comparable to those gained from mapping the involuted marital coastlines of large numbers of fur trade families from more aerial perspectives. They also provide critical depth and insight; sometimes close-up views can in fact broaden our vision. Nelson's journals and reminiscences are outstanding sources for fur trade and Native history and culture in the regions of Wisconsin, Lake Winnipeg, Moose Lake (Manitoba) and Lac la Ronge (Saskatchewan); they repay close study.[6] From 1802 to 1823, Nelson served almost continuously as a clerk in three successive companies. In the spring of 1802, he left his home town of Sorel (then called William Henry) in Lower Canada for Grand Portage on Lake Superior, marking his sixteenth birthday on the voyage. The relatively well educated son of a schoolmaster, he served the XY Company, otherwise known as Sir Alexander Mackenzie and Company, until the 1804 merger of the XY and North West companies brought him into the Nor-Westers' employ. Then in 1821, when the North West and Hudson's Bay companies merged, he lasted a further two years until found redundant under the new regime of HBC Governor George Simpson.

Nelson's two fur trade marriages were both with Ojibwa women; the first lasted for about nine months, and the second for 23 years until his wife's death in Sorel. He wrote in different ways at different times and places about them, and his alternate versions pose a variety of questions. How do we define these "connexions"? In what senses and at what stages were they marriages, and in whose views? Nelson's writings let us look at them in some depth because they offer intimate, almost photographic views of what happened at particular moments. He openly set down his perceptions and his partial or expanded memories of how these ties came about (he too suffered from headnotes). The zones of silence are also interesting.

"Custom" is a term needing some discussion. European and Euro-Canadian fur traders' unions with Native women began, functioned, and ended in many different ways. The phrase, "custom of the country," implies a misleading degree of uniformity and consensus—a shared set of forms and rituals legitimated by widespread recognition and repetition among all parties involved. If such a unitary marriage custom were found to prevail in the fur trade north from the Great Lakes to Rupert's Land and beyond, it would simplify research and analysis. Any time that we came across a trader's Native family, we could make assumptions about how it got started and evolved, and about what patterns and norms guided it, even in the absence of documents on particular cases. But such assumptions are just that—

assumptions. What if there were multiple customs, or custom on one side of the relationship and confusion or indeterminacy on the other? Were fur traders often coping in various ad-hoc ways with immediate personal situations, needs, and demands, rather than sharing a practice widely valorized and a ritual based on common moral understandings? If they partook of "Indian custom," to what extent did they know or care what it was, or what it entailed from a Native perspective? Or did their awareness of that perspective come rather later, if at all?

It is possible, in fact, that "the custom of the country" was a relatively late construct born of hindsight, as nineteenth-century traders and twentieth-century scholars brought retrospective symbolic order to a receding social world. It would be interesting to track its conception and (re)formulations in detail from the early nineteenth century forward. Looking back, we can certainly find fur trade unions that became characterized by serious, lasting loyalty and mutual affection. These examples evoked James Douglas's phrase of 1842: "the many tender ties, which find a way to the heart," and Van Kirk's conclusion that, "In spite of its many complexities and complications, 'the custom of the country' should be regarded as a bona fide marital union."[7] Yet even these unions did not necessarily begin with any visible ritual or contractual agreement; often, we have no clue about how they began, though some of them evolved into long-term ties. In any case, these examples do not cover the territory; as Van Kirk and I also found, Hudson's Bay Company governor George Simpson and a good many others before and after him acquired "tender ties" which they did not view as marriages. Scholars looking at the more negative aspects of the fur trade have found ample grounds to argue that abuse of women, neglect, prostitution, family breakup, and other social problems were also part of fur trade life.[8]

George Nelson's writings offer insights into both the European and the Native sides of fur trade marriages, helping us understand traders and their Native partners on their own terms, in the contexts of their own times and places. When Nelson and other traders first came together with their Native companions, many of them, both male and female, were still teenagers. Crossing profound gulfs of culture, language, and experience, they could not have had a clear sense of what sorts of unions they were getting into. Nor did they know at the outset what would happen to their relationships; indeterminacy was the order of the day. And of course, they are not around to tell us what "really happened." When we tell their stories for them, the dead cannot contradict us if we misrepresent, oversimplify, or misjudge them. We have to read attentively the incomplete and subjective sources that we have, and we can only imagine and try to allow for all that we have lost.

Nelson's stories of his first fur trade connection survive in two accounts written 25 years apart. They tell, in somewhat different ways, about how he was pressed into it in the fall of 1803 in what is now northern Wisconsin, south of Lake Superior, and then of how the relationship ended. What can we learn from his accounts, putting them together? Was his union an example of what Van Kirk has called "an indigenous marriage rite which evolved to meet the needs of fur-trade society"?[9] For whom was it marriage, sanctioned by whom, and on what models? In the fur trade, as in our own times, definitions of marriage and its meanings were important issues, rarely discussed openly.

The first version comes from Nelson's edited journal of 1803–1804, which he rewrote in 1811 while stationed on Lake Winnipeg and sent to his father in Lower Canada. We do not have his original journal, or as anthropologists would say, the "fieldnotes," written on the spot. Nelson was impressively frank in all his writings, and he emended the 1811 version with useful annotations. But he clearly also recast and amplified this text (on the basis of an original with headnotes added) to make it intelligible, and his past actions defensible. After all, his schoolteacher father was to be its prime reader.

The journal starts at Grand Portage. On 13 July 1803, Nelson, aged 17, left that place for the Sauteux River (Wisconsin) with three men and an interpreter under his charge. He was still a novice, with one difficult winter behind him. His superior in 1803–04 was Simon or Simeon Chaurette, who was to be based up the Montreal River, south of Lake Superior. Nelson described Chaurette as actively looking out for his own wellbeing. He encouraged Nelson to give his men whatever they wanted, "as it was for his interest that they should take up their wages & even more in Goods liquor, tobacco or any other such articles as we had on board our Canoes"; that is, Chaurette would profit from their being in debt to him (15 July 1803).[10]

A week later, at Fond du Lac (the west end of Lake Superior), Chaurette, Nelson, and the others met an Ojibwa whom they called "Le Commis" because, as Nelson explained, "formerly, traders would give him about a 9 Gallon keg of rum & other things & send him trading among or with the other indians; he was always sure to make good returns." (This French word is related to "commission" in English; it is often translated as "clerk," a meaning which does not apply here.) Le Commis had a large family, and Nelson observed,

Here I beleive I may date the beginning of my troubles for this year. Among the rest of his Children he had a daughter who was about 15 years old (but was not here at the time being with her other relations at a few leagues from here.) This old fellow either took a fancy for me, or Chaurette took a fancy for my little wages [i.e., if Nelson acquired a wife his expenses would put him in debt to Chaurette]. I beleive both to be the case. But as for myself, it never came the least into my thoughts to take a woman & I beleive that I should never have perceived this meanness—if I had not been told—but a long time after this.[11]

On 23–24 August, while encamped on the way to his wintering ground, Nelson had "frequent visits & conversations with old Commis—But [I] not being able to understand him Chaurette told me that the old *fellow* wanted to give me his daughter." Nelson was upset at this proposal and "told Chaurette that it was impossible—; that if my father was to know it he would be in the greatest rage with me; that besides I was yet only a boy; & that the Knight [Alexander Mackenzie] would never endure the sight of me...but all this would not do, he always had ready answers which he was Good enough to tell me the Indian made." He finally started avoiding Le Commis, and told Chaurette categorically that he refused the offer. Soon, however, he was obliged to backtrack: "At last to pacify them I told [Chaurette] to tell the old man to keep his daughter 'till next year when I would have wherewith to cloth[e] [her] at least for a time. This appear'd to quieten him a little—but I am sorry to say that it was not so intirely."[12]

After Chaurette departed for his wintering place, Nelson was on his own, dealing with Le Commis whom he badly needed as a guide. His problems continued:

> There has not passed a single day since Chaurette left me...that I have not been teased & troubled on every side—sometimes to take his (Commi's) daughter & other times [he] menaces to leave me if I did not give him rum—He drank much of my rum...but was setting off as soon as he seen the men arrive. this troubled me, particularly, as I could not find any others [to] guide me to my Wintering ground—, being afraid that if I prevailed upon him to remain with me he might perhaps leave somewhere on the road &...I might starve...particularly as my provisions were now exceeding short...& [with] the men & every one else after me I at last was prevailed upon to take *her*. I did not much relish the thought; & was sure that the Knight would be enraged at me (as it did not fail to happen).... I do not or have I any intentions whatever of screening myself from censure when I write this—: ...I know tho', that if I had known as much of [the] manners & customs & trade of the country as I do at present [1811]—this should never have happened me—.[13]

In 1836, Nelson again wrote about these events. Having left the fur trade in 1823, he was living a life of poverty and struggle in his home town of Sorel,

Lower Canada. In 1825, he began keeping a desultory record of his activities. On page 21 of this intermittent diary, however, a remarkable change occurred. A chance meeting with an old fur trade friend, Dominique Ducharme, on 12 September 1836, released a flood of memories of his former life, and suddenly the text became a reminiscence of those times. These recollections complement Nelson's rewritten journal record of 1811 in important ways.

Nelson in 1836 opened his account of 1803–1804 this way: "About the 12th August 1803 I was shipped off for Riviere des Sauteux on the S. side of Lake Superior, & the next Post east of where I had wintered the preceding year. A Canadian by the name of Chaurette, a very harmless and peaceable little man, had taken an outfit upon his own account for the Rivr des Sauteux & Lac Du Flambeau. I was sent as his clerk."[14]

Chaurette was not the only personage to change character in this memoir. Le Commis, in this account, was first mentioned not at Fond du Lac but when Nelson and Chaurette were encamped at the *Mauvaise Riviere* (Bad River, east of Ashland, Wisconsin), and he too became a more benign and appealing figure. Nelson, now aged about 50 and no longer writing for his father, also modified his rendering of himself, admitting that he had been attracted to Le Commis's daughter:

> As none of us had ever been in that quarter, an old Indian who had been very frequently employed as guide, clerk &c. and who well deserved the confidence reposed in him, was detained by Chaurette to guide me in to my winter quarters. He had a very nice young daughter that both he & Chaurette wished me much to take as wife! A whelp, not yet 18 to marry! Whatever might have been my own bent, which, to tell the truth, was far from averse to it, yet the respect for my fathers injunction...& the dread of the Knights censure were so powerful as to effectually curb and humble my own dear Passions. Fear prevailed for a long time. The old father became restless & impatient: frequently menaced to leave me, & at last did go off. I sent out my interpretor to procure me another guide. In vain.—my provisions being very scanty, my men so long retarded, fear of not reaching my destination; and above all the secret satisfaction I felt in being *compelled* (what an agreable word when it accords with our desires) to marry for my safety, made me post off for the old man. He was already several miles on his way. I think I still see the satisfaction, the pleasure the poor old man felt. He gave me his daughter! He thought no doubt that it would be the means of rendering him happy & comfortable in his old days. What a cruel disappointment!—It is strange how our passions, our desires, do blind our reason and pervert our understanding![15]

This account diverges from the earlier one in its tone as well as in its character sketches. It outlines more clearly Nelson's relation to Chaurette. It admits to his own desire and temptation. It also reflects, doubtless after the fact, Nelson's improved understanding of Ojibwa culture, or more specifically, the motives of Le Commis in pursuing this alliance. Ojibwa marriages commonly started out as matrilocal: that is, a new son-in-law who behaved appropriately would stay with and assist his wife's family and assume a range of kin-based roles and obligations. Nelson in retrospect, after a later lengthy experience with Ojibwa familial ties, appreciated what Le Commis must have expected from him, and realized how he had fallen short.

The 1836 text also exhibits interesting omissions. It makes no reference to translation difficulties or to Chaurette's meddling and self-interest, and the main actors are reduced to two, Nelson and a rather more dignified Le Commis. The events of the moment are condensed and polished with a light sheen of romance and nostalgia—a general stylistic feature of these late reminiscences. The earlier (1803/1811) version conveyed a vivid picture of Nelson "teased & troubled on every side"; anyone familiar with the Ojibwa sexual joking behaviour that classically surrounds potential marriage mates can imagine both the humour he was exposed to and the embarrassment and culture shock this young English-Canadian must have felt. And the voyageurs did not spare him either: "the men & everyone else [were] after me [until] I at last was prevailed upon to take her." But all this pressure from his companions has disappeared in the 1836 account. In other respects, however, the versions are similar. Both leave entirely to our imaginations whatever ritual may have marked the occasion, once Nelson consented; and in both, silence surrounds the voice (and name) of the young girl involved. Yet both accounts contain clues about the importance of Le Commis and his family in the following months and confirm that for Nelson, that Ojibwa kinship tie was of critical aid for both subsistence and survival. They also reveal Le Commis's views of the importance of the matter.

We also have two accounts of how he left this relationship, again from the 1803–04 journal rewritten in 1811, and from the reminiscence of 1836. As before, the earlier account is the fuller one. Nelson and his people returned from their wintering grounds to Grand Portage on 29 June 1804. Negative gossip about Nelson had preceded his arrival; that night, he "was sorry, & troubled...to hear the men say that they had heard that the Knight said, he was quite displeased with a young Fondulac Clerk for taking a woman." Nelson feared "a severe set down from the Knight upon that account." The next day, he met with Mackenzie:

> I had no need of a Telescope to see what was the matter with him. He only asked me a few Cross Crabbit questions in a Crabbit manner

which I answered as well as I could: he did not make the least mention to me about the woman; & and I am quite sorry for it, for I am found [fond] enough yet of myself to think that he would not have been quite so displeased with me as he was; &...would not have said of me what he did; at least not so much [that is, if Nelson had had a chance to explain himself].[16]

During the rest of Nelson's time at Grand Portage, until 22 July, the Knight, who had been as kind as a father the previous summer, scarcely spoke to him. Nelson's account ended on a gloomy note, describing how he at last clumsily detached himself from the company of Le Commis's daughter:

It is a very true Proverb in my humble opinion, "that he who hears only one side of the story hears nothing" — but the worst of it was there was more than half a proof against me —; that is she being Yet with me, altho I often tried to get her to take a dislike to me — I often sent her away &...I would not put up my own tent but slept in Chaurette's & under this pretext I sent her to her father's lodge — but even when I had my tent pitched in the fort with the other Clerks she yet came twice to me; but at last I got rid of her, for an interpretor took her.[17]

The 1836 telling of Nelson's return to Grand Portage offers some different perspectives. "We were no sooner arrived than I was congratulated upon my *fine choice* of a wife! — a brat of just 19 [18] indeed, the age I had attained or completed a few days before our arrival." As in the first version, Nelson anticipated reproof from the Knight. This account added a new element, however: Mackenzie's reproof was intensified by false reports of Nelson's behaviour passed on by another trader with whom he had previously had trouble. This man, intent "to *curry* favour, & to show a devotion [to his superiors] always pretended and never sincere" spread stories about Nelson's "unfortunate sickness of the preceding year [a result of an injury], when I passed blood in my urin...in corroboration of my corrupt morals! Wretch — and that *wretch* has injured me more than once since."[18]

As for Alexander Mackenzie, Nelson wrote in 1836, "he should have called me & examined me, he would have discovered the truth: but his intercourse with men had afforded him[so] many opportunities of seeing wickedness...I suppose he considered it useless." After a time, Mackenzie did send for Nelson. "He reprimanded me in a true fatherly manner," Nelson recalled, "...and told me to prepare to go in to the North Lake Winnipick. I thanked him as was my duty....the word *north* passed through my soul like a sword...*Lake Winnipick* too, where all our people suffered so much every year, where so many had died of hunger in all its most frightful shapes — was not calculated to reassure me."[19] The next paragraph sees Nelson on his way to the Lake Winnipeg region where he would spend the next decade of his life. The text of 1836 is silent about Nelson's severing of his tie with Le Commis's daughter; she disappears without remark. But the implication is clearly that Nelson's posting to Lake Winnipeg was the penalty for his getting entangled with her, and a consequence, too, of false and malicious reports that he was not allowed to refute.

Nelson's versions of this relationship raise two points for contemplation. First, they suggest how much we lose whenever an event is described in only one document from one time and place. History is like a patchwork quilt; we construct it from partial truths, bits of fabric that reveal only snippets of patterns, people, and events. Or to invoke another metaphor, we must apply the land surveyor's technique of triangulation, taking sightings on our subjects from several angles and perspectives in time and space. Nelson lets us view his life from different angles in his writings, and it is worth exploring them all, for we learn something from each.

Second, they pose questions about interpreting Nelson's experience in 1803–04. Did it involve both "marriage" and "custom"; and if so, in whose terms? To answer this question, we need to look at his relationship not only from the angles he provides, but from the vantage points of both his fellow fur traders and the Ojibwa people involved, Le Commis and his family.

The XY Company fur traders of 1803–04, including Nelson, left no evidence that they viewed Nelson's connection as a true marriage. Alexander Mackenzie did not want Nelson to get involved with a woman at all and had evidently warned him not to; his attitude must have been a key factor leading Nelson to end the relationship. Mackenzie's stand on this matter was likely a harbinger of a policy put in place just two years later; in 1806, the North West Company, then recombined with the XY Company, made its ruling that no trader should take a woman from among the Indians (not that the new rule was to be closely obeyed by Nelson or his superiors).[20] Nelson did not view the relationship as meeting either his parents' or his notions of a proper marriage. The views of Simon Chaurette, Nelson's superior in 1803–04, are not on record. Chaurette had an Ojibwa family, but his overall approach seems to have been highly opportunistic, emphasizing such things as selling many goods to his men to secure their wages as debt. In the end, Nelson had no choice but to be opportunistic himself. He badly needed Le Commis's help in the fall and winter of 1803 and felt that he had no other option (1811), while also allowing (by 1836) that the imposed opportunity held some personal attraction.

On the Ojibwa side, Le Commis was surely not innocent of opportunism, for himself and for his "large family." But Nelson's 1836 account suggests there was more to it than that. From an Ojibwa perspective, trade as such was not hived off as a domain separate from alliance, friendship, and kin ties.[21] Nelson proposed to winter in Le Commis's lands, among his people. Although he would not have understood Le Commis's expectations until much later, and no one explained them to him, he in effect took on an obligation to offer gifts and hospitality such as rum; and the Ojibwa would have had in mind the aim of making him into a kinsman who would take on the responsibilities and reciprocities of a relative rather than remaining a stranger. Nelson as a young, unattached, male outsider fitted easily into the Ojibwa cross-cousin category of eligible mate.[22] And, as Nelson himself noted in 1836, Le Commis must have had some hope that this callow and serious son-in-law would be helpful with trade goods and support for some time into the future. In sum, this relationship was a marriage in Ojibwa terms.

As for its ending in 1804, the fact that at Grand Portage, Nelson both wished to leave the girl, and was under pressure to do so without further obligation, suggests again that neither he nor the other traders considered the connection to be a marriage, even though they sometimes casually used such terms as "wife" and "father-in-law." There is no sign that Nelson followed any formal custom of "turning off" such as Van Kirk has identified in a number of instances;[23] he recorded no role in providing for her or finding her another mate.

On the other side of the cultural divide, however, Nelson's ending of the tie was compatible with the Ojibwa definition of marriage as a relationship that could break up. Within their frame of reference, Le Commis and his daughter would still have viewed the connection as a marriage, just as the fur traders carried on with their view that real marriage was something else. And of course, the traders and the Ojibwa did not sit down together to study the issue but carried on with their own distinct values and outlooks.

To what extent, then, can we speak of a custom or a "fur trade society" encompassing these parties? A community of Euro-Canadian men based at Grand Portage shared and fostered certain interests and values, enforcing a degree of conformity on their members. But the Ojibwa men who traded with them and the women who (in Ojibwa terms) married them had no occasion to be familiar with or to share those values. No missionary had yet introduced them to marriage as a Christian rite and a lifelong relationship, and the traders' own actions did not present such a model. Native people of the time also kept largely to their own ways; they were not becoming Europeanized any more than the traders were "going Indian." These thoughts have led me generally to find it more helpful to think of the fur trade not as a society, but as a semi-autonomous (not free-standing) "partial or incomplete social sphere" intersecting with both the European and

Canadian societies and economies that supported it, and the Native communities (still largely autonomous) who made it possible.[24]

Nelson's second Ojibwa marriage took place in 1808, two years after the North West Company partners, meeting at Fort William on Lake Superior, had set their hands to a resolution against the further taking of women from among the Indians. The expenses of the traders' domesticity were a growing concern. But so too was the problem of finding suitable mates for their own numerous daughters; thus, the resolution also stipulated, "It is however understood that taken the Daughter of a white Man after the fashion of the Country, should be considered no violation of this resolve."[25] This ruling represents an early formal construction of these relationships as being a common pattern, but it offered no guidelines for the forming or mainte-nance of these ties, and no definition of their status. On the ground, Nelson and his fellow traders continued to cope with or make the best of their immediate situations, options, and constraints.

For 1808 as for 1803–04, we have both a journal (original, this time) and reminiscences in Nelson's hand. This time, though, the contrasts between the two are striking. In early September, Nelson was at Bas de la Riviere (Fort Alexander) near the mouth of the Winnipeg River, where he and many other Nor'Westers were readying themselves and their supplies for travel to their winter outposts. The NWC partner or "bourgeois" of the district, Duncan Cameron, arrived on 1 September to winter there. Nelson's journal was mainly business; he noted, however, that on 3 September, everyone stopped work early to "prepare for a dance (which is now the third) on honour to Mr. Seraphin's wedding—Mr. McDonald played the violin for us and Mr. Seraphin played the flute alternately." His entry for 9 September affords the only hint that another dance was held that week for Nelson himself and a new partner. That day, several groups departed for their winter quarters. They included a party of six bound for Nelson's post on River Dauphine (the Little Dauphin River): four voyageurs and "myself & woman," unnamed and unexplained.[26]

The almost total silence of Nelson's journal on this topic contrasts remarkably with the vivid recollections about it that he set down perhaps thirty years later:

> [September 1808] I must here mention an event, perhaps the most momentous in the life of man—"taking a wife."—
>
> There was a young woman, a cousin of Mr [Duncan] Cameron's wife, living with the family. She was an orphan, about 20 years of age, & in whom C. took great interest, he wanted to provide for her, & pitched upon me![27] He had thrown out many hints when we met in the Spring. I carefully avoided her; & all my conduct & conversations

sufficiently showed how very averse I was to connexions of that sort. — I considered them in the light of "open, or public Adultery", & the dread I had of that was vastly increased by "what will my father (& mother) say to this, a man so stern & unyielding in his morality? — my mother! how she will fret!" The very idea of living with a woman, in adultry was intolerable — my spirits were prostrated, & my heart so pinched it hardly throbbed. — "How can I after this pray to God! Surely his malediction will follow me wherever I may go or whatever I may undertake!" — My prospects were blasted; my hopes of prosperity at an end. — I saw but penury, want & wretchedness staring me for the remainder of my days! I told Mr C. my scruples but he derided them. — I was alone, friendless, & no one to advise with. I had not that energy of character that make some rise above every difficulty, & absolutely lacked that clear perception & sound judgement the result of good common sense. In short, I had not been taught to *think*; — I had indeed been taught to read & cypher but had not been instructed how to apply these essentials to the purposes of morality & human actions — these were to be developped of themselves according to their circumstances. I was then (& ever have been) the child, the mere tool of natural impulse & circumstance, as water poured on the ground seeks or runs into hollows & holes where it is lost, or of no benefit but to its immediate localities & the advantages of which it often destroys or injures. — I was not, however, better than my neighbors; the Sex had its charms for me as it had for others; But there always remained a sting, that time only wore away.

I gave way, & went as the ox to the Slaughter. A ball was given on the occasion by Mr C. — I had to go and see them two or three times; but my heart overflowing I had to retire to give vent to my feelings. It was a time (if not a subject) of gayety to the others, who, to serve craving lusts, thought nothing, & cared nothing for the consequences, of the poor creatures who they took from [as?] young indians with whom they would pass their lives with their children & families, to cast them off afterwards with those to whom they had given birth to linger in want & wretchedness. But I must leave this subject, for quires of paper, nay reams, would be required to write all the painful, sad & sorrowful results. — There is surely a Providence ruling, or at least watchful of the ways of man; &, not withstanding his perverseness averts the woes that he so blindly, & often wantonly, works for his own misery. — *Yes! there is!* — for I have too often seen it.[28]

From the Christ Church (Anglican) registers of Sorel, we know that the woman who thus came into Nelson's life was an Ojibwa of the Loon clan, from north of Lake Superior. Nelson brought her and their children to Sorel in the summer of 1816, when he took leave of fur trading for two years. She was baptized Mary Ann on 29 July 1818, and she and Nelson were married by Anglican rite in 1825. She died in Sorel in November 1831, having borne eight children of whom one daughter survived to adulthood. The union endured for 23 years, including a period from 1818 to 1823 in which Mary Ann and their children must have lived with Nelson's family in Sorel while he returned west to resume his fur trade employment.[29]

These records, along with the journal, the reminiscences and other clues, allow us to look at this relationship as a process, the meanings and patterns of which evolved over time. Its beginning, to judge by the silence of the journal and the outburst in the reminiscences, was traumatic. Nelson liked and respected his bourgeois, Duncan Cameron, and evinced some sympathy for the latter's concern to support his Ojibwa wife's young cousin. Yet the personal crisis he had faced over his first Ojibwa connection and its ending was still vivid to him, both in 1808 and when he recalled it about three decades later. During his long service, he saw other fur trade familial problems and abuses that distressed him; by 1808, he probably knew, too, of his employers' official stance against alliances with Indian women. His terminology suggests that he remained deeply ambivalent about these fur trade unions. His journal of 1808 spoke of Mr. Seraphin's "wedding" and his reminiscences referred to Mr. Cameron's "wife"; but his own companion was "woman," not wife, and "connexions of that sort" were "open, or public Adultery."

Nonetheless, the tie, over the years, became a significant part of Nelson's life despite the "sting, that time only wore away." As he became increasingly familiar with Ojibwa culture and language, he learned that, for better and worse, his marital connection enmeshed him in a wide network of Native kin extending from Lake Superior to Lake Winnipeg; as he wrote some years later on being accosted by an Ojibwa kinswoman near Fort William, "there is no end to relationship among the Indians."[30] At any moment across the region, encounters with his wife's relatives might occur. Perhaps the most dramatic came while Nelson was stationed at Manitounamingan Lake (near Longlac, Ontario). On 30 April 1815, Nelson recorded, "Two strange indians from Nepigon [Lake Nipigon] peep in, they are brothers to the woman I have — it is a rencounter pleasing to both, but a little reflection ought to render it *sorrowful*; 'for here are my brothers' — 'here is my sister; but where are our Parents?'" The brothers brought news of the brutal stabbing murder of their father some time before and of their mother suffering the same fate a year or two later, "leaving several very young children to the care of *their* murderers & their abbettors, who a short time after made food of some of them. This has been a remarkable unfortunate family. — "[31] Trade relations were fostered by kinship, but with those ties also came obligations to offer aid and support.

From 1816 onward, the evolving status of the relationship is traceable mainly in entries appearing in the registers of Christ Church, Sorel; Nelson's own references to it were few and often oblique. On 10 October 1816, the rector baptized Mary and Jane, "daughters of Mr George Nelson a Clerk in the North West Company by an Indian Woman"; six of Nelson's own family signed as godmothers and godfathers (a suggestive hint of their moral support), but the unnamed mother did not sign. She herself was then baptized as Mary Ann on 29 July 1818. On 17 April 1819, three more daughters were baptized in Nelson's absence. This time, Mary Ann was listed as "an Indian Woman of what is called the Loon Tribe" and she signed with an X under the name, "Mary Ann Perusa" which apppears nowhere else. A sheerly speculative guess is that the rector may have been trying to write the Ojibwe word, *binesi* (bird), a common personal name, without benefit of Nelson's interpretive fluency in Ojibwe.[32] Finally, on 16 January 1825, a year and a half after Nelson's retirement from the fur trade, he and Mary Ann were "Married by License," in a ceremony witnessed by his father and several of his sisters.[33] He left no evidence about why this act came so long after her 1816 arrival in Sorel.

The records of George Nelson's second marriage recall some conclusions drawn earlier about his first one; they also lend themselves to further analysis and comparison because of the length of the union. First, it seems clear that in Ojibwa terms, this, like his first, was a marriage. Nelson learned, too, as Duncan Cameron had before him, that such a relationship brought him many kin who ranged from being helpful trading partners and allies to making claims for aid and support.

For the Euro-Canadian traders of 1808, however, the status of these ties was more open and indeterminate. Those who defined them as without moral standing ("adulterous" in Nelson's terms) might either exploit them opportunistically, or try to avoid them as Nelson did. Those who became entangled anyway, yet remained attached to Christian backgrounds and church-going families, might go through a long series of doubts and decisions before admitting their unions as marriages; Nelson and one of his North West Company contemporaries, Daniel Williams Harmon, are two of the best documented examples in the period from 1800 to the 1820s.[34] Yet even they offer only occasional small bursts of introspection and few explanations of their motives and actions. We can only guess, for example, why Mary Ann lived for almost nine years in Sorel without the church recognition of her union that Sorel's Anglican community and Nelson's upright English father might have expected, and why, for that matter, the church marriage did come about in 1825.

In fact, to judge by a later court decision concerning a similar union, Nelson and Mary Ann's marriage would have been found legal in Quebec once they settled together in Sorel, even with no church rite. In 1867, eight years after Nelson's death, the Quebec Superior Court ruled that the marriage of a former NWC trader, William Connolly, and a Cree woman "according to the usages and customs of the country" was valid in Quebec, Connolly having brought her to Montreal as his wife by Indian custom.

The Connolly case parallels George Nelson's story in that Connolly was Nelson's immediate contemporary; he joined the North West Company in 1801. (Unlike Nelson, however, he was commissioned a chief trader when the NWC combined with the Hudson's Bay Company in 1821.) Their fur trade marriages are comparable too, up to a point. In 1803, while in charge of the post of Rat River near Nelson House (Manitoba), he took a Cree wife, Suzanne. He left no record of how that union began; but it lasted 29 years. In the summer of 1831, after several years in charge of the district of New Caledonia (B.C.), Connolly returned to Montreal with Suzanne and their six children. In May of 1832, however, he left Suzanne and married Julia Woolrich, securing a dispensation from the Roman Catholic Church (which the church required of him not because of a prior marriage but because Julia was his second cousin). Connolly then took Julia to his new posting at Tadoussac. Suzanne and her family continued in Montreal until 1841 when she was sent to live out her days in the Grey Nuns' convent in Red River (Winnipeg).[35]

Connolly died in Montreal in 1848. In 1864, Connolly's and Suzanne's eldest son, John, sued for his share of his father's estate, all of which was willed to Julia. The case went through several courts until John won the suit in 1867. The testimonies arguing both sides of the issue are fascinating. They echo the ambiguities and cross-currents that surrounded Nelson's relationships, as various witnesses found themselves obliged to give evidence to support or dismiss the validity of such marriages. Ultimately, the judges concluded that the marriage met the tests specified in clause 6 of their final ruling: "That a marriage contracted where there are no priests, no magistrates, no civil or religious authority, and no registers, may be proved by oral evidence, and that the admission of the parties, combined with long cohabitation and repute will be the best evidence."[36]

The 1867 majority decision from the Superior Court in Montreal, while it upheld John Connolly's claim, was not, however, a vindication of fur traders' Indian marriages as binding in all circumstances (indeed the Quebec courts in the 1880s rejected the validity of former Nor'Wester Alexander Fraser's fur trade union).[37] Rather, it was a recognition of Indian custom as *ius gentium* (law of the people), that is, as customary law valid in a region where more formal legal structures were absent. In clause 8, the court explicitly acknowledged Cree marriage customs as having legal status for all who practised them in Cree country:

> 8. That an Indian marriage between a Christian and a woman of that [Cree] nation or tribe is valid, notwithstanding the assumed existence [among the Cree] of polygamy and divorce at will, which are no obstacles to the recognition by our Courts of a marriage contracted according to the usages and customs of the country.

That is, fur traders could marry Cree women on the principle of *ius gentium*. But the next clause went one step further to reveal a key reason for the court's support of John Connolly's claim. Clause 9 stated: "That a Christian marrying a native according to their usages, cannot exercise in Lower Canada the right of divorce or repudiation at will, though...he might have done so among the Crees."[38]

The decision would have surprised William Connolly, as it did the Woolrich family in 1867. Connolly in 1832 had clearly decided that his Cree marriage was not binding; and evidently the Catholic clergy agreed when they granted his dispensation for cousin marriage and consecrated his marriage to Julia Woolrich. But in fact, from the point of view of Julia and her heirs, he unknowingly made a grave mistake in bringing Suzanne to Lower Canada and putting her aside while they resided in that jurisdiction, if he had no intent to recognize her as his wife. As the final court opinion pithily concluded, Mr. Connolly could not "carry with him the common law of England to Rat River in his knapsack, and much less could he bring back to Lower Canada the [Cree] law of repudiation in a bark canoe."[39] Separation under country custom in Cree territory would have been legal; a Cree-style divorce in Lower Canada was not.

Connolly in 1832, however, unquestionably saw his actions as sanctioned not only by the church but by two of his respected superiors, Governor George Simpson and Chief Factor John George McTavish, in 1829–30. Their setting aside of Native partners to bring white brides to Rupert's Land, and in particular, Simpson's repudiation of Margaret Taylor, brought strong censure from some colleagues. Connolly, however, evidently drew encouragement from their actions in 1832, even though he had earlier stated "it was 'a most unnatural proceeding' to desert the mother of one's children." Simpson and McTavish acted in blatant defiance of the views of those who considered "the custom of the country" as a "bona fide marital union."[40] Yet paradoxically, if the court had tested Simpson and McTavish by the criterion applied to Connolly's marital separation, it would probably not have held their unions as still valid, since such repudiations were within the limits of "custom" in Cree country.[41] Unlike Connolly, they had not tried to bring Cree *ius gentium* to Lower Canada "in a bark canoe."

To conclude, it seems useful to reassess the "custom of the country" by looking closely at individual instances of Native/fur trader unions where sources allow, exploring their dynamics and their different trajectories over time, in both Rupert's Land and beyond. Their definitions and meanings were commonly not fixed, or even articulated by or agreed upon by the participants of either gender, or by their contemporary observers. In mapping these "inlets or rocks on the shore" (fractal graphics again), our attention turns to the fine points of texture, nuance, negotiation, and process in these relationships, and to the ambiguities and indeterminacies facing those who entered into them. The sources never offer more than partial truths, but analysis and understanding advance considerably if we take into account all the texts and clues we have.

In a recent restudy of the fabled encounter between Pocahontas and Captain John Smith in Virginia in 1607–08, Frederic Gleach demonstrates how we can amplify our understandings of that event beyond the inevitably partial views afforded by Smith's writings (or by Disney). Gleach outlines what he calls "controlled speculation" as a method involving detailed comparative study, "to infer crucial information that may be missing or obscured in the historical record of a particular situation." Inferences from such speculation can be controlled "by being carefully and explicitly grounded in the ethnographic, historical, and/or archaeological records." The method helped him to develop new insights about the Powhatan Indians' side of their interaction with John Smith, weighing their perspectives equally with those of the English. As he notes of such contacts, "We can forget too easily that...both sides were living, acting co-creators of the events recorded in those accounts."[42]

Gleach's emphasis on understanding the diverse views and actions of the groups involved in these early cross-cultural encounters calls to mind some perspectives that John Foster developed in his articles on Plains Metis ethnogenesis. Looking at the fur trade, he observed that the roles of adult males, both within the trading posts and within Aboriginal communities who came to trade, need more attention. He by no means played down the importance of women; he simply argued that gendered analyses should not be applied only to them. As he wrote in 1985, "Perhaps a number of the institutions that arose in the fur trade post owed as much to the fact that the society consisted almost solely of adult males as it did to the needs of a commercial trade and *Canadien* tradition."[43] In 1994, he went on to focus more closely on the relationships that male traders found key to their lives. "The first and foremost" of them was the country marriage between the leader of a trading party and "an Indian woman closely related to the prominent males of the band." A second essential tie was the trader's relationship with "the adult males of the band"; that link "would determine the level of acceptance extended to the outsider." For the trader's success, "it was essential that adult Indian males view the outsider as one of themselves."[44]

In Foster's analyses of the fur trade and the Métis, the dynamic processes of interaction, feedback, and on-the-ground negotiation of relationships and identities were key matters of curiosity and interest demanding ongoing restudies of all the available sources. We must regret the writings he did not finish, the headnotes lost, the lines of discussion he could not pursue. But his contributions and ideas will continue to open these fields to fresh explorations by coming generations of scholars. His legacy is one of expanding mental horizons across the plains; it is not one of closure or endings.

Acknowledgements

Parts of this essay formed bases for talks given to historians at the University of Alberta in March 1997, and to the Friends of Grand Portage in Minneapolis and to the interpretive staff at Old Fort William in Thunder Bay in May 1997. I am grateful to Theodore Binnema and Gerhard Ens for the invitation to be a part of this volume and for the opportunity it provides to develop these ideas further.

Notes

1. Sylvia Van Kirk, *"Many Tender Ties": Women in Fur-Trade Society, 1670–1870* (Winnipeg: Watson & Dwyer, 1980), and Jennifer S.H. Brown, *Strangers in Blood: Fur Trade Company Families in Indian Country* (Vancouver: University of British Columbia Press, 1980).

2. Our four dissertations are sometimes cited together in overviews of fur trade historiography; see, for example, Michael Payne, "Fur Trade Social History and the Public Historian: Some Other Recent Trends," 494, n. 1, in Jennifer S.H. Brown, W.J. Eccles, and Donald P. Heldman, eds., *The Fur Trade Revisited: Selected Papers of the Sixth North American Fur Trade Conference, Mackinac Island, Michigan, 1991* (East Lansing/Mackinac Island: Michigan State University Press and Mackinac State Historic Parks, 1994).

3. James Clifford, "Introduction: Partial Truths," in Clifford and George E. Marcus, eds., *Writing Culture: The Poetics and Politics of Ethnography* (Berkeley: University of California Press, 1986), 7.

4. In Roger Sanjek, ed., *Fieldnotes: the Makings of Anthropology* (Ithaca: Cornell University Press, 1990), 139–60.

5. Marilyn Strathern, *Partial Connections* (Savage, Maryland: Rowman & Littlefield Publishers, 1991), xx–xxi, 122 n. 9.

6. Besides Van Kirk's publications, see Jennifer S.H. Brown and Robert Brightman, *The Orders of the Dreamed: George Nelson on Cree and Northern Ojibwa Religion and Myth, 1823* (Winnipeg: University of Manitoba Press, 1988). The most detailed biographical account of Nelson available in print is in the introduction to this volume, and details of his life given here derive from that source unless otherwise credited. Nelson's writings pertaining to his Wisconsin years (1802–1804) have been edited by Laura Peers and Theresa Schenck, and will be co-published by the Minnesota Historical Society Press and McGill-Queen's University Press in the Rupert's Land Record Society documentary series.

7. Van Kirk, *"Many Tender Ties,"* 36, 51.

8. See Edith I. Burley, *Servants of the Honourable Company: Work, Discipline, and Conflict in the Hudson's Bay Company, 1770–1879* (Toronto: Oxford University Press, 1997), 123–27, and for a stronger view, Ron G. Bourgeault, "The Indian, the Metis and the Fur Trade: Class, Sexism and Racism in the Transition from 'Communism' to Capitalism," *Studies in Political Economy* 12 (Fall 1983).

9. Van Kirk, *"Many Tender Ties,"* 28.

10. Nelson, 1803–1804 journal redrafted in 1811. Manuscript. Nelson Papers, Metropolitan Public Library of Toronto. On Chaurette's identity, see "A Wisconsin Fur-Trader's Journal, 1804–05, by Francois Victor Malhiot" in Reuben Gold

Thwaites, ed., *Collections of the State Historical Society of Wisconsin*, Vol. 19 (Madison: State Historical Society of Wisconsin, 1910), 170 n. 33.

11. Nelson, 1803–1804 journal redrafted in 1811, 21 July 1803.

12. Nelson, 1803–1804 journal redrafted in 1811, 23–24 August 1803.

13. Nelson, 1803–1804 journal redrafted in 1811, 3 September 1803

14. Nelson, Sorel journal and reminiscence, 35. Manuscript. Nelson Papers, Metropolitan Public Library of Toronto.

15. Nelson, Sorel journal and reminiscence, 35–36.

16. Nelson, 1803–1804 journal redrafted in 1811, 30 June 1804, ff.

17. Ibid.

18. Nelson, Sorel journal and reminiscence, 55.

19. Ibid.

20. Brown, *Strangers in Blood*, 96.

21. For valuable context, see Bruce White, "Give us a Little Milk: The Social and Cultural Meanings of Gift-Giving in the Lake Superior Fur Trade," *Minnesota History* 48, no. 2 (1982).

22. On Nelson's finding himself placed in the cross-cousin category, and on the scope of Ojibwa familial relations generally, see Laura Peers and Jennifer S.H. Brown, "'There is no End to Relationship among the Indians': Ojibwa Families and Kinship in Historical Perspective," *The History of the Family: An International Quarterly* 4, no. 4 (2000): 529–55.

23. Van Kirk, "*Many Tender Ties*," 50–51.

24. Brown, *Strangers in Blood*, xvi–xvii.

25. Ibid., 97.

26. Nelson, journal, River Dauphine, 1808. Nelson Papers, Metropolitan Toronto Public Library.

27. Nelson's description, in his reminiscences, of the woman as an orphan as of 1808 does not conform with his 1815 journal description (see infra) of having just received the news of her parents' deaths. It was common for Ojibwa offspring to be fostered by and live with other relatives even if their parents were alive; this was evidently the case in 1808. Writing about three decades later, Nelson confused the sequence of events.

28. Nelson, Reminiscences, 206–7. Nelson Papers, ibid.

29. Brown and Brightman, "*The Orders of the Dreamed*," 13, 20.

30. Peers and Brown, "'There is no End to Relationship among the Indians," 1.

31. Nelson, journal, Manitounamingan. Nelson Papers, Metropolitan Toronto Public Library.

32. Initial 'p's and 'b's are soft in the Ojibwe language and are often interchanged in transcriptions. There is no 'r' in Ojibwe; spoken 'n' is soft and nasalized. The long 'e' in *binesi* could be readily transposed with the final vowel, yielding a final long 'a' in the rector's "Perusa." (Note: most linguists currently use the spelling, 'Ojibwe,' when referring to the language.)

33. Christ Church (Anglican), Sorel, Quebec. Registers of baptisms and marriages. Montreal, Archives of the Synod of the Diocese of Montreal.

34. On Harmon, see W. Kaye Lamb, ed., *Sixteen Years in the Indian Country, the Journal of Daniel Williams Harmon 1800–1816* (Toronto: Macmillan of Canada, 1957), and summary in Brown, *Strangers in Blood*, 103–7.

35. Bruce Peel, "Connolly, William," in *Dictionary of Canadian Biography*, Vol. 7 (Toronto: University of Toronto Press, 1988), 204–6; see also Brown, *Strangers in Blood*, 90–92, 94–96.

36. See Connolly v. Woolrich and Johnson et al. Superior Court, 1867, Montreal, 9 July 1867, *Lower Canada Jurist* 11, 197–265, for the full report of the case.

37. Brown, *Strangers in Blood*, 90–93.

38. *Lower Canada Jurist* 11, 197.

39. Ibid., 215.

40. Van Kirk, *"Many Tender Ties,"* 188, 51.

41. One question, however, is whether the fact that the women involved were only half Cree would have made a difference in a hypothetical court ruling. That seems unlikely, however, since the court acknowledged Native *ius gentium* as the only available standard pertaining to traders' Native marriages in Rupert's Land at the time. (The only exception by the 1820s would have been Red River Settlement where Roman Catholic and Church of England missionaries were providing church marriages, beginning in 1818 and 1820 respectively.)

42. Frederic Gleach, "Controlled Speculation: Interpreting the Saga of Pocahontas and Captain John Smith," in Jennifer S.H. Brown and Elizabeth Vibert, eds., *Reading beyond Words: Contexts for Native History* (Peterborough, ON: Broadview Press, 1996), 22, 39.

43. John E. Foster, "Some Questions and Perspectives on the Problem of Métis Roots," in Jacqueline Peterson and Jennifer S.H. Brown, eds., *The New Peoples: Being and becoming Métis In North America* (Winnipeg: University of Manitoba Press, 1985), 84.

44. Foster, "Wintering, the Outsider Adult Male and the Ethnogenesis of the Western Plains Metis." *Prairie Forum* 19, no. 1 (1994): 10, reprinted in this volume as Chapter 8.

4

"A Most Important Chain of Connection"

Marriage in the Hudson's Bay Company

HEATHER ROLLASON DRISCOLL

IN 1830 George Simpson married his 18-year-old British cousin Frances and brought her to live with him in Rupert's Land. The news of their union spread quickly amongst George's fellow employees because it represented a break from a 150-year-old tradition. The cause of the sensation was not the fact that George had married nor was it Frances's age; rather, it was her place of birth.[1] George's employer, the fur trading enterprise known as the Hudson's Bay Company (HBC), had prohibited all employees from bringing British-born wives and daughters with them into fur trade country since 1684.

Scholars have interpreted the marriage of George and Frances as evidence of a significant shift in the state of social relations at fur trade posts. In their seminal studies of fur trade society Jennifer Brown and Sylvia Van Kirk noticed that over a number of generations traders' spousal preferences changed from Native to mixed-blood and finally to British-born women. In explaining the shifts, particularly the one associated with Frances's arrival, they focused upon racism as the chief causal factor. Sylvia Van Kirk proposed that "[w]ith the appearance of women of their own race, the fur traders began to exhibit prejudices toward native females which had previously been dormant."[2] Similarly Jennifer Brown suggested that traders found British-born women desirable because "[g]enetically, culturally, and in their social affiliations, they exhibited fewer Indian traits."[3] Based upon their work, other scholars have argued that racial prejudice increasingly determined traders' marriage partners. This thesis has been highly influential in the evolving canon of scholarship. More recently Veronica Strong-Boag described the significance of the arrival of British women to fur trade country in terms much stronger than ever used by Brown or Van Kirk:

While early fur-trade society offered significant opportunities to native women, its long term heritage included a racism and sexism that would consign native and mixed-blood women to special victimization by male and white society well into the twentieth century.[4]

Unlike Brown or Van Kirk, Strong-Boag excludes all other elements contributing to the shift in marriage patterns.

Racism undoubtedly contributed to the shift, but as the dominant explanation it falls short. First, the appearance of these "dormant" racist beliefs coincides with economic events without which these racist notions would have taken hold. The economic situation characterizing the first two decades of the nineteenth century pushed the fur traders into new ways of thinking about their business; namely, it brought about the amalgamation of the rival HBC and North West Company (NWC), and the granting of permission for development of British-styled settlement within the heart of fur trade country. Both Brown and Van Kirk identify the joint influence of George Simpson and the Red River settlement (particularly the influx of clergy) as providing the environment in which racism could flourish.[5] It is assumed that Simpson's motive for marrying the British-born Frances instead of one of the women of Rupert's Land derived solely from his disdain for the latter. Yet there is evidence that his motive may have been multi-faceted. Furthermore, it is argued here that amalgamation of the HBC and NWC affected marriage practices in ways other than the need to standardize conduct between the two former companies. Brown and Van Kirk acknowledge that traders' views about who to marry changed after amalgamation, but overlook its role in these very same changes. Second, the impact of amalgamation and settlement upon marriage patterns can only be understood in the context of the fur trade's social milieu: a hybrid of British and Native practices and values. The marriage of George and Frances represents the product of all these events, beliefs and practices. It may be possible to identify the increasingly strong presence of racist beliefs associated with the choice of marriage partners around the time of the Simpson wedding, but this is best explained through the impact of changes to the business of the fur trade upon long established social practices in Rupert's Land.

This study represents a preliminary attempt to explore the relationships between an array of factors that affected a shift in marriage practices, and it focuses more on the social environment characteristic of the HBC than the NWC. A more thorough exploration of the primary sources is required to support these initial conclusions. By demonstrating the existence of parallel and persuasive explanations for the change in marriage patterns between the 1820s and 1840s, this paper may stimulate future research into this topic. To understand the chain of relationships that permitted George to wed

Frances it is necessary to examine the first link in the chain: the HBC's use of British and Native marriage practices to further its business.

Analysis of the post managers' journals and minutes from meetings of company directors reveals similarities between the corporate structure of the HBC and a patriarchal household. The resemblance between the patterns of life on the Hudson Bay and British domestic life was not the result of an unconscious or accidental process; rather, right from the early stages of the company's existence, the London Committee intended its employees to recognize these similarities and behave accordingly.

From the moment of its incorporation in 1670, the HBC chose to model its field operations upon an idealized image of the patriarchal family.[6] The British style of patriarchal family consisted of a married couple, their children, and workers or servants. According to the ideal image of this family structure, the husband formally represented the head of the household, followed by the wife. Below them, in terms of social and economic status, came their children and then the household servants.[7] The status conveyed by marriage was key to differentiating the patriarch and his wife from the rest of the household. The act of marriage signalled a couple's economic independence from their previous households, for upon marrying it was expected that the couple would set up and finance their own household. Household servants entered a contract typically while in the state of bachelorhood and remained so until they were ready to leave the residence of their employer because it was assumed that marital obligations would compromise their loyalty to the household. In exchange for this demonstration of the servant's commitment to the patriarch's household, he or she received lodgings, clothing, and food; the servant could also apprentice a trade or benefit from the patriarch's business and social connections.[8] At the end of a period of service, the patriarch gave the servant a financial reward, similar to a dowry, that provided a measure of economic independence thereby aiding the former servant to establish his or her own household.[9] There are two observations of particular relevance to understanding the HBC's vision for the structure of trading post social relations. First, the head of the household was the only male supposed to be having sexual relations, let alone be married. Second, servants married only when they had achieved a measure of economic independence, typically occurring upon completion of an apprenticeship or contract of service.

The HBC's decision to use the patriarchal family as a model for organizing trading posts was not unprecedented; many institutions, including the British army and the merchant marine, had chosen to model their organizations upon this family style because of its familiarity to those working within the institution, its ability to enforce discipline over vast geographical distances, and the perception that it was a moral and humane method of controlling people.[10] Even the organizing interests of the Massachusetts Bay Company in the mid 1600s stipulated that:

> For the better accommodation of businesses, wee have devyded the servants belonging to the Company into severall famylies, as wee desire and intend they shall live together...Our earnest is, that you take spetiall care, in settlinge these families, that the chiefe in the families (at least some of them) bee grounded in religion; whereby morning and evening famylie dutyes may bee duely performed, and a watchfull eye held overall in each famylie to by appointed thereto, that so disorders may be prevented, and ill weeds nipt before they take too great a head. It wilbe a business worthy your best endeavours to looke unto this in the beginninge.[11]

The HBC chose to institute this model because of a series of management problems specific to the company's activities.

According to the HBC's charter, the organization was to be run by a committee of seven elected investors, known as the London Committee, and overseen by an eighth investor known as the governor.[12] These persons met weekly in London to oversee the creation of company policy and direct activities at trading posts along the shores of Hudson Bay. With the body of the company employees working across the ocean, the committee needed a method to ensure employee loyalty, hard work, and deference. Yet the HBC's operational problems were greater than controlling employee activity and behaviour over great geographical distances; it also had to overcome limited communication between the body and head of the company. Ships travelled from London to Hudson Bay but once a year, arriving at the bay in August or September and departing soon thereafter. Thus the London Committee communicated with its post managers solely on an annual basis. From the time the ships left the bay until they returned the next year, post operations and employee behaviour were beyond the committee's direct control. Furthermore, the company was anxious to ensure maximum profitability and thus needed to prevent its employees from idling during the workday, keeping furs for private trade, or breaking their contracts to start independent businesses along the bay. The London Committee needed a method to enforce discipline and encourage activity in the environment of the trading post.

The company's management problems stood to be compounded by the characteristic worker recruited into service. In the early years of the company's existence, the London Committee hired the vast majority of employees from the London area. However, it began to look elsewhere, particularly for labourers, when London recruits used the competitive labour market in London to ask for higher wages. Beginning in 1702, the HBC contracted men from the village of Stromness in the Orkney Islands located north of mainland Scotland. The London Committee's decision to switch recruiting grounds to Scotland was logical for a variety of reasons. Orkneymen were reputed to be literate, amenable to harsh living conditions, and willing to work for lower wages than their London counterparts.[13] Stromness was a convenient recruitment centre as it was the last port of call to pick up supplies before company ships sailed across the ocean to Hudson Bay. As well, the Orkneys were home to a sizeable population of young poor men interested in new economic opportunities. Indeed, the majority of HBC recruits in the Orkneys came from the lower end of the economic scale.[14] The large difference in yearly wages between what one could earn in Orkney and in the HBC suggests a rational economic motivation for signing an overseas contract with the HBC; the most a ploughman could earn on Orkney was two to three pounds per year, whereas the HBC offered from six to 18 pounds for a labourer and from 20 to 36 pounds for a carpenter.[15] By the late eighteenth century, approximately three-quarters of all employees hired, or 416 out of 530, were Orcadian.[16] In other words, over 400 Orkney men, likely between the ages of 18 and 30, were in fur trade country at a time when they otherwise would have been apprentices or contracted to a household in Orkney.[17]

The company's directors hoped that employing the patriarchal family as the model for social relations at its trading posts would solve all of the problems posed by the circumstances of the bay. The problem of isolation could be minimized with a post patriarch who could watch over the men's activities on a daily basis. As most of the workers were at the fur trade posts when their peers were contracted into a household, they were familiar with the household concept and the patriarch as an authority figure. One of the main advantages for the HBC in using the patriarchal family as its model for post structure was that it limited employees' ability to rise up against the company or to quit it all together. By organizing employees in small "family" units, each employee was closely supervised by someone possessing a higher rank. Thus an employee's most important relationship was with a superior, not a peer. Furthermore, because there was a good distance between each trading post, an employee's working relationships were mostly with others at his post who filled very different positions; those who held ranks like his own most likely were scattered at other posts.

A more detailed analysis of the company's structure reveals that from the beginning the London Committee organized each post hierarchically, roughly mimicking the patriarchal household.[18] During the HBC's first years, the top position was that of governor who was responsible for overseeing the general affairs at all trading posts.[19] This governor's domain consisted of field operations and is to be distinguished from the governor of the company proper. Though the title "field governor" gradually disappeared as a distinct position in the early eighteenth century, it returned in the nineteenth century when the HBC underwent major structural changes. Significantly, the reappearance of this position coincides with other changes related to the appearance of Frances Simpson.

The factor, or chief factor as he was also called, was the patriarch of the trading post. It was to him that the London Committee sent their annual instructions. In turn, he was responsible for creating the yearly report on trading activities, employee behaviour and anything else he thought might interest his superiors. He set daily tasks for the servants and monitored supplies. As the head of the post, the factor had the privilege of leading the procession to welcome trading Natives and participating in the ceremonial smoking of the calumet. Besides ensuring a profitable trade, the chief factor filled the roles of patron, father-figure, and teacher to the employees below him.[20] He was responsible for the spiritual and physical welfare of the men at his post.[21]

Henry Sergeant, field governor and chief factor of York Fort beginning in 1683, wholeheartedly embraced his patriarchal role; at this time he was the only employee who brought his wife and a minister to fur trade country. Since the HBC structured the organization of employees at its trading posts based upon practices used in the navy and merchant marine, Mrs. Sergeant's presence seemed in line with the expectations associated with the role of a captain: the patriarch of a ship. Furthermore, as the company was still in the process of setting up its operations, the London Committee would have perceived positively any method of reinforcing the association of chief factor as post patriarch. Being the only man permitted to have his wife standing by his side certainly would have achieved this goal. Henry Sergeant's decision to bring the minister John French signified his patriarchal obligation to care for the spiritual sustenance of those under his watch and care.[22] That the HBC allowed him to bring the minister demonstrates again the company's determination to instill an image of its field leaders as patriarchs. Indeed, while the company soon altered its position on the presence of wives in fur trade country, it continued to support chief factors' role as caretakers of employee's souls.

Further evidence that the company's management of the posts reflected the patriarchal household exists in early directives from the London Committee to field governors and chief factors. When the committee appointed James Knight chief factor of Chichewan Fort in 1682, in light of his station they also gave him permission to bring along his brother, Richard, as his man-servant.[23] Like Sergeant's wife, Richard's presence would have helped to distinguish brother James's rank from the rest of the employees. Only the patriarch would have the company's permission for such a luxury.

The London Committee encouraged these men to take responsibility for the apprenticeship and training of their subordinates, thus mimicking the idealized patriarch's responsibilities toward his household servants. In 1710 the London Committee sent Chief Factor Henry Kelsey official encouragement for his attempt to educate York Fort's servants: "You doe well to Educate the men in Literature but Especially in the Language that in time wee may send them to Travell...We have sent you your dixonary Printed, that you may the Better Instruct the young Ladds with you, in ye Indian Langage."[24] Considering these examples, it seems clear that the HBC intended that the social structure of its trading posts and the behaviour of its employees resemble the patriarchal household. Further analysis of the organizational structure of the posts reinforces this conclusion.

Directly below the chief factor was the position of second who was apprenticed to the chief. Among other things, the second assisted in the keeping of the journals and account books. When the London Committee appointed William Grover as second at Churchill Fort in 1763, part of his new duties included learning a number of specialized trades. In a letter to Grover, the committee suggested that "at all convenient Seasons instruct Yourself in Mr Potts's method of keeping his Medicines and their particular Virtues...in case any Accident should happen when his ill state of health deprives you of his assistance."[25] Like the chief factor, the person selected for this position often had years of experience working in the fur trade. Grover had worked for the HBC in the fur trade for six years before receiving the appointment of second. Some of the larger posts had councils, akin to the arrangement between the head governor and the London Committee. The main part of the council consisted of the post's surgeon and writer, and if the post had any ships, its captains, and the second. These men constituted the immediate "family" of the symbolic patriarch.

The company referred to the remainder of the post's employees as "servants," who worked as tradesmen and labourers.[26] The company's directors expected servants to behave in similar ways to household servants, particularly in regard to the status of bachelorhood. Indeed, for many reasons the HBC preferred to hire bachelors over married men.[27] First, company officials believed that these men were more likely to stay in fur trade country for extended periods and that they did not have conflicting sets of loyalties, as would be implied by the existence of a distant wife and children. Second, since the majority of HBC servants were brought up in an environment where the status of bachelorhood involved living in another's household, acting in deference to the head of the household, and maintaining one's single status until enough wages had been saved, it is likely that they carried such expectations into their employment at fur trade posts. As well, the company expected them to adhere to a working code of strict discipline and "to live virtuous, celibate lives" while in Rupert's Land.[28]

It is clear that the similarities between the structure of the HBC's trading posts and patriarchal household were deliberate and enduring. Yet there remains one large difference between the trading post and the household model. Company policy contained no sanctioned role for women at trading posts. Indeed, women's official absence led Jennifer Brown to contend that "[c]learly the company did not plan these posts to be households, for there were no women and children."[29] Originally the company did not have policies governing its employees' relationships with women; however 14 years into its existence the HBC revoked its flexible stance to forbid the presence of all women at trading posts.

When the London Committee prohibited women it acted in what it believed to be the best interests of the company. In 1684, one year after Henry Sergeant, his wife, her companion, and their daughter arrived in Rupert's Land, the HBC prohibited employees' wives and families from accompanying them.[30] No documentation survives explaining the company directors' rationale; however, it seems likely that the London committee had decided there were less expensive methods to reinforce the authority of chief factors. Furthermore, the company was not a colonizing venture; its focus was on resource extraction, be it fish, furs, or minerals. The presence of women and children would have encouraged colonization and perhaps distracted chief factors' efforts from the company's primary goals. Most importantly, the HBC may not have wanted the added responsibility of ensuring the health and welfare of employees' families particularly in a place where Native people's actions were unpredictable and the environment could be harsh and unforgiving.

The ensuing experience of the Sergeant family reinforced the London Committee's conviction of the appropriateness of its policy. In part due to the new restrictions in 1687 they requested that Henry Sergeant and "the whole parcell of Women appertaineing to him" return to London.[31] Meanwhile the French engineered the capture of all the company's bayside posts. During the attack, Mrs. Sergeant's companion, Mrs. Maurice, was wounded. She was reunited with the rest of the family on Charlton Island where the French temporarily kept all HBC prisoners. As winter drew near the French then transferred their prisoners to the HBC's main post of Port Nelson since it was impossible to send them to England until the spring thaw. When that time arrived the Sergeant household sailed for London, never again to see the shores of Hudson Bay.[32] The departure of Mrs. Sergeant, her daughter, and Mrs. Maurice, signalled the last formal approval of British-born women's presence until Frances Simpson's arrival in 1830. In order to establish the possibility that reasons other than racism factored into the company's decision to revoke its policy on British-born women, it is necessary to look at its stance toward another group of women present at Hudson Bay.

When recruits signed their contracts with the HBC, their new work environment would be unlike anything they had encountered in Britain.[33] Rather than working in a trade shop or on a farm, these recruits would be entering the social milieu of the fur trading post.[34] While the patriarchal family served as the model for structuring relationships among the HBC employees, it did not govern the behaviour of the company's Native trading partners. Because the HBC depended upon Native peoples to trap, prepare, and transport the pelts to the trading post, and to procure the majority of fresh provisions for all HBC employees, Native peoples exerted considerable influence on post affairs. The presence of Native women in particular challenged the HBC's strict adherence to the patriarchal family as its operational model.

As with the prohibition of British-born women, the company's directors produced a similar conveyance pertaining to Native women. In 1682 the London Committee sent the following directive to field Governor John Nixon:

> We are very sensibly that the Indian Weoman resorting to our Factories are very prejudiciall to the Companies affaires, not only by being a meanes of our Servants often debauching themselves, but likewise by embeazling our goods and very much exhausting our Provisions, It is therefore our positive order that you lay strict Commands on every Cheife of each Factory upon forfiture of Wages not to Suffer any wooman to come within any of our factories, and that none of our Servants may plead ignorance, Wee doe hereby require, you to cause a writeing to bee affixed in Some publick place in every Factory intimateing our Commands herein, and the penalty in disobeying them: and if not withstanding all this, there shall be any refactory Persons that shall Presume to entertaine, any Weamon, let us have an account of them by the first Opertunity and wee will not faile to send for them home fore wee cannot never Expect good Servises from such, whome neither the Lawes of God or Man can restraine from Wickedness.[35]

Apparently the London Committee believed that Native women not only were a drain on post provisions but a distraction to its employees. Directors may have also feared that unrestricted relations with Native women could jeopardize peaceful relations with Native traders and hunters. Indeed, in the early eighteenth century, employees at Churchill Fort learned that local

Natives had killed French fur traders for mistreating Native women. These fears led chief factor James Knight to imprison Thomas Butler for "[a]gainst my Orders lyeing with a Woman of this Country to the Endanger of our Lives wch Sevll of the french was killd."[36] Clearly, the London Committee did not understand how their enterprise depended on Native women's work and therefore their policy, though understandable from a business perspective, was impracticable.

Native women occupied many roles in this trading post society; their skilled repertoire included serving as interpreters and diplomatists, preparing pelts, making clothing and snowshoes, transporting furs, and procuring food for the company's stores.[37] The Inuit woman Doll (as she was known in HBC correspondence) was a favoured interpreter who accompanied northern trading expeditions setting out from Churchill in the mid-eighteenth century. She was also responsible for negotiating a peace between the Inuit and the Chipewyan in the 1760s.[38] The HBC desired harmonious relations between different Native groups because it believed Native people would then concentrate on procuring furs rather than making war. Native women also represented the means to extend the company's trade.

When a fur trader formed an alliance with a Native woman, their union signalled more than an agreement between two individuals to co-habitate; it also symbolized the obligation of the trading post and the band toward one another. Typically, the band members hoped the alliance would gain them prestige amongst their own people and garner them preferential treatment during trade with the HBC, but they also believed the marriage committed the trader to provide them with assistance in times of need and protection in times of conflict. From the perspective of the HBC field operators, these alliances were valuable for similar reasons. A trader hoped the woman's male relatives would decide to hunt for the trading post in order to be near her, but primarily he wanted the band to bring their trappings exclusively to his post.[39] Thus, these unions represented an indispensable method of ensuring a continuing source of pelts.

The mentality of the household servant provides insight into HBC servants' perception of their relationships with Native peoples, particularly women, while residing in fur trade company. Company servants appeared to accept the association between the patriarchal household and their work with the HBC not only by their recognition of the hierarchical structure of company management, but also in regard to their contract with the company representing a stepping stone to being able to marry and establish their own household. William Thomson noted in his *History of Orkney* that eighteenth-century Orcadians tended to delay marriage until the couple possessed a reasonable degree of economic stability, often achieved by working as a servant or apprentice.[40] John Nicks found that the Orkney

HBC servants mirrored their countrymen's behaviour by saving their wages until they could return home; thus, they tended "to view their work in the fur trade as a means to an end: a way of accumulating capital so that they might realize ambitions within their own society."[41] Many retired Orcadian employees bought farms or invested in businesses in their homeland. This mentality suggests that besides any sense of personal attachment to Native women, servants' perception of these relationships in the long-term was guided by economic rather than ethnocentric motives. For the most part, servants approached relationships with Native peoples in the context of work, particularly since they knew that upon completion of their contract(s) the company required them to leave Rupert's Land.

Herein lies one of the central conflicts between the HBC's operational model and the realities of the fur trade. According to the patriarchal model, only the head of the household should be having sex with women. However, as any employee who had worked for some time in the fur trade knew, ties with Native women were key to establishing good trading relations. The company's directors would have questioned the chief factor's morality if they thought he was "establishing good trading relations" with a Native woman from every band that came to the post. In turn his actions would not have been worthy of the rest of the employees' respect and deference, thereby decreasing his ability to govern effectively. As well, the company did not want its rank-and-file employees debauching themselves or, more importantly, having the opportunity to create another set of loyalties other than to the chief factor and the HBC. Remember that the HBC preferred to hire labourers of bachelor status because they had less reason to prematurely break their contracts. Because of official company policy, HBC records contain scanty and vague references to alliances between its employees and Native women, as post officers were reluctant to reveal that they were disobeying instructions in order to further trade.

While the London Committee maintained its position on forbidding Native women on post premises, it eventually came to accept, if only unofficially, the existence of alliances between traders and Native women. Chief Factor Andrew Graham commented on this contradiction between official policy and unofficial practice when he wrote reflectively in 1771 that "[t]he intercourse that is carried between the Indian ladies and the Englishmen is not allowed, but winked at."[42] In 1763 the London Committee sent surgeon John Potts the following directive:

We observe with much Concern Venereal Complaints are not uncommon among our Servants at Prince of Wales's fort and that the same Disorder has made its appearance among the Indian Women there also. Which we think to be of the worst Consequence as the

Natives already not sufficiently Numerous, may be greatly reduced by means thereof, if not prevented. Therefore we strongly enjoin you to use your utmost endeavours to Eradicate that Disease, in every object that shall present, who is affected therewith."[43]

The following year Potts received another letter on the subject: "We are glad you was able to effect the Cure of the two persons You mention and we rely on Your promised endeavours to eradicate the Veneral Distemper whenever it offers."[44] Obviously sexual relations between HBC traders and Native women existed in spite of any official company directives. Indeed, as Brown and Van Kirk have documented, by the end of the eighteenth century not only were these alliances common, but there was a growing population of mixed-blood children and future wives resulting from these unions.[45]

In the language of the fur trade, these alliances were known as country marriages, or *marriage à la façon du pays*. By definition, the union, symbolized by the exchange of words and gifts between a male fur trader and a Native or mixed-blood female, was an agreement to co-habitate for an unspecified period of time. Country marriages were usually temporary although some lasted until death or end of contract separated the couple. In economic terms, the marriage existed as long as the trader was stationed at the post where the woman's family traded; if either party moved or became displeased, the union dissolved. There was an unwritten code among traders that at the time of separation, or "turning off," the trader should assume some form of continuing responsibility for his former wife and any of their children.[46] Often when an HBC employee retired he attempted to ensure the continuing welfare of his country family, for when an employee chose not to renew his contract he had no choice but to leave fur trade country. This could be done by establishing accounts for them as Matthew Cocking did or by annuities established for them in a trader's will.[47] On the fourth of May in 1785 the London Committee recorded the payment of £10 in accordance with the will of Chief Factor Ferdinand Jacobs "being a Legacy left to his Daughter in Hudson's Bay."[48] Over time the London Committee appeared to accept, though still unofficially, the necessity of these marriages and the existence of an increasing number of families. Indeed, by 1808, the company's directors decided that schoolmaster should be sent to each major trading post for "the Religious and moral Education of the Children."[49]

As alluded to by the HBC's quiet acceptance of this practice, by the end of the eighteenth century significant social changes had occurred in the fur trade. These changes were rooted in the growth of economic competition between the HBC and its rivals coming out of the St. Lawrence River watershed. After the British takeover of New France in 1763, various groups of fur traders based in Montreal mounted a serious challenge to the HBC's hold on fur-producing territories west of Hudson Bay.[50] These traders travelled far inland, circumventing the HBC's posts, to seek out interested Native trappers and traders. In response to the aggressive trade strategy of these Canadian "pedlars" or "Nor'Westers," as they variously were called in the HBC correspondence, field officers such as Andrew Graham suggested that the HBC also open inland posts.[51] Prior to this point the HBC operated only seven posts, but with the opening of Cumberland House in 1774 the company commenced a program of rapid post construction and hiring to support their campaign in the North-West. Between 1774 and 1821 the HBC opened 242 new inland posts and increased the number of its employees from 200 to 900.[52] When the London Committee sanctioned this departure from its traditional coastal operations, and strove to match the Nor'Westers post for post, country marriages became all the more common amongst HBC men. The increased frequency of relations between Native women and traders was due to the inability of chief factors to supervise travelling inland servants and to the heightened importance associated with these marriages, in terms of creating loyal ties with families of Native trappers during a period of intensive competition.

Up to this point, mainly senior officers had entered into these unions. Labourers and tradesmen may have had liaisons with women outside post walls, but they could not enjoy the prestige and access to protection and privileges enjoyed by the post patriarch and his immediate family of officers.[53] However, when secondary officers and lower ranked men began to travel inland to winter with Native bands or to set up new posts, for the first time these men had something to offer to Natives. Now these lower ranked men were the ones leading Native traders back to the coastal posts or negotiating trades at the newer inland posts. Thus, marriage ceased to be a defining symbol of the post patriarch's authority as governing head of the trading post household.[54] Yet the HBC continued to rely upon the patriarchal house-hold as its model for post organization and as a method to reinforce the chief factor's authority. Throughout the late eighteenth-century and into the nineteenth century, the company maintained its traditional management structure while it expanded its operations westward.

The HBC faced other challenges to ensuring its survival and profitability which in turn affected its stance on country marriages. The ongoing Napoleonic Wars carried serious repercussions for the HBC's ability to put pelts on the market. The company was unable to sell any furs between 1806 and 1809 because the war effectively shut the HBC out of European markets. In the meantime, HBC directors fretted over how they would continue to provide "supplies which were necessary for the Subsistence of Six Hundred European Servants their Wives and Children, dispersed over a vast and extended Field of the North American Continent."[55] Over the next couple of years the directors solved the problems faced by the HBC using a twofold approach. First, they acquired a loan from the Bank of England for £50 000 to help the company weather the war.[56] Second, the directors resolved to lessen the company's expenses, including the burden of supporting traders' families.

In 1810, Thomas Douglas, Lord Selkirk presented a radical proposal to the London Committee. He knew of the HBC's financial concerns and offered a means to alleviate some of these pressures by creating an agricultural colony within company territory. Though he intended to populate the colony with the poor from the Scottish Hebrides, there would also be room for retired HBC servants. His proposal was attractive to the committee because the families of HBC servants could farm land in the new colony and thus provide for themselves. The company had the option to acquire surplus food from the colony with the added benefit of saving transportation costs associated with shipping goods across the ocean. The colonists would also provide a protected market for company goods, a further financial boon. Although the directors initially rejected Selkirk's proposal, they eventually acquiesced particularly because of the potential financial relief presented by the colony. Committee member Charles MacLean argued if families could be removed from company territory to the colony, they would be able to shift funds formerly used for support of these families to hiring much needed men to compete with the Nor'Westers.[57] Thus on 11 June 1811 the London Committee gave its approval for the creation of the colony of Red River in the territory of Assiniboia.[58]

In 1821 the nearly disastrous competition between the HBC and the North West Company (NWC) led the two rivals to amalgamate into one company, still to be called the HBC. This act, more than anything else, created the environment in which George Simpson could break tradition by bringing Frances to fur trade country. Simpson, like many of his fellow fur traders, had intimate relations with Native women soon after his arrival to fur trade country. The combination of selected written descriptions by Simpson on his female relationships and then his move to bring his new wife Frances to Rupert's Land has persuaded scholars that Simpson's actions were governed by racial prejudice. But, when understood in the context of the immediate needs and the strategy of the HBC, and the practice of country marriages, it becomes apparent that other factors contributed to Simpson's decision to marry Frances and bring her to Rupert's Land.

George Simpson entered fur trade country in 1820 as a trader for the HBC. The very next year, the HBC appointed Simpson governor of the Northern Department. With only two seasons of experience George faced the challenge of overseeing the amalgamation of the rival companies. The former HBC and NWC used decidedly different management styles and corporate structures. They agreed to base the new organization upon the combination of the HBC's administrative and financial structure and the NWC's field expertise.[59] The directors aimed to streamline company operations, eradicate mismanagement and duplication, and rationalize the mechanics of trade.

With these goals in mind, Simpson worked over the next few years to standardize the prices of furs and reduce the number of employees, the wages of those who remained, and the HBC's financial commitment to the families of retired or departed traders. Simpson's report evaluating the management of the Columbia District contained the following suggestions:

> no question exists in my mind that by introducing economy and regularity with the necessary spirit of enterprize and a disregard to little domestic comforts it may be made a most productive branch of the Company's Trade...it must however be understood that to effect this change we have no petty coat politicians, that is, that Chief Facters and Chief Traders do not allow themselves be influenced by the Sapient councils of their *Squaws* or neglect their business merely to administer to their comforts and guard against certain innocent indiscretions which these frail brown ones are so apt to indulge in. The extent of evil arising from this source strangers can have no conception...[60]

One of Simpson's greatest management challenges involved establishing his authority and rank among approximately two-thirds of the officers in the new HBC, who had come from the old NWC and were used to a much less authoritarian system.[61]

During this time, George already had become involved with local women. In 1822 Simpson's first country-born daughter, Maria, was born and then baptized in February. Her mother, Betsy Sinclair, was the mixed-blood daughter of a chief factor and a Cree woman. Soon thereafter he terminated their brief relationship.[62] Just prior to departing on a lengthy tour of the company's territory, Simpson wrote to his good friend and fellow fur trader John George McTavish informing him to eradicate the traces of this last affair.

> My Family concerns I leave entirely to your kind management, if you can dispose of the Lady it will be satisfactory as she is an unnecessary & expensive appendage. I see no fun in keeping a Woman, without enjoying her charms which my present rambling Life does not enable me to do; but if she is unmarketable I have no wish that she should be a general accommodation shop to all the young bucks at the Factory and in addition to her own chastity a padlock may be useful.[63]

Caution is required in interpreting Simpson's words, for the intimate details of his relationship with Betsy are not known, nor does Betsy record her own perspective of the affair.

Using Simpson's attitudes toward women and marriage to symbolize and epitomize the changing trend in fur trade marriages and the status of Native, mixed-blood and British-born women is problematic for a number of reasons. First, Simpson's history of relationships with women is complex and ranges beyond those he had in fur-trade country. He was an illegitimate child. As well, he fathered two daughters, not necessarily by the same woman, before he joined the HBC.[64] Thus, the scholarly belief that his behaviour toward his country-wives was guided by racism seems to be derived from scholars' predisposition to examine Simpson's life solely within the context of the fur trade. Second, Simpson's colourful and derogatory commentary in regard to his country wives, and the women born into fur trade country in general, can be found primarily within private letters to longtime male friends, such as John George MacTavish. It is difficult to judge, from the letters alone, Simpson's frame of mind when he composed these words. Perhaps they were intended as banter, perhaps they were reflections of frustrating situations, or perhaps these words indeed represented his deepest beliefs about Native and mixed-blood women. Deciding which of these scenarios most aptly fits Simpson's true demeanor remains difficult.[65]

Significantly, Simpson's exit from the tryst coincides with his first concrete expression of concern regarding the connection between his interactions with women and his status in the company. The more persuasive rationale for Simpson's action is this connection to his status rather than Betsy's behaviour, particularly given her subsequent history with husband Robert Miles.[66] Several months after the christening of Maria, Simpson confided in another private letter to McTavish, that "I suspect my name will become as notorious as the late Gov. in regard to plurality of wives."[67] In spite of his worries about Betsy, George apparently proceeded to become involved in a number of other relationships. He clearly expressed his concern about the effect specifically on his reputation in a subsequent letter to McTavish: "had I a good pimp in my suite I might have been inclined to deposit a little of my spawn, but have become so vastly tenacious of my reputation..."[68] Simpson's comment in the first cited letter to McTavish "I have no wish that she should be a general accommodation shop to all the young bucks at the Factory" also reflects his apprehension about the effect upon his reputation of Betsy's future behaviour with men from lower ranks. To be so involved would have created the intolerable state of placing the status-obsessed Simpson on the same level as these other men.

Simpson's anxiety about how his relationships with women could compromise his ability to command the respect of employees may have derived from his personality, but it also reveals the impact the HBC's corporate structure had on its employees' frame of mind. As the highest ranked man in the district, Simpson had to appear to those from lower positions as a model of decorum, discipline, and gentlemanly character. He had the added challenge of creating this persona in the unsettled environment of the recently amalgamated company. All of Simpson's trysts and entanglements with women had the potential to create a problematic working environment; not only could he lessen the social distance between himself and others by sharing the same woman, but he could also lose his employees' esteem or incur their anger depending on the details of the triangle.

As if to terminate the problems with employee relations associated with his connections to the women in fur trade country, in 1823 Simpson resolved to leave Rupert's Land in search of a British wife who could help create an aura of social propriety.[69] Given Simpson's complaints about his difficulty in maintaining a gentlemanly reputation, he likely believed his future wife would help distinguish and elevate him from the other employees. However, the trading post environment had changed from the time when Henry Sergeant had brought his wife to Rupert's Land as a method to reinforce his patriarchal authority, which meant that Simpson's marriage needed to be different.

Not only had the former HBC gradually, but unofficially, relaxed its prohibition on traders' involvement with Native and mixed-blood women, Nor'Westers had always been free to intermix with the women in fur trade country. The NWC did not use marriage as a method of instilling a sense of hierarchy and authority; rather, the Nor'Westers had relied upon marriage chiefly as a building block to establishing an ever expanding trade network. Thus if the HBC was to maintain the patriarchal household model as an effective method of reinforcing its post managers' authority, somehow it had to distinguish these officials from the rest of the employees. Because marriage had become so common, it seemed an unlikely device, but in fact it was one of the most striking tools at the company's disposal.

Meanwhile, the London Committee rejected Simpson's request to travel to London. Instead, Simpson continued to become involved with the women of fur trade country despite his concerns about such activities upon his ability to govern effectively. In 1823, the same year of Simpson's initial request for leave to London, he fathered a son. The identity of the mother has not survived in the documentary record. A few years later, and likely after a number of other relationships, he entered into a stable country marriage with Margaret Taylor, a mixed-blood woman.[70] While involved with Margaret, in 1826 Simpson attained the pinnacle of the HBC's field positions by becoming governor-in-chief of all the company's territory.[71] According to one of Simpson's biographers, John Galbraith, about this time

Simpson consciously cultivated the pomp and splendour associated with his position of field governor, and he carefully designed his public appearances to emphasize his elevated status. For example, in 1827 Simpson hired Colin Fraser to play the bagpipes in the governor's canoe, particularly when the boat neared a trading post. The addition of Fraser to Simpson's crew helped to distinguish the arrival of the governor's boat from all others.[72] Now, more than ever, he sought ways to demonstrate his elevated status.

The governor had not abandoned his quest in search of a British-born wife, in spite of the evidence that he shared an enduring and emotionally positive relationship with Margaret. Just as Margaret gave birth to their second child, Simpson left for London in August of 1829.[73] He was accompanied by his friend McTavish, and the chief purpose of their trip was to search for wives who could reflect their sense of their heightened position in the HBC. Both men achieved this goal. On 24 February 1830 Simpson and Frances were wed, and subsequently he brought her into fur trade country, as did McTavish with his new wife Catherine. The act of marriage to a British-born woman while under contract to the HBC itself was not a threat to the status quo of trading post life; a number of prominent HBC officers, such as Moses Norton, predated Simpson by having British wives while still working in Rupert's Land.[74] Rather, it was Simpson's decision to have Frances accompany him into fur trade country that upset the established pattern of marriages.

Evidence of a multi-faceted rationale for the marriages lies in the effect these two women had upon trading post society.[75] When Frances and Catherine arrived, all the wives of lower ranked employees were Native or of mixed-blood. In this way traders' changing marital preferences and the ethnicity of their wives appear related, even though the documentary evidence indicates the reasons for the connection were based just as much in corporate strategy as any personal preference. Jennifer Brown contended that the impact on social relations at Moose Factory of Catherine McTavish's presence reinforced Chief Factor John MacTavish's status, "[f]or the next four years, MacTavish and his Aberdeenshire wife were the highest ranked residents at Moose, and like the Simpsons…, interposed new social barriers between themselves and the natives of the country."[76] Thus the need of highly ranked HBC officials to reinforce their status in this age of company reorganization appears to be directly related to the appearance of British-born wives in Rupert's Land.

Further evidence that business concerns shaped Simpson's attitude towards marriages to Native, mixed-blood and British-born women is revealed by his seemingly contradictory stances on whom traders should marry. While Simpson contravened the HBC's traditional ban on bringing British-born wives to Rupert's Land for himself, he simultaneously advocated that other traders continue to marry Native and mixed-blood women in the interests of the fur trade:

> the restrictions which the Honble. Committee have put on Matrimonial alliances and which I consider most baneful to the interests of the Company are tantamount to a prohibition of forming a most important chain of connection with the Natives, so we have solely to depend on the Indians who have no other feelings than those which interest and mercenary views create towards us; it is never matured to attachment and a price is only required to make those on whom our existence depends our inveterate Enemies.[77]

The only way to make sense of why Simpson encouraged some traders to marry British women while suggesting that others marry Native or mixed-blood women is to consider what distinguished these two groups of traders, and that factor was their rank. If Simpson's decision to abandon Margaret in favour of Frances was rooted in racism alone, he would not have continued to support country marriages of officers located in key fur-providing territories. He would have created policies requiring all HBC officials and servants to marry only British women; instead, Simpson encouraged just a few high-ranking friends to choose British wives. Considering the historic importance of women to the fur trade, and Simpson's ability to comprehend the workings of the fur trade in such a short time (as evidenced by his rapid promotion at such a crucial time), Simpson's actions are best explained in terms of his business acumen.

British-born wives distinguished the post patriarch in ways that Native or mixed-blood women could not. They looked and behaved differently from the rest of the women in fur trade country, and their marital status was permanent and formally sanctioned by the church. All employees from lower ranks either had country marriages, which were perceived as temporary in nature and informal, or had British wives who were unable to join their husbands. Thus, while the post patriarch no longer was distinguished by marriage, he could at least be differentiated from the majority of married employees by the aura of contrast surrounding his wife.

When Chief Factor Colin Robertson attempted to have his mixed-blood country-wife, Therisa Chalifoux, befriend Frances Simpson, predictably George forbade the meeting between the two women: "Robertson brought his bit of Brown with him to the Settlement this Spring in hopes that she would pick up a few English manners before visiting the civilised world; but it would not do — I told him distinctly that the thing was impossible, which mortified him exceedingly."[78] Seen within the context of maintaining the position of post patriarch, George's words signify more than discrimination based on race. To maintain this new distinguishing feature of the fur trade patriarch, George could not afford to have his new British wife undermine her unique status by socializing with women married to anyone from a lower station in the company.

It is clear that the rationale for the marriage pattern of fur traders cannot be sufficiently explained by racial motives alone. If "shock waves"[79] were sent throughout fur trade country as a result of the appearance of British-born women at the fur trade posts, then the move by officers to differentiate themselves from those in the lower ranks had succeeded. By the time of amalgamation Native and mixed-blood women no longer helped to symbolize the patriarchal structure necessary to maintain authority and control in the HBC. There is enough evidence to suggest that officials' decision to bring their British-born wives to Rupert's Land was associated with a period of crisis in which it was necessary to create new ways of differentiating the head of a post from his inferiors.[80] Ideally employed as powerful, visible symbols in maintaining status differentiation, these marriages helped to reinforce the concept of the patriarchal family, which was implicit to the corporate structure of the HBC. As the company's own age-old directives suggest, it had utilized the model of the patriarchal family as the chief method for instilling discipline and reinforcing employee ranks almost from the moment HBC traders arrived on the shores of Hudson Bay.

Notes

1. Historians are unsure of the exact year of George Simpson's birth. He married at either age 38 or 43. See respectively Arthur Silver Morton, *Sir George Simpson, Overseas Governor of the Hudson's Bay Company, A pen picture of a man of action* (Binsfords-Mort, 1944), 3; Frederick Merk, "Editor's Introduction," *Fur Trade and Empire: George Simpson's Journal*, rev. ed. (Cambridge, Mass: The Belknap Press of Harvard University Press, 1968), xliii.

2. Sylvia Van Kirk, *"Many Tender Ties": Women in Fur Trade Society in Western Canada, 1670–1870* (Winnipeg: Watson and Dwyer Publishing Ltd., 1980), 201.

3. Jennifer S.H. Brown, *Strangers in Blood: Fur Trade Families in Indian Country* (Vancouver and London: University of British Columbia Press, 1980), xvi.

4. Veronica Strong-Boag, "Writing About Women," in John Schultz, ed., *Writing About Canada: A Handbook for Modern Canadian History* (Scarborough: Prentice-Hall Canada, Inc., 1990), 185. For other similar summaries of the significance of the arrival of British-born women see Brian Gallagher, "A Re-examination of Race, Class and Society in Red River," *Native Studies Review* 4 (1988): 38; Frits Pannekoek, "The Anglican Church and the Disintegration of Red River Society, 1818–1870," in Carl Berger and Ramsay Cook, eds., *The West and the Nation: Essays in Honour of W.L. Morton* (Toronto: McClelland and Stewart, 1976); Arthur J. Ray, "Reflections on Fur

Trade Social History and Métis History in Canada," *American Indian Culture and Research Journal* 6, no. 2 (1982): 91–107.

5.   Brown, *Strangers in Blood*, 214; Van Kirk, *"Many Tender Ties,"* 117, 119.

6.   E.P. Thompson cautions historians when they use terms like "patriarchal" to be aware of the difference between the "actual" and the "ideal." For example, he notes that between the mid-seventeenth century and well into the eighteenth century, the idea of patriarchy remained a popular choice as an effective management system; however, in actuality it was waning a method of economic control over the labour force, primarily due to the increased geographic mobility of labourers. See E.P. Thompson, *Customs in Common* (London: Penguin Books, 1991), 37–38; see also Rosemary O'Day, *The Family and Family Relationships, 1500–1900: England, France, and the United States of America* (New York: St. Martin's Press, 1994), 24.

7.   Readers interested in examining the scholarly debate surrounding the role and influence of this type of family structure upon society, should begin by consulting the following sources: Peter Laslett, *Family Life and Illicit Love in Earlier Generations: Essays in Historical Sociology* (Cambridge: Cambridge University Press, 1977); Alan Macfarlane, *The Origins of English Individualism: The Family, Property and Social Transition* (New York: Cambridge University Press, 1978); Steven Mintz, *A Prison of Expectations: The Family in Victorian Culture* (New York: New York University Press, 1983). Though somewhat dated, this list forms the basis from which more recent debates have developed. For a more recent interpretation of this debate see Mary Abbott, *Family Ties: English Families, 1540–1920* (London and New York: Routledge, 1993).

8.   According to Alan Macfarlane, the majority of marriages in England occurred after a contract or apprenticeship had been completed. Macfarlane claims that desirable female marriage partners were those who had access to economic stability either through personal wealth, or through a connection to the most influential person in the future husband's life, his patron. See Macfarlane, *The Origins of English Individualism*, 175; Laslett, *Family Life*, 217–19.

9.   O'Day, *The Family and Family Relationships*, 175–76.

10. Gerhard Ens, "The Political Economy of the 'Private Trade' on the Hudson Bay: The Example of Moose Factory, 1741–1744," in Bruce G. Trigger, Toby Morantz, Louise Dechene, eds., *Le Castor Fait Tout: Selected Papers of the Fifth North American Fur Trade Conference, 1985* (Montreal: Lake St. Louis Historical Society, 1987): 387, 398; John E. Foster, "Trading-Post Social Organization," Lecture, History 663, University of Alberta, 17 March 1995.

11. *Massachusetts Records*, I, 397, as cited in O'Day, *The Family and Family Relationships*, 57. See ibid., 58, for other examples from American colonies.

12. The charter specifically states that "the said Governor and Company shall or may elect seaven of theire number in such forme as hereafter…shall bee called the Committee of the said Company…" See "Charter of the Hudson's Bay Company, 1670. The Royal Charter for incorporating The Hudson's Bay Company, A.D. 1670," *Charters, Statutes and Orders in Council relating to the Hudson's Bay Company* (London: Hudson's Bay Company, 1931), 5. The first governor and committee were appointed.

13. Brown, *Strangers in Blood*, 24–25; Van Kirk, *"Many Tender Ties,"* 11.

14. John Nicks, "Orkneymen in the Hudson's Bay Company," in Carol Judd and Arthur J. Ray, eds., *Old Trails and New Directions: Papers of the Third North American Fur Trade Conference, 1978* (Toronto: University of Toronto Press, 1980), 122. He suggests that

these men joined the HBC with the hope of improving their economic and social status, either saving enough money to create a new position for themselves upon returning to the Orkneys or by working their way through the ranks of the HBC and returning with an already improved status.

15. J. Storer Clouston, *The Orkney Parishes: Containing the Statistical Account of Orkney, 1795–1798. Together with a General Introduction and Notice of each Parish* (Kirkwall: W.R. Mackintosh, The Orcadian Office, 1927), 112, 121. I realize that a ploughman and a carpenter may not be equivalent occupations; however, I could find information on yearly wages for only some occupations in Orkney and in the HBC. No identical occupations for both the HBC and the Orkney Islands were listed. As of 1811 the London Committee proposed that labourers be contracted for £18 per year for a three-year contract and £20 per year for a five-year contract. See HBCA, A.5/5 fo. 37.

16. Carol Judd, "'Mixt Bands of Many Nations,': 1821–70," in Carol Judd and Arthur J. Ray, eds., *Old Trails and New Directions: Papers of the Third North American Fur Trade Conference, 1978* (Toronto: University of Toronto Press, 1980), 129; William P.L. Thomson, *History of Orkney* (Edinburgh: The Mercat Press, 1987), 218. For more information on the relationship between the Orkney Islands and the HBC see; Nicks, "Orkneymen in the Hudson's Bay Company"; and *The Orkney Parishes: Containing the Statistical Account of Orkney*; Bruce S. Wilson, "The Orkneymen and the Hudson's Bay Company," in Patricia A. McCormack and R. Geoffrey Ironside, eds., *Proceedings of the Fort Vermillion Bicentennial Conference, September 23–25, 1988* (Edmonton: Boreal Institute for Northern Studies, 1990).

17. HBCA, A.5/5 fo. 31, 8 December 1810. The company contracted apprentices often around the age of 13 or 14 years.

18. Edith Burley's recently published version of her doctoral dissertation examines evidence of resistance by HBC employees to the company's authority. In the context of her study she similarly observes on the parallels between the ideal conception of the patriarchal family and the HBC's style of operations. See *Servants of the Honourable Company: Work, Discipline, and Conflict in the Hudson's Bay Company, 1770–1879* (Don Mills, Ontario: Oxford University Press, 1997), 2.

19. The HBC maintained five posts during the seventeenth century: Charles Fort, later known as Rupert was built at the mouth of the Rupert River; Port Nelson, located at the mouth of the Nelson River would become known as York Fort or Factory; Hayes Fort, later called Moose Factory, was found at the mouth of the Moose River; Severn Fort was positioned near the mouth of the Severn River; and Chichewan Fort, eventually known as Fort Albany, was stationed at the mouth of the Albany River. See Ernest Voorhis, *Historic Forts and Trading Posts* (Ottawa: Department of the Interior, 1930), 4; and "Appendix A: Posts," *Copy-Book of Letters Outward, 1679–94*, edited by E.E. Rich, assisted by A.M. Johnson (Toronto: Champlain Society, 1948), 345–69.

20. Brown, *Strangers in Blood,* 33. On the same page she provides documentary evidence that traders perceived the chief factor in this light.

21. There are other examples of chief factors attending to the spiritual needs of their charges, but in all other cases the factors carry out the services themselves. Churchill Post Journal entries throughout the eighteenth century document the chief factor's performance of the ritual Sunday sermon. Chief factor Richard Norton of Churchill included weekly notices of his reading of prayers to the employees; see the entries dated 1 and 8 September 1723. HBCA, B.42/a/4 fos. 5, 6. Similarly chief factor Captain Anthony Beale wrote for his entry dated Sunday 20 August 1727 that

he "Read Prayers to According to the Liturgy of the Church of England:" see HBCA, B.42/a/8 fo. 3. For other such entries in the latter part of the eighteenth century see HBCA, B.42/a/34 fo. 26d and B.42/a/42 fo. 1d. The London Committee's minute books from the latter part of the eighteenth century include orders for religious tracts they intended to distribute to the various chief factors for their men's use. See HBCA, A.1/46 fos. 21 and 87d, London Minute Book 1783–88.

22. Henry Sergeant's orders to depart for Hudson Bay are dated 24 January 1683. See "Appendix B: Biographies," *Letters Outward, 1679–94*, 388.

23. On Knight's appointment as chief factor see letter to Knight from the London Committee, 23 May 1682, *Letters Outward*, 51. On Knight's manservant see Ernest S. Dodge, "James Knight," *Dictionary of Canadian Biography*, Vol. 2 (Toronto: University of Toronto Press, 1969), 318.

24. Letter to Henry Kelsey at York, from the Governor and London Committee, 29 May 1710, Letterbook 603, 199, as cited in *The Kelsey Papers*, intro. by Arthur G. Doughty and Chester Martin (Ottawa: Public Archives of Canada and the Public Record Office of Northern Ireland, 1929), xxvii.

25. Regarding Grover's appointment to second at Churchill, see the letter to William Grover from the London Committee, 31 May 1763, HBCA, A.5/1 fos. 55, 108. For the reference to his new duties see the letter to Grover from the London Committee, 15 May 1765, HBCA, A.5/1 fos. 68, 135.

26. The company also hired boat crews, but as they were not necessarily permanent residents at the trading posts and therefore will not be included in this discussion.

27. Brown, *Strangers in Blood,* 10–11. Here Brown relates some of the difficulties encountered by the HBC when it employed married men and those with dependents.

28. Van Kirk, *"Many Tender Ties,"* 11.

29. Brown, *Strangers in Blood,* 20–22.

30. The daughter is first mentioned as a passenger aboard the HBC's yacht *Colleton* in the spring of 1786. Either the Sergeants brought her with them from England or she was born in Rupert's Land. See E.G.R. Taylor, "Introduction," *Letters Outward*, xxxiii. On the 1684 policy see Brown, *Strangers in Blood*, 11.

31. *Letters Outward,* 235, dated 3 June 1687.

32. *Letters Outward*, 390.

33. HBC contracts were for three-year periods, with the exception of apprentices who signed on for seven years. At the end of the contract the company and employee could negotiate another three-year renewal.

34. Foster, "Trading-Post Social Organization." Van Kirk describes trading post society as a combination of European and Native cultural elements, resulting in a "distinctive, self-perpetuating community, *"Many Tender Ties,"* 5.

35. Letter to Nixon from the London Committee, 15 May 1682, *Letters Outward*, 40–41.

36. HBCA, B.239/a/2 fo. 11, York Factory Post Journal 1715–16, 27 December 1715.

37. HBC trader and explorer Peter Fidler reported in a journal entry from 1790: "An Indian woman at a House is particularly useful in making shoes, cutting line, netting snow shoes, cleaning and stretching Beaver skins &c." As cited in *Journals of Samuel Hearne and Philip Turnor*, edited by J.B. Tyrrell (Toronto: Champlain Society, 1934), 327, footnote 6. For an in-depth examination of their varied roles and influences in the fur trade see Van Kirk, *"Many Tender Ties,"* specifically chapter three, "Your Honors Servants."

38. The first reference to Doll's use by the HBC as an interpreter occurs in Chief Factor Moses Norton's instructions to Captain Magnus Johnson, 17 July 1764. The letter directs Johnson to take the "Eskimo Woman Doll, who is sent wth you as a Linguist." HBCA, A.11/14 fo. 1. On 14 September 1769 Doll died at Churchill Fort of an unnamed illness. Chief Factor Norton entered the following remark in the post journal to mark her passing: "the Death of the Woman I doubt will be a Loss to the Northern Trade with the Esquimaux as she has been of great Service on Assisting to make Peace between the Northern Indians and her Country People." HBCA, B.42/a/77, fo. 2d, Churchill Post Journal.

39. Daniel Harmon comments frequently in his journal about these alliances. Soon after he had entered the fur trade a Cree chief approached him: "who appeared very desirous that I should take one of his Daughters to remain with me...he wished to have his Daughter with the white people...I was sure that while I had the Daughter I should not only have the Fathers hunts but those of his relations also, of course [this] would be much in the favor of the Company & perhaps in the end of some advantage to me likewise." Though Harmon was a "Nor'Wester," his perception of alliances with Native women reflects the shared views of HBC traders. See *Sixteen Years in the Indian Country: The Journal of Daniel Williams Harmon*, edited by W. Kaye Lamb (Toronto: Macmillan, 1957), 62.

40. Thomson, *History of Orkney*, 220.

41. Nicks, 123.

42. Andrew Graham, *Observations on Hudson's Bay*, HBCA, E.2/7 fo. 24d; as cited in Van Kirk, *"Many Tender Ties,"* 41. Concerning this document, readers will be interested to note that there are 10 different volumes under the title of Graham's *Observations*. Some are in Graham's handwriting, others are not. There are substantive differences between the versions in terms of content and length. A detailed study comparing these versions has yet to be performed and may prove useful in revealing Graham's changing portrayal of Native peoples. In the meantime, interested readers are instructed to examine Glyndwr Williams's edited version of Graham's *Observations* for his understanding of this complex mass of manuscripts.

43. Letter to John Potts from the London Committee, 31 May 1763, HBCA, A.5/1 fo. 55, 108–9.

44. Letter to John Potts from the London Committee, 23 May 1764, HBCA, A.5/1 fo. 60, 118.

45. Brown, *Strangers in Blood,* 70; Van Kirk, *"Many Tender Ties,"* 45. Brown provides 15 documented examples of country marriages involving HBC employees; see *Strangers in Blood*, 52–58.

46. There is sufficient evidence that many Native and mixed-blood women did not act as victims of abandonment. Rather, they operated out of self-interest to ensure their own futures. When Joseph Colen left York Factory in 1798 for Britain, his former Cree wife and children re-allied themselves with another employee "who had long since been in the habits of her attention and Affection." See Brown, *Strangers in Blood,* 68. Consider the case of the Native woman Betsy who had a number of company employees as husbands. Throughout the course of her alliances she had saved 88 pounds, which allowed her a measure of financial security. She told British-born Letitia Hargrave that she would never marry again because the men would probably be after her money. See Letitia Hargrave to Mary MacTavish, 1 September 1840, *Letters*, 72; Van Kirk, *"Many Tender Ties,"* 89–90.

47. Van Kirk covers this topic in far greater detail in chapter two, "Customs of the Country" of her *Many Tender Ties."* See also John S. Galbraith, *The Little Emperor: Governor Simpson of the Hudson's Bay Company* (Toronto: Macmillan, 1976), 67.

48. The minutes from the London Committee's weekly meetings during the 1780s and 1790s include a few references to chief factors' provisions for their families after death. Jacob's wishes are recorded in HBCA, A.1/46 fo. 51d. Other similar references are contained in HBCA, A.1/46 fos. 89, 89d and A.1/47 fos. 36d, 92d and 113.

49. HBCA, A.5/5 fo. 14d, Letter to David Geddes from the London Committee, 30 March 1808.

50. During the late eighteenth century and early nineteenth century, the Nor'Westers formed a number of competing companies; however the rivalry with the larger HBC eventually drove them to form a coalition known as the North West Company. An introduction to the history of the various Montreal-based companies is contained within Gerald Friesen, *The Canadian Prairies: A History* (Toronto: University of Toronto Press, 1984); Harold A. Innis, *The Fur Trade in Canada* (Toronto: University of Toronto Press, 1930).

51. Glyndwr Williams, ed., "Appendix A," *Andrew Graham's Observations on Hudson's Bay 1767–1791,* Hudson's Bay Record Society, Vol. 27 (London: Hudson's Bay Record Society, 1969), 346–47.

52. Burley, *Servants of the Honourable Company,* 5. She also notes that during this same period the Nor'Wester organizations opened 342 posts. Most of the HBC and Nor'Wester posts lasted no longer than five years before being abandoned.

53. For example it was noted in the Churchill Post Journal that on the 14th of March 1724, "3 of our men gone over the River to the Hunters tent to lye there for 1 Night." The next morning they returned back to the post. Though it was not recorded why they spent just one night in the hunters' tent instead of in their regular lodgings, the existence of such events points to the opportunity for sexual relations with Native women. See HBCA, B.42/a/4 fo. 21

54. Brown, *Strangers in Blood,* 51; Van Kirk, *"Many Tender Ties,"* 38, 45. There are two points to be made here. First, both authors agree that as marriage occurred with increased frequency throughout the ranks of the HBC, officers began to marry mixed-blood women in a similar frequency. This pattern of preference should not be surprising, if one considers the influence the patriarchal model had upon employees. These mixed-blood women were the daughters of post patriarchs. For employees seeking to rise in the ranks there was no better way to confirm one's "rightful place" in his immediate household than to be adopted into the patriarch's family by marriage to his daughter. Second, though not proven, it seems plausible that there would be a correlation between the increase of HBC posts and the number of country marriages. Interested readers should consult instead both Brown's *Strangers in Blood* and Van Kirk's *"Many Tender Ties"* that contain extensive documentation of country marriages, though neither author correlates the frequency of marriage with the number of posts particularly since this was not their purpose. Perhaps future research in this area could sustain, or challenge, the argument for the economic and social motivations for these marriages in opposition to the argument reliant on ethnicity.

55. HBCA, A.1/49, fo. 93, letter from the London Committee to the Commissioners of the Royal Treasury, 21 December 1809. The full letter, including references to the impact of the Napoleonic Wars, consists of folios 91d–94d. Another reference to the

effect of the war upon the HBC is located in HBCA, A.1/147, fo. 40d–41, London Committee Minute Books, dated 15 March 1809.

56. HBCA, A.1/49 fo. 102d, minutes from meeting of the London Committee, 20 September 1809.

57. HBCA, A.5/5 fos. 35–35d.

58. For the London Committee's discussion and Selkirk's original proposal, see HBCA, A.1/50 fos. 34–38.

59. Friesen, *The Canadian Prairies*, 83.

60. Merk, *Fur Trade and Empire*, 58.

61. Friesen, *The Canadian Prairies*, 84; Merk, *Fur Trade and Empire*, xlvi. For examples of how the Board of Governors and Simpson formulated the new policies examine the following references in *Journal of Occurrences in the Athabasca Department by George Simpson, 1820–1821, and Report*, edited by E.E. Rich, Vol. 1 (Toronto: The Champlain Society, 1938): on reduced wages see 2 February 1822, p. 306, 8 March 1822, p. 314, 16 July 1822, p. 339; on support for families see 2 February 1822, p. 311, 8 March 1822, pp. 314–15, 31 July 1822, p. 354. On the reduction of posts, Burley states that by 1821 the HBC operated 68 posts and the NWC ran 57. In the merged company the number of posts would be reduced to a total of 52. See Burley, *Servants of the Honourable Company*, 6. For a general discussion of the policies following amalgamation see Galbraith, *The Little Emperor*, 73–75; Morton, 64.

62. Galbraith, *The Little Emperor*, 69. Galbraith believes that the relationship between Betsy and George is better characterized as a brief fling than a country-marriage.

63. Private letter from Simpson to John George McTavish, 12 November 1822, as cited in *Minutes of Council Northern Department of Rupert Land, 1821–31*, edited by E.E. Rich and R.H. Fleming (Toronto: Champlain Society, 1940), 424.

64. See Galbraith, *The Little Emperor*, 68; Merk, *Fur Trade and Empire*, xliii.

65. Readers interested in Simpson's biography and in examining the various depictions of his character are advised to consult the following list: Merk, *Fur Trade and Empire*; Galbraith, *The Little Emperor*; *Journal of Occurrences in the Athabasca Department*; *Minutes of Council Northern Department of Rupert Land, 1821–31*; and Morton, *Sir George Simpson*.

66. Galbraith, *The Little Emperor*, 70.

67. Letter from Simpson to McTavish, 4 June 1822, as cited in *Minutes of Council*, 424.

68. Galbraith, *The Little Emperor*, 68.

69. Galbraith, *The Little Emperor*, 75.

70. See Galbraith, *The Little Emperor*, 95; Van Kirk, *"Many Tender Ties,"* 161.

71. Merk, *Fur Trade and Empire*, xliv.

72. Galbraith, *The Little Emperor*, 95–96.

73. During Simpson's last tour of fur trade country before he left for England, he referred affectionately to Margaret as "my fair one." See Galbraith, *The Little Emperor*, 100. It is not known if Simpson forewarned Margaret of his intentions to terminate their relationship.

74. Evidence that Norton was married to a British woman while still in the employ of the HBC is contained in HBC official correspondence to him. For example, see the letter to Moses Norton from the London Committee, 15 May 1760, HBCA, A.5/1 fo. 36. In this letter the committee informs Norton that they "have paid your Wife the Ballance of your Account as you desired."

75. Galbraith, *The Little Emperor*, 102, 104.

76. Brown, *Strangers in Blood,* 133.

77. Simpson, 1821 Athabasca Report, *Journal of Occurrences,* 395–96.

78. HBCA, B.135/c/2, 15 Aug 1831; as cited in Brown, *Strangers in Blood,* 129–30.

79. Brown, *Strangers in Blood,* xv.

80. It has been necessary to focus upon the merger as a crisis in the new company's organization in order to illuminate the implications of policy changes on fur trade social relations. However, by highlighting a period as the turning point in social relations, it is easy to overlook long-term continuities. Part of this paper's argument hinges upon the assertion that the change in policy to allow British-born women at fur trade posts reflects the desire to maintain a long-term mode of operation. There are other continuities; for example, the percentage of officers married to mixed-blood women remained fairly stable (there was actually a small increase by three percent) well past the middle of the nineteenth century. See Gallagher, "A Re-examination of Race, Class and Society in Red River," 28–29, 31.

II

METIS HISTORY

5 Metis Studies

The Development of a Field and New Directions

FRITS PANNEKOEK

UNTIL RECENTLY, sources for Metis studies have been few both for classroom use as well as academic reflection. Lately, there has been a virtual explosion of interest, although largely among non-Metis historians. Now this too has begun to change. A new dynamic is also forcing Metis historiography out of the bog of Red River in which some argue it has been mired for too long. The writings of the previous decades have already been examined from a historiographical perspective in several excellent articles.[1] Rather than updating these useful exercises, an alternative is to examine the new literature from a topical perspective, posing questions and suggesting new avenues of investigation.

The current literature is the reflection of scholarly concerns of the last two decades and fit into six basic themes or areas: the origins of the Metis people, the historic Metis of the fur trade period of the eighteenth and early nineteenth century, the Metis Diaspora of the mid to late nineteenth century, the revival of Metis consciousness in the twentieth century, Metis land claims, and Metis women's history. A case could be made that the beginning point in each of these areas are the great icons of Metis historiography: W.L. Morton, G.F.G. Stanley, and Marcel Giraud.[2] However, their studies have been well assessed and often reinforce stereotypes, so it is best to look to more recent literature.

ᨙ Metis Identities and Origins

Much of the current debate in Metis studies, whether cultural or legal, but particularly those relating to land rights, centres on who is Metis. This interest in Metis identity and origins was in no small way sparked by the work of John Foster. In the late 1970s and 1980s Foster examined, in some detail, the origins of the various Metis communities in the Canadian West.[3] His last essay on this subject, "Wintering, the Outsider Adult Male and the Ethnogenesis of the Western Plains Métis," goes a long way in detailing the complexity of Metis origins. Since the 1980s scholars have also begun to investigate the emergence of Metis communities in other parts of North America. These studies enhance our understanding of the complexity of Metis identity and provide some insight as to why some of these communities were so short lived.[4]

Several questions are current with regard to Metis identity and its origins. First, precisely who are the Metis and how are they defined? This question is particularly relevant given the 1982 identification of the Metis as Aboriginal people under the Canadian constitution. At one time, some suggested that only those who could claim ancestry to the historic Metis, that is those from Red River, could claim Aboriginal rights. Where, some asked, would this leave the Saskatchewan and Alberta Metis? In 1983, depending upon the definition of Aboriginal Metis, there could be as many as one-million or as few as one-hundred-thousand Metis in Canada. Second, why do the Metis have a strong collective identity in Western Canada, but only a weak sense of one in Eastern Canada or in the United States? John Foster in his "Some Questions and Perspectives on the Problem of Metis" argues rather cogently and with a great deal of common sense that you are Metis if you say you are, and, as important, you are Metis if others who identify themselves as Metis say you are.[5] Unfortunately both conditions can not always be met, and from that springs much current conflict. Trudy Nicks in "Mary Ann's Dilemma: The Ethnohistory of an Ambivalent Identity," brings the issues of identity home by examining the very personal dilemma of a Cree Metis woman. She identified herself as Cree, until her material culture was identified as Metis by a Provincial Museum of Alberta curator. She then opted for a new identity. Little has been done with the use of material culture to identify Metis ethnicity, and it is obvious from the Nicks article that while the exercise may have its rewards there will be many pitfalls along the way.[6] There is, however, innovative new work being done in Metis cultural history, much of which still has not been published. The recent work on the Michif language is a good indication of the promise this work holds.[7]

The role of governments in the formation of Metis identity is very evident in the writings Olive Dickason, Jacqueline Peterson, Vern Dusenberry, and David Boisvert and Keith Turnbull. In their article, "Who are the Metis?"[8] the latter two authors focus on the impact of government regulation and law on the creation of a Metis identity. In particular, they attempt to deal with the question of who are the "historic Metis." Can the past and the current identity of the "historic Metis": or those with roots in Red River form a realistic foundation for a new Canadian Metis identity? Where does this leave the Saskatchewan, the Alberta and the Territorial Metis whose roots do not extend there? Yet their point about the importance of government policy in determining identity is worth pursuing, and in fact emerges in a number of other writings by senior scholars. Olive Dickason argues in her "From One Nation"[9] that the Metis did not emerge in New France because of government policy to assimilate any mixed-bloods into French culture. Peterson also argues in her article, "Many Roads to Red River; Metis Genesis in the Great Lakes Region, 1680–1815,"[10] that if the Metis did find their roots in the Great Lakes area, it was also because government regulation was tempered with isolation. Vern Dusenberry's observation of the American situation in his "Waiting for a Day That Never Comes: The Dispossessed Metis of Montana"[11] may be the most telling. He provides clear evidence that government refusal to recognise the Metis, and the Metis acceptance of the fact, relegated most to the status of Indians. More recent work on the American Metis in Montana and North Dakota adds some complexity to this picture showing how the Metis were able maintain some sense of a separate identity within the context of tribal structures.[12]

◇ The Red River Metis

In the last decade much ink has been devoted to the historic or Red River Metis. The debate is often acrimonious and some might argue not relevant to the Metis situation today. But it is critically relevant because so much of Canada's Metis identity is tied to what happened at Red River. For this reason it is imperative to understand the formation of the Red River Metis and their subsequent dispersal and move into the western interior. One particular event that has been re-examined recently involves what has come to be known as the "Seven Oaks Massacre." This incident, that ended in 22 deaths, only one a Metis, is often cited as the single event that acted as the catalyst that shaped the Metis identity and proved their rights to Manitoba's plains. Even so, until 1992, the incident received little close attention. Lyle Dick in a provocative article, "The Seven Oaks Incident,"[13] argues that the killings were not planned, and that it was to the advantage of the settlers and other Canadians to call Seven Oaks a "massacre." By doing so, they justified the subjugation of the Metis. The word "massacre" confirmed the image of the Metis as a barbaric and savage people. This same image of the Metis as a less than "civilized people" was reinforced by a generation of historians like George Stanley in his interpretations of the 1869 and 1885 rebellions as inevitable clashes between a civilised and primitive society.

Other questions that are being asked by scholars and by the Metis Community include: What was the nature of this society? What caused the society to change over time? In particular, what were the economic and social pressures inside Red River that precipitated the Riel Resistance of 1869? The writings of W.L. Morton, Marcel Giraud, G.F.G. Stanley, Gerhard Ens,[14] Irene Spry,[15] Frits Pannekoek,[16] and Sylvia Van Kirk[17] address these questions. While the particular events of the Riel resistance of 1869 are not currently subject to much debate, the importance of the resistance in alienating the Metis from the Canadian mainstream is an area to be studied.

The interpretation of the two armed uprisings will always be central to an understanding of the dynamic of the historic Metis. The publication in 1985 of *The Collected Writings of Louis Riel*[18] has made it much easier to examine some of the crucial sources related to these uprisings and to evaluate some of the interpretations that have arisen regarding them. The appendix to this volume, by Thomas Flanagan and Glen Campbell, updates this collection including some of Riel's writings that were not included in the published five volumes, as well as providing a commentary to these sources.

The first interpretation of the Metis uprisings was that of George Stanley who saw the Metis as being a half-wild, half-civilised people, incapable of facing the modern world. In his view the Metis resistance and rebellion against the Canadian state in both 1869 and 1885 represented a last stand against racial and economic absorption.[19] W.L. Morton, in his classic interpretation in the introduction to Alexander Begg's *Red River Journal and other papers relative to the Red River resistance of 1869–1870*,[20] believed that Red River was an island of civilisation within the wilderness, and that the Metis were the ultimate expression of the balance that could be achieved between the barbarous and civilised halves of the settlement. Morton argues that the Rebellion of 1869 was an attempt on the part of Red River to secure its dual cultural and political reality within a Canadian Protestant and Anglophone expansion. The causes of the resistance were to be sought not in Red River but in outside forces, particularly the bigotry and racism of the Canadians.

More recently, historians argue that Red River should be explored on its own terms rather than in the dual schizophrenic cultural assessment offered by Morton, Giraud or Stanley. Perhaps the Rebellion was an outward manifestation of a growing social unease within the settlement. I argue in *A Snug Little Flock* that perhaps the mixed-bloods of Red River should not be seen as a monolith, but rather as two communities with two separate identities. The one, the English speaking mixed-bloods, sided with the Canadians, while the French speaking mixed-bloods, the Metis, accepted Riel's leadership against the cultural and racial bigotry of the Canadians and, unfortunately, their own English speaking mixed-blood brothers. This argument has not been widely accepted. The best refutation is by Irene Spry, in her article in *New Peoples: Being and Becoming Metis in North America*, who saw the mixed-bloods, regardless of heritage, as united. They were a classless and free society working in complete harmony with nature.[21]

◆ The Metis Diaspora
More important are the arguments in the recent literature that relate to the great Metis Diaspora, that is the migration and dispersal of the Metis after

the 1869 resistance in Manitoba, and the Riel Rebellion of 1885 in the North-West Territories. A great deal has been written to explain what precipitated the Metis exodus from Red River. Traditional thinking was that it was a result of the callous economics and racism of the incoming Canadians. If this was the case then perhaps much of what Stanley has stated might be true. He argues that the Metis could not cope with the new sophisticated economic environment and that combined with a new virulent racism pushed the Metis further into the interior. Stanley saw 1885 as the end of the Metis nation, the last stand. Even today, historians like George Woodcock second Stanley's interpretation in his biography of the great Metis general, Gabriel Dumont.[22] John Foster and Gerhard Ens argue rather that the situation that precipitated the Diaspora from Red River to the Saskatchewan country and to the United States was more complex. As early as 1850 the Metis had become commodity manufacturers, particularly of buffalo robes for eastern capitalist markets. Both Ens and Foster demonstrate that the Metis were divided into a merchant class and a buffalo-hunting class who worked almost entirely on the production of buffalo hides for the Eastern markets. In turn the Metis were paid in manufactured goods, upon which they increasingly relied.

The Metis then were not pushed out of Red River, rather they were attracted by opportunity to move into the Western interior.[23] Many like Diane Payment now accept Ens's thesis but argue as well that racism and economic hardships imposed by unfair land allocation practices contributed to drive the Metis into the South Saskatchewan area. She notes in her book that the Metis adapted well to their new economic realities and achieved considerable success as farmers, merchants and professionals particularly with the demise of the buffalo.[24] To Gerald Friesen, whose summary interpretations can be found in *The Canadian Prairies: A History*, the Metis had to adapt to a market economy and did so with variable success after 1885.[25] But all accept that the dream of a sovereign Metis Nation ended in 1885.

What is also worth noting is that little has been added to the interpretation of the Riel rebellions over the last few years.[26] There continues to be an interest by military and Parks Canada historians in the battles of 1885, but the precise nature of this event has been relegated to antiquarianism. Some events related to the rebellion have become laboratories for other subjects, including women's studies. But the debate over the Diaspora from Red River has yet to become the foundation for a much more important issue, the emergence of the new Metis consciousness of the twentieth century. The assumption is still that with the end of the buffalo robe trade, the Metis became a peripheral people. The suggestion is that the importance of a people is directly related to the viability of their economic base. The implication is that as the buffalo robe trade became marginal, so did the Metis. The history of the Metis is too easily confined to the period when they were on centre stage.

ᐁ A New Metis Consciousness

The real future in Metis studies lies not in Red River, or in the early North West, rather it lies in determining the roots of the new Metis consciousness of today. These roots can be discerned in the mythology of 1869 and 1885, but more importantly in the 50 years of marginalisation following 1885. Until recently there was not a great deal of material on the Metis from 1885 to the Depression. Enough now exists however, so that the legal process that led to the marginalisation of the Metis in Western Canada can be discussed. More importantly, there is enough critical literature that allows evaluation of the events that led to the formation of the Ewing Commission, the single event that ultimately led to the establishment of the Alberta Metis colonies and to the reassertion of Metis nationalism. In addition, recent literature allows the contribution of Jim Brady and Malcolm Norris to the resurrection of that nationalism to be further explored. However, the historiography is still sufficiently fragile that it will need to be nurtured if healthy and critical scholarship is going to emerge in the next decade.

Mike Brogden's "The Rise and Fall of the Western Metis in the Criminal Justice Process"[27] attempts to prove that the Metis were purposely marginalised by the Euro-Canadian manipulation of the criminal justice system in the period following 1885. "Criminality" was a social artefact used to marginalise and segregate the Metis who "hindered the thrust of eastern Canadian and European capitalism." He argues that, regardless of time, the Metis were marginalised or criminalized whenever they attempted to seek their economic freedom. With the defeat of Riel in 1885, Brogden further argues that the Canadian government deliberately used the justice system to criminalize the Metis political and social structures through "vagrancy" and "sturdy beggar" laws. The Metis became a marginalised class, kept in their place through the criminal justice system and used as cheap labour in the new agriculture of the Canadian West.

In a more biographical vein Murray Dobbin's *The One-and-a-Half Men*[28] documents the hopelessness and despair of the Alberta and Saskatchewan Metis after 1885. Dobbin's analysis focuses almost entirely on issues of class and on the intersection of class and nationalism with Metis relations with the state. Dobbin traces the careers of Malcolm Norris and Jim Brady, both middle-class Metis from northern Alberta, who were instrumental in organising the Metis after the Depression and bringing their concerns to the forefront. Throughout their lives, both Norris and Brady urged Metis communities to undertake their own economic development along cooperative lines and to minimise dependence on government. Their ideal was an empowered community that would determine its own economic and cultural future, collectively and cooperatively. Dobbin argues that the works of Norris and Brady led to the resurrection of the Metis identity and to the creation of the first Metis homelands in northern Alberta and later, northern Saskatchewan. Equally importantly, Dobbin argues convincingly that current day political action and organisation resulted from their work. In so doing, he was one of the first scholars to assign agency to key Metis leaders of the twentieth century.[29]

⚜ Land Claims

The legal relationships of the Metis to the land is linked to their standing as Aboriginal peoples, and will determine their cultural well-being as a nation and their economic well-being as individuals. The troubles in Manitoba in 1869, in the North-West Territories in 1885, and in Alberta in the 1930s all had their origins in land. The similarities and differences between Metis, Non-Status, and Indian rights and claims are now the subject of numerous court cases and this should generate a new spate of studies on Metis scrip, land, and rights to complement the work of D.N. Sprague and Thomas Flanagan.

Considerable scholarship has already been published concerning the nature of Metis "Aboriginal" claims. Do the Metis have the same land claims as Indians or Inuit? Thomas Flanagan concludes that Metis rights are subordinate to those of the Natives and the Inuit. Metis rights flow from Indian claims. Flanagan limits even these unique rights of Western Canada to the old North-West Territories. He believes that no Metis rights exist in the rest of Canada. Flanagan's strongest arguments are marshalled in his *Metis Lands in Manitoba*[30] in which he maintains that when Manitoba entered Confederation, the Metis were British subjects with full civil and political rights. Unlike Indians, they could own land, enter into contracts, vote and hold public office. Flanagan argues that the Canadian Government consciously respected that status when it gave Metis scrip to extinguish whatever Aboriginal title to land they may have had. Scrip was private property, to do with as the Metis wished.

Doug Sprague and Joe Sawchuk, historians for the Alberta and Manitoba Metis federations, disagree with Flanagan. Sawchuk points out that the concept of Aboriginal title is a European one that has been accepted by Metis and Natives only because it is useful in the new society, not because it is rooted in Native tradition. Sawchuk's analysis also calls Flanagan's conclusions into question by noting that the Metis were included in the treaty process in Ontario, particularly Treaty No. Three. The differences between Flanagan and Sawchuk are in the interpretations of the Manitoba Act. Sawchuk sees Section 31 as acknowledging Native title; Flanagan sees it as a political expedient. However, Flanagan notes that Riel wanted to have the Metis dealt with by the federal government as a nation, not as individuals. Sawchuk comes closer to Flanagan in his careful outline of how the Metis became increasingly subordinate to the Native treaty process. Aboriginal title had to be extinguished first, and only then could the Metis be offered Crown land to extinguish whatever rights they might have.[31]

The real debate in land claims is between Sprague and Flanagan. Sprague argues that the federal government conspired to deny the Metis their rights under the Manitoba Act. He contends that the "introduction of the Manitoba Act was duplicitous" and that the Metis were deliberately dispossessed and dispersed.[32] Most historians do not agree with Sprague. Flanagan argues that the federal government generally fulfilled and possibly over-fulfilled the land provision of the Manitoba Act. Flanagan provides evidence that Metis families generally did extremely well, particularly with the lands allotted to Metis children. He accuses Sprague of being guilty of the historical crime of "animism" or "anthropomorphism," ascribing human qualities to the federal government as a whole. Sprague sees a "government conspiracy." Flanagan argues that there was neither an overall conspiracy nor a single government mind set. Metis lands were handled by a number of bureaucrats, who often worked in isolation to each other. Each responded to unique circumstances.

Flanagan admits, as has Sprague, that the question of the Manitoba lands centres on whether the Metis could make informed choices on whether to stay or to sell. Sprague maintains that many of the Metis left because of racial prejudice and the pressure of speculators. Flanagan argues that the federal government was caught in a dilemma. Since the Metis did not want to be treated paternalistically, the government issued land either in money scrip or land scrip, an act that, in turn, opened the door to speculation. Flanagan claims that the Metis made individual decisions based on what was best for them economically at the time the scrip was issued.

Metis leaders do not agree with Flanagan's findings. The Metis Association of Alberta argues that Metis claims will have to be settled by the courts. Issues surrounding individual money scrip and land scrip rights will have to be dealt with. Metis leaders argue that extinguishing individual rights with payment of scrip did not and does not extinguish national rights. They contend that scrip was designed to benefit the speculator, not the Metis and the federal government was guilty of breach of trust. The Metis argue that the extinguishment of their Aboriginal rights was not compensated for by scrip. A major point to be explored is that the ending of Metis Aboriginal rights was imposed by Order in Council and Statute, not by negotiation. The Metis could be construed to be Indians under the terms of the British North America Act and are entitled to the same rights as Indians. As well, Metis rights were recognised by the Manitoba Act and by the various

Dominion Lands Acts and these rights were never fully extinguished. As a nation, the Metis argue that they have the right to negotiate directly with federal government but the Canadian Government refused to recognize the political and national identity of the Metis in 1870. The courts must decide on these issues concerning the human and national rights of the Metis.[33]

As land issues are resolved, and they eventually will be, cultural issues will become of greater concern to the Metis and to the scholars involved in their interpretation. This has already started to happen, but the issues tend to focus too much on the character of Louis Riel. The persistence and nature of Metis culture, family life and gender relations will become increasingly of interest. There are signs this is already starting to happen.

❧ Women, Gender, and the Metis

Generally mainstream historians like Morton, Giraud, Stanley, Flanagan, and even Sprague have all worked within a context in which men created the issues that were important to history. Issues such as child-rearing, gender, ageing or patterns of life were not addressed. The impact of the industrial colonisation of the Canadian West on women, and more impor- tantly, on Native women was simply not an issue. The role of women in forming mixed-blood communities and Metis identity is currently an important area of study. Another area being explored is the role of the churches, education, and racism in contributing to the changing role of Metis women.

Only in the 1970s with the work of Sylvia Van Kirk and Jennifer Brown did the history of the mixed-blood women and mixed-blood families become a legitimate focus of historical scholarship. Van Kirk's *"Many Tender Ties"* and Brown's *Strangers in Blood*[34] were published first as fur trade studies, and secondarily as contributions to native studies and women's history. Brown's most important point, other than her analysis of fur trade marriages, is her discussion of the role of women in forging a distinctive identity in her article "Women as Centre and Symbol in the Emergence of Metis Communities." Brown argues that some Metis men attached a special importance to their maternal ancestry. Brown observes that the daughters born to European fur traders and their Indian wives were more likely to marry and stay in the West than were the sons born to these couples. The sons tended to go to England or Montreal to be educated. Brown observes that newly married couples tended to live with the wives' relations for a period of time.[35] Brown asks several important questions that historians would be wise to consider in their future research. Did Metis women main- tain the matrilocal tendency of their mothers in their own marriages? How important were the daughters who stayed behind in the interior? What impact did the absence of fathers and young men have on family structure?

Sylvia Van Kirk in her article on the well documented English speaking mixed-blood Alexander Ross family of Red River observes the opposite that the male, not the female, had the greatest impact on a family's choice of identities. She notes that in the Ross family, the mother's influence in the family particularly on its choice of identity was marginal. The father made the critical cultural decisions. This observation may well be subject to interpretation in the near future. It can be argued that Van Kirk was captive of letters by those trying to emulate a "patriarchal" and "Imperial" culture.[36] On this question readers should also consult John Foster's "Wintering, the Outside Adult Male and Ethnogenesis of the Western Plains Métis."[37]

Diane Payment's and Natalie Kermoal's articles "La Vie en Rose"[38] and "Les Rôles et les souffrances des femmes métisse lors de le Résistance de 1870 et de la Rébellion de 1885"[39] are key to an understanding of the new emerging discussions on such issues as the impact of the Church on the position of Metis women, the impact of racism on the status of women, and the impact of the events of 1869 and 1885. Kermoal sees Metis women as passive participants. Their role was private, one of keeping the family intact and providing domestic support for the political or public activities of their men. Women were subordinate, suffering within the confines of a world controlled by men. She sees little change in women's status between 1869 and 1885. Diane Payment, using Batoche as an example, argues that the persistence and survival of the Metis is due equally to the Metis men and women. She makes particularly interesting observations about the role of women in securing compensation for losses incurred during the rebellion. Payment also emphasises that there was change from 1869 to 1885. Payment recognises the growing influence of the Roman Catholic Church, which encouraged the subordination of women. However, she points out that while the Catholic Church saw the family as a patriarchy in which women had the nurturing, child rearing and domestic roles, after 1885 there was a growing sisterhood amongst Metis women. Particularly with the expulsion of their men folk following 1885, they experienced their struggles as a group, met with one another socially, and supported each other through their trials. According to Payment, Metis women believed they were equal to men, even if Euro-Canadians did not.

While Metis women's history is still in its infancy and has many themes that need to be explored, insights can be gleaned from the contemporary writings of Metis women. Amongst the best is Maria Campbell's *Halfbreed*.[40] This autobiography is an intensely personal story of Campbell's struggle against prejudice and poverty, and her ultimate discovery of herself.

☙ Conclusion

Where Metis studies will head in the next decades is not certain. However, an examination of the recently completed dissertations in the social sciences and humanities gives us some idea where scholarship might turn. The preponderant interest, particularly of scholars in American institutions, would seem to focus on issues of identity, and the interplay of gender, race and class. Lucy E. Murphy's "Economy, Race and Gender Along the Fox-Wisconsin and Rock Riverways, 1737–1832,"[41] examines a northern borderland region's economy during the gradual transition from Indian and Metis to white hegemony through the filters of race, ethnicity and gender. Melinda M. Jette, "'Ordinary Lives': Three Generations of a French-Indian Family in Oregon, 1827–1931,"[42] argues that individual circumstances determined how three generations of her family adapted from fur trade to urban life.

There is a continued interest in childhood, first established in Canada by Brown and Van Kirk. Juliet T. Pollard's, "The Making of the Metis in the Pacific Northwest Fur Trade Children: Race, Class and Gender,"[43] albeit an earlier thesis, argues that much can be determined about the historical process by the investigation of childhood experiences, which shape the lives of the next generation of adults. Pollard's examination of the contours of class, race and gender on the Metis children at Fort Vancouver, during from 1800 to 1850, years of rapid social change, determines that most children, rather than becoming "victims of 'higher civilization,'" became successful member of the dominant Euro-American culture. Elizabeth Scott, "'Such Diet as Befitted His Station as Clerk:' The Archaeology of Subsistence and Cultural Diversity at Fort Michilimackinac, 1761–1781,"[44] examines cultural remains to determine how the interplay of environment, socio economic position, ethnicity and gender might have accentuated or muted differences amongst the French, English, mixed-bloods and natives at Michilimackinac. Scott finds that the subsistence patterns at the site at once reflected and reinforced social and economic differences. Brad Jarvis's "A Woman Much to be Respected: Madeline LaFramboise and the Redefinition of a Metis Identity,"[45] argues that LaFramboise constructed her identity in nineteenth century Mackinaw to maximize her economic and social status in the various ethnic groups comprising her society. However, the best of the dissertations undertaken at American institutions relates to contemporary issues of Metis identity. Evelyn I. Legare "Nobody Speaks for the Nation Anymore: Canada's Problems with Itself,"[46] argues that Canadian nationalism "represents real Canadians as a culturally unmarked citizens." Within this identity the Metis are allowed a subordinate role within but not as full members of the Canadian nation—they are not "real" Canadians.

The scholarly interests at Canadian institutions tends to be more diffuse, although the debates of the 1980s and 1990s still seem to grip the historiography with little relief in sight. John Frederick Shore's "The Canadians and the Metis: The Re-Creation of Manitoba 1858–1872,"[47] argues that the use of the Red River Expeditionary Force by the new Ontario elite marginalized the Metis position in Manitoba. He argues that the Metis had managed to gain political hegemony during the 1860s to the point where they dominated the politics of the new province. However the intimidation tactics employed by the Force soon ensured that this position soon ended to allow for the dominance of the new Ontarians. Margaret Louise Clarke's "Reconstituting the Fur Trade Community of the Assiniboine Basin, 1793 to 1812,"[48] positions itself within the Spry-Pannekoek debates on the nature of the divisions between the English and French speaking mixed-bloods. She found that geographic location more than ethnicity was the key determinant in intermarriage.

There is evidence as well that Metis studies will move increasingly beyond Red River in the next decades. Paul Thistle, in "The Twatt Family, 1780–1840: Amerindian, Ethnic Category, or Ethnic Group Identity?"[49] studies the mixed-bloods of the lower Saskatchewan River to determine whether their identities were self-formed or formed by external perceptions.

The issues of land is a greater issue generally in Canadian historiography than American. One of the more interesting studies on land issues from an Aboriginal perspective is Elmer Nelson Ghostkeeper's "'Spirit Gifting': The Concept of Spiritual Exchange,"[50] which describes the impact of changing Metis attitudes in Paddle Prairie towards the land from one based on a spiritual values in the early 1960s to one based on commercial values in the late 1970s. The interest by Ruth Swan on border Metis,[51] and that by Heather Devine on transborder families and the factors shaping identity is more indicative of recent scholarship, and is comparable in scope to that undertaken by their American counterparts.

Some of the best new scholarship is in political history. If these become base line studies there is great promise of the Metis beginning to realize the power of historical agency. Laurie Meijer Drees, " History of the Indian Association of Alberta, 1939–1959,"[52] argues that while to date historiography has suggested that Aboriginal (including Metis) involvement in WWII precipitated political action, in fact it was prewar concerns over land, hunting and fishing rights, education and health that were the real root. While the dissertation accepts Metis agency, it also argues that non-Native support was critical in determining the nature of political action. Another valuable contribution to the understanding of Metis politics is Shannon M. Avison's "Aboriginal Newspapers: Their Contribution to the Emergence of an Alternative Public Sphere in Canada,"[53] that determines that while Metis and native newspapers did establish an alternate arena for political and social debate, its effectiveness was circumscribed by its government funders.

There is an increasing interest in cultural issues particularly in literature, music and material culture. In "Case Study: Bob Boyer the Artist,"[54] Barbara E. Pritchard explored the traditional Metis roots of Bob Boyer's art from 1971 to the present. This exploration of cultural traditions carries much hope. Annette Chretien's, "Mattawa, Where the Waters Meet: The Question of Identity in Metis Culture,"[55] examines music as evidence of identity. She argues that music provides evidence that there are "multiple" Metis identities based on class, geography and language. Karl Neuenfeldt, "First Nations and Metis Songs as Identity Narratives,"[56] studies Metis popular songs and argues that they have a critical role in both creating and reinforcing identities. Blending both traditional music and Riel's historic writings, Normand Guilbeault has produced a musical on Riel, based on Metis uprisings in Manitoba and Saskatchewan, entitled *Riel Plaidoyer musical / Musical Plea*.[57] Joan Reid Acland, "The Native Artistic Subject and National Identity: A Cultural Analysis of the Architecture of the Canadian Museum of Civilization, Designed by Douglas J. Cardinal,"[58] is an intriguing work that attempts to determine the interplay between Cardinal, his Aboriginal heritage, his building and his nation in a post colonial and post modern environment.

If there is an exciting future that continues to be still relatively unexplored is the interdisciplinary and comparative study of mixed-blood peoples, although there are important forays into the field. Perhaps it is here we will find new insights for the future. One example is Laura Caso Barrera, "The Canadian Metis and the Mexican Maya as a Cross Cultural Study of Native Land Struggles."[59] This comparative research on the Maya Caste War of Yucatan (1847–1901) and the Riel Rebellions (1869–1885) attempts to demonstrate that the rebellions were both efforts to preserve indigenous social organization and autonomy in the face external pressures.

As Metis studies continue their focus on cultural and political identities, there will be attempts by "main stream" historians like Gerald Friesen, in for example the earlier cited "Labour History and the Metis" to place Metis studies within the context of larger Canadian historiographical concerns, in this case the history of the left. However, if those who completed their recent dissertations and theses continue to publish in the refereed literature, it is very likely that the focus will continue to be on the issues relating to identity formation. This will steer debate, and future research, and even determine the direction taken by generational and gender concerns of an increasing number of Metis scholars. The major research gaps that continue to exist are in the period from 1900 to 1950, the decades in which the roots of today's politics, culture and identity were formed. It will be in these decades, rather than the "Genesis" fur trade years, that today's Metis will find the roots of the issues most relevant to them today. It is also in these years that today's Metis will find the traditions for their current leadership and themselves. And never forget the pain that some Metis continue to go through as they discover their heritage. This pain will continue to produce great pieces of Canadian literature like Gregory Schofield, *Thunder Through My Veins Memories of a Metis Childhood*.[60]

Notes

1. Jennifer Brown, "People of Myth, People of History: A look at Recent Writings on the Metis," *Acadiensis* XVII (Autumn 1987): 150–63; Dennis F.K. Madill, "Riel, Red River and Beyond: New Developments in Metis History," in Colin G. Calloway, ed., *New Directions in American Indian History* (Norman: University of Oklahoma Press, 1987), 19–78; Gerald Friesen, "Labour History and the Metis," in Gerald Friesen, ed., *River Road: Essays on Manitoba and Prairie History* (Winnipeg: University of Manitoba Press, 1996), 79–89.

2. See W.L. Morton's extensive introductions to two set of published documents: *Eden Colvile's Letters*, edited by E.E. Rich (London: The Hudson's Bay Record Society, 1956), and *Red River Journal and other papers relative to the Red River resistance of 1869–70*, by Alexander Begg (Toronto: Champlain Society, 1956). Marcel Giraud, *The Metis in the Canadian West*, 2 vols., translated by George Woodcock (Edmonton: University of Alberta Press, 1986). Originally published in French in 1945. George F.G. Stanley, *The Birth of Western Canada: A History of the Riel Rebellions* (Toronto: University of Toronto Press, 1970), originally published in 1936.

3. See John E. Foster, "The Indian Trader in the Hudson Bay Fur Trade Tradition," in Jim Freedman and J.H. Barkow, eds., *Proceedings of the Second Congress, Canadian Ethnology Society* (Ottawa: National Museum of Man, 1976); John E. Foster, "The Origins of the Mixed-Bloods in the Canadian West," in L.H. Thomas, ed., *Essays on Western History* (Edmonton: University of Alberta Press, 1976); John E. Foster, "The Métis: The People and the Term," *Prairie Forum* 3, no. 1 (1978); John E. Foster, "The Plains Métis," in Bruce Morrison and C.R. Wilson, eds., *Native Peoples: The Canadian Experience* (Toronto: McClelland and Stewart, 1986); "John E. Foster, "Wintering, the Outsider Adult Male and Ethnogenesis of the Western Plains Métis," *Prairie Forum* 19, no. 1 (Spring 1994). (Also included in this book as Chapter 8.)

4. See Jacqueline Peterson, "Prelude to Red River: A Social Portrait of the Great Lakes Metis," *Ethnohistory* 25 (Winter 1978): 41–67; "Ethnogenesis: Settlement and Growth of a New People in the Great Lakes Region, 1702–1815," *American Indian Culture and Research Journal* 6, no. 2 (1982): 23–64; Tanis Thorne, *The Many Hands of My Relations: French and Indians on the Lower Missouri* (Columbia: University of Missouri Press, 1996); Susan Sleeper-Smith, "Furs and Female Kin Networks: The World of Marie Madeleine Réaume "L'archevêque Chevalier," in Jo-Anne Fiske, Susan Sleeper-Smith, and William Wicken, eds., *New Faces of the Fur Trade: Selected Papers of the*

Seventh North American Fur Trade Conference, Halifax, Nova Scotia, 1995 (East Lansing: Michigan State University Press, 1998), 53–72; Keith R. Widden, *Battle For the Soul: Métis Children Encounter Evangelical Protestants at Mackinaw Mission, 1823–1837* (East Lansing: Michigan State University Press, 1999).

5.   John E. Foster, "Some Questions and Perspectives on the Problems of Metis Roots," in Jacqueline Peterson and Jennifer S.H. Brown, eds., *New Peoples: Being and Becoming Metis in North America* (Winnipeg: University of Manitoba Press, 1985), 73–87.

6.   Trudy Nicks, "Mary Anne's Dilemma: The Ethnohistory of an Ambivalent Identity," *Canadian Ethnic Studies* XII, no. 2 (1985): 103–14.

7.   Peter Bakker, *A Language of Our Own: The Genesis of Michif, the mixed Cree-French Language of the Canadian Métis* (Oxford: Oxford University Press, 1997).

8.   David Boisvert, David and Keith Turnbull. "Who are the Metis?" *Studies in Political Economy* 18 (Autumn 1985): 107–45.

9.   Olive Patricia Dickason, "'From One Nation' in the Northeast to 'New Nation' in the Northwest: A Look at the Emergence of the Metis," in Jacqueline Peterson and Jennifer S.H. Brown, eds., *New Peoples: Being and Becoming Metis in North America* (Winnipeg: University of Manitoba Press, 1985), 19–36.

10. Jacqueline Peterson, "Many Roads to Red River; Metis Genesis in the Great Lakes Region, 1680–1815," in Jacqueline Peterson and Jennifer S.H. Brown, eds., *New Peoples: Being and Becoming Metis in North America* (Winnipeg: University of Manitoba Press, 1985), 37–71.

11. Verne Dusenberry, "Waiting for a Day That Never Comes: The Dispossessed Metis of Montana," in Jacqueline Peterson and Jennifer S.H. Brown, eds., *New Peoples: Being and Becoming Metis in North America* (Winnipeg: University of Manitoba Press, 1985), 119–36.

12. More recent work on the marginalization of the American Metis includes: Gregory Scott Camp, "The Turtle Mountain Plains Chippewa and Metis, 1797–1935" (Ph.D., University of New Mexico, 1987); Gerhard J. Ens, "After the Buffalo: The Reformation of the Turtle Mountain Métis Community, 1879–1905," in Jo-Anne Fiske, Susan Sleeper-Smith, and William Wicken, eds., *New Faces of the Fur Trade: Selected Papers of the Seventh North American Fur Trade Conference, Halifax, Nova Scotia, 1995* (East Lansing: Michigan State University Press, 1998), 139–52.

13. Lyle Dick, "The Seven Oaks Incident and the Construction of a Historical Tradition, 1816 to 1870," *Journal of the Canadian Historical Association* 2 (1992): 91–112.

14. Gerhard J. Ens, *Homeland to Hinterland: The Changing Worlds of the Red River Metis in the Nineteenth Century* (Toronto: University of Toronto Press, 1996).

15. Irene Spry, "The Tragedy of the Loss of the Commons in Western Canada," in A.L. Gerry and Antoine S. Lussier, eds., *As Long as the Sun Shines and Water Flows*, (Vancouver: University of British Columbia Press, 1983).

16. Frits Pannekoek, *A Snug Little Flock: The Social Origins of the Riel Resistance of 1869–1870* (Winnipeg: Watson & Dwyer, 1991).

17. Sylvia Van Kirk, *"Many Tender Ties": Women in Fur Trade Society in Western Canada, 1670–1870* (Winnipeg: Watson and Dwyer, 1980).

18. George F.G. Stanley, gen. ed., *The Collected Writings of Louis Riel*, 5 vols. Vol. I, *1861–1875*, Raymond Huel; Vol. II, *1875–1884*, Gilles Martel; Vol. III, *1884–1885*, Thomas Flanagan, Vol. IV, *Poetry*, Glen Campbell; Vol. V, *Reference*, George F.G. Stanley, Thomas Flanagan, Claude Rocan (Edmonton: University of Alberta Press, 1985).

19. Stanley, *The Birth of Western Canada*, 18.

20. W.L. Morton, "Introduction," to *Red River Journal and other papers relative to the Red River resistance of 1869–70*, by Alexander Begg (Toronto: Champlain Society, 1956).

21. Irene Spry, "The Métis and Mixed-Bloods of Rupert's Land Before 1870," in Jacqueline Peterson and Jennifer S.H. Brown, eds., *New Peoples: Being and Becoming Metis in North America* (Winnipeg: University of Manitoba Press, 1985).

22. George Woodcock, *Gabriel Dumont: The Metis Chief and His Lost World* (Edmonton: Hurtig, 1975).

23. Gerhard J. Ens, "Dispossession of Adaptation? Migration and Persistence of the Red River Metis, 1835–1890," *Historical Papers* 1988 (Ottawa: Canadian Historical Association, 1988): 120–44. John E. Foster, "The Metis and the End of the Plains Buffalo in Alberta," *Alberta Studies in the Arts and Sciences* 3, no. 1 (1992): 61–77. (This article also appeared simultaneously in John Foster, Dick Harrison and Ian MacLaren, eds., *Buffalo*, Alberta Nature and Culture Series (Edmonton: University of Alberta Press, 1992).)

24. Diane Payment, *"The Free People—Otipemisiwak" Batoche, Saskatchewan 1870–1930* (Ottawa: National Historic Parks and Sites, 1990).

25. Gerald Friesen, *The Canadian Prairies: A History* (Toronto: University of Toronto Press, 1984).

26. An excellent synthesis of the 1885 Rebellion is Bob Beal and Rod Macleod, *Prairie Fire: The North-West Rebellion* (Edmonton: Hurtig Publishers, 1984). An excellent study of the military tactics themselves is Walter Hildebrandt, *The Battle of Batoche: British small warfare and the entrenched Metis* (Ottawa: National Historic Parks Service, 1989). It challenges several key interpretations in the Beal/Macleod volume.

27. Mike Brogden, "The Rise and Fall of the Western Metis in the Criminal Justice Process," in Samuel W. Corrigan and Lawrence J. Barkwell, eds., *The Struggle for Recognition: Canadian Justice and the Metis Nation* (Winnipeg: Pemmican Publications, 1991), 39–51.

28. Murray Dobbin, *The One-and-a-Half Men: The Story of Jim Brady and Malcolm Norris, Metis Patriots of the Twentieth Century* (Vancouver: New Star Books, 1981).

29. A more recent examination of Alberta Metis political leadership and organizations from the 1930s to the 1980s is Joe Sawchuk, *The Dynamics of Native Politics: The Alberta Metis Experience* (Saskatoon: Purich Publishing, 1998).

30. Thomas Flanagan, *Metis Lands in Manitoba* (Calgary: University of Calgary Press, 1991). See also his "The History of Metis Aboriginal Rights: Politics, Principle, and Policy," *Canadian Journal of Law and Society* 5 (1990): 71–94; and "Louis Riel and Aboriginal Rights" in A. L. Getty and Antoine S. Lussier, eds., *As Long as the Sun Shines and Water Flows* (Vancouver: University of British Columbia Press, 1983), 247–62. Flanagan has also recently published *First Nations? Second Thoughts* (Montreal: McGill-Queen's University Press, 2000).

31. Joe Sawchuk, "The Metis, Non Status Indians and the New Aboriginality: Government Influence on Native Political Alliances and Identity," *Canadian Ethnic Studies* 17, no. 2 (1986): 133–46.

32. D.N. Sprague, *Canada and the Metis 1869–1885* (Waterloo: Wilfred Laurier University Press, 1988). See also his "The Manitoba Land Question, 1870–1882," *Journal of Canadian Studies* 15, no. 3 (Fall 1980): 74–84; and *The Genealogy of the First Metis Nation: The Development and Dispersal of the Red River Settlement 1820–1900* (Winnipeg: Pemmican Publications, 1983).

33. Joe Sawchuk, Patricia Sawchuk, and Theresa Ferguson, *Metis Land Rights in Alberta: A Political History* (Edmonton: Metis Association of Alberta, 1981).

34. Jennifer S.H. Brown, *Strangers in Blood: Fur Trade Company Families in the Indian Country* (Vancouver: University of British Columbia Press, 1980).

35. Jennifer S.H. Brown, "Women as Centre and Symbol in the Emergence of Metis Communities," *The Canadian Journal of Native Studies* 3, no. 1 (1983): 39–46. See also her "Fur Trade as Centrifuge: Family Dispersal and Offspring Identity in Two Company Contexts," in Raymond J. Demaillie and Afonso Ortiz, eds., *North American Indian Anthropology* (Norman: University of Oklahoma Press, 1994).

36. Sylvia Van Kirk, "'What if Mama is an Indian?' The Cultural Ambivalence of the Alexander Ross Family, " in Jacqueline Peterson and Jennifer S.H. Brown, eds., *New Peoples: Being and Becoming Metis in North America* (Winnipeg: University of Manitoba Press, 1985), 207–17.

37. Foster, "Wintering, the Outsider Adult Male and Ethnogenesis of the Western Plains Metis."

38. Diane P. Payment, "'La Vie en Rose?' Métis Women at Batoche, 1970–1920" in Christine Miller and Patricia Chuchry, eds., *Women of the First Nations: Power, Wisdom, and Strength* (Winnipeg: University of Manitoba Press, 1996), 19–38.

39. Nathalie Kermoal, "Les Rôles et les souffrances des femmes métisses lors de la Résistance de 1870 et de la Rébellion de 1885," *Prairie Forum* 19, no. 2 (Fall 1993): 153–68. See also her "'Le Temps De Cayoge': La Vie Quotidienne Des Femmes Métisses au Manitoba De 1850 à 1900" (Ph.D., Université d'Ottawa, 1996).

40. Maria Campbell, *Halfbreed* (Toronto: McClelland and Stewart, 1973).

41. Lucy E. Murphy, "Economy, Race and Gender Along the Fox-Wisconsin and Rock Riverways, 1737–1832" (Ph.D., Northern Illinois University, 1995).

42. Melinda M. Jette, " 'Ordinary Lives': Three Generations of a French-Indian Family in Oregon, 1827–1931" (M.A., University of Oregon, 1996).

43. Juliet T. Pollard, "The Making of the Metis in the Pacific Northwest Fur Trade Children: Race, Class and Gender" (Ph.D., University of British Columbia, 1990).

44. Elizabeth Scott, "'Such Diet as Befitted His Station as Clerk:' The Archaeology of Subsistence and Cultural Diversity at Fort Michilimackinac, 1761–1781" (Ph.D., University of Minnesota, 1991).

45. Brad Jarvis, "A Woman Much to be Respected: Madeline LaFramboise and the Redefinition of a Metis Identity" (M.A., Michigan State University, 1998).

46. Evelyn I. Legare, "Nobody Speaks for the Nation Anymore: Canada's Problems with Itself" (Ph.D., Duke University, 1997).

47. John Frederick Shore, "The Canadians and the Metis: The Re-Creation of Manitoba 1858–1872" (Ph.D., University of Manitoba, 1991).

48. Margaret Louise Clarke, "Reconstituting the Fur Trade Community of the Assiniboine Basin, 1793 to 1812" (M.A., University of Manitoba, 1997)

49. Paul Thistle, "The Twatt Family, 1780–1840: Amerindian, Ethnic Category, or Ethnic Group Identity?" *Prairie Forum* 22, no. 2 (1997).

50. Elmer Nelson Ghostkeeper, "'Spirit Gifting': The Concept of Spiritual Exchange" (M.A., University of Alberta, 1995).

51. Ruth Swan and Edward A. Jerome, "The History of the Pembina Metis Cemetery: Inter-Ethnic Perspectives on a Sacred Site" *Plains Anthropologist* 44: 70–81.

52. Laurie Meijer Drees, "History of the Indian Association of Alberta, 1939–1959," (Ph.D., University of Calgary, 1997).

53. Shannon M. Avison's "Aboriginal Newspapers: Their Contribution to the Emergence of an Alternative Public Sphere in Canada" (M.A., Concordia University, 1997).

54. Barbara E. Pritchard, "Case Study: Bob Boyer the Artist" (M.A., University of Manitoba, 1998).

55. Annette Chretien, "Mattawa, Where the Waters Meet: The Question of Identity in Metis Culture" (M.Mus., University of Ottawa, 1996).

56. Karl Neuenfeldt, "First Nations and Metis Songs as Identity Narratives," *International Journal of Canadian Studies* 12, 1995.

57. Normand Guilbeault, "Riel Plaidoyer musical / Musical Plea" (AM 073 2CD), Dame, Montreal, Quebec. "With Riel, Plaidoyer musical / Musical Plea, Normand Guilbeault and his large group of outstanding musicians invite us to discover a historical and musical epic set on the Manitoban frontier. Original compositions, native chants, gigues, reels, songs of the period, military marches and improvisation are woven to create the fabric of a vibrant work that combines politics and poetry. Music, chants, political texts and poetry surprise, delight and assert without compromise."

58. Joan Reid Acland, "The Native Artistic Subject and National Identity: A Cultural Analysis of the Architecture of the Canadian Museum of Civilization, Designed by Douglas J. Cardinal" (Ph.D., Concordia University, 1994) .

59. Laura Caso Barrera, "The Canadian Metis and the Mexican Maya as a Cross Cultural Study of Native Land Struggles" (M.A., University of Calgary, 1992).

60. Gregory Schofield, *Thunder Through My Veins Memories of a Metis Childhood* (Toronto: Harper Collins, 1999).

Les Desjarlais

The Development and Dispersion of a Proto-Métis Hunting Band, 1785–1870

HEATHER DEVINE

∿ The Role of the Freeman in Métis Ethnogenesis

The process of Métis ethnogenesis[1] has become one of the central topics in the study of fur trade social history. As John Foster has pointed out, the scholarship in this field has moved from the views of Marcel Giraud, who offered essentially biological explanations for the development of Métis ethnic identity, to a more sophisticated view that takes into account factors of ethnicity, religion, and class in the formulation of variable biracial ethnic identities.[2]

Unfortunately, the primary sources for fur trade social history on which we have based our understanding of ethnogenesis—the post journals, officers' correspondence, and servants' financial accounts—have intrinsic shortcomings. First of all, they are commercial documents that reflect the economic preoccupations, class prejudices, and cultural biases of the British officers who created them. As a result, they present incomplete and stereotypic portrayals of the labouring classes of the fur trade. Over the past 25 years, this problem has been ameliorated by studies that have focused on biracial populations designated as 'country-born'—groups descended primarily from British labourers and officers of the North West and Hudson's Bay companies. However, there continues to be a paucity of literature concerning the lives of the non-British labouring groups, particularly the large numbers of seasonally or irregularly employed *Canadien*, Indian, and biracial boatmen, freighters, provisioners, guides, and winterers on which the industry depended.[3]

The scarcity of usable data is particularly acute when attempting to understand the lives of freemen in the fur trade. The term 'freemen' was used to describe those *Canadien* and eastern Indian *engagés* who chose to end their employment in the direct service of the major trading companies and live independently, hunting and trapping alongside local native groups with whom they had established kin relations. It is the freeman populations of Rupert's Land from whom Plains Métis populations, by and large, are derived.[4]

Other biracial populations in other parts of North America were never completely successful in establishing themselves as separate ethnic entities apart from their European and aboriginal parent cultures. Why then, were separate and distinct Métis populations able to emerge and proliferate out of the roving bands of itinerant freemen in Rupert's Land?

John Foster suggested that the development of individual and groups as Métis, or as "country-born" lies in identifying and understanding the collective experiences shared by adult males, adult females, and family groups which translate into an ethnicity separate from that of other populations.[5] Jennifer Brown would appear to concur with this view, noting that the "relative importance and consistency of paternal and maternal ties, and the nature and strength of their attachments to the broader communities in which they were enmeshed, determined the trajectories these children would follow, moving outward from the variable contexts of their fur trade origins." Brown also notes that only the study and understanding of a wide range of individual and group experiences will lead to a broader understanding of the development of distinct mixed-race corporate identities.[6]

One way to approach these topics is to undertake a chronological study of a representative freeman family whose descendants occupy the racial and ethnic categories identified by Foster and Brown. Such a case study would highlight the environmental factors that influenced the cultural labels applied to (or adopted by) various family members.

With this goal in mind, this study explores the fur trade activities of one extended group of *Canadien* freemen, specifically the Desjarlais family in the Lesser Slave Lake region of Athabasca (now northern Alberta) between 1800–1830. The family's responses to stresses brought about by the years of competition between the Hudson's Bay Company (HBC) and the North West Company (NWC) will be examined, with particular emphasis on the cultural origins of the various adaptive behaviours adopted by particular family members. The paper will conclude by focussing on the dispersion of the family and the eventual fate of two brothers—the shaman Baptiste "Nishecabo" Desjarlais and his brother Antoine Desjarlais.

Baptiste "Nishecabo" Desjarlais, biracial son of Joseph Desjarlais, affiliated himself with Saulteaux culture and values, while his brother Antoine followed a typically Métis life course. This ethnic divergence within the same family suggests that the development of ethnic identity is a complex, dynamic process determined less by biology and initial socialization, and more by the individual survival strategies adopted in response to various environmental factors.

◆ The Freeman Ethos and Survival in the North West After 1760

Prior to 1760, the *Canadien* fur trade was carried on by small commercial partnerships that were granted *congés*, or trading licenses, for specific destinations for set periods of time. These small trading companies employed *engagés* to transport goods and people between the settlements on the St. Lawrence and their inland military posts. By the onset of the Seven Years' War (1754), French fortifications and settlements were established throughout the Great Lakes region and along the banks of the Mississippi. In addition to the establishments founded under the auspices of the French authorities, there existed several ad hoc communities established by traders deemed 'outlaws' by the French colonial authorities. In these communities, *habitant*s-voyageurs who had migrated southward from the St. Lawrence valley lived in peaceful coexistence with local aboriginal bands. There they practised subsistence agriculture and carried on commercial activities, both legal and extra-legal.[7]

After the 1760 capitulation of Montreal by the French during the Seven Years' War, the British eventually secured their claim to eastern North America via the Treaty of Paris and the Royal Proclamation of 1763. This signalled the end of *Canadien* domination of the inland fur trade.[8] For the small-scale *Canadien* merchants and their *engagés*, making the social connections and behavioural adjustments needed to compete successfully with the Anglo-Canadian traders was a difficult, if not impossible, task. First of all, the *Canadien* was French and not British. He was Roman Catholic and not Protestant. He had an affinity towards cohabitation and intermarriage with Native people, aided and abetted for generations by the clerics and governors of New France. His heritage and his upbringing prevented him from any real prospect of economic and social mobility in a British-dominated system, and he knew it. The *Canadien* was completely at odds with the values, attitudes, and modes of behaviour espoused by the British, and he was shrewd enough to realize that even in the unlikely event that he would willingly choose to adopt the behaviours expected of him, doing so would offer few, if any, tangible benefits.[9]

However, the role of cultural broker in the hinterland provided prestige, wealth (by wilderness standards), independence, and a surprising degree of power over the lives of both Europeans and Natives. As a result, many *Canadien engagés* directed their efforts towards establishing their autonomy as freemen—independent traders living outside the control of trading companies. In order to assume the role of broker apart from the trading company however, the freeman had to be successful in establishing an influential relationship with an aboriginal hunting band.

The dynamics of aboriginal hunting band formation[10] suggests that bands depended on the assumption of leadership by one or more male group members who possessed the combination of personal and spiritual attributes needed for group survival. It also suggests that an outsider, such as a *Canadien* male, would be required to demonstrate that he had personal qualities complementary to, but not supplanting, those already possessed by existing male members of a band before he would be permitted to marry one of their women *a la façon du pays*.

For most Euro-Canadians, their most attractive personal qualities were their race and language skills, which could be employed in a broker capacity with other Euro-Canadian traders if the stranger joined the group. Once admitted as a member of the band via union with a female band member, the *engagé* could assume a position of autonomy outside of the trading post sphere. His membership in the band provided him with protection from hostile natives and also insulated him from the violence of other Euro-Canadian traders who might wish to coerce him back into direct service. His membership in an aboriginal hunting band also provided him with access to the trade goods he needed to survive in the wilderness independently—at least until he was able to establish a family and create another band apart from his aboriginal kinsmen.

Until the freeman was able to establish himself independently, however, he had to establish himself with his Indian wife's relatives. To do this successfully he had to be contributing to the band's survival, which meant maintaining its dominance of hunting territories within a geographical region. These obligations required the freeman and his mixed-blood children to cultivate the cultural and spiritual attributes most admired and feared by other Native people.

Once a freeman had established himself and his mixed-blood children in a band apart from the aboriginal parent band, they continued to cultivate aboriginal values, attitudes, and modes of behaviour. These "proto-Métis" family groups were compelled to operate as aboriginal hunting bands, not only to maintain solidarity with their Indian relations but also to establish dominance over their own hunting territories.

The boundaries of band hunting territories became less fluid and more rigid as hunting pressures engendered by the fur trade compelled hunters to supply specific numbers of pelts based on externally determined exchange values for furs and not on the carrying capacity of the land. This in turn forced the newly-developed "proto-Métis" hunting bands to aggressively define and protect their hunting territories by establishing a position of dominance. This dominant position was maintained by its members demonstrating physical and spiritual power through the practise of aboriginal spirituality, physical dominance through warfare and individual tests of strength, and continued usufruct dominance of a region through maintenance of continued hunting success. Their dominance was reinforced and enhanced by the European traders, who designated successful hunters—of all ethnic stripes—as trading chiefs and bestowed upon them the symbols of dominance in the European context.

From the mid-eighteenth century to the end of the nineteenth, male members of the Desjarlais family of Louiseville, Quebec found work as *engagés* on the Great Lakes, in the territories along the Mississippi and Missouri rivers, and in the Hudson's Bay watershed. Only a few of these men, however, were able to establish separate lives for themselves outside the direct employ of the fur trade companies. These were the Desjarlais family members living as freemen in loosely knit bands in the remote regions of Rupert's Land. The lives of these freemen, well documented in the post journals of the Hudson's Bay Company, provide useful insights into the development and dispersion of freemen bands in response to various social and economic forces.

The Desjarlais clan, by and large, operated as a proto-Métis hunting band in an Ojibwa cultural tradition. The activities of the Desjarlais family in northern Alberta between 1800 and 1825, illustrate how they developed and employed the symbols of power in aboriginal and Euro-Canadian contexts to maintain their regional dominance. The eventual dispersion of branches of the Desjarlais clan in the Lesser Slave Lake region can, in turn, illustrate a significant stage in the process of Métis ethnogenesis—the moment when social upheaval caused individuals to coalesce into collectives apart from larger groups, to pursue different economic and political goals.

ᴂ Development of the Desjarlais Freeman Band

Joseph Desjarlais, Jr. (born 3 September 1754 at Contrecoeur, New France), the first son and namesake of Joseph Desjarlais, Sr. and Marie-Marguerite Hervieux, was the first Desjarlais known to have gone to Rupert's Land. Surviving records suggest that Joseph Desjarlais, Jr. contracted an alliance *a la façon du pays* with an Ojibwa woman named Okimaswew[11] within two years of his receipt of a trading pass to Grand Portage in 1783.[12] His brother Antoine Desjarlais (born ca. 1760 at Contrecoeur), engaged with David and Peter Grant in early 1792, and spent the next several years working for different firms affiliated with the NWC. He became a freeman in 1805 after the coalition of the NW and XY companies, trapping and trading in the vicinity of Red River.[13] In 1792 François Desjarlais, a relative, from Rivière-du-Loup, entered the service of McTavish Frobisher, and Company to go to the North

West.[14] By the early 1800s, Joseph, Antoine and François Desjarlais lived as freemen along the eastern slopes of the Rocky Mountains and on the shores of Lesser Slave Lake and Lac La Biche.

The elder Desjarlais brothers and their mixed-blood offspring soon enjoyed regular employment and success as fur suppliers, as hunters, as fishermen, as interpreters, and as guides with the NWC and later the HBC in the Athabasca region. To the chagrin of the Euro-Canadian *bourgeoisie* and clerks compelled by necessity to woo the Desjarlais and other freemen families wintering in the Athabasca hinterland, the success of these *hivernants* in hunting, trading, and forging alliances with local native groups gave the freemen the leverage over the English traders needed to extract trade goods, temporary employment, and other benefits from the competing trading firms as needed.

Because the Euro-Canadian fur traders were prevented from employing the usual methods of physical coercion that could be applied to recalcitrant servants in their employ, they were compelled instead to use persuasion, deception, and bribery to manipulate the behaviour of the freemen.

In July of 1810, Alexander Henry noted that members of the Desjarlais family and their hunting companions had come to borrow horses to go to Rocky Mountains and then to the Columbia, "where they hoped to find beaver as numerous as blades of grass on the plains." Henry attempted to thwart their plans, commenting, "I took much trouble in trying to make a division among those freemen, to prevent them from crossing the mountains, where they will be even a greater nuisance to us than they are here." A few days later, a frustrated Henry reported "Troubled with those mongrel freemen and Indians all day. No dependence is to be placed upon them; they have neither principles, nor honor, nor honesty, nor a wish to do well; their aim is all folly, extravagance, and caprice: they make worse mischief that the most savage Blackfeet in the Plains."[15] Although Henry did manage to discourage some from travel, by 3 September Joseph Desjarlais, Sr. (a.k.a. Old Joseph) and his stepson Tullibii[16] had arrived at White Earth House to borrow horses for the overland trip to the Columbia. Henry noted that:

> ...they propose to go toward the Rocky Mountains for the winter, and thence to the Columbia. These Freemen have formed extravagant ideas of the numbers of beaver to be found on the W side of the mountains. I fain would prevent them from going there, but in vain; they are bent on the undertaking, and no persuasion will change their minds.[17]

Prior to 1815, the activities of the freemen in the Lesser Slave Lake region appeared untouched by the struggle for control of the Athabasca fur trade.

There was occasional social intercourse between employees of both posts, and freemen appeared able to move freely between the two companies' establishments. However, this was to change, as the HBC, under the direction of ex-Nor'Wester Colin Robertson, spearheaded a push into Athabasca territory to establish for the first time a tangible company presence in the form of outposts manned by personnel ready and able to battle the NWC on its own terms.

The isolated skirmishes that had heretofore characterized the era of fur trade competition turned violent as the companies destroyed their competitors' buildings, stole their furs and trade goods, scared away the game needed for food, and threatened employees. Although, the freemen ostensibly benefitted from aspects of this competition, the fight for control of the trade also threatened to destroy their livelihood, and with it, the very existence of their families, as the stresses of competition undermined the social structures upon which their hunting bands were based.[18]

Prior to 1815 the NWC accounts, such as those of Alexander Henry the Younger, indicate that the family was affiliated primarily with that concern, though Antoine Desjarlais (a.k.a. Old Antoine) had begun to trade with the HBC by 1810.[19] However, by 1815, Antoine Desjarlais, mixed-blood son of Old Joseph Desjarlais, had engaged with the HBC. The abrupt switch in loyalty implies that the presence of two competing companies in the area made it possible for freemen to negotiate, for the first time, the best possible financial and labour arrangements for themselves, and also suggests that the much-heralded affection of *Canadien engagés* and freemen for the NWC was, in all likelihood, a union of convenience broken when the opportunity presented itself.

Clerk John Lewes of Lesser Slave Lake frequently recorded the comings and goings of two generations of Desjarlais family members in the period 1817–18. The elder generation consisted of *Canadien*-born brothers Old Joseph Desjarlais, whose home base was the east end of Lesser Slave Lake, Old Antoine Desjarlais, who settled at Lac La Biche, and their relative François Desjarlais. The second generation, most of whom appear to be Joseph's sons also camped at the east end of Lesser Slave Lake. They include Tullibii, the eldest (step) son of Old Joseph (born ca. 1784), Joseph Desjarlais, Jr., Baptiste (born ca. 1790), and Martial (a.k.a. Marcel). Only one brother, Antoine (born ca. 1792) lived apart from the family; his position of Fort Interpreter required him to reside at the post, but he appeared to have spent some time wintering with his family as well.

Old Joseph Desjarlais's son Antoine was employed as Fort Interpreter at Lesser Slave Lake during this period, a situation which benefitted both Lewes and *Les Desjarlais* in several ways. Lewes employed the versatile Antoine as interpreter at the post and as an *en derouine* trader to secure the furs of Plains Indian bands before the NWC could reach them. Through Antoine, Lewes also monitored the activities of Antoine's brothers and other relations, and used Antoine's influence to keep them away from NWC advances.[20]

John Lewes's journal entries for the period indicate that he sent Antoine and other men to the Desjarlais lodges to secure their furs and bring them to the posts safely. Whether these steps were taken to prevent the family from being robbed by the NWC on the way to the post, or because Lewes was unsure of their willingness to direct their hunts to him, is not clear. However, by mid February of 1819 Lewes had taken steps to bring the Desjarlais family securely within his sphere of influence.

> 17th Feb.... This afternoon François and Rochbleau returned from the Tulibiis tent by whom I Rec'd the following Furs sixteen Beaver, eighty Martin, two Otters two Foxes One Pound Castoreum. François informed me that he had left Baptiste Desjarlais in the Lake and that he wished People to be sent to meet him with Dogs to assist him to the House as he was obliged to have a Sledge himself. The cause of this young man's coming here is on account that I sent for him to engage to the HBCo. This step I have taken upon myself providing that it will meet with the approbation of the Governor when he is informed that it is out of mere necessity which obliges me to do so.

> Feb. 23. Sent off Antoine the Interpreter and François to meet Bapt. Desjarlais they returned in the Evening with the whole Family...

> Feb. 25... I this day had Baptiste Desjarlais engaged at the sum of two Thousand Livres pr Annum. This salary I make no Doubt will appear Enormous to the Eyes of the Governor in Chief and Committee but it was out of mere necessity which makes me take it upon myself to engage him for we are so unfortunately situated that unless we have him to hunt this Post as well as the Lives of the Companys Servants will be inevitably in danger, the Former of being abandoned and the Latter of Starvation.[21]

For the remainder of the winter of 1819 Baptiste was employed as Fort Hunter, while his brother Antoine acted as Interpreter and traded *en derouine* with the Iroquois and other aboriginal groups. Baptiste also appears to have acted as Fort Interpreter in his brother's absence. The post remained in constant communication with Desjarlais family members, who visited the post throughout the winter to bring furs and provisions, but also to report on their living conditions. Food shortages—a by-product of the overhunting engendered by trade competition—were common, and Lewes sent off provisions and ammunition to Lesser Slave Lake to ease the starvation of the families of Joseph Desjarlais, Jr. and Tullibii.[22]

Lewes's patronage of Desjarlais family members extended beyond provisions of employment and goods, as he appears to have designated Joseph Desjarlais's step-son Tullibii the Lesser Slave Lake trading chief by the spring of 1819.

> Sun. May 2—Men sent off with Bapt. they had met with Tolibee & Band coming to the House. I received by these two men Tolibii's Spring hunt consisting of 35 Beaver skins, and 7 lbs. of Castoreum... they soon arrived. I had the Tolibee Saluted with several discharges of Fowling Pieces as he is the Chief Trader of this Place & a man most interested for the Interest of the Company. I gave him a Chief's Equipt with a View to intice the Crees of this Place to put confidence in his greatness and to Listen to his Orations with more zeal in our Cause the Natives of this Place are all except three waiting his return at the East End of the Lake.[23]

The Lesser Slave Lake District Report provides this description of Tullibii:

> The name of the HBCo chief is Tulibii a Soteux by birth and of 34 years of age in Nature 5 feet 11 inches. His countenance denotes good nature and intelligence. He speaks French like a Canadian and dresses the same as the white people. In spring and fall he receives a full suit of the finest articles of clothing brought up (and a Keg of Indian Rum).[24]

The importance of the trading ceremony in cementing the leadership status of a band chief should not be underestimated. Although the presentation of a suit of European clothes might ostensibly mark the recipient as someone of importance in European eyes, the costume had important supernatural implications as well. One of the most influential spirit helpers in Ojibwa mythology is a character called the Sun. When the Sun appeared to a person in a dream, "he was dressed like a Gentleman, i.e. a short coat, waist coat, short breeches, stockings, boots a hat and a beautiful feather in it. He speaks English..." A chief "rigged" in these clothes might also be viewed as having received additional supernatural power.[25] A freeman such as Tullibii could enhance his stature and extend his influence amongst the regional hunting population simply by acquiring and manipulating these symbols of supernatural power.

Over time John Lewes had developed a firm friendship with Tullibii, and had tented with him and his family outside of the fort. In later years, Tullibii acknowledged his personal debt to John Lewes in a trading speech:

...I will always remain attached to you as I find myself well off—I am extremely proud that my conduct has been represented in so flattering a manner to the Company and approved of—I intend this year if success attends my hunting to go below to see the New Govr. I had thought before I entered here to receive your bounty of immediately returning it as none of my relations are now with me but upon further consideration I take them as the NW might make a scandal of it to ridicule me to relations and the Indians. I am ashamed to take the Presents as none of my relations are here to share it with me. But in spring I expect that many of them shall be here and then I shall use all my influence to prevent them going to war.—I heartily thank the Company for what they now give me and particularly you their Representative. I love you as I love myself for all your past kindnesses. I have served many traders but none like you.[26]

Tullibii's growing influence with John Lewes aided and abetted the ambitions of his younger half-brother Baptiste, who had already demonstrated prowess as a hunter and talent as an interpreter.

...all the Evening they Deverted themselves drinking. Bapt the Interpreter also Joined them, as the Tolibii is his Brother by the Mother's side. Late at night they all went over to the NW Fort where they all got fighting & Baptiste being intoxicated came off but second best.[27]

Journal entries for the following days describe Baptiste's subsequent dealings with the Nor'Westers:

Mon. May 3 ...Several Iroquois arrived this day at the NW Fort. One of this tribe sent over a challenge to Fight Bapt. but he was stopped from going to accept it as they are all intoxicated.

Tues May 4 ...Bapt. accordingly went over to the NW Fort to see if the Iroquois was in readiness to put his threats in execution he accordingly fought Bapt but could not keep his Ground as he was too weak. Bapt afterwards went into one of the Men's Houses when one of the NW men rushed into the House & struck Bapt who immediately returned the Compliment & knocked Him Down several others ran in & Held Bapt. while the others struck him McDonnell & Henry whe were Present Encouraging their People to this unequal Contest. But Bapt soon put an end to this unequal Contest by a compleat Victory over them all.[28]

The next day Lewes sent Baptiste to join his family at the east end of the lake, presumably to avoid further battles.

It is not clear whether Lewes allowed Baptiste to fight with the Iroquois as an indulgence, or whether it was done as a calculated move to establish Baptiste's influence over natives who might possibly be persuaded to join the HBC cause. In any case, Baptiste's stature in the eyes of both the Iroquois freemen and the Hudson's Bay British seems to have grown. By June of 1819 Baptiste Desjarlais was identified as the Fort Interpreter, and was trading *en derouine* with Iroquois freemen on behalf of the post. In the post journal of 7 August 1819, the clerk, William Smith, noted that Baptiste Desjarlais traded goods to an Iroquois *already* indebted to the Company, implying that Desjarlais should have extracted the skins without payment and applied them to the Iroquois outstanding debt. An exasperated Smith writes that he hopes Mr. Lewis will "impinge" upon Baptiste to "understand better not to do it again."[29]

Smith's frustration suggests that he was not in total agreement with John Lewes's management of the freemen under his employ, hinting that Baptiste had overstepped his bounds in negotiating deals with the Iroquois. The Lesser Slave Lake District Report provides an interesting perspective on Baptiste's rise to power:

> The Master of this District was under the disagreeable necessity of making (Nishecabo) Bapt. Desjarlais a half brother of Tulibiis a chief of the same consequence as the NWCo had made great offers to him to be their Chief—he is a very powerful man and of a daring ambitious disposition and on these accounts much feared by the Indians if he had not been made chief by Mr. Lewes he would have accepted the NWCo offers and left the HBCo with all his brothers and relations and by his influence among the Indians have put the HBCo to double the expense. These people know well how to take advantage of the times but it is to be hoped that a time will very soon come when these fellows will be more kept under by the power of a single trader...[30]

Although Baptiste's hunting abilities and physical strength impressed the Europeans, it is unlikely that his status among the traders was sufficient to establish him outside the post as a man of power in the eyes of the Indians. The possibility that Baptiste took steps to impress upon the natives of the region that his power was of supernatural origin should not be discounted.[31] It is only *after* Baptiste's exploits of 1819–20, when he assumes the mantle of trading chief, that he is identified by the name Nishecabo in the trade records. His assumption of his aboriginal name at this time suggests that he wished to impress upon others his supernatural links with his "spirit helpers."[32]

Although some of Joseph Desjarlais's métis sons were establishing them-selves as chiefs in the aboriginal tradition, others, such as Antoine Desjarlais the interpreter, chose to identify with their *Canadien* ancestry rather than their aboriginal heritage. This process was probably facilitated by the elder genera-tion of Desjarlais men, who maintained contact with their relatives in Quebec. Old Antoine Desjarlais, Master of the Post at Red Deer's Lake (Lac La Biche), was receiving letters from family members resident in Varennes.[33] There is other documentation that suggests that Old Antoine and Old Joseph Desjarlais travelled to Quebec for occasional visits. In the Lesser Slave Lake Post Journal of 1820, accountant Robert Kennedy recorded the following entry:

> ...Old [Joseph] Desjarlais who came up from Montreal with the NW canoes, he is the father of our interpreter and of several halfbreeds attached to the HBCo, he returned to the house with me to remain here for his family...[34]

This evidence flies in the face of most historic and modern depictions of *Canadien* freemen, who are portrayed invariably as northern "squawmen" who had abandoned all ancestral ties for an indolent life in the wild.[35]

The preference in cultural identification exhibited by Antoine Desjarlais —in sharp contrast to his brothers—appears to have caused Euro-Canadian observers such as Robert Kennedy to draw a distinction between Joseph Desjarlais's offspring. Antoine's behaviours also suggest that at least some of the first generation of "proto Métis" continued to identify with Euro-*Canadien* values and attitudes, a choice no doubt facilitated by their fathers' maintenance of family ties to Quebec. As long as mutual relations with kin and community were maintained, the mixed-race children of *engagés* were considered to be an extension of the much larger kinship network origi-nating in the French settlements on the St. Lawrence and the outposts along the Mississippi and Missouri, a tradition which was well-established by over 200 years of frontier exploration and diplomacy. From an "ethnogenesis" standpoint, mixed-race children were not yet a separate people.

For the Desjarlais family, maintaining Euro-Canadian links in the trading post via acculturated siblings was an important survival mechanism as well as a matter of personal preference for young Antoine. During times of hard-ship, having kin in the post ensured that pressure could be brought to bear to release ammunition, medicines, and other necessary provisions if needed.

Employment in a trading post also served to socialize the biracial chil-dren of freemen to Euro-Canadian values, attitudes, and behaviours, enhancing their ability to move freely between both cultures. Biracial *engagés*, and their sisters who had married Euro-Canadian traders, were able to exert a further socializing influence on their siblings and cousins living away from the post. Over time, these prolonged and intimate exposures to *both* cultural milieus served to distinguish mixed-race wintering families from Indian wintering groups, despite the hunting and gathering lifestyle that they both shared.

ᎬᏴ The Dispersion of the Desjarlais Freeman Band

The competition for control of the Athabasca fur trade caused animal populations to plummet. The HBC employees and freemen suffered constant harassment from the NWC. In addition to the threat of physical violence, disease took its toll on the Indians. During the fall and winter of 1819–20, a measles epidemic raced through the native population of Athabasca, killing 39 men, women and children, including five of Lewes's best hunters. Predictably, the supply of pelts from the winter's trade was small, and Lewes blamed the NWC, whom he suspected of deliberately introducing the disease into Athabasca to punish the natives for trading with the HBC.[36] This placed added stress on the freemen, particularly the trading chiefs, who were compelled by both pride and outstanding debt to produce pelts and provisions regardless of their own privations.

Over the winter of 1820–21, misfortune continued to dog both the HBC traders and the freemen. Reports of starvation and disease from isolated freemen bands wintering away from the post were not encouraging. Many of these freemen had contracted debts prior to the winter in anticipation of a successful winter's hunt. Their misfortunes over the winter resulted in a reduction of pelts and an outstanding debt in the spring that could not be paid off. The Desjarlais family fared no better. As accountant Robert Kennedy stated in the annual District Report:

> Nishecabo who was made chief last fall for the seasons then mentioned—
> Rec'd his usual presents at Red Deer Lake—and gave as a present in
> return 25 beavers—the Hunt of himself and his Band was not so much
> as was expected he himself gave 50 Beaver Skins but was unable to
> exert himself as he had promised as he had the venerial disease.—He
> with his Brothers and relations have since gone to L.S. Lake where
> they will remain.[37]

By 26 March 1821, the HBC and NWC officially amalgamated, ending the vicious competition that had characterized the Athabasca trade. John Lewes was appointed to the position of Chief Trader and transferred to the Columbia Department, while William Conolly became Chief Trader at Lesser Slave Lake, a post he assumed in August of 1821.[38]

Under the direction of Governor George Simpson, the traders began the task of systematizing and regularizing the day-to-day operations of the company with an eye to cutting staff and reducing expenses, which had ballooned out of control during the years of competition. Simpson had his eyes on the activities of the freemen for some time, and as early as 1820 had discouraged his traders from giving in to the freemen's demands for provisions, and had, in fact, encouraged his staff to avoid doing business with the freemen altogether.[39]

The new chief trader at Lesser Slave Lake, William Conolly, complied with these orders and began the task of scaling back privileges to freemen at the semi-annual trading ceremony of October 1821:

> Three of Desjarlais Sons, his son-in-law, Cardinal's son...the Old Tondre and 2 sons arrived with colors flying, firing....As these freemen took every advantage of the times & was completely spoilt during the opposition I thought it best to let them feel...that times had altered by receiving them rather coolly & presenting them with nothing more than each a foot of tobacco per man. In fact they got goods [at such a] cheap rate that its impossible to afford them anything greater....this of course they will not like....Most of the freemen in this quarter are greatly indebted to either, and some of them to both, the companies.[40]

By 10 December 1821 William Conolly had met Tullibii, the HBC trading chief, for the first time, noting sourly:

> ...This Tolibee was in immense debt which is absolutely impossible he will ever pay, he was one of Mr. Lewes *chiefs* & has been more spoilt than I believe any other. *He will of course feel* the changes that have taken place more severely than others.[41]

Over the winter of 1821–22 the freemen managed to improve their hunts, but not enough to alter Conolly's treatment of them.

> ...Their hunts are not great but Suffice to pay their Debts of this year. This Tullibii was one of Mr. Lewes chiefs and appears greatly disappointed at not meeting with his [former] treatment. Be this as it may he must endeavor to content himself with what he can get.[42]

Conolly appears to have dispensed with the spring and fall trading ceremonies shortly thereafter, as they do not appear in the records for 1821–22. The Desjarlais's fall from grace was not only rapid, but must have been humiliating as well. As Conolly notes in his District Report of 1821–22:

> ...the People who go under the Dinomination of Free Men....were, during the late opposition, accustomed to get goods to any amount

they pleased, and at very reduced prices. Besides this, several of those who traded with Mr. Lewes were Cloathed as Chiefs, received Large Kegs of strong Liquor as presents. And Many other things.— Moreover their Brains were stuffed with So many promises that their disappointment at not finding their expectations realized is scarcely to be described.[43]

In his report Conolly also made specific reference to Antoine Desjarlais, commenting that Desjarlais

...is a man of good abilities as an Interpreter, but being also a very good Hunter, the Company will reap more benefits from his labors as such than in a capacity in which his services are not now required.[44]

One can only imagine how the Desjarlais family must have reacted to the rapid collapse of their collective fortunes. In two short years Tullibi and Baptiste Desjarlais, the half-brothers who had achieved success as trading chiefs, had been stricken with starvation and disease and public humiliation, and stripped of the honours to which they had become accustomed. Joseph Desjarlais's son Antoine, who had chosen to pursue a life in the Euro-Canadian trading sphere, found his options for advancement within the HBC reduced, if not completely eliminated by his arbitrary demotion to hunter from interpreter by William Conolly.[45]

Antoine's reaction to the curtailment of his opportunities was swift. In the District Report of 1821–22 William Conolly reported:

Antoine Desjarlais and Primeau have both come out. The object of the former's trip is, I believe, to determine what encouragement the Red River holds out to people of his description, and if it answers his expectations, himself, his Brothers & and Brother-in-Law would retire thither, an act which would deprive Slave Lake of Six or Seven good hunters.[46]

It is not clear whether Antoine's fact-finding mission was an immediate success. Over the years that followed, the family began trapping with renewed zeal and, according to Conolly, "were determined to exert themselves to pay their debts."[47] The winter of 1823, however, brought with it the same bad fortune that had plagued the family in the previous winters:

About 11:00 a.m. Bte Desjarlais arrived half dead with hunger, he left his brother Joseph & their families yesterday morning in so weak a state that they were unable to move. The object of his trip is to beg a supply of provisions....Starvation is not the only misfortune they have....having lost 100 skins 80 of which were from Beaver, that were destroyed by Wolverines...year after year Caches are destroyed by wood animals, yet will these stupid Free Men, & particularly the Iroquois, continue to expose their furs in this foolish way...[48]

On 14 March 1823, Conolly reports on the Desjarlais family's declining fortunes further:

...They saw old Desjarlais & family at the East end of the lake almost dead with hunger & begging for God's Sake that I should send him some assistance without which they must surely perish.[49]

Conolly advanced the family some provisions and ammunition to relieve their distress. Despite the evidence of continued hardship among the freemen, Conolly persisted in his belief that the miniscule returns were the result of laziness on the part of the freemen.

...the rascals might have done much better had they been inclined to work....I attempted this spring to punish some for their laziness by refusing them a supply of ammunition for the Summer. This I am confident would have had a good effect were there no other place from whence they could obtain that article.[50]

By spring the Desjarlais families had moved to Lac La Biche in search of better hunting opportunities. Tullibi and his half-brother Antoine Desjarlais chose other pursuits:

Reached Lac La Biche at 2 p.m. and the Big Island at 6 where we found Old Desjarlais, his son Martial and Pembrook. They informed me that Tolibii, with Antoine Desjarlais and Antoine Allarie had joined a party of Crees...on a war expedition...[51]

The participation of Tullibii and Antoine Desjarlais in a Cree war expedition suggests that there was a need for the members of the Desjarlais family to reestablish their status with their native neighbours. It also suggests that they may have been attempting, along with the Crees, to expand their hunting territories by forcibly removing rival bands out of hunting areas they coveted for themselves.

As far as William Conolly was concerned however, the actions of the freemen were yet another example of their irresponsibility.

...The Coalition has had a good effect with regard to the Indians who saw the necessity of staying Industrious....But the Freemen are incorrigible. They are addicted to all kinds of vices. I have tried fair means with them in vain and I fear that nothing but the severest of measures will bring them to their senses. They are now anxiously expecting an American opposition,[52] and endeavor to instill the same notions into the minds of the Indians. As such stories tend to nourish that spirit of independence which was excited by the late Opposition, they must of course be injurious, and the propogation of them ought to be punished.[53]

By the fall of 1824 the same group of freemen was preparing to make war again, this time in the Columbia region, an area where, 14 years earlier, they had gone in search of beaver "as numerous as the grass on the plains." In George Simpson's journal entry of 21 September 1824 he reports on his visit to

...the Banks of Lake la Biche, where we found old [Antoine] Dejoilais the Freeman and his Family likewise Cardinals Family and a posse of Freeman and their followers. These people with a few Cutonais and Soteux were preparing to go on a War Expedition against a poor helpless inoffensive tribe of Indians "Shewhoppes" natives of the North branch of the Thompsons River knowing them to be weak and unprovided with the means of defense and solely with a view to plunder and gain renown as Warriors by taking a few Scalps without incurring danger. On these poor wretches they made a War a few Years ago and treacherously massacred a whole camp in the Mountain on their way to the Fort.[54]

However, Simpson would not tolerate such incursions because it interfered with his own plans to encourage the Shushwaps to cross the mountains to visit Rocky Mountain House in Athabasca Pass. Indeed, Simpson and his associates had finally recognized, to their dismay, that the freemen had become a serious threat to the long-term survival of the Company. Over time, trading relations with aboriginal groups had evolved to the point that *Canadien* and Iroquois *engagés*, speaking aboriginal languages and living *en derouine* with their native relatives, who were exercising control over the critical aspects of the trade. It was *Canadien* and Iroquois *engagés* who were agitating for improved working conditions and creating labour unrest in the firm. And it was *Canadien* and Iroquois freemen—mobile, skilled, and disloyal—who were encouraging desertion and inviting competition from the Americans to the south.[55] It was clear that something had to be done to neutralize the influence of the freemen and reestablish Company control over their activities. In the meantime, Simpson dealt with his most immediate problem—the Desjarlais family and their plans to make war in the Rocky Mountains.

> ...I therefore spoke my Mind very plainly to those freemen, told them we meant to protect the Shewhoppes and if they did not instantly abandon their cruel intentions they should not this winter have even a particle of ammunition at any of our Establishments and that next Season they should be bundled down to Canada where starvation & misery would follow them. This lecture had the desired effect and they promised that they would no longer entertain hostile feelings towards those people.[56]

During the July 1825 meeting of the governing council of the HBC's Northern Department, the following resolution was introduced into the Minutes:

> 89. That all Freemen Half breed or Iroquois Trappers having no other means of paying (for) their supplies than with their Hunts to be treated on the footing of Indians, unless where otherwise specially provided for by Council and that Freemen not coming under that description having Funds in the Companys hands and unable to pay their supplies with Furs, be charged 200 p. Cent on the District Inventory prices and that no money in payment of furs or other articles be allowed either class without directions from Council.[57]

It is probable that this policy targeting freemen, combined with Simpson's prior ban on their raiding activities, marked the end of the Desjarlais family's influence in the Lesser Slave Lake region. Their lack of outstanding fur returns had diminished their stature in the eyes of the new regime of traders, who were not prepared to develop the kind of patronage relationship they had enjoyed in the past with John Lewes. As a result Tullibii and Nishecabo lost their privileges as trading chiefs, and with it the favours and trade goods needed to maintain status among their followers. Their public diminishment by the traders, compounded by their lack of sustained hunting success, their loss of already harvested pelts through destruction of caches compounded by their bouts with starvation and serious illness, would have convinced their Indian allies and relations that the leaders of the various Desjarlais bands—particularly Tullibii and Nishecabo—had lost their spiritual power.

As A. Irving Hallowell has noted, there was no formalized mechanism for meting out punishment to individuals in Ojibwa society.[58] The "spirit helpers" in Ojibwa religion did not act to punish. Instead, the Ojibwa believed that a "spirit helper" withheld assistance from individuals who had morally transgressed. If a hunter committed a moral offense, it was believed that the hunters "spirit helpers" would not allow animals to be caught. There were also sanctions against cruelty to animals in Ojibwa culture. Unnecessary killing of animals, or causing them unnecessary suffering, was subject to sanction by spirit helpers, who would withdraw assistance to hunters guilty of this offense. In the Ojibwa worldview, the harvesting of animal pelts to exchange for trade goods (rather than to meet the basic needs for food and clothing), and the accidental destruction of pelts through carelessness could very easily be interpreted as a form of cruelty to animals. The downward spiral of game populations as a result of overhunting would be proof positive, from an aboriginal perspective, that the spirit helpers were punishing the hunters responsible for this unnecessary cruelty and waste.

The effect of Nishecabo's bout with venereal disease on his stature as a trading chief and shaman should not be discounted. In Ojibwa culture, it was believed that sickness was a punishment for bad conduct on the part of an individual. In particular, any serious illness of unknown origin which proved resistant to treatment was believed to the result of immoral or unethical dealings or the violation of taboos. His contemporaries would have assumed that he was being punished for misconduct as a hunter, or for abusing his powers as a shaman, or for not exhibiting the qualities of generosity expected of a band leader.[59]

Governor Simpson's ban on warring against rival groups effectively prevented *Les Desjarlais* from renewing their status as leaders or gaining access to new hunting territories where they might experience renewed hunting success. As a result, the family was denied the only mechanism remaining that would have enabled them to retain their followers and maintain their cohesion in that region. As Roger McDonnell has concluded:

> ...bands were political units that assembled around the promise of benefits associated with the abilities of particular individuals. These abilities were understood to be a manifestation of spiritual powers that were employed for the benefit of others. If such benefits diminished—so, too, might the band: if they increased—so might the number of would-be beneficiaries.[60]

Simpson's threat that the Desjarlais would "be bundled down to Canada where starvation & misery would follow them" was strangely prescient. In

1825 Marguerite Desjarlais Langevin[61] (b. 1766), the sister of Old Joseph and Old Antoine Desjarlais, had applied for curatorship[62] over her siblings' landholdings in the parish of Varennes, stating that her male relatives had no intentions of returning to Lower Canada to live. Had the now-elderly Desjarlais brothers attempted to return to Lower Canada with their native wives and children, they would have found themselves disinherited. Their choices had run out.

For the Desjarlais family, the opportunities for bettering themselves and their families had ended in the Lesser Slave Lake area, and in Lower Canada as well. Over the next few years the names of Desjarlais family members disappear from the Lesser Slave Lake post records, suggesting that their regional political influence diminished and that the bands headed by the two former Desjarlais trading chiefs disintegrated. By April of 1827 a new HBC trading chief, Le Maigre, was rigged in chief's clothes and given rum.[63]

Where the various branches of the Desjarlais family went is unclear. Some Desjarlais who had intermarried with other freemen families, such as the Cardinal family, remained on the shores of Lesser Slave Lake and Lac La Biche, where their descendants can be found today.[64]

However, there is ample evidence to confirm that Joseph Desjarlais and his sons *did* eventually choose to travel eastward in search of new opportunities. References to various members of the Desjarlais family appear in the post journals for Cumberland House (1827–28); Carleton (1828–30), at Fort Pelly (1830–34), and at the Fishing Lakes along the Qu'Appelle River (1833–34).[65] Old Joseph's son, Antoine Desjarlais, established two independent trading establishments. The first was a large stockade called Fort Desjarlais on the Souris River near present-day Brandon, Manitoba, which he operated with his brother Marcel, his son, Baptiste, his sons-in-law, Charles DeMontigny, Eusebe Ledoux and Simon Blondeau, and over 70 other inhabitants. The second one was a small post on the Souris River near present-day Minot, North Dakota.[66] Those family members that chose not to trade settled at the mission of St. Paul-des-Sauteux (a.k.a. Baie St. Paul and later St. François Xavier in the Red River Settlement).[67] Here they raised their families and participated in semi-annual buffalo hunts with other Métis hunters resident in the parish.

After the Red River Resistance of 1869, several Desjarlais families migrated to the Qu'Appelle Valley in Saskatchewan from Baie St. Paul, among them the family of Baptiste "Nishecabo" Desjarlais who settled at Little Fork, Qu'Appelle Lake. Despite having settled in more-or-less Christianized surroundings after leaving Lesser Slave Lake in the 1820s, there is evidence to suggest that Baptiste "Nishecabo" continued to practise aboriginal spirituality while at Red River,[68] and later in Saskatchewan.

Former HBC clerk Isaac Cowie provides this interesting, but poignant description of Nishecabo's last days:

Among the freemen wintering about the lake was one of the wide-spread Disgarlais families, but decidedly more Saulteau than French in tongue and tone. The father, named Wah - ween - shee - cap - po, was a giant in size and ancient in days and devilment. When one of his grandchildren had died during the previous summer, in his grief and rage old Disgarlais, arming himself with his long flintlock, with powder-horn and ball-pouch slung over his shoulders, commenced blazing away at the sun, challenging the power up there to "come down and fight him like a man instead of killing innocent children". As a professor of Indian medicine and black art in general he was dreaded, and he appeared to have the faculty of either hypnotizing or putting himself in a trance, lying so long in that state that during that winter his sons twice though he was really dead and came to the post for material to bury him. On both these occasions he came to life again after two or three days, during which he said he had visited spirit-land, of which he related his experiences to his fascinated and awestruck family and audience. By the time he fell into the third trance, or actually died that winter, his sons had no occasion to come to the post for winding sheet or coffin nails. The grave had also been dug ready; so, when he once more became apparently dead, his sons lost no time in nailing him down in the coffin and sinking him in a deep grave and covering him with earth. Then they poured water thereon so as to freeze him down in case he should come to life once more to terrorize his panic-stricken and superstitious descendants.[69]

It is apparent that Nishecabo Desjarlais continued to cling to an aboriginal *persona* throughout his life, and remained a Saulteux in his soul despite the fact that most members of the Desjarlais family, including members of his immediate family, would be legally designated as Métis after 1885.[70]

For Nishecabo Desjarlais, the gravitation to a life as a Saulteux shaman was a natural response to an environment where options for personal well being were expanded or diminished by factors outside of one's control. The lure of shamanism (or what may have seemed like the "dark side" to his Christianized kinsmen) offered an opportunity to overcome obstacles and become a person of power, a "man of consequence," In exchange for this power, Nishecabo was compelled by Ojibwa beliefs to treat animals and human being with respect. During the years of competition in Lesser Slave Lake, when violence against animals and man was the rule rather than the exception, Baptiste appeared to violate these beliefs, and suffered the life-long consequences of these spiritual violations through disease and loss of influence. That Baptiste believed this himself is suggested by his reaction to his grandchild's death.[71] Why else would he vent his anger by shooting at the Sun—the Ojibwa "spirit-helper" most associated with European traders?

Antoine Desjarlais, the brother who appeared to identify most closely with his Euro-Canadian ancestry, also found his way to the Qu'Appelle Valley. By 1871 Old Antoine came to live at Father DeCorby's mission at Lebret, on the shores of Qu'Appelle Lake, where he survived by doing "odd jobs." In the winter of 1872, "faithful to the end" he burned to death trying to save objects from the mission, which was completely destroyed by fire.[72]

❧ Their Own Boss: the Emergence of the Métis People

Canadien freemen were *engagés* who had managed to establish a measure of commercial autonomy for themselves apart from the established trading companies. In doing so, they were heirs to the entrepreneurial *ethos* fostered in the early days of New France, where only those who were daring, ambitious, and skilled could achieve the notoriety and wealth needed to become "a man of consequence" in *Canadien* society. In order for freemen to maintain their independence, enhance their status, and ensure the physical and social well-being of their families, it was necessary for them to establish their dominance over the fur trade in the areas where they lived. Freemen bands functioned best when they could maintain familial relations with adjacent Indian bands and with personnel at Euro-Canadian trading companies *simultaneously*, a task best accomplished when individual family members contracted marriages *à la façon du pays*, secured employment in trading posts, and wintered with Indian bands. Having family members in both environments facilitated the free flow of goods back and forth, enabling individual freemen to profit from their role as fur brokers between their Indian kin and Euro-Canadian traders, while ensuring a steady and generous supply of the desired European trade goods through their relatives employed in the posts.

Should real or fictive kin relations not enable freemen to achieve the economic goals of themselves or their relatives, their strategies would be adjusted accordingly. In choosing alternative methods, they selected from both the aboriginal or Euro-Canadian cultural repertoire, as individual inclination, talent or immediate circumstances dictated. One or two family members might seek power and influence amongst local Indian bands as shamans, hunters or warriors, forcibly moving into hunting territories through the threat of physical violence, sorcery, or hunting skill. Other family members, in the meantime, applied pressure to the trading companies by threatening to work for opposing firms, by withdrawing their service as *engagés*, interpreters, and hunters, or by pressuring other *engagés* to desert.

They used their mobility to avoid Euro-Canadian trade sanctions, and manipulated their kin connections to foment discontent amongst the local natives.

These techniques, however, only worked in an environment where freemen's services were deemed to be essential and irreplaceable, or where the freemen could gain access to alternative, competing markets or employment. Unfortunately for the Desjarlais and other families like them, the ability to manipulate working conditions in their favour began to disappear as Anglo-North American corporate monopolies took the place of Montreal-based companies, and as the national boundaries of Canada and the United States shifted to annex and subjugate wilderness areas.

The temporary decline of the Desjarlais family fortunes were, in large part, due to new policies implemented by the HBC after 1821 intended to "systematize and regularize" its business practices, and consolidate its trade monopoly in Rupert's Land. To achieve this objective, the company needed to control the activities of individuals both inside and outside of the direct employ of the firm. A key element of its strategy was the development of policies targeted at individuals and groups identified as "freemen," "half-breed," or "Indian," intended to undermine their power, influence and autonomy by restricting access to essential goods and services. In doing so, the HBC inaugurated a lengthy tradition of corporate and government ascription of aboriginal identity, and indigenous resistance to same.

In the eyes of the politicians and company officials who assumed almost complete control over the lives of the inhabitants of Rupert's Land,[73] the *Canadien* freemen and their mixed-race descendants were anachronisms, holdovers of a defunct French empire which had been supplanted by Anglo-Scots in the North and Anglo-Americans to the south. The new rulers of the West were imbued with the positivism of an emerging industrialism and the nascent racism of the nineteenth century. They could not understand or accept a people who were accustomed to moving freely between one set of cultural practices and another, and did so willingly. They were not prepared to allow freemen and their mixed-race children a destiny that would enable them to sustain their ties with their Indian kin. Nor were they prepared to accept these mixed-race people into their settlements to live on an equal footing with their fellow citizens.

The period between 1821 and 1830 was a time of economic and social transition for the Desjarlais family and other freemen in Rupert's Land. Despite the initial hardships brought about by the HBC monopoly, however, the unique skills of the freeman remained indispensable. The continued trade in pemmican and buffalo robes, so essential to the survival of the HBC, soon brought a degree of economic prosperity to those freemen who chose to remain in Rupert's Land with their native wives and children. As time and distance slowly eroded their kin relations with their families in Lower Canada and their tribal kin in Rupert's Land, stronger kinship bonds were established with other freemen families. In one or two generations, thriving new communities whose cultural, political, and economic *ethos* embodied the nexus of European and aboriginal values, attitudes, and behaviours had become well established.

Subsequent economic and political policies, hostile to the very survival of these fledgling mixed-race communities, aggravated the widening social distance between their aboriginal and European parent communities, culminating in military and political conflicts that further strengthened their sense of separateness. In retrospect, it was inevitable that these separate biracial groups would coalesce into a corporate entity that could mobilize to protect the economic, cultural and political interests they shared. This new people would come to be known to the Europeans as Métis. To their Cree relations, however, they remained *Otipemsiwak*—"the people who own themselves."

Notes

1. The term "ethnogenesis" has been used by scholars "to refer to a people who seem to come into being as a definable group, aggregate, or category at some point in history—The concept of syncretism—the blending of distinct, even contrasting, systems of culture to form a novel system—is a salient feature of ethnogenesis, when the phenomenon dealt with is a definable or stipulated people, rather than an institution or set of institutions." See Norman E. Whitten, Jr., "Ethnogenesis," in David Levinson and Melvin Ember, eds., *The Encyclopedia of Cultural Anthropology* (New York: Henry Holt and Company 1996), 407–10.

2. John E. Foster, "Some Questions and Perspectives on the Problem of Métis Roots" in Jacqueline Peterson and Jennifer S.H. Brown, eds., *The New Peoples: Being and Becoming Métis in North America.* (Winnipeg: The University of Manitoba Press, 1985), 73–91. See also Sylvia Van Kirk " 'What if Mama is an Indian?' The Cultural Ambivalence of the Alexander Ross Family" in Jacqueline Peterson and Jennifer S.H. Brown, eds., *The New Peoples: Being and Becoming Métis in North America* (Winnipeg: The University of Manitoba Press, 1985), 207–8.

3. Foster, "Some Questions and Perspectives," 74; Jacqueline Peterson and John Anfinson, "The Indian and the Fur Trade: A Review of Recent Literature," in William R. Swagerty, ed., *Scholars and the Indian Experience: Critical Reviews of Recent Writing in the Social Sciences* (Bloomington: Indiana University Press, 1984), 244, 248.

4. John E. Foster, "Wintering, the Outsider Adult Male and the Ethnogenesis of the Western Plains Metis," *Prairie Forum* 19, no. 1 (Spring 1994): 3–4. (Also included here as Chapter 8.) For a contemporary description of freemen, as viewed by Hudson's Bay Company personnel, see Hudson's Bay Company Archives (HBCA), B.115/e/3 *Lesser Slave Lake Report on District 1819–1820.*

5. Foster, "Some Questions and Perspectives," 82–87.

6. See Jennifer Brown, "Diverging Identities: The Presbyterian Métis of St. Gabriel Street, Montreal," in Jacqueline Peterson and Jennifer S.H. Brown, eds., *The New Peoples: Being and Becoming Métis in North America* (Winnipeg: The University of Manitoba Press, 1985), 204.

7. See Jacqueline Peterson, "Many Roads to Red River: Métis Genesis in the Great Lakes Region, 1680–1815," in Jacqueline Peterson and Jennifer S.H. Brown, eds., *The New Peoples: Being and Becoming Métis in North America* (Winnipeg: The University of Manitoba Press, 1985), 39–46.

8. See Harold A. Innis, *The Fur Trade in Canada* (Toronto: The University of Toronto Press, 1956), 188–200. See also Gordon Charles Davidson, *The North West Company* (New York: Russell & Russell, 1967), 3–31.

9. A detailed discussion of the closely-knit and conservative Montreal merchant élite and its failure to adjust to the new economic climate after the British Conquest is featured in José Igartua, "The Merchants of Montreal at the Conquest: Socio-Economic Profile," *Histoire Sociale-Social History* 8, no. 16 (November 1975): 275–93. For a comparison of *Canadien* versus British relations with Amerindian groups see Robert J. Surtees, "Canadian Indian Policies," in Wilcomb B. Washburn, ed., *Handbook of North American Indians: History of Indian-White Relations*, Vol. 4 (Washington: Smithsonian Institution, 1988), 81–88.

10. There is an extensive literature devoted to band societies and their subsistence cycles which provides background documentation to this theoretical discussion of Euro-Canadian integration into aboriginal hunting bands. Sources cited for this article include A. Irving Hallowell, "Northern Ojibwa Ecological Adaptation and Social Organization," and "Ojibwa Ontology, Behavior, and World View," from *Contributions to Anthropology: Selected Papers of A. Irving Hallowell* (Chicago: University of Chicago Press, 1976), 334–36; 383–85, and A. Irving Hallowell, *The Role of Conjuring in Saulteaux Society* (Philadelphia: University of Pennsylvania Press, 1942), 7–29. See also Jennifer S.H. Brown and Robert Brightman, eds., *"The Orders of the Dreamed": George Nelson on Cree and Northern Ojibwa Religion and Myth, 1823* (Winnipeg: University of Manitoba Press, 1988), 8–9, 71, 120, 145; Roger McDonnell, "Paper on Band Formation Used as Supporting Evidence in the Bill C-31 Litigation," (Unpublished manuscript on file, Department of History and Classics, University of Alberta, n.d.), 37–48, 50, 51–54; G. Williams, ed., *Andrew Graham's Observations on Hudson's Bay, 1767–91* (London: Hudson's Bay Record Society, 1969), 169–70, as quoted by Arthur J. Ray and Donald Freeman in *'Give Us Good Measure': An Economic Analysis of Relations Between the Indians and the Hudson's Bay Company Before 1763* (Toronto: University of Toronto Press, 1978), 15, 17. The detailed analysis of NWC clerk George Nelson's kin relations with, and obligations to, his native family, as provided in Jennifer S.H. Brown's "Partial Truths: A Closer Look at Fur Trade Marriage" in this volume, supports this author's contention that acceptance by male band members was a prerequisite to any marriage *à la façon du pays*.

11. See Fr. Pierre Picton to Mr. Coté, Saint-Norbert, Manitoba dated 12 September 1947. Desjarlais Family File. *Pierre Picton Papers*, La Société St. Boniface, St. Bonifaee, Manitoba.

12. In 1783 there is record of a trading pass to Grand Portage granted to Joseph Desjarlais and Baptiste Plante, who were permitted to take one canoe with "five men, 60 gallons of rum, 4 fusils, 70 pounds gunpowder, one cwt. shot, etc. valued at £100". See Gordon Charles Davidson, *The North West Company* (New York: Russell & Russell, 1967), 23. See also Innis, *Fur Trade in Canada*, 198.

13. Harry Duckworth, Winnipeg, Manitoba to the Author, Monday 30 March 1998 re engagements of Antoine Desjarlais. Private Correspondence in the Collection of the Author. See also *Rapport de la Province du Québec (RAPQ)* 1942–43: 318, 356. As Elliott Coues noted, there were at least two *Canadien* Antoine Desjarlais in the North West

in this period. See E. Coues, ed., *New light on the early history of the greater Northwest: The Manuscript Journals of Alexander Henry the Younger and David Thompson 1799–1816*, 2 vols. (Minneapolis: Ross & Haines, Inc. 1965), 1: 237, n.6. See also W. Kaye Lamb, *The Journal of Gabriel Franchère* (Toronto: The Champlain Society, 1969), 167–68.

14. See *RAPQ 1942–43*: 313, for the 14 June 1792 engagement of François Desjarlais with McTavish Frobisher to "aller au Nord". Previous genealogical research by Father Pierre Picton has identified François Desjarlais as the younger brother of Joseph and Antoine Desjarlais, baptised at Contrecoeur on 7 August 1771 in the presence of his parents Joseph Desjarlais and Marie-Marguerite Hervieux. However, a burial certificate, dated 27 February 1784 for François Jarlais, aged eleven, son of Joseph Jarlais of Rivière-du-Loup, suggests that Joseph and Antoine's younger brother died during childhood. Therefore, the *engagé*-turned-freeman named Antoine Desjarlais may not be the sibling of Joseph and Antoine, but is a relative, probably a first cousin. See *Programme De Récherche en Démographie Historique* (hereafter PRDH), website (2001) http://www.genealogy.umontreal.ca l'Université de Montréal, Québec, Record #727141—Baptismal Record of François Desjarlais; and PRDH Record #548536—Burial Record of François Jarlais.

15. See Elliott Coues, *New light*, Vol. II, 609–14.

16. According to surviving accounts Tullibii was 34 years of age in 1820, which would place his birthdate approximately 1786. Because these accounts indicate repeatedly that Joseph Desjarlais's sons by this woman were Tullibii's half-brothers, Tullibii would appear to be Joseph's stepson. See HBCA, B.115/e/1, Lesser Slave Lake Report on District 1819–1820, sec. III for a description of Tullibii.

17. By 26 September 1810 Henry was headed towards the mountains, where various members of the Desjarlais family, including Joseph Sr., his son Baptiste (born ca. 1787), and Joseph's brother (or nephew) Francois were wintering with David Thompson at Rocky Mountain House and engaged in hunting and trading with the Peigans and Sarcees. See Elliott Coues, *New light II*: 659–91.

18. There are several scholarly monographs that discuss the activities of freemen (and the Desjarlais in particular) in the Lesser Slave Lake area. One article that focusses exclusively on the effects of trading competition and monopoly on freemen bands is Trudy Nicks "Native Responses to the Early Fur Trade at Lesser Slave Lake" in Bruce Trigger, Toby Morantz, and Louise Dechêne, eds., *Le Castor Fait Tout: Selected Papers of the Fifth North American Fur Trade Conference* (Montreal: Lake St. Louis Historical Society, 1987), 278–310. See also D.R. Babcock, "Lesser Slave Lake: A Regional History" (unpublished manuscript on file, Historic Sites Service, Historic Sites and Cultural Facilities Division, Alberta Community Development); W.P. Baergen, "The Fur Trade at Lesser Slave Lake, 1815–1831" (M.A. Thesis, University of Alberta, 1967); and Edward J. McCullough and Michael Maccagno, *Lac La Biche and the Early Fur Traders* (Edmonton: Canadian Circumpolar Institute, 1991).

19. Harry Duckworth to the Author, Monday 30 March 1998.

20. On 9 December 1817, Lewes notes "This evening Joseph Desjarlais arrived from his father's tent." On 11 December, Lewes states "This morning Jos. Desjarlais returned to his tent and three NWt. with him. I accordingly sent off Antoine and one man after them." See HBCA, B.115/a/1, Lesser Slave Lake Post Journal 1817–1818; B.115/a/2, Lesser Slave Lake Post Journal 1818–1819.

21. HBCA, B.115/a/2, Lesser Slave Lake Post Journal 1818–1819.

22. Ibid., see entries for 10 March and 3 April 1819.

23. Ibid.

24. HBCA, B.115/e/3, Lesser Slave Lake Report on District 1819–1820.

25. As described by trader George Nelson in Brown and Brightman, *"The Orders of the Dreamed,"* 50. Brown and Brightman also noted that George Nelson was the first person to place on record the only known identification of The Sun with the Euro-

Canadian traders, as this spirit speaks English, wears English clothing, and possesses the power to repair firearms. See page 113.

26. HBCA, B.115/a/4, Lesser Slave Lake Post Journal 1820–1821. In this passage it is clear that Tullibii was well aware of his responsibilities as chief and benefactor to his followers, in that he expressed regret at not being able to immediately redistribute the wealth among them.

27. HBCA, B.115/a/2, Lesser Slave Lake Post Journal 1818–1819.

28. Ibid.

29. HBCA, B.115/a/3, Lesser Slave Lake Post Journal 1819–20.

30. HBCA, B.115/e/3, Lesser Slave Lake Report on District 1819–20.

31. Northern Algonkians believed that spirit helpers could take on a variety of human, animal, or other forms in real-life encounters. From a spiritual perspective, the seemingly impossible victory of Baptiste Desjarlais in a trading post brawl over impossible odds is the kind of everyday event which assumes supernatural implications when other corroborating events take place. See Brown and Brightman, *"The Orders of the Dreamed,"* 120.

32. Ojibwa children were always given names by their grandfathers, or a member of their grandfathers' generation; "the name carries with it a special blessing because it has reference to a dream of the human grandfather in which he obtained power from one or more of the other-than-human grandfathers." See A. Irving Hallowell, "Ojibwa Ontology, Behavior, and World View," in *Contributions to Anthropology: Selected Papers of A. Irving Hallowell*, 360.

33. See W.K. Lamb, *The Journal of Gabriel Franchère*, 167–68, where Franchère encounters Antoine Desjarlais and reads his letters for him, due to his illiteracy. It is possible that Antoine Desjarlais made this request of Franchère due to shared family and community ties. Gabriel Franchère's cousin, Thercille Franchère, married Jean-Baptiste Picotte, son of Jean Picotte and Hélène Desjarlais. Hélene Desjarlais, the daughter of Louis Desjarlais and Catherine Banliac Lamontagne, was a first cousin to both Antoine and Joseph Desjarlais. See PRDH Record # 361435 — Marriage of Jean Baptiste Picot and Hélène Dejarlais, 20 October 1775, Louisville, P.Q.

34. HBCA, B.115/a/4, Lesser Slave Lake Post Journal 1820–21. See also "List of Families Supported at the Company's Establishments in English River District," HBCA, B.89/a/7, Ile-à-la-Crosse Post Journals 1823–24, where Antoine Desjarlais, steersman at Lesser Slave Lake, is identified as residing in Canada during 1823–24.

35. Frederick Merk described freemen as follows: "They were usually worn-out voyageurs...[who]...chose to remain in the Indian country living among the natives. Shiftless and irresponsible, they found in the Indian country refuge both from the necessity of regular labor and the restraints of civilized life." See Frederick Merk, *Fur Trade and Empire*, rev. ed. first published in 1931 (Cambridge, Mass.: Harvard University Press, 1968), 20.

36. McCullough and Maccagno, *Lac La Biche and the Early Fur Traders*, 95–102.

37. HBCA, B.115/e/2, Lesser Slave Lake Report on District 1820–1821.

38. See R. Harvey Fleming, ed. *Minutes of Council Northern Department of Rupert Land, 1821–31* (Toronto: The Champlain Society, 1940), 2–7. See also McCullough and Maccagno, *Lac La Biche and the Early Fur Traders,* 103–4.

39. See Rich, ed., *Journal of Occurrences in the Athabasca Department*, 68.

40. See HBCA, B.115/a/5, Lesser Slave Lake Post Journal 1821–22.

41. Ibid.

42. Ibid., 18 March 1822.

43. HBCA, B.115/e/3, Lesser Slave Lake Report on District 1821–22.

44. Ibid.

45. In the post-coalition HBC, mixed ancestry hampered one's opportunities for advancement. As the uneducated son of a *Canadien freeman*, Antoine would have had

no future whatsoever outside of a labouring capacity. See Jennifer Brown, *Strangers in Blood: Fur Trade Company Families in Indian Country* (Vancouver: University of British Columbia Press, 1980), for her discussions of social mobility and mixed-blood populations. See also Frederick Merk, *Fur Trade and Empire*, xli–xliii, for a summary of the organizational hierarchy of the Hudson's Bay Company after 1821.

46. HBCA, B.115/e/3, Lesser Slave Lake Report on District 1821–22.

47. HBCA, B.115/a/6, Lesser Slave Lake Post Journal 1822–23.

48. Ibid., Friday, 25 February 1823.

49. Ibid.

50. HBCA, B.115/e/4, Lesser Slave Lake Report on District 1822–1823.

51. HBCA, B.115/a/6, Lesser Slave Lake Post Journal 1822–23, 9 June 1823.

52. See HBCA, B.89/a/7, Ile-a-la-Crosse Post Journals, where George Keith notes on Sunday 14 December 1823 that "the Plains Cree of the Saskatchewan acquaint them [the local woodland Cree] that there is an American Party (probably the Scientific & Exploratory Expedn that reached Red River in August last) have reached the skirts of the Rocky Mountain and is selling large Blankets for only 5 Muskrats apiece and other articles in a like proportion! Hence they conclude and were strongly assured by the above informants, that they will soon see an opposition in this Country." It is obvious that this news was spreading like wildfire amongst the natives and freemen of Rupert's Land.

53. HBCA, B.115/e/4, Lesser Slave Lake Report on District 1822–1823.

54. See Merk, *Fur Trade and Empire*, 20.

55. For a regional perspective on these issues, see William R. Swagerty and Dick A. Wilson, "Faithful Service Under Different Flags: A Socioeconomic Profile of the Columbia District, Hudson's Bay Company and the Upper Missouri Outfit, American Fur Company, 1825–1835", in Jennifer S.H. Brown, W.J. Eccles, and Donald P. Heldman, eds., *The Fur Trade Revisited: Selected Papers of the Sixth North American Fur Trade Conference, Mackinac Island, Michigan, 1991* (East Lansing: Michigan State University Press, 1994), 243–67. See also Edith I. Burley, *Servants of the Honourable Company: Work, Discipline and Conflict in the Hudson's Bay Company, 1770–1879* (Toronto: Oxford University Press, 1997), 85–96; and Fleming, ed., Minutes of Council Northern Department of Rupert Land, xi–lxxii, which discuss, in some detail, the strategies adopted by the Hudson's Bay Company to manage *Canadien engagés*, curtail costs and neutralize American competition.

56. Merk, *Fur Trade and Empire*, 22.

57. Fleming, ed., Minutes of Council Northern Department of Rupert Land, 120.

58. A. Irving Hallowell, "Ojibwa World View and Disease," 391–444.

59. Ibid., 418–19.

60. McDonnell, "Paper on Band Formation Used as Supporting Evidence in the Bill C-31 Litigation," 67–68.

61. Marguerite Desjarlais (born at Sorel on 28 February 1766) married Isidore Langevin at Varennes on 9 July 1782. Another sister, Judith (born at Sorel August 29, 1758) married her second husband, Louis-Augustin Fontaine dit Bienvenu at Varennes on 7 May 1802. See Société Canadiennes Français, "Généalogie de Gerlaise-Desjarlais," 81–82. One of these sisters was writing to Antoine while he was at Lac La Biche, as Gabriel Franchère noted in June of 1814: "He [Desjarlais] asked me to read two letters that he had in his possession for two years without finding anyone able to read them. They were dated from Varennes and were from one of his sisters." See Coues, ed., *New light*, 1, 237, n.6. See also Lamb, *Journal of Gabriel Franchère*, 167–68.

62. See Curatelle #525, dated 21 October 1825. "Tutelles et Curatelles," Archives Nationales du Québec à Montréal (microfilm #s 1800–1841), as quoted in "Absents-Curatelles de Personnes Absentes du District de Montréal du 03-09-1794 -

30–03–1830." Unpublished manuscript on file, St. Boniface Historical Society, Winnipeg.

63. HBCA, B.115/a/8, Lesser Slave Lake Post Journal 1826–1827.

64. Historian Marcel Giraud noted that by 1880, the 300 Metis who lived around Lac La Biche could all trace descent, mainly through marriage between relatives and in-laws, from the old *Canadien* freemen Cardinal and Desjarlais. As quoted in McCullough and Maccagno, *Lac La Biche and the Early Fur Traders*, 84–85.

65. These references are summarized in Laura Peers, *The Ojibway of Western Canada, 1780 to 1870* (Winnipeg: University of Manitoba Press, 1994), 104–7, 109–14.

66. Although an elderly Métis informant named Filoman Lafontaine identified Fort Desjarlais as having been built by one Joseph Desjarlais, the men she identifies as Joseph Desjarlais's sons-in-law are actually the sons-in-law of his brother *Antoine* Desjarlais, according to genealogical data. Moreover, parish records for Joseph Desjarlais, Jr., his wife Josephte Cardinal and their children indicates that Joseph Jr., his wife and children remained in the Lac La Biche area during the period when Fort Desjarlais was in operation (ca. 1836–1856). Joseph Desjarlais, Jr. died at Lac La Biche in 1854. For genealogical information on Joseph Desjarlais, Jr., see Glenbow Archives (GA), C.D. Denney Papers, Family charts for Joseph Desjarlais and Josephte Cardinal (#1156.000); Antoine Desjarlais and Catherine Allary (#1228.000). See also the Fort Des Prairies BMD Register, 1842–1851, which records the marriage of Joseph Desjarlais and Josephte Cardinal, and the subsequent baptism and marriages of their adult children on 4 November 1844 at Lac La Biche (*Fort Des Prairies Registre, 1842–1851*, Acc: 71.220 — Item 5214; Oblate Archives, Provincial Archives of Alberta (PAA), Edmonton, Alberta. For information on Fort Desjarlais see G.A. McMorran, *Souris River Posts and David Thompson's Diary of His Historical Trip Across the Souris Plains to the Mandan Villages in the Winter of 1797–98* (Souris, Manitoba: Souris Plaindealer, 1953): 12–13; and Bruce Wishart, "Archaeology on the Souris River: Fort Desjarlais" (Parts Two and Three of a four-part newspaper article, n.d.). Manuscript on file at the Provincial Archives of Manitoba (PAM).

67. Old Joseph Desjarlais died at Riviere du Cygne (Swan River) on 22 October 1833 at the age of 80 years of age. An Antoine Desjarlais, assumed to be his son, was present at his burial. In the registers of St. Francis Xavier de la Prairie du Cheval Blanc (White Horse Plain), well into the 1840s, the marriage records of Joseph's sons, and the baptismal records of their children, are recorded. In 1869 members of the Desjarlais family were featured in the parish records of Baie St. Paul, St. Laurent, and Whitemud River. See the file for the Desjarlais family, and Father Picton's correspondence re: Joseph Desjarlais and his sons, in the Desjarlais Family File, *Father Picton Papers*, unpublished manuscript collection on file, St. Boniface Historical Society, Winnipeg, Manitoba.

68. In W.J. Healy, *Women of Red River* (Winnipeg: Russell, Lang and Co. Ltd., 1923), Mrs. William Cowan of Winnipeg recalls being present at the performance of a shaman, or as she calls him a "magician", a buffalo hunter by the name of Desjarlais, ca. 1840.

69. Isaac Cowie, *The Company of Adventurers* (Toronto: William Briggs, 1913), 416–17.

70. Whether their designation as Métis was voluntary or forced is not known. However, it should be noted that several members of different Desjarlais families, including Nishecabo's son Benjamin Desjarlais, (who was struck off the Muscowequan Band list) had withdrawn from treaty on 1 June 1888. See *List of Halfbreeds Who Have Withdrawn from Treaty June 1, 1888*. NAC, RG10, Series B-8-m, Volume 10038. See also records of 1900 Scrip Affidavit, P. 510, recording claims of various members of Baptiste Desjarlais's family, as recorded in the Desjarlais Family file of the C.D. Denney Papers (GA). This record also confirms the birthplace of Baptiste as being Lac La Biche ca. 1790, and his marriage to Charlotte Cardinal ca. 1815 at Baie St. Paul

(St. Paul-des-Sauteux), and Baptiste's death in the winter of 1871 at Little Fork, Qu'Appelle Lakes.

71. It was believed by the Ojibwa that children's illness or death was a result of the wrongdoing of their parents or grandparents. See Hallowell, "Ojibwa World View and Disease," 391–444

72. See Isaac Cowie, "Editorial Notes" (#21) for *The Journal of Daily Occurrences at the Hudson's Bay Company's Fort Ellice, Swan River District—From 1st May 1858 to 27th April 1859*: 39, which states: "Antoine Desgarlais was a Metis employee, who in the days of conflict between the H.B. and N.W. Companies had been employed by the H.B.C. to take out letters from Athabasca to Red River during the winter. He had to avoid being taken prisoner by the N.W.C. on his long solitary journey, full of privations, but succeeded eventually. As a very aged man he became attached to the Rev. Father Decorby's mission at Qu'Appelle Lakes (now Lebret), 'doing chores.' He was burned to death, when faithful to the end, he attempted to save something from the mission building which was gutted by fire in the winter of either 1870/1 or 1871/2." Unpublished manuscript on file, PAM.

73. As Roger McDonnell correctly points out, the fluidity of band formation and dissolution, and the inclusionary nature of band societies, was entirely at odds "with the exclusionary and relatively static diagnostic tendencies that separated Indian and Metis." Historical evidence suggests that Indians and Métis themselves did not draw rigid membership boundaries until the imposition of these Euro-Canadian, exclusionary determinants of ethnic identity. See McDonnell, 61–65.

✒ *Johnny Grant circa 1865. Johnny was 35 years old when this photo was taken.*
Montana Historical Society

7

Metis Ethnicity, Personal Identity and the Development of Capitalism in the Western Interior

The Case of Johnny Grant

GERHARD J. ENS

The concept of a single exclusive, and unchanging or cultural or other identity is a dangerous piece of brainwashing. Human mental identities are not like shoes, of which we can only wear one at a time. We are all multi-dimensional beings. Whether a Mr. Patel in London will think of himself primarily as an Indian, a British citizen, a Hindu, a Gujarati-speaker, and ex-colonist from Kenya, a member of a specific caste or kin-group, or in some other capacity depends on whether he faces an immigration officer, a Pakistani, a Sikh or Moslem, a Bengali-speaker; and so on.

ERIC HOBSBAWM, 1996[1]

DURING THE COURSE of a long and illus-trative trading career on the northwestern plains, Johnny Grant assumed a number of different personal and ethnic identities that ranged from Euro-Canadian, to Metis,[2] to Indian. His business career, which spanned the last half of the nineteenth century, likewise showed great variability with Grant amassing a small fortune by the 1860s and 1870s, and losing nearly all of it by the end of the 1880s. These two phenomena, although somewhat unique to Grant, are also symptomatic of trends that affected many Metis merchant traders at the end of the nineteenth century. The decline of the Metis trading class[3] was closely connected to specific economic changes that were transforming the western interior in the last three decades of the nineteenth century, and that these economic changes also affected Metis identity and ethnicity.

This marginalization of Metis merchants was not due to a lack of initial capitalization as many were wealthy by any standards often worth anywhere from $10,000 to $100,000, nor was it a case of their inability to adapt to an early form of capitalism as their assets attest to. While the racism and discriminatory attitudes of the incoming Canadian and American settlers and institutions had something to do with the withdrawal of the Metis from the commercial sphere,[4] the case of Johnny Grant illustrates that this was not a crucial determinant in their withdrawal from commerce in the late 1880s.

The commercial niche the Metis carved out for themselves in the nascent capitalism of the 1840s to 1870s was essentially that of intermediaries between the pre-capitalist native economy of the northern plains and the developed capitalism that began making inroads into the region by the 1840s. The Metis adaptation to capitalism flourished while both native economies and developed capitalist economies co-existed on the northern plains. This is what some economists have called a dual economy or society. This concept argues the co-existence of two different sectors divided by different cultures, laws of development, technology, and demand patterns within the same economy.

In a dual society one of two prevailing socio-economic systems is imported from the outside (usually capitalism), but is unable to immediately eliminate or assimilate the divergent system that is indigenous to the region. The result is that neither of the systems becomes general and characteristic for that society as a whole. The interaction of the two distinct social systems within the borders of one society is what one might call a dualistic economy. In dual societies generally the native element or producer does not trade beyond the boundaries of the region. The purchaser, therefore, is obliged to acquire trade goods at the point where production takes place. This creates the function of an engrosser or middleman—a typically dualistic figure who bridges the chasm between native economies and capitalism. This role of middleman in the dual economy of the northwestern plains was often assumed by the Metis.[5]

Those Metis that fulfilled these middlemen roles in the western interior had particularly multidimensional individual and group identities. This is not surprising as their trading activities took them across most of the northwestern part of the continent, and they were moving continually between Indian and Euro-Canadian economies and communities. Most historians who have studied the Metis, however, have tended to essentialize Metis

ᑎᔆᐧ Richard Grant circa 1850–1860.
K. Ross Toole Archives, The University of Montana -Missoula #75-6060.

ethnicity after having established their historic roots. Metis identity is usually seen as a fixed set of cultural attributes into which one is born. This tendency was reinforced by government policy that tended to define Metisness on racial lines. Metis ethnicity in the last half of the nineteenth century, however, was much more contingent than this.

The contingent nature of Metis ethnicity is illustrated by those Red River Metis who returned from Montana after the buffalo disappeared in the late 1870s and early 1880s, and congregated at Turtle Mountain in northern North Dakota. They returned because they believed they could acquire land from the American government during the treaty negotiations with the Ojibwa of that region. The American government, however, did not legally recognize the Metis and so they redefined themselves as the Turtle Mountain Chippewa (Ojibwa), entered treaty and obtained a reservation in the Turtle Mountains.[6] Similarly, individual Metis in Canada could and did enter treaty in the 1870s both as a strategy of survival and because they had relatives in various bands that took treaty. Later, after the 1885 Rebellion, when land and money scrip were offered to those Metis born in the North-West Territories, many of the same Metis left treaty to be eligible for Scrip—in effect, becoming Metis again. This type of instrumental ethnicity[7] and identity was much more common than is usually recognized.

These themes of instrumental ethnicity, personal identity, and economic marginalization are not only related but are personified in the life of Johnny Grant. During the last decades of the nineteenth century when market capitalism was transforming the western interior, Grant shifted his identity in such a way to maximize his economic opportunities. He had family ties in both Euro-Canadian and Native groups, and he emphasized those ethnic aspects that gave him a business advantage. For a time, a "Metis" identity was instrumental to a trading enterprise within a dual economy that existed on the northern plains but, later when this dual economy disappeared, Grant increasingly emphasized his Canadian connections, which were crucial to the new economy in Manitoba in the 1880s. Eventually, when these connections failed to gain him entrance into the Canadian commercial elite and he lost his fortune, he began to feel himself more of an Indian. While Grant is clearly not representative of all Metis merchants, his life and contingent ethnic identity is symptomatic of trends found in other Metis merchant families. As well, his career spanned almost the entire era from the 1840s to the 1890s, and his business locale shifted from Montana to the Red River Settlement, and ended in Northern Alberta.[8]

John Francis Grant was born 7 January c. 1833[9] at Fort Edmonton to Richard Grant, a Hudson's Bay Company trader from Montreal and Marie Ann Breland the Metis daughter of a sometime Hudson's Bay Company employee and freeman.[10] He was related to some of the most famous Metis of the British North West. Through his mother's side he was related to Pascal Breland, one of the leading free traders in the Red River Settlement in the period from the 1840s to 1870s and to Cuthbert Grant, Jr.[11] A short time after his birth, Johnny's mother died and he along with his siblings were sent to Quebec to be brought up by their grandmother and aunt. He stayed in Quebec until 1847 when he returned to the North West to rejoin his father. During these Quebec years he received his only education, which included four years in a seminary, and he formed his identity as a *Canadien*. His ties to Canada were still felt after a 20-year absence when he returned to Quebec to visit his former friends and relatives, but he could no longer live in the city. As he wrote, "I felt myself too much of an Indian..."[12]

In 1847, Johnny and his brother Richard left to join their father at Fort Hall, Idaho where the Hudson's Bay Company had stationed him. The reunion with his family was a mixed blessing. While happy to see his father, he lived in fear of the 6'2", 225 pound man with a voice like thunder, and felt uncomfortable with his stepmother. As he later noted "I was treated like a stranger in that family."[13] The first few winters at Fort Hall were spent learning to trap and hunt, and he sometimes accompanied his father on trading expeditions. In 1849 his father sent him to Fort Vancouver to be trained in the trade and made a man. Johnny's brother suggested he go to California where gold had been discovered, but Johnny preferred the trading life in the North West and proximity to family. On returning to Fort Hall his father gave him a $100 trading outfit with the proviso that he not trade within a mile of Fort Hall. Johnny quickly broke this regulation and was encouraged to leave the post by his father.[14] He eventually took up with some traders and trappers living in a lodge about eight miles from the Fort and began his independent trading career.

After leaving Fort Hall Grant lived with a Shoshoni woman partly, he said, to spite his father, partly because she helped him cement trading ties to her Indian band, and partly because she was good at leather work, which could be traded to immigrants passing through the region.[15] This was the beginning of a recurring pattern for Grant—that of forming liaisons with native women who would further his trading career. Popular legend has it that when Grant set up his trading operations on the Little Blackfoot River in Montana, he had wives[16] among all of the seven different Indian groups that hunted in the vicinity.[17] Whether or not this was strictly true, he did have relations with four different native women in the Montana/Idaho region who bore him at least a dozen children.[18] These kinship connections not only ensured good relations with the various Indian groups but enhanced his trading relations.

In 1859 Grant built a temporary home on the Little Blackfoot River in the Deer Lodge Valley and in 1861 built a more permanent ranch site and settlement at Cottonwood (Deer Lodge).[19] He was, he said, too lonely on the Little Blackfoot where his nearest neighbour was 130 miles away,[20] so he recruited a number of French fur traders and their native families to settle with him at Cottonwood. Amongst those who followed him were Louis Descheneau, Leon Quesnelle, Louis Demers, David Contois, and Michael Leclair.[21] A visitor to Grant's ranch in 1862 described both Grant and the Settlement.

John Grant, or as he is called here, Johnny Grant, is a man I should judge of 32 or 33 years of age, tall and well formed, with less of the Indian than American in his features, of a dark swarthy complexion, increased no doubt by exposure and his habits of life. He had, I understood, three Indian wives, and seven or Eight, perhaps more children, that he treats with affectionate fondness of manner that the children of many white men might envy.... Here in this luxuriant grassy valley, abounding with game and fish—the finest brook trout I ever saw—possessed of large herds of cattle and Horses, surrounded by his half breeds, Indian servants, and their families, with a half dozen old French mountaineers and Trappers who have married Indian women for his neighbours, Grant lives in as happy and free a manner as did the ancient Patriarches.[22]

This settlement, then, resembled the Metis communities of the Great Lakes and Red River regions.

In the 1850s and early 1860s, Grant's method of operation was fairly consistent: during the winter, he traded furs and robes with the Blackfoot, Shoshoni, Bannock and Flathead Indians; during the spring and summer, he went up to the Immigrant trail (Oregon Trail) and traded cattle with the immigrants. He offered immigrants $10 a piece for their lame cattle and then fattened them up in the Deer Lodge Valley before reselling or trading them. Alternatively he would trade one fat cow for two lame ones.[23] By the late 1850s, he had over 1000 head of cattle grazing in the Deer Lodge Valley protected from the predations of neighbouring Indian bands by his kinship connections and his generosity.[24] By 1857 he was making large profits trading cattle to the United States army troops and Mormons passing through the region. Granville Stuart noted in 1858 that Grant had herds of several hundred cattle and horses. These cattle fattened on the native grasses and "in spring they were fat and fit for beef and were driven back to the Emigrant road and traded for more foot sore and worn out animals which in turn were driven back to winter range in Montana..."[25] The market for beef skyrocketed during the Montana gold rush in 1861, and Grant became rich. He claimed that in the early 1860s his cattle and house were worth $110,000. While this valuation may be somewhat overstated, a traveller passing through in 1863 noted that, "Mr. Grant owns some 4,000 head of cattle, and some 2,000 or 3,000 ponies. The miners of Bannock and Virginia cities get most of their beef from him."[26] By this time there was a small settlement of French Metis, miners and mechanics around Grant's place in the Deer Lodge Valley, and Grant expanded his business by opening a store, saloon, dancing hall, grist mill, and blacksmith shop.[27] All of these operations, however, lost money except for his fur and cattle trading business, and his freighting operation between Deer Lodge and Fort Benton.[28]

The reasons for Grant's successes and failures in Montana are not hard to deduce. In those operations that depended on face-to-face relations, cross-cultural mediation, courage, trust and initiative, Grant was successful. As an intermediary in the dualistic economy and society of Montana of the 1850s and 1860s Grant was unrivalled. Those of Grant's operations, however, which depended on careful management, bookkeeping, and a knowledge of business and contracts were typically disasterous. Grant spent lavishly outfitting his saloon with French Mirrors and billiard tables which did little to increase business but drained his cash reserves. He lent large sums of money to individuals on trust only to be disappointed when they did not pay him back, and he never kept any accounts of his business activities.[29] As he noted,

> All my accounts I kept in my head. Sometimes I would get a little mixed up and it gave me some trouble, so I got a book and pencil to keep my accounts; but after putting them down, I could not understand my own writing. I concluded to hire a bookkeeper. The first one was James Arnold. He was not a competant man, for I could reckon mentally quicker than he could with a pen. But I had no choice. I soon learned, however, that as soon as I had to depend on others I lost money.[30]

Apparently, few Metis merchants and traders in the nineteenth century kept written business accounts. To date, I have yet to find even the faintest trace of the business records of Metis merchants. One of the more astute and successful Metis merchants, Xavier Letendre of Batoche Saskatchewan, admitted "I never took stock of my goods, I always made my own business...I have no education for such purposes...and had to depend on my memory....[31] Grant spent a large sum of money buying and bringing a grist mill to Deer Lodge only to realize that he did not have the aptitude to run it effectively and, he eventually sold the mill for a huge loss. He later claimed in his memoirs that he had been duped because he could not read or understand the bill of sale—that he had been promised one thing verbally but the bill of sale had said something else.[32]

By the late 1860s Grant was anxious to leave the Deer Lodge Valley. The ostensible reason given in his memoirs was that the region had become too rough and dangerous with the discovery of gold. He left, he said, to take his children away from robbers and gamblers and raise them in more peaceful parts of the country.[33] In interviews and newspaper accounts, however, he suggested another reason. The Gold Rush had not only brought thieves and criminals into the area, but had necessitated law and order, and government. Up until this point Grant had paid no taxes, and his failure to keep any accounts had not created any problems other than some financial losses. With the coming of law and government, Grant noted with disgust, had come the tax assessor and tax collector asking for a detailed accounting of his property.

> I'll tell you. I had been raised in an Indian country since I was 15 years old. I got along well. My door was open to every one and my table free to all who came. I harmed no man, nor did any harm me. My stock ranged the valleys and hills unmolested, and my money, at much at times as $10,000 or $20,000, lay in my cabin unmolested. I needed no protection. I cost nobody a dollar. After a time the Territory was established, then counties, and then officers were elected. Then came Assessors and the Collectors annoying me with their lists and tax collections and laws for this, that and the other, and I concluded to leave for Manitoba.[34]

It is interesting to note that the year Johnny left Montana, the United States revenue officers seized his entire stock of alcohol—some 700 gallons. This piece of bad luck, coming on the heels of a fire that destroyed his livery stable worth $3,000, prompted Grant to tell a reporter for the *Montana Post* that if his luck did not change he "would clear up and go among the Indians again."[35] Whatever his reasons for leaving, Grant sold the remainder of his herd and houses to Conrad Kohrs for $19,000 in 1867 and moved to the Red River Settlement in the British North West.[36]

Grant chose the Red River Settlement, a colony of some 10,000 Metis, as his new home because of the proximity of relatives who encouraged him to relocate,[37] the opportunity to educate his children there, and the economic opportunities. On arrival he bought some real estate in what is now the City of Winnipeg, scouted for land to settle on, and examined the business possibilities.[38] Grant and his family settled on land just south of the Parish of St. Charles at a location known as Riviére aux Ilets des Bois (today the site of Carman, Manitoba). Here he staked out land for himself, family and friends who had followed him to Manitoba.[39] He arrived in Manitoba driving a herd of 500 horses, 62 wagons, 12 carts, and accompanied by 106 men who he had organized along the lines of a Metis buffalo hunt. He subsequently bought cattle from the American territories hoping to start a ranching operation as he had done in Montana. He also brought supplies in from the United States opening a store at Sturgeon Creek, and began a fur trading operation. By 1870 he operated a saloon in the St. Charles parish, and had married Clotilde

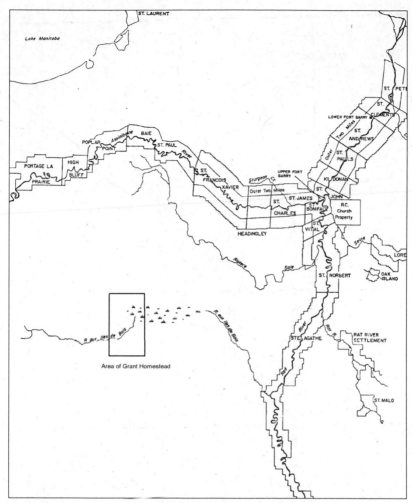

◈ *The Red River Settlement circa 1870 showing the location of the Johnny Grant farm.*

Bruneau, the Metis daughter of a former judge in the Red River Colony.[40] These actions, in effect, duplicated the strategy that he had developed in Montana. His closest friends and relatives, the Brelands, the McKays, the Rowands, and the Leveilles were all Metis connected to the fur-trading economy of the northwest.

Grant, like most Metis residents of the Settlement, was apprehensive with the prospect of the annexation of Rupert's Land by Canada and the arrival of Canadian surveyors in 1869, but he did not join Louis Riel's resistance to Confederation. Grant, and many other Metis merchants and traders

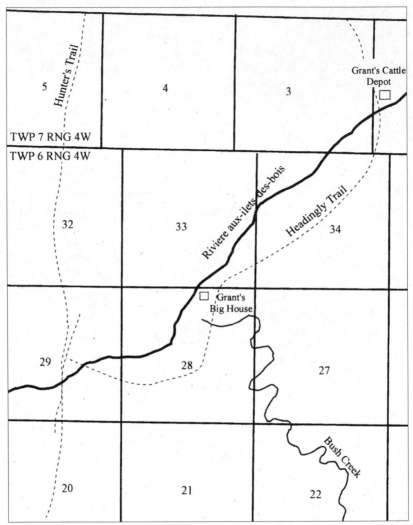

Location of Johnny Grant's homestead and cattle depot.

in the Colony tried to remain neutral or resisted Riel. For them Riel was far too imperious and arrogant insisting that he would be the sole interpreter of events for the Metis. Riel's seizure of property and goods eventually turned Grant against Riel especially when his own horses were seized by Riel's men. When Donald A. Smith, the chief officer of the Hudson's Bay Company in Canada and Canada's emissary, arrived in Red River to negotiate with Riel in January of 1870, Grant immediately put himself at Smith's disposal.[41] Grant, Pierre Leveille, and Angus McKay were sent to protect Richard Hardisty who had gone to Pembina to retrieve Smith's official papers. For these actions and his opposition to Riel, Grant would later be imprisoned by Riel for eight days.[42]

It did not take Grant long to recoup his fortunes after the Resistance and eventual Confederation with Canada. Grant quickly realized that the new opportunities were in the land market. Under the terms of the Manitoba Act, which brought the Red River Settlement into Canada, the Metis of Manitoba were granted about 2.5 million acres of land. Dissatisfied with many aspects of life in the new province many Metis left the province to move further west. This created tremendous opportunities in land speculation. Grant made use of the connections he had established with Donald Smith and was loaned $1900 by the Hudson's Bay Company. Grant's entrepreneurial and interpersonal skills, and his family and kin connections to many of the Red River Metis allowed him to quickly amass a small fortune in land. By 1882 Grant owned 13,000 acres of land in the province of Manitoba.[43] His home site consisted of a 640-acre section of land on the Riviére aux Ilets des Bois (later renamed the Boyne). Here he constructed a substantial two-storey house measuring 40 feet by 28 feet finished in lumber of the best quality, a cattle depot, and a water-powered saw and shingle mill.[44]

Although Grant was successful in building up this fortune through speculative land dealings, he was much less successful in managing his fortune. When the Manitoba land boom collapsed in 1882, Grant owned thousands of acres of land, but had gone into debt to acquire it. To hold on to his most valuable land he mortgaged his home properties to pay interest on his loans, and began selling off selected properties at a loss. He managed to retain most of his land for three years but by 1885–86 his estate was crumbling. He lost 1600 acres for a mere $600 because he had not bothered to or was unable to read a mortgage or loan document. If Grant had reading skills, he certainly had no expertise, training, or interest in legal transactions. He would later blame his financial decline in Manitoba on the dubious money lending practices and legal maneuvers of the lawyers and bankers that had come into the province after 1870.[45]

From the early 1870s to the early 1880s Grant had tried to become a member of the new commercial elite in Manitoba, and he tried hard to build alliances with this group. He helped get Donald Smith elected in the Federal elections of 1871 and 1872 by canvassing the parishes of St. James, St. Charles, and Headingly using his saloon to buy votes in these neighbourhoods. It was in part for these services that Smith secured a loan for Grant from the Hudson's Bay Company. While Grant considered himself a part of Smith's inner circle, it is quite probable that Smith patronized Grant for his influence amongst the French Metis voters along the Assiniboine River. In effect, Grant was still acting as a broker in the dual society that existed in Manitoba in the early 1870s. When Grant realized that his services to Smith did not provide him with adequate compensation nor entry into the elite, he changed candidates supporting Andrew Bannatyne's candidacy in the Federal election of 1874 opposing Smith. In retaliation Smith had the Hudson's Bay Company call in Grant's loan.[46] Grant would later claim that Smith also robbed him of $1260 when, as executor of James McKay's estate, he refused to make good McKay's debt to him.[47]

These and other setbacks eventually broke Grant who lost even his home, 640 acres, through a defaulted mortgage and he was forced to live on land owned by his wife. The straw that broke the camel's back, Grant claimed, was when Manitoba passed a herd law prohibiting the running of cattle at large. This hurt his cattle operation since he now owned little land himself and could no longer graze his cattle on the open range. Shortly thereafter Grant decided to leave Manitoba. Disgusted and nearly broke, Grant sold the rest of his cattle in 1891 and moved to the North West in 1892.[48]

Grant and most of his immediate family moved to Bittern Lake, Alberta where he homesteaded. He lived there eight years and then went to Grande Prairie where he re-entered the fur trade and opened a stopping place, but things went poorly. He moved again, this time to Athabasca Landing, and finally to Deep Creek [Waugh, Alberta] where he kept a stopping place. When Treaty Eight was signed in Northern Alberta in 1899 Johnny and his family were living in the area ceded by the treaty, and Johnny became a spokesman for the children of Manitoba Metis who were disqualified from taking scrip because their parents had taken scrip earlier. In a five-page petition, Grant reviewed the history of Metis land grants in Manitoba and the North-West Territories, and made an eloquent case for the children of "Manitoba Halfbreeds" living in the Treaty Eight area.[49] These efforts, however, came to naught and by 1907, too ill to take care of himself, Grant returned to Edmonton with his wife to live out his last days with his daughter and son-in-law. He died 1 May 1907.[50]

The life of Johnny Grant is representative of many Metis traders and merchants in the last half of the nineteenth century. This was an era when native economies coexisted with an incoming nascent capitalism in the western interior, and Grant and other Metis were quick to spot an economic opportunity as intermediaries between the two economies and societies. Adapting at a certain level to this incoming capitalism, these Metis traders were able to carve out an entrepreneurial niche on the northern plains. They travelled out to the various Indian bands buying up furs and buffalo robes with goods and alcohol, and selling them in turn to the various Canadian and American fur concerns. These Metis merchants, including such families as the Brelands, Grants, McGillis, Gingras, Fishers, Letendres, and Hamelins, had adapted to a number of features of the incoming market capitalism while at the same time maintaining their social and cultural ties to their native heritage. As long as dual societies and economies prevailed on the northern plains, these Metis traders were influential and flourished. Some built up a chain of trading and mercantile operations, and became wealthy in the process. As long as interpersonal and intercultural skills, and entrepreneurial initiative were at a premium, these traders and merchants prospered. However, when the various native economies in the northwestern United States and the Canadian prairies began to be marginalized in the 1880s and 1890s, with the disappearance of the buffalo and the move onto reserves, these traders were themselves marginalized.

The skills that bred success in the new commercial and business arena of developed capitalism (regularized management, accounting, planning, and a knowledge of contracts and corporations) were generally lacking among the Metis merchant class. The rapid demise of the native economy on the plains coincided with the very abrupt disappearance of the buffalo in the late 1870s, and gave them very little time for adjustment. Lacking the technical skills of the new commercial elite coming into the region, and not having the financial connections or access to capital in Canada that were so important,[51] Metis merchants were pushed to the side. Irene Spry, in detailing the business affairs of other Metis entrepreneurs in Rupert's Land, dates their decline to exactly the same period that Johnny Grant failed financially in Manitoba. She writes that the death of James McKay in 1879,

> marked the end of an era, the end of the restless individualism of the native entrepreneurs of Rupert's Land. They had accumulated their own personal capital. Those who had achieved wealth, status, and influence had done so on the basis of their own ambition, courage, initiative, energy, and shrewd intelligence and also of their prowess in the chase, on the trail and in boat brigades, and their intimate knowledge of the plains and the peoples of the plains. Now strangers were arriving in increasing numbers. They...brought with them new and different skills—sophisticated commercial and technical skills—and had access to outside sources of capital, to partners with funds, to corporate finances, or to bank loans.[52]

Johnny Grant tried to make that transition but was checked by his unfamiliarity with cost-accounting, knowledge of contracts, and access to capital markets.

The existence of a dual economy or society on the western plains had created the social and economic space that permitted, even encouraged, the elaboration of a Metis identity as a "people in-between." It was an ethnic positioning that was economically advantageous. When this dualistic economy disappeared from the northern plains in the 1880s and 1890s, a Metis identity was no longer instrumentally advantageous. It was during this period that many Metis began drifting back to their native roots (entering treaty or reserves), or assimilating to a Euro-Canadian identity. Shortly before his death Johnny Grant told a reporter that he felt "as though he himself were an Indian."[53] Within the space of a lifetime Grant's own personal identity had fluctuated from Euro-Canadian, to Metis, to Indian. Although Metis communities and Metis peoples did not cease to exist after the 1880s, there was a clear retreat from self-identification as "Metis" from the 1890s to the 1930s. Being Metis during these decades was no longer economically nor socially advantageous.

Notes

1. Eric Hobsbawm, "Language, Culture, and National Identity," *Social Research* 63, no. 4 (Winter 1996): 1067.
2. Following the increasing common practice of the Metis themselves, the word "Metis" is written without an accent except when quoting texts or titles where the accent is found. The term "Metis," for the purposes of this paper, includes all mixed-blood communities who regarded themselves as distinct from Indian peoples on the one hand and white communities on the other regardless of whether they referred to themselves as *métis* or halfbreeds. The term Metis is used in this generic sense because it facilitates theoretical formulation and does not carry the pejorative connotations of the word "halfbreed."
3. This paper is part of a larger study having to do with Metis merchant families on the northern plains in the last half of the nineteenth century and early twentieth century. The study examines the life courses of about two dozen Metis merchants who came of age in the 1840s and 1850s.
4. This argument has been used with some effectiveness by Diane Payment in her study of the Metis of Batoche, Saskatchewan. See her *"The Free People—Otipemisiwak": Batoche, Saskatchewan 1870–1930* (Ottawa: National Historic Parks and Sites, Parks Service, Environment Canada, 1990), 75–76, 215–16.
5. This brief summary of some aspects of dual economies is based on a reading of: J.H. Boeke, *Economics and Economic Policy of Dual Societies* (New York: Institute of Pacific Relations, 1953); W.A. Lewis, "Economic Development with Unlimited Supplies of Labour," *Manchester School* 22 (May 1954); Benjamin Higgins, "The Dualistic Theory of Underdeveloped Areas," in *Economic Development and Cultural Change*, 5 (1956); W.A. Lewis, "Unlimited Labour: Further Notes," *Manchester School* 26 (1958); Gustav Ranis and John C.H. Fei, "A Theory of Economic Development," *American Economic Review* (1961); Amartya K. Sen, "Peasants and Dualism with or without Surplus

Labor," *Journal of Political Economy* (1966); William Barber, "Dualism Revisited: Economic Structures and the Framework of Economic Policy in a Post-Colonial Setting," in Paul Streeten, ed., *Unfashionable Economics: Essays in Honour of Lord Balogh* (London, 1970); H.W. Singer, "Dualism Revisited: A New Approach to the Problems of the Dual Society in Developing Countries," in Sir Alec Cairncross and Mohinder Puri, eds., *The Strategy of International Development: Essays in the Economics of Backwardness* (White Plains, New York, 1975).

6. For a more extensive examination of the reformulation of the Turtle Mountain Metis identity see: Gerhard J. Ens, "After the Buffalo: The Reformation of the Turtle Mountain Metis Community," in *New Faces of the Fur Trade: Selected Papers of the Seventh North American Fur Trade Conference, Halifax, Nova Scotia, 1995* (East Lansing: Michigan State University Press, 1998), 139–52.

7. Instrumental ethnicity, also referred to as 'situational' or 'subjectivist' ethnicity "posits that what really matters is a people's definition of themselves as culturally or physically distinct from others. Their shared descent is secondary and, if necessary, may be manufactured and manipulated. Ethnicity is, therefore, flexible, adaptable and capable of taking different forms and meanings depending on the situation or perceptions of advantage. Consequently ethnic groups emerge, merge, and split constantly." Sammy Smooha, "Ethnic Groups," in Adam Kuper and Jessica Kuper, eds., *The Social Science Encyclopedia* (London: Routledge, 1985), 268.

8. Grant is one of the few Metis merchants who has left behind a fairly detailed account of his life and business dealings. Grant's last wife, Clotilde Bruneau, wrote his autobiography as dictated to her by Johnny Grant at the end of his life in Edmonton. Entitled "Very Close to Trouble," this manuscript was completed in 1909. Copies of this manuscript are in the possession of the National Parks Service, at the Grant-Kohrs Historic Site in Montana and the descendants of Johnny Grant. Recently a part of this manuscript was published as *Very Close to Trouble: The Johnny Grant Memoir*, edited by Lyndel Meikle (Pullman: Washington State University Press, 1996). In addition to this autobiography there are a number of recorded interviews with Johnny Grant, and records of his land transactions can be reconstructed from records in the various land titles offices in Manitoba.

9. There is some question regarding the date of Johnny's birth. While most sources list him as born in 1831, his baptism in Trois-Rivières on 16 November 1836 listed him as three years of age. That would make his birth date 1833.

10. Grant's genealogy has been reconstructed from information found in parish registers and census materials. The author is also very grateful for family information received from Anita Steele, a descendent of Johnny Grant. For more detailed information on the Grant genealogy see Anita Steele, "Canadian Grant Family," (http://www.televar.com/-gmorin/grant.htm).

11. Richard Grant was born in 1794 in Montreal. His father was William Grant of Three Rivers. Marie Ann Breland was the daughter of Pierre Breland and the sister of Pascal Breland. Pierre Breland had several wives. As mothers and children have not all been linked, it is unknown if Pascal and Marie Ann were full siblings.

12. *Very Close to Trouble: The Johnny Grant Memoir*, 143, 147.

13. Ibid., 7.

14. Ibid., 25–26.

15. Ibid., 31–32.

16.   While Grant was not legally married to any woman prior to marring Clotilde Bruneau in the Red River Settlement, these women were regarded as country wives and married "according to the custom of the country."

17.   John Francis Grant, Montana Historical Society, Small Collections #764. These Indian bands included Blackfoot, Shoshoni, Bannock, Flathead, and Pend d'Oreille.

18.   This information comes from parish registers, newspaper accounts, oral histories, and Grant's memoirs.

19.   These last buildings still exist and form the focal point of the Grant-Kohrs Ranch National Historic Site.

20.   *Very Close to Trouble: The Johnny Grant Memoir*, 72–73.

21.   Ibid., 76.

22.   Edwin Rutheven Purple, *Perilous Passage: A Narrative of the Montana Gold Rush, 1862–1863,* edited by Kenneth N. Owens (Helena: Montana Historical Society Press, 1995).

23.   *Very Close to Trouble: The Johnny Grant Memoir,* 48–50, 62–64, 71–82.

24.   Ibid., 93.

25.   Granville Stuart, *Pioneering in Montana: The Making of a State, 1864–1887*, edited by Paul C. Phillips (Lincoln: University of Nebraska Press, 1977), 97.

26.   Capt. James L. Fisk quoted in Merrill G. Burlingame, *Montana Frontier* (Helena: State Publishing Company, 1942), 264.

27.   *Montana Post*, 16 December 1865. "John Francis Grant," Montana Historical Society, Small Collection #764.

28.   *Very Close to Trouble: The Johnny Grant Memoir*, 125–30.

29.   Ibid.; "Johnny Grant," Montana Historical Society, Small Collection #764.

30.   *Very Close to Trouble: The Johnny Grant Memoir,* 98.

31.   Quoted in Diane Paulette Payment, *"The Free People—Otipemisiwak": Batoche, Saskatchewan 1870–1930*, 212.

32.   *Very Close to Trouble: The Johnny Grant Memoir,* 127–28. The complaint that he was duped or swindled by unscrupulous operators or lawyers is a recurring complaint throughout Grant's later career.

33.   *Very Close to Trouble: The Johnny Grant Memoir*, 134.

34.   Account of an interview with Johnny Grant in 1886 in *The New North-West*, 16 April 1886. See also "Johnny Grant," Montana Historical Society, Small Collection #764.

35.   *Montana Post*, 17 February 1866.

36.   *The Rural Municipality of Dufferin, 1880–1908* (Rural Municipality of Dufferin, 1982), 481.

37.   By the 1860s the Metis of Red River were regularly travelling to Montana to hunt buffalo and they would no doubt have had some regular contact with Grant.

38.   *Very Close to Trouble: The Johnny Grant Memoir*, 151–58.

39.   Ibid., 184–85. Those that had followed him from Montana included Alex Pambrun, Thomas Lavetta, and David Contois.

40.   Ibid., 186–89; *The Rural Municipality of Dufferin*, 481–82. *The Nor'Wester*, 19 January 1868.

41.   Grant would later claim that Smith had made promises to himself and other loyal Metis that they would be compensated. This compensation, Grant complained, never arrived.

42.   Johnny Grant memoir (manuscript). *The Rural Municipality of Dufferin*, 482–83.

43. Provincial Archives of Manitoba, GR 174, Box 12b #1, Unpublished Sessional papers. Testimony of John F. Grant 22 November 1881 to the Commission of Inquiry into Infant Metis Lands.

44. *The Rural Municipality of Dufferin*, 483.

45. Johnny Grant Memoir (manuscript).

46. The preceding account is summarized from Grant's unpublished memoirs.

47. Ibid.

48. Ibid.; *The Rural Municipality of Dufferin*, 483.

49. Petition of Manitoba Metis for the rights of their children. The original of this petition is in the possession of Anita Steele, a descendent of Johnny Grant. The petition itself is written in long hand on long pages of parchment in Clotilde Bruneau's handwriting. No record of this petition could be found in various archives which suggests that either it was never sent, never received, or was lost. The petition is undated but since it is addressed directly to Frank Oliver, the Minister of the Interior, it was undoubtedly written in either 1905 or 1906.

50. *Edmonton Journal*, 2 May 1907.

51. As Jay Gitlan has shown in his study of the French fur-trade merchants in the American Midwest, commercial success after the arrival of American settlers depended on having friends and contacts in both the federal and local governments, and crucial credit connections. Jay Gitlan, " ' Old Wine in New Bottles': French Merchants and the Emergence of the American Midwest, 1795–1835," *Proceedings of the Thirteenth and Fourteenth Meeting of the French Colonial Historical Society*, edited by Philip P. Boucher (New York: University Press of America, 1990), 37–52.

52. Irene Spry, 'The "Private Adventurers" of Rupert's Land," in John E. Foster, ed., *The Developing West: Essays on Canadian History in Honor of Lewis H. Thomas* (Edmonton: University of Alberta Press, 1983), 62–63.

53. *Edmonton Bulletin*, 29 April 1907.

8 Wintering, the Outsider Adult Male and the Ethnogenesis of the Western Plains Métis

JOHN E. FOSTER

OVER THE PAST half century the historical assessment of the nineteenth-century Plains Métis experience has altered from that of "losers" to that of "winners." The appearance of *les hivernants* (winterers) on the western Plains in the 1840s was, for Marcel Giraud, evidence that "primitivism" had won out over "civilization" in the lives of many of the Plains Métis.[1] More recently, for Gerhard Ens, the same evidence suggests a highly effective entrepreneurial response to an industrial market opportunity.[2] With the emergence of this scholarly reassessment historians have exhibited heightened interest in the fate of the Métis with the onset of settlement in the last decades of the nineteenth century. Métis primitivism is no longer an acceptable explanation for the marginalization of the Métis in this period. This same historical reassessment has heightened interest as well in the questions of what were, a century earlier, the circumstances and processes which gave rise to the Métis. As scholars have come to appreciate mixed Euro-Canadian and Indian ancestry as simply a biological fact, shared among many individuals who may choose to identify culturally as Indian,[3] Métis or Euro-Canadian, their interest has sharpened in terms of the circumstances and processes which constitute Métis ethnogenesis.[4] No longer are mixed ancestry and the social circumstances which gave rise to it sufficient explanation for the origins of the Métis on the western Plains.

The context for the processes and social relationships which gave rise to the Plains Métis was wintering as it was practised by Montreal-based fur traders in the last quarter of the eighteenth century in *le pays sauvage* (Indian country).[5] The focal person was the *coureur de drouine* (itinerant trader) or *commis* (clerk), the "outsider" from an Indian perspective, who led a trading party seeking to make contact with Indian hunters on their wintering grounds. The process of establishing this trade constituted the first step in the two-step process that gave rise to the Métis. During the first step three critical relationships were formed. The first was the country marriage of the outsider to a prominent woman of the Indian band. The second relationship involved the outsider in a kin relationship with the adult males of the Indian band. And the last relationship involved the *coureur de drouine* in association with his fellow *engagés* (servants) as comrades and work mates. The shared experiences of these relationships gave expression to the Métis when the outsider with his country wife and family chose to live apart from both the trading post and the Indian band.

L'homme libre, the freeman, looms large in the process of Métis ethnogenesis. His historical importance in part lies in his social ties to indigenous Indian bands who came to consider this outsider as one of themselves. Rarely of British origin, the *Canadien* or "eastern Indian" freeman was a phenomenon of the Montreal-based fur trade and its *en drouine* (itinerant peddling) system of trade. Usually he was an *engagé* who had established himself as a man of consequence among his fellows. Physical prowess counted for much, but not all; generosity and a penchant for an evocative song and an entertaining story were recognized as well. The man of consequence influenced others and affected the image of being less influenced by others. The man of consequence acted to become a "master" of his own affairs and circumstances. The logic of this ethos among the fur trade *engagés* led some to end their relationship with the trading post as *engagés* and become *les hommes libres.* This means of expressing their sense of consequence, by becoming free, was the beginning of the second stage in a two-step process which was intimately and critically involved in the emergence of the Plains Métis.

Particular behaviours distinguish the historical Plains Métis from indigenous Indians and from Euro-Canadians. The nature of these distinguishable behaviours in significant measure may well be "degree" rather than "kind." Further, such behaviours can be said to be central to the culture of these people. To explain their cultural origins it is useful to acknowledge the enculturation of children as a fundamental mechanism in the transmission of culture generationally. Thus the critical feature in explaining Métis ethnogenesis is not mixed ancestry; rather, it is the historical circumstances and processes which saw some children enculturated differently than those children associated with Indian bands or with the very few Euro-Canadian communities that could be said to exist in the presettlement West. Few would quarrel with the observation that children born to Indian mothers and enculturated in Indian bands did, and do, function culturally as Indians. In the closing decades of the eighteenth century on the western Plains there were only Indian mothers. Thus to have some children experience a different enculturation, to the extent that the historical actors themselves recognized them as culturally distinct from Indians, it is necessary to posit an enculturation circumstance for these children apart from indigenous Indian bands. The freeman, the outsider adult male, was a critical factor in creating these historical circumstances.

Two scholars in particular have offered insight in this area. Jacqueline Peterson, in her article "Prelude to Red River: A Social Portrait of the Great Lakes Métis," details an historical mechanism which would see some children enculturated in circumstances apart from an Indian band.[6] Her focus is the early eighteenth-century Great Lakes fur trade and the small party of traders dispatched *en drouine* by a *bourgeois* (merchant) at a major trading post.[7] The trading party of perhaps four to six men, led by a *commis*, sought out Indian bands on their home territories. Frequently the basis for a commercial trade between the two was a sociopolitical tie linking the traders, particularly the *commis*, to the principal adult males of the band. The vehicle for such a relationship in most instances was the "country marriage" of the *commis* and a principal woman in the band. Peterson goes on to suggest that should the *commis* enjoy success, emerging in time as a *bourgeois* and contracting a more enduring marriage from his own social circle, he could still gather some of the children of his previous country marriages to be raised in his own home circumstances. Peterson's article argues that sufficient experiences of this nature over two or three generations contributed significantly to the rise of the Great Lakes Métis. In terms of the western Plains, the immediate question arising from Peterson's article is whether a similar process can be identified which would have some children enculturated, as were some children of the *commis*, in circumstances distinct from Indian bands.

Jennifer Brown, in her book *Strangers in Blood*, offers the concept of patrifocality to explain why most children in the families of fur trade officers and their Native wives in the nineteenth century did not emerge as Métis.[8] Brown argues that the dominant position of fur trade officers in their families allowed them to influence the enculturation of their children to the extent that they did not become Métis. An implication for readers of Brown's book is whether matrifocality rather than patrifocality would explain the appearance of the Métis. Were the Métis the cultural product of children enculturated apart from the band in a family in which the wife and mother was the dominant factor in their enculturation? In part Brown returned to this discussion in a later article, "Woman as Centre and Symbol in the Emergence of Métis Communities."[9]

The historical record argues persuasively for the significance of the outsider male in the historical processes that gave rise to the Métis. Further, a noteworthy number of these males would appear to be characterized as assertive in terms of their behaviour with others. An example is Jean Dumont, the founder of the Dumont family among the Métis in western Canada. Having "turned off" his country wife, Suzette, the Sarcee-Crow woman, and family to another freeman, Paul Durand, Jean left for Lower Canada in 1802, only to return two or three years later to challenge Durand for his family: "mais Paul Durant [sic] refusait de rendre la femme à son premier propriétaire, Jean Dumont dut la prendre de irve force."[10] Durand's name would disappear from documents until his son by Suzette reached maturity and married. Quite possibly a similar assertiveness expressed itself in the family lives of these men and in their relations with their children, particularly sons. Whether or not such assertiveness in family life consti-tuted "patrifocality" or "man centrality," it does argue for significance in terms of the circumstances in which the young in such families were encul-turated. Equally significant in arguing the importance of the husband and father in proto-Métis households one is not implying the unimportance of the wife and mother.

In attempting to identify the particular historical circumstances and processes which gave rise to the western Plains Métis attention is directed to the wintering villages which first captured Giraud's attention.[11] Within a generation of their first appearance, numbers of these villages dotted the western Plains. Among the most westerly was Buffalo Lake in what is today the province of Alberta. At its height as a wintering village of Métis buffalo hunters it had over eighty cabins, numbering close to 1,000 inhabitants.[12] It is to wintering in the fur trade, not in the 1870s, however, but in the 1770s, that scholars must look to identify the circumstances and the processes which gave rise to the Métis on the western Plains.

Wintering in its broadest sense is the complex of individual and community behaviours invoked in response to factors rooted in climatic circumstances. The behaviours are those necessary for survival when on occasion a benign or challenging environment can become threatening. But wintering behav-iours involve more than simple survival: they involve the full interplay of individuals and groups in small, face-to-face communities. In the context of the St. Lawrence-Great Lakes fur trade in the eighteenth century, wintering differentiated *les bons hommes* who wintered in the interior from *les mangeurs de lard* who bound themselves to the constraints of society in the environs of Montreal and elsewhere in French Canada.[13] Those *engagés* who remained in the interior were *les hivernants*. They met the challenge of wintering in the Indian country, not simply by surviving but by becoming persons of consequence among their fellows and in the Indian bands. Thereby they gained reputation and full entry into the adult male fraternity of the St. Lawrence-Great Lakes fur trade. For the officers wintering was the prerequisite, after appropriate social circumstances, for membership in the famous, and at times infamous, Beaver Club.[14] Others of their social and ethnic milieu could be guests at the club's functions, but only winterers of appropriate social circumstances could be members. For those officers and servants in posts in the North Saskatchewan River valley, in the last quarter of the eighteenth century, *hivernement* (wintering) had an even more specialized meaning.

While the discussion of the circumstances and processes of wintering is sparse in the fur trade literature it is noteworthy that Giraud provides the most detail. The image of wintering that emerges in Giraud suggests two cardinal factors determining circumstances. The first factor is the *en drouine* trading system, developed in the St. Lawrence-Great Lakes trade during the closing decades of the seventeenth century.[15] Jacqueline Peterson has explained that the system involved small parties of men sent from a regional trading fort to trade with Indians on their home hunting and trapping territories. These peddlers would find winter a most appropriate time for their travel not only because the season facilitated travel in areas away from canoe-navigable rivers but because it would be the best circumstance in which to encourage Indians to emphasize trapping activities. Giraud explains:

> the employees of the Canadian companies, as soon as they reached their wintering places, provided themselves with trade goods and scattered among the Indians in the hope of securing their furs and gaining their allegiance through the mutual sympathy that was born of such a shared experience....the Canadians already had recourse to this procedure, which they found to their advantage as well as to that of the Indians.... The "coureur de drouine," as such an employee-trader was called, became the essential cogwheel in the trading post. Many of the Canadians shared...the life of the natives, choosing to live over winter in their tents, next to their families, without caring about the rigorous cold or the uncomfortable quarters....such a dispersion might have an added importance of conserving the fort's scanty resources of food.[16]

In effect, wintering in the posts of the *en drouine* fur trade system involved travel to the Indian bands and some period of residence among them.

The practice of *en drouine* trading in winter provided the bourgeois of the trading post with a means of addressing the perennial problem of the cost of surplus labour during the winter months.[17] *Engagés* were hired primarily to transport trade goods into the interior and furs out to market. With winter this labour force had to be directed towards other activities. Those *engagés* with crafts such as carpentry and smithing could be profitably employed in most instances. Others less technically skilled could be directed for a time to such activities as cutting firewood. As extensive as this activity might be during a Plains winter the usual course of action was to have as much wood as possible cut, transported and stacked before the onset of cold weather. In effect a number of *engagés* could be relatively idle for extended periods during the winter months; and thus, they would be a drain on the post's stores of provisions and, of course, on the profitability of the trade. While hunting activity could be encouraged for a few appropriately skilled servants, it could be cost effective as well to dispatch small parties of men with a limited supply of trade goods to winter with residential bands of Indians. Their trade goods would permit them to exchange goods for food and other necessities from the Indians. In effect the *en drouine* system could be combined with the practice of encouraging small parties of men to winter with the bands. Such parties could encourage the bands to act in a manner that favoured their home fort. In competitive circumstances they could direct furs and provisions to their *bourgeois* at the trading post. At the same time they would provision themselves through their own efforts and/or through the efforts of the band with whom they were temporarily residing.

Such wintering practices involved *engagés* intimately in the affairs of the band. On first contact the leader of the trading party would lay the basis for a trading relationship, using all of his social and political skills and his knowledge of Indian ways. In most instances his actions could be described as an "assertive bonhomie" in which gifts were offered and conversation would introduce the names of personages who could be said to offer a link between the *commis* and the adult males of the band.[18] As with many cultural traditions hunting Indians seemed to have preferred conducting trade with "family." The trader would emphasize conversations that would serve to have him considered in this context. Preferably a common kinsman would be discovered in the course of conversation. In the early period both parties would have to be satisfied with a social link to an Indian or trader of well-deserved reputation. It was out of a successful initial meeting that a social relationship could emerge between the *coureur de drouine* or *commis* and the adults of the band. A country marriage to an eligible woman of the band would cement this relationship. Although evidence is very sparse other circumstances at a later date suggest that women of the band were not necessarily simply passive observers in this decision.[19]

Other members of the *en drouine* party might form marriage relationships with women of the band, but the continuation of these relationships in succeeding winter seasons was far more problematic. Members of the trading party other than the *commis* would be much less likely to have the status that would keep the country wife's interest when the winter and the trade ended. Similarly the *engagé*, should he have the inclination, would be less able than the *commis* to persuade his *bourgeois* to allow him in succeeding winters to return to the band of the previous year's country wife. The country marriages which led to the Métis appear in large measure to be those that were sustained over several trading seasons.

The country marriage was critical to the *commis's* trading success because it included him in the social system of the residential band. Kinship determined appropriate privileges and responsibilities in relations with others. By virtue of his marriage the *commis* was enmeshed in this social system. Every person in the residential band and in the surrounding "neighbourhood" was a "parent" (relative) who owed him obligations and to whom he owed obligations. A failure to behave appropriately in this area could be fatal to a *commis's* commercial interests and, in some instances, to himself and his compatriots.[20] The advice of a country wife on this subject as well as others could be critical to the long-term success and health of the *commis* and his compatriots.

At first glance the spousal relationship involved in wintering suggests "bride service," that is, the newly married couple living with the bride's parents until the birth of the first child. The advantages for the males involved in this practice were the opportunity for the outsider male to learn a new hunting and trapping territory under the skilled tutelage of the bride's male relatives and the opportunity for the males of the band to acquire an ally who could further their economic and political interests. The advantages for the bride were equally obvious. The new "country husband's" skills as a "provider" could be evaluated while she was still close to the bosom of her natal family. No doubt for many young brides the birth of a first child among female relatives in whom she had confidence was far more preferable than a birthing experience away from her kinswomen. Should the outsider male be found wanting either as a provider or as a work mate and ally of her kinsmen the spousal relationship could be terminated. On the other hand, relationships which emerged and endured over the course of several winters could be said to have some depth and stability.

The gender-based roles and skills of the woman in the freeman family were crucial to its survival and success. Perhaps as critical as this spousal relationship was the relationship between the outsider adult male and his country wife's male relatives. In point of fact the two relationships were intertwined. A spousal relationship with a woman of consequence which was established in intimate association with the band required her relatives to accept the outsider country husband as a kinsman. Such an acceptance would always be conditional on the outsider's appropriate behaviour towards his wife's kin. In time, instances of genuine affection between the outside male and his "in-laws" could emerge. In most instances the relationship no doubt remained somewhat formal and distant. The lack of harmony in some instances may have led to violence.[21] For the successful freeman and his family, however, the essential requirement accompanying a country wife was the acceptance of his presence by her kinsmen and their neighbouring connections. The tragic fate of the twelve Iroquois and two *Canadien* freemen who journeyed to Chesterfield House in the autumn of 1801 is clear testimony to the sociopolitical understanding that were necessary for survival.[22] The fourteen were a trapping party hoping to base themselves at Chesterfield House near the confluence of the Red Deer and South Saskatchewan rivers, when they were set upon by Atsina, sometimes known as Gros Ventres, who viewed them as interlopers.

A critically important relationship in the emergence of the Métis was that involving two or three outsider males. With the adult males of this wintering group functioning as hunting, trapping and fishing work mates and partners for extended periods of the year their families came to constitute a social milieu in which the succeeding generation would choose marriage partners. A perusal of some freeman genealogies demonstrates that individuals did marry into indigenous Indian bands but the large majority in most regions would appear to have taken spouses from other freeman families and bands.[23] It is noteworthy that the families of freemen who failed to form these work mate partnerships became part of the indigenous Indian tradition. Two particular examples are George Sutherland, said to be the founder of the Willow People among the Down-River Plains Cree, and Alexis[?] Piché, the progenitor of several prominent families among the Rocky Mountain-Beaver Hills People of the Up-River Plains Cree.[24] Without the relationship with other outsider males a winterer and his household might well enjoy success, but the generational legacy in the nineteenth century would be overwhelmingly in an Indian, not a Métis, tradition.

Among the distinguishing behaviours of some freemen descendants in the North Saskatchewan River valley was the practice of a "folk" Roman Catholicism which predated the appearance of Roman Catholic missionaries by more than half a century.[25] Roman Catholic missionaries after 1840 encountered infant baptism and Roman Catholic prayer among Native laity who had had no previous experience with church-sanctioned religious instruction. Such practices originated in an earlier generation of work mates who sustained some behaviours of the community of their origin, Lower Canada. They were shared among families who shared similar progenitors. In time some of these families would become distinct communities. In terms of ethnogenesis the work mate or outsider male relationship was as important as the other two relationships.

The cultural significance of the processes involved in the three relationships of the first step should not be underestimated. If these processes are ethnogenesis, what then is the relationship between particular experiences in wintering and the emergence of the Métis as a distinct sociocultural entity in the fur trade West? The anthropologist Fredrick Barth suggests a useful "model" to depict the interconnection of behaviour and culture:

> The simplest form of this interconnection would seem to depend on sharing: individual behaviour produces experience, a confrontation with reality which may or may not seem consistent with pre-existing conceptualizations and thus may sometimes tend to confirm, sometimes falsify them. If a number of persons in communication share a similar opportunity situation, experience the same confrontations with reality, and have the same conceptualizations falsified, one would expect them to develop shared understandings and modify their collective culture and expectations in accordance with this.[26]

The shared experiences in wintering were the behaviours involved in establishing the three critical relationships; the country marriage between an outsider male and an Indian woman of the band, the sociopolitical alliance relating the outsider male to the male kinsmen of the woman and the friendship that bound outsider males in an economic and social relationship. All of these relationships and the experiences that engendered them and the experiences that they in turn engendered constituted the first stage in the two-stage process of Plains Métis ethnogenesis.

While Giraud's description of the factors determining the circumstances of wintering appear to be clear the historian will find the process of wintering far more problematic. Brief references to particular activities at the trading post can be found in the various trading post journals. But life outside the trading post in the wintering bands is much more dimly perceived. In order to garner some insight into this experience, the first of two stages in the ethnogenesis of the Plains Métis, it is necessary to examine the second stage, the time when the Métis were emerging as a distinct cultural entity.

The opportunity of going free or becoming a freeman was not an option that would be available to many *engagés*. Most would lack the technical and sociopolitical skills necessary for survival. Not only would a freeman have to know how to hunt, fish and trap successfully while living apart from the fort and the Indian band but he would require the sociopolitical skills necessary to have the surrounding bands view him as one of themselves in so far as the resources of the region were concerned. Strangers were interlopers who were not tolerated. Such survival skills were acquired over time and required appropriate circumstances for their expression. For several "eastern Indians" who had been hired by the Montreal-based fur trade companies and who were numerous in the Athabasca country, particularly the Lesser Slave Lake and Jasper House neighbourhoods, freeman status proved to be a quick and natural process.[27] Their skills as hunters and trappers and their ability to achieve acceptance on the part of neighbouring Indians suggested they would be more profitable to the fur trade as free trappers and hunters rather than as contracted servants. Similarly Euro-Canadian servants who contemplated freeman status would have to have the necessary skills to function as a hunter and/or a trapper and to negotiate acceptance on the part of neighbouring Indians.

A critical factor in the transition from *engagé* to freeman was motivation. Elsewhere I have argued the existence of an adult male ethos among French Canadian males of this era that emphasized the necessity of being a man of consequence in one's own eyes and in the eyes of one's fellows.[28] A most dramatic expression of this sense of consequence is found in Alexander Ross's familiar account of the words of an old *engagé* whom Ross met in 1825 in route to the Red River Settlement:

> I have now been forty-two years in this country. For twenty-four I was a light canoe man.... No portage was too long for me; all portages were alike. My end of the canoe never touched the ground till I saw the end of [the portage].... Fifty songs a day were nothing to me, I could carry, paddle, walk and sing with any man I ever saw.... No water, no weather, ever stopped the paddle or the song. I have had twelve wives in the country; and was once possessed of fifty horses, and six running dogs, trimmed in the first style. I was then like a Bourgeois, rich and happy; no Bourgeois had better dressed wives than I; no Indian chief finer horses; no white man better harnessed or swifter dogs.... I wanted for nothing;...I should glory in commencing the same career again. I would spend another half-century in the same fields of enjoyment. There is no life so happy as a voyageur's life; none so independent; no place where a man enjoys so much variety and freedom as in the Indian country.[29]

Enduring status as a lowly *engagé* was incompatible with the ethos of a man of consequence. The expression of such an ethos in *le pays sauvage* required in time promotion, possibly to the rank and status of interpreter, and subsequently for some, freeman status. Others might become freemen earlier in their careers. It would appear that a similar if not identical ethos influenced those eastern Indians who chose to remain in the West to live as freemen. It is the existence of such an ethos which may well explain, in significant part, why the majority of freemen chose to live apart from indigenous Indian bands. Some of the particulars of their sense of a man of consequence would not be shared with the males of the indigenous Indian bands. While each could acknowledge kinship with the other their respective expressions of consequence limited the time that they and their families could spend in each other's company. A successful freeman as well as his "in-laws" may well have understood the limits of each other's tolerance of "different" behaviours. Living apart from kinsmen for significant periods could well have been an important element in a successful freeman's repertoire of behaviours. In living with his family apart from the Indian band and the trading post, the freeman laid the basis for his children to be enculturated in circumstances distinct from that of the band or the post. The process of enculturation in such circumstances was the second stage of a two-stage process which gave rise to the Plains Métis.

Wintering in the fur trade in the valley of the North Saskatchewan River and its tributaries in the latter decades of the eighteenth century was the basic context in which, for some Métis, processes of Métis ethnogenesis began. In all probability similar experiences marked behaviour in the valleys of the Red, Assiniboine and Athabaska rivers. The *en drouine* trading tradition and the bourgeois' interest in controlling labour costs were the twin wintering factors that encouraged the formation of the three essential relationships. These relationships in turn were critical to the success of the freeman and his family or, if you will, the proto-Métis. The first and foremost of these relationships was the country marriage between the servant, who by virtue of reputation and favour led the *en drouine* party and an Indian woman closely related to the prominent males of the band. The second critical relationship was that between the leader of the *en drouine* party, and the adult males of the band.[30] Resting upon the marriage relationship with the Indian woman, the relationship with the males of the band would determine the level of acceptance extended to the outsider. For purposes of exploiting the resources of the region it was essential that adult Indian males view the outsider as one of themselves. The third critical relationship that would see the freeman's family emerge distinct from the Indians was the relationship formed among some of the members of the *en drouine* party. While examples can be found of freemen and their families living with Indian bands the overwhelming impression from the sources emphasizes freeman families neighbouring with each other for extended periods of the year.[31] Such second-stage associations suggest friendships built up over time, dating from a period when circumstances encouraged close cooperation among some outsiders. While such associations reflected mutual self-interest in terms of economic activities they also reflected the freeman's preference for those with whom he shared a similar ethos and all that such sharing entailed.

The second stage in the process of Métis ethnogenesis in the Saskatchewan country emerged with the decision of the experienced *engagé* to become a freeman. With the support of his *bourgeois* who encouraged his pursuit of the material markers of consequence, the freeman claimed his family from the band or possibly the fort and began his assiduous pursuit of provisions and furs in surplus amounts. His ethos and the behaviour that manifested it made him and his family distinct from the indigenous Indians. He naturally grouped with those who suggested compatibility with his ways. With the marriage of his children to the children of other freeman families and with their pursuit of his ways, the process of Métis ethnogenesis on the western Plains, as early as the first quarter of the nineteenth century, was complete.

Gabriel Dumont the elder, the eldest son of Jean Dumont and Suzette, the Sarcee-Crow woman, witnessed the Métis of the upper North Saskatchewan becoming a community. He married Suzanne Lussier, the daughter of freeman François Lussier, the subject of a Paul Kane portrait. Members of his extended family were residing at Lac Ste-Anne when the Roman Catholic missionary Reverend J. Thibault visited there in the 1840s. In 1861 some followed the mission to Big Lake (St-Albert), a few miles north of Fort Edmonton. Already the Métis of the region were responding to the opportunities becoming apparent in the buffalo robe trade. From their base at St-Albert the Métis hunted south and southeast through the parkland to the prairie. In the 1870s at Buffalo Lake they established one of the largest *hivernement* villages. The husband of a granddaughter, Louison Montagnais, became the principal *Chef Métis* in the village. Kinsmen from the lower South Saskatchewan River at *Petite Ville* (ancestral to the village of Batoche) joined them at Buffalo Lake some winters. Dumont himself witnessed the demise of the village when the robe hunt swept southward and the resource on which it was based collapsed.[32] An aged patriarch at the time of his death in 1880 he was finally laid to rest a few miles south of Buffalo Lake on a bluff overlooking another wintering village site at the confluence of Tail Creek and Red Deer River. In his lifetime he would have witnessed the events that marked the processes that constituted the birth of a people.

The foregoing analysis has focussed on the outsider adult male in the circumstances and processes of becoming western Plains Métis. In this process no single act has more consequence than the individual *engagé's* decision to go free. The action is a powerful statement of self-definition and self-assertion. In this light concepts of patrifocality and male centrality suggest explanative insight into which freemen families would succeed as Métis. The bias of the historical sources themselves encourages this focus. What remains to be addressed in more detail is the nature and consequence of the wife and mother from the indigenous Indian band in the process of Métis ethnogenesis.

Editor's Note

This article originally appeared in *Prarie Forum* 19, no. 2 (Spring 1994): 1–13.

Notes

1. Marcel Giraud, *The Métis in the Canadian West,* 2 vols., translated by George Woodcock (Edmonton: University of Alberta Press, 1986), 2: 159. Originally published as *Le Métis Canadien* (Paris: Institut d'Ethnologie, Musée Nationale d'Histoire Naturelle, 1945). Giraud's view is comparable with "the problem of the frontier, namely the clash between primitive and civilized peoples" in G.F.G. Stanley, *The Birth of Western Canada* (1936; Toronto: University of Toronto Press, 1960), vii, and the Red River Settlement as "an oasis of civilization...amid the surrounding barbarism of forest and plain," in W.L. Morton, *Manitoba: A History* (Toronto: University of Toronto Press, 1976), 56.

2. Gerhard Ens, "Dispossession or Adaptation? Migration and Persistence of the Red River Metis, 1835–1890," *Historical Papers* (Ottawa: Canadian Historical Association, 1988), 121–22. Also see Gerhard Ens, "Kinship, Ethnicity, Class and the Red River Metis: The Parishes of St. Francois Xavier and St. Andrew's" (Ph.D. Dissertation, University of Alberta, 1989).

3. While terms such as "Aboriginal" and "Amerindian" have received support from academics and political activists it is my impression that among most elders in a reserve context in western Canada these terms are not used. Further, in many instances they are viewed as needless, ostentatious affectations. Perhaps in time this popular, community-rooted opposition will cease. At the moment, however, "Indian" would appear to be the preferable term.

4. Charles Winick, *Dictionary of Anthropology* (Totowa, NJ: Littlefield, 1968), 193, "ethnogenic. Relating to the beginning of ethnic groups." Also see Jacqueline Peterson and Jennifer S.H. Brown, "Introduction," in Jacqueline Peterson and Jennifer S.H. Brown, eds., *The New Peoples: Being and Becoming Métis in North America* (Winnipeg: University of Manitoba Press, 1985), 3–16.

5. In this article French terms and phrases used historically in the western fur trade will be acknowledged with italics.

6. Jacqueline Peterson, "Prelude to Red River: A Social Portrait of the Great Lakes Métis," *Ethnohistory* 25 (1978): 58.

7. *"En drouine"* varies in spelling. This form is used in Giraud, *Métis in the Canadian West,* 1: 216. Also see *Trésor de la Langue Française: Dictionnaire de la langue du XIXe et du XXe siècle (1789–1960)* (Paris: Editions du Centre national de la recherche scientifiques, 1979), vol. 17: 526a.

8. Jennifer Brown, *Strangers in Blood: Fur Trade Families in Indian Country* (Vancouver: University of British Columbia Press, 1980).

9. Jennifer Brown, "Woman as Centre and Symbol in the Emergence of Métis Communities," *The Canadian Journal of Native Studies* 3, no. 1 (1983): 39–46.

10. Provincial Archives of Alberta (PAA), Congrégations des oblats de Marie Immaculée (OMI), Fonds oblat de la province d'Alberta-Saskatchewan, Paroisse Duck Lake, "Liber Animarum des Indiens et Métis...jusqu'en 1940," boîte 1, item 1, p. 725. Suzette, the Sarcee-Crow woman, was also known as Josette. "Turning-off" was the process whereby an individual leaving *le pays sauvage* induced a younger man to replace him as husband and father by turning over to him one's "outfit" such as horses, traps and other accoutrements. Jean Dumont had apparently acquired Suzette in a similar fashion early in the 1790s from a Jean Baptiste Bruneau. In the process of "turning-off," the country wife was not necessarily a passive participant.

11. Giraud, *Métis in the Canadian West,* 2: 152–58.

12. John E. Foster, R.F. Beal, and L. Zuk, "The Métis Hivernement Settlement at Buffalo Lake, 1872–77," report prepared for Historic Sites and Provincial Museums Division, Department of Culture, Government of Alberta, 1987.

13. Grace Lee Nute, *The Voyageur* (1931; St. Paul: Minnesota Historical Society, 1966), 5.

14. Marjorie W. Campbell, *The North West Company* (1957; Toronto: Macmillan, 1973), 163–64.

15. Nute, *Voyageur,* 93; note the spelling "dérouine." See Giraud, *Métis in the Canadian West,* 1: 216.

16. Giraud, *Métis in the Canadian West,* 1: 215–16.

17. Ibid., 263.

18 Unfortunately the detailed descriptions of trade negotiations which have survived in the Hudson's Bay Company tradition are not matched for the winter camps in the Montreal-based trade for this period.

19. H.M. Robinson, *The Great Fur Land* (New York: G.P. Putnam's Sons, 1879), 258–59. In describing courtship among the Métis a century later Robinson suggests that the daughter and mother would indicate to the father whether a proposal was acceptable.

20. Giraud, *Métis in the Canadian West,* 1: 200–201.

21. Occasional references to incidents of violence involving peddlers and Indians in winter camps in HBC documents cannot be confirmed.

22. Alice Johnson, ed., *Saskatchewan Journals and Correspondence: Edmonton House 1795–1800, Chesterfield House 1800–1802* (London: Hudson's Bay Record Society, 1967), 311, 314.

23. PAA, OMI, Paroisse Duck Lake, "Liber animarum," vol. 1: 1, demonstrates this point in the genealogies of the Jean Dumont and François Lucier families.

24. William A. Fraser, "Plains Cree Assiniboine and Saulteaux (Plains) Bands 1874–84," manuscript (n.p., 1963), 12–13, copy in possession of author.

25. Foster, Beal and Zuk, "Métis Hivernement Settlement," 65.

26. Fredrick Barth, "Descent and Marriage Reconsidered," in Jack Goody, ed., *The Character of Kinship* (London: Cambridge University Press, 1973), 5.

27. Gertrude Nicks, "The Iroquois and the Fur Trade in Western Canada," in C.M. Judd and A.J. Ray, eds., *Old Trails and New Directions: Papers of the Third North American Fur Trade Conference* (Toronto: University of Toronto Press, 1980), 90.

28. John E. Foster, "The Plains Métis," in R. Bruce Morrison and C. Roderick Wilson, eds., *Native Peoples: The Canadian Experience* (Toronto: McClelland and Stewart, 1986), 384.

29. Alexander Ross, *The Fur Hunters of the Far West,* 2 vols. (London: Smith, Elder and Co., 1855), 2: 236–37. As quoted in W.J. Eccles, *The Canadian Frontier 1534–1760* (Toronto: Holt, Rinehart and Winston, 1969), 191.

30. Giraud, *Métis in the Canadian West,* 1: 255–56 suggests Indian women preferred marriage relationships with Euro-Canadians. Sylvia Van Kirk, *"Many Tender Ties": Women in Fur Trade Society in Western Canada, 1670–1870* (Winnipeg: Watson and Dwyer, 1980) is a useful corrective.

31. Giraud, *Métis in the Canadian West,* 1: 267.

32. Gabriel Dumont the elder (sometimes Alberta) was the uncle of the more famous Gabriel Dumont the younger (sometimes Saskatchewan). Also see John E. Foster, "The Métis and the End of the Plains Buffalo in Alberta," in John E. Foster, Dick Harrison and I.S. MacLaren, eds., *Buffalo* (Edmonton: University of Alberta Press, 1992), 61–78.

THE IMAGINED WEST

9

The Imagined West

Introducing Cultural History

GERALD FRIESEN

HISTORICAL WRITING, like history itself, does not end. The next day dawns, the next articles and books are published, and the human processes of creation and reflection simply carry on. John Foster's writing and teaching played a central part in the re-imagining of western Canada that took place between the 1960s and the 1990s. This volume is testimony to his influence. Indeed, many of the articles in *From Rupert's Land to Canada* illustrate the range of his interests and the persistent challenge to accepted the wisdom that he represented while other articles move onto new ground, expanding on Foster's curiosity about how societies see and depict themselves.

Cultural history is a relatively new kid on the block. It follows three great waves of historical interpretation in English Canada that are discussed in Carl Berger's *The Writing of Canadian History*.[1] Two of these, which took shape between 1900 and the 1960s, were dominated by professional historians, most of them located in the country's metropolises, who debated vigorously among themselves but, in retrospect, seem to have worked within common methodological assumptions. Supporters of a British nationality, of a distinctive Canadian economy and polity, or of a North American destiny, they wrote histories that were accessible to lay readers. Indeed, in the finest writing such as that of a Creighton or a Lower, a national pantheon was created that delighted several generations of Canadian citizens.

The third wave of national histories is still rolling in. Commencing in the 1960s, it drew upon the worldwide enthusiasm for social history and a large optimistic generation of new Canadian scholars, among whom John Foster was prominent, to paint a canvas populated by ordinary folk. Aboriginal and fur trade studies, labour and women's history, the biographies of cities and regions and ethnic groups, proliferated in the 1970s and 1980s. This spate of new stories could not easily be assimilated into the previous generation's narrative line that relied on national autonomy and the development of a national economy. Rather, the new social history delighted in contradicting the impression conveyed by a single national narrative. John Foster was one who relished such skirmishes. Implicit in his writing was advocacy for a new, honoured place for First Nation and Metis people within Canadian society. Thus, the social history approach elicited from him, and from many of his colleagues, sympathy for less-favoured groups, whether immigrant miners, suffragist women, or Metis boatmen. Inevitably, their interest in the country's erstwhile minorities, and their apparent neglect of overriding national narratives, provoked criticism from those who held different allegiances or who simply worried about national unity and history's role in preserving it.[2]

Social history has now lost the sheen that comes with being the latest fashion. It has been challenged not only by those who assert the primacy of elites in a community but also by historians of "culture." The latter approach inquires into a society's "signifying system," understood as the "repertoire of interpretive mechanisms and value systems" by which a group of people "communicate their values and their truths."[3]

Cultural history borrows from anthropology and literary theory. It moves beyond exclusively economic and social explanations of past events to ask how groups of people perceive meaning and communicate values. An important pioneer in this field, the Italian Communist, Antonio Gramsci, who wrote a series of notebooks while in prison during the interwar years, suggested that an elite exercises power in society by shaping the cultural context within which everyone operates. Conventional assumptions about the exercise of power, which focus on military, economic, or political forces, must be expanded, Gramsci suggested, to consider the elite's role in the development of "hegemony." Gramsci was proposing that, in democratic societies, the needs of the "ruling class" are secured through the public's consent to certain dominant ideas, not the overt exercise of force.[4]

The Gramscian thesis folded into a larger assault upon Enlightenment conventions that gathered strength in international academic circles between the 1960s and 1980s. For Michel Foucault and other poststructuralists, previous histories had been revealed as ideological constructions. Such critics concluded that because the tenets of the sciences and social sciences during the age of modernity (roughly from the seventeenth to the mid-twentieth century), were tendentious products of class interests, they should be subjected to an all-out attack. In their view, knowledge was not objective, language was neither stable nor reliable, science was at the mercy of hegemonic interests, and even the autonomous self ("the subject") was a myth.[5]

The postmodern and poststructural approaches have emerged only slowly in western Canadian studies, partly because of the demographic composition of the small group of professional scholars who contribute to the field, partly because the cultural context differs. In recent years, however, a number of western cultural histories have reflected the "linguistic turn" of this poststructural approach. Elizabeth Vibert's *Traders' Tales: Narratives of Cultural Encounters in the Columbia Plateau, 1807–1846* is an interesting representative work that deconstructs the narratives written by fur traders to uncover the cultural assumptions within which they lived and worked. Jeffery Taylor's *Fashioning Farmers: Ideology, Agricultural Knowledge and the Manitoba Farm Movement, 1890–1925* offers a similarly-challenging perspective on farm knowledge. What is interesting about a juxtaposition of the two works is that the former focuses its attention upon the margin between the worlds of Aboriginal and European, while the latter examines the point where ancient perspectives upon agricultural economy and peoples' resistance movements confront modern capitalist institutions. Foucault would have been delighted to see the sharp edges of the tectonic plates—the clash of worldviews—represented in each book. An adventurous study that bridges the subject matter covered by Vibert and Taylor is Sarah Carter's *Capturing Women: The Manipulation of Cultural Imagery in Canada's Prairie West*. Carter places gender at the forefront of her story but, inevitably, the contrasts between European Canadian and Aboriginal, and between noncapitalist and capitalist worlds, play a fundamental part in the narrative.[6]

Postmodern language does not figure prominently in the essays on "The Imagined West" that follow but poststructural notions of meaning and cultural difference do underlie the ambitions of each. Ted Binnema, Ian MacLaren, Rod Macleod and Heather Rollason Driscoll are precise in their definitions of the texts to be examined, careful in the elucidation of the world views that shaped them, and specific in the lessons they draw. They imagine that truth, or a closer approximation of it than was previously available, will emerge from their research. They do not sink into the despair that seems to be the counsel of many fashionable postmodernists.

A map, says Binnema, is a kind of text, as much the distinctive product of a society as language or music. He argues that map-making was a long-standing tradition in the Blackfoot world. Sketched roughly and provisionally on hides, snow, or in the dust, Blackfoot maps constituted remarkable outlines of vast territories. But to understand such a map, Binnema writes, later observers must come to terms with the specific qualities of the Blackfoot way of life. These distinctive qualities included the vantage points established by an equestrian and pedestrian mode of travel and by the military and diplomatic network that constituted the plains as familiar terrain, the mountains as alien ground. The purpose of the map was to guide travellers safely, to indicate the distances between water sources (a crucial matter in summer), and to estabish the relations among the various territories of friends and enemies.

Binnema contends that the Old Swan map of 1801 conveys truthful, useful impressions. His task, as a student of cultural history, has been to learn how to "read" the map in the way that was originally intended. His carefully-planned steps across a vast cultural divide render a seemingly-indecipherable or apparently inaccurate sketch both comprehensible and valid. Moreover, his empathetic reading of the map enables the modern student to appreciate the forces that prevailed in a distant—and yet not so very distant—culture. Binnema's success illustrates the remarkable diversity of cultural conventions that may underlie the superficially transparent matter of map-making. It is an example, too, of cultural history's sensitivity to the dramatic differences in perspective that can prevail among social groups in contemporary Canada.

The same pattern of cultural forces is evident in Ian MacLaren's essay. However, in approaching this paper, the reader should beware the simplicity and apparent opacity of the opening paragraphs. Carefully chosen by Professor MacLaren to convey a neutral impression, these innocent phrases hide some fascinating duplicities in the career of the artist-author, Paul Kane, the stories in his purported journal, and the society in which these texts appeared. According to MacLaren, Paul Kane's memoir of his travels to the North-West in the 1840s is not what it seems.

It is the gulf between the seeming factuality of the texts handed down to us and the more complicated truths about their context, as revealed by MacLaren's careful research, that makes this essay a wonderful example of cultural history. The reader learns very quickly that Kane's book, and others of similar ilk dating from the eighteenth and nineteenth century, are tendentious constructions. They promote the interests of some groups while undercutting the status and fortunes of others. They even misrepresent the author's own experiences, though the reader is never certain whether Kane has given his consent to this dishonesty. One eventually concludes that the commercial and political goals of the imperial-colonial elite were furthered by the revisions buried in the text and that Aboriginal authority was diminished. The story uncovered by MacLaren is, as the Victorians might have said, a tonic; its bracing properties might just offer a cure, or at least a palliative, for what ails society today.

The law, like the map and the travel volume, is a highly-refined social construction that can be examined as a cultural text. It expresses a country's ideals, distinguishes acceptable from unacceptable behaviour, and conveys strong, clear impressions about the fears of the dominant groups in a society. The newspaper, by contrast, though also a cultural text, is a much more spontaneous product, written quickly and, it might be thought, just as quickly forgotten. Macleod and Rollason Driscoll demonstrate that the newspaper and the law offer quite different testimonies about a society, particularly at a tense moment of change when the population was sharply—and evenly—divided between Aboriginal and European Canadian elements.

The pressure upon the police, the courts, and the jails of the North-West must have been intense in the late 1870s and early 1880s. During this era of great instability, when two vastly different cultural groups tried to control the same space, Canadian officials were treading difficult ground. They belonged completely in one of the groups but were trying to ensure that citizens in the other adapted quickly and were not crushed in the process. Significantly, Macleod and Rollason Driscoll demonstrated in an earlier essay that European Canadians were over four times more likely than Aboriginal people to be charged with crimes in the Territories in these years. In the essay in this volume, they now turn to the newspapers to see what the daily climate of opinion might have been like. The result is interesting: in the northern districts of Battleford and Edmonton, where economic development was slow, newspaper discussion of crime was less inflammatory and treatment of Aboriginal offenders was more personal and individual; in the south, where the arrival of the railway ensured that the economy changed much more rapidly, crime was more prevalent (two to three times as many convictions as in the north) and the newspaper discussions of Aboriginal offenders were much more extensive and more likely to inflame anti-First Nation prejudice among the incoming European Canadians.

As in the discussions of Blackfoot maps and Paul Kane's book, the newspapers appear in this article as a text under examination. To understand the messages hidden within the newspaper columns, the reader must step back from the printed page to ask about the circumstances in which it was prepared. Macleod and Rollason Driscoll mention an historical article written in the 1970s that actually believed the crime stories reported in the Calgary newspapers and attributed much of the region's crime to Aboriginal people. That article simply reported one side's view of the overheated cultural wars of the 1880s. Macleod and Rollason Driscoll, by contrast, have undertaken a careful two-stage research project. First, they examined the court records that constitute the best source of information on numbers of charges and convictions. Second, they utilize a variety of newspapers in order to assess the factors that led to overheated anti-Aboriginal rhetoric in some communities but not others. This is trustworthy history, an excellent illustration of how sensitivity to cultural difference should be built into one's perceptions of the world.

Each of these articles deals with western Canadian texts of the nineteenth century. In each, the gulf between Aboriginal and European Canadian societies is a central part of the inquiry. In each, the authors identify blind spots in the vision of some western Canadians today. Finally, in each, the central issue of cultural perspective is addressed: how a Blackfoot would have perceived Old Swan's map; how Paul Kane's experiences were re-invented to meet the expectations of his book's audience; how the differences between southern and northern Territorial newspapers' depictions of crime responded to the economic and social tensions in the two districts, not to the actual crime rates or to actual ratios of Aboriginal/ European Canadian participation in criminal acts.

The new cultural history reflects the changing concerns of Canada at the start of the twenty-first century. It exists not simply for its own sake, though some scholars believe that is reason enough to do what they do, but because our sense of direction depends on our awareness of where we were and where we are. Like any landscape, the past takes on different textures and outlines when we change our vantage point.[7] In an age preoccupied by rapid changes in communications and cultural industries, cultural history enables us to understand the present by recasting the image of the past. John Foster enjoyed this process of revision.

Notes

1. Carl Berger, *The Writing of Canadian History: Aspects of English-Canadian Historical Writing 1900–1970* (Toronto: Oxford University Press, 1976).
2. J.L. Granatstein, *Who Killed Canadian History?* (Toronto: HarperCollins, 1998).
3. Raymond Williams, *Culture* (Glasgow: Fontana, William Collins, 1981), 13; Joyce Appleby, Lynn Hunt and Margaret Jacob, *Telling the Truth About History* (New York: W.W. Norton, 1994), 218; I discuss these issues in the last five essays in my *River Road: Essays on Manitoba and Prairie History* (Winnipeg: University of Manitoba Press 1996), 165–239.
4. David Forgacs and Geoffrey Nowell-Smith, eds., *Antonio Gramsci: Selections from Cultural Writings* (Cambridge: Harvard University Press, 1985); Raymond Williams, *Keywords: A vocabulary of culture and society* (London: Fontana, HarperCollins, 1976, 1988), 144–46.
5. A helpful short introduction to these questions is presented in Appleby et al., chapter 6, "Postmodernism and the Crisis of Modernity," 198–237.
6. Elizabeth Vibert, *Traders' Tales: Narratives of Cultural Encounters in the Columbia Plateau, 1807–1846* (Norman: University of Oklahoma Press, 1997); also Vibert and Jennifer S.H. Brown, eds., *Reading Beyond Words: Contexts for Native History* (Peterborough: Broadview, 1996); Jeffery Taylor, *Fashioning Farmers: Ideology, Agricultural Knowledge and the Manitoba Farm Movement, 1890–1925* (Regina: Canadian Plains Research Centre, 1994); Sarah Carter, *Capturing Women: The Manipulation of Cultural Imagery in Canada's Prairie West* (Montreal: McGill-Queen's University Press, 1997).
7. This analogy is borrowed from the British historian, R.H. Tawney.

10

How Does a Map Mean?

Old Swan's Map of 1801 and the Blackfoot World

THEODORE BINNEMA

ON 22 NOVEMBER 1800, a group of Blackfoot warriors left the fur trade posts at Chesterfield House to seek out their Shoshoni enemies in the upper Missouri River basin. Forty-nine days later, the unsuccessful party returned to that location at the confluence of the Red Deer and South Saskatchewan rivers. Fur trader, Peter Fidler, may have been inspired by reports of this expedition to ask Siksika headman, Old Swan (Ak ko mokki), to draw him a map of the northwestern plains showing the route the war expedition had taken (Figure 10–1).[1] That same February, Fidler collected maps from three other Native informants at Chesterfield House. A year later, Old Swan drew another map for Fidler. These maps were potentially very valuable to the British because they depicted a large area with which Euroamericans were unfamiliar. Nevertheless, Fidler kept all of the maps for himself until his death in 1822 when, in accordance with his will, they were turned over to his former employer, the Hudson's Bay Company (HBC). Fidler did redraft Old Swan's 1801 map and sent the copy, now known as the Ac Ko Mok Ki Map (Figure 10–2), to HBC officials in London during the summer of 1802. These officials instantly recognized the value of the map and sent it to Aaron Arrowsmith, the leading British cartographer at the time.[2] Arrowsmith incorporated the new information into his 1802 map of North America (Figure 10–3). Three years later, when Captains Meriwether Lewis and William Clark made their way up the Missouri River on behalf of the United States government, they took several maps but apparently considered the Arrowsmith map their most reliable.[3]

The connection between the Ac Ko Mok Ki map and the Lewis and Clark expedition is probably what has drawn scholars to Fidler's copy of Old Swan's map. Ironically, the information gained from the Ac Ko Mok Ki map

		Tents			Tents
1	Choque - Muk House	150	18	Ne chick a hah soy particular foot	60
2	Do sap poo - Crow Mountain	200	19	Nuo che tap he Woody	100
3	ams cape sox sue - Scissors neck	70	20	Sox six chicks sin na tap he Scissor foot	50
4	Lip pe tah he - Wrinkled	90	21	Poo can nam a tup he Pearl shell	70
5	Kix tah ka tap pee - Bruise	50	22	Six too te tup he Black	200
6	Choque - Go to war with Pee 1	160	23	Cut tux pee too hin Flat heads	50
7	Nee coo chis ah ka - Tattoed	80	24	Cum min na tup pe Blue eyed	60
8	An ne po tap pe - Gray fox	40	25	ap pa tup pe Tamin or white	90
9	Ke ta kap sum Garter	30	26	So he pee tup pee, thos that collect shells	
10	Do koo is too ye Hairy or Beard	50	27	Oe cook sa tap he Pablos	30
11	eth hin nex sa tup pe	40	28	At cha tap pee Snare mer	18
12	Tick et a tup pe Rib	100	29	Cut tux in nah mi Weak Bow	18
13	oo apo six sa tup pe Thigh	20	30	Patch now	12
14	oe sa tup pe scabby	100	31	Cotton na	22
15	Nae que a tup pe Wolf	200	32	Pum nuo pee tup pin Long Hair	100
16	Mut tah yo que Goap Tents	180			
17	mem me ous you First Father	20			

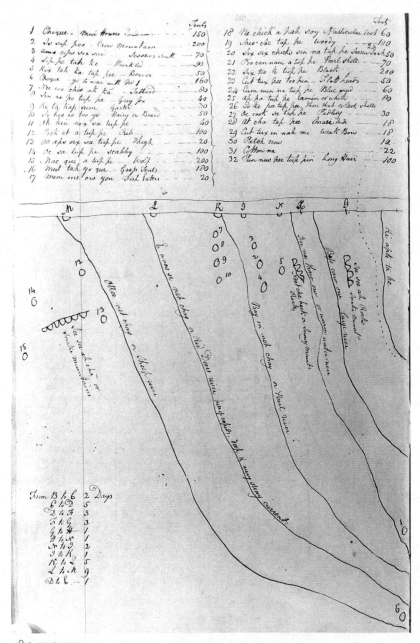

FIGURE 10-1

Old Swan's original 1801 map.

N4348 Hudson Bay Company Archives, Provincial Archives of Manitoba

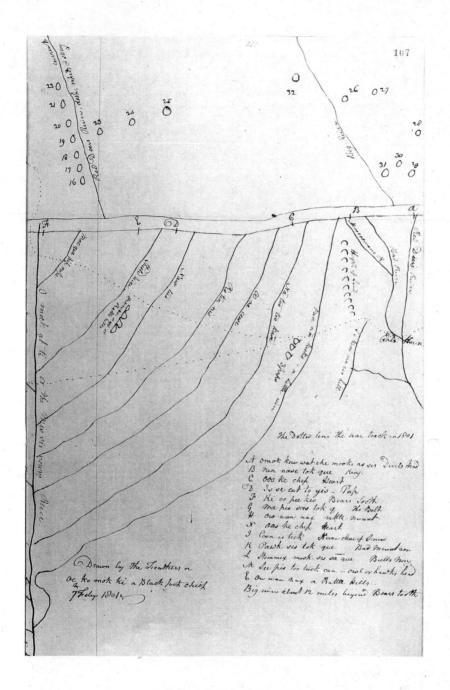

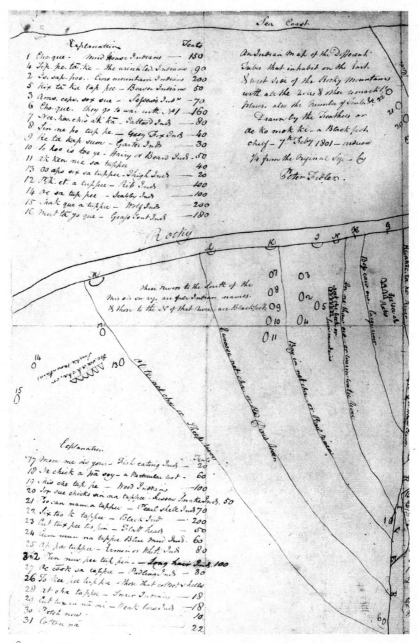

FIGURE 10–2

Fidler's redrawn map of Old Swan's 1801 map, known as the Ac Ko Mok Ki Map.
N4157 Hudson Bay Company Archives, Provincial Archives of Manitoba

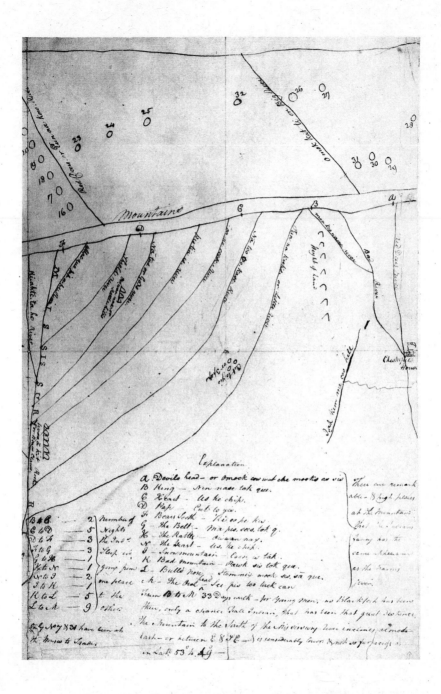

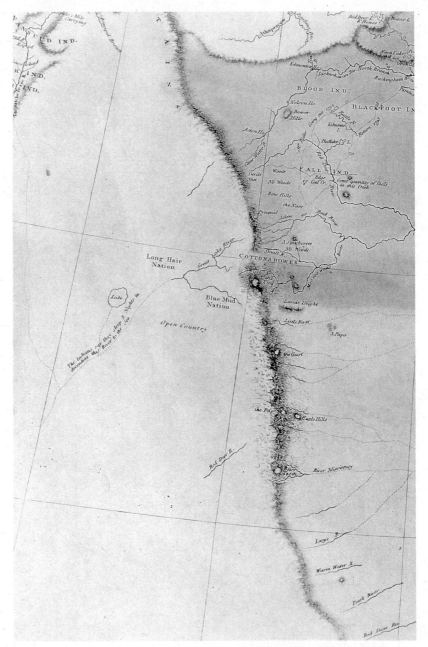

&ℓ *FIGURE 10–3*

Detail of Arrowsmith's 1802 map of North America based on the Ac Ko Mok Ki
Map of 1802. N6493 *Hudson Bay Company Archives, Provincial Archives of Manitoba*

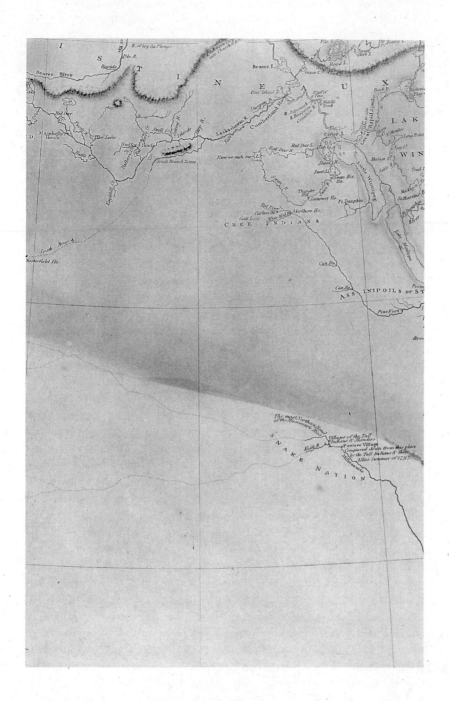

actually only confused Captains Lewis and Clark. By the time they contemplated Arrowsmith's map while travelling up the Missouri in 1805, several layers of misunderstanding had so distorted Old Swan's original information that Lewis and Clark would have been better off without it. Since 1802, others have tried to understand the Ac Ko Mok Ki map (thus, by extension, the Old Swan original), but with limited success.[4] This persistent failure to understand the map stems from observers' attempts to understand *what* the map means without first enquiring about *how* Blackfoot maps convey meaning. Only by analysing the cartographic style of the maps can we begin to understand the maps.

Recent work by historians of cartography reveals that all maps are prone to misinterpretation when not approached, like any other historical documents, as products of a particular time, place, and society.[5] In order to appreciate indigenous maps we must acknowledge that "a single map is but one of an indefinitely large number of maps that might be produced for the same situation or from the same data."[6] We *must* assume that other societies devised sophisticated cartographic styles that members of the community readily understood even if modern Western readers find them baffling. If maps are historical artifacts, knowledge of the individuals and societies that produced the maps, of the contexts in which the maps were produced, and of the landscapes portrayed in the maps should help us interpret them.

Had Peter Fidler attempted to interpret Old Swan's map rather than merely convey it to London, he would probably have been much more successful than Arrowsmith, for Fidler had far more pieces of the puzzle than Arrowsmith did. Fidler had five Native maps, not one. A competent surveyor, Fidler had visited part of the region depicted in the maps, and had gathered oral accounts of other parts. Perhaps most important, Fidler seems to have appreciated that the Plains Natives had a cartographic tradition very different from Western cartography. Sitting at his desk in London pondering but one of the maps, Arrowsmith knew little of the context in which the map was drawn. Given the information that Fidler submitted with the map, Arrowsmith should have done better than he did, but Arrowsmith was so steeped in Western cartographic traditions that he was ill prepared to understand how culturally specific his own cartographic concepts, and those of Old Swan, were. And so, Arrowsmith was the first, but not the last, to attempt to decipher Old Swan's map without trying to understand Blackfoot cartographic conventions. Not surprisingly, Lewis and Clark, thinking that the Arrowsmith map was based on Peter Fidler's observations, were baffled by the discrepancy between the map and the reality before them.

The context in which Fidler collected the maps suggests that the confusion caused by Old Swan's map cannot be attributed to a deliberate attempt by Old Swan to withhold or obscure knowledge from Fidler. The Blackfoot reached the height of their military dominance and confidence on the northwestern plains around the turn of the nineteenth century. They easily regulated contact between Euroamerican fur traders and any of the rival Native groups whose locations were portrayed on the map. The Blackfoot also enjoyed a cordial relationship with Peter Fidler and the Saskatchewan River traders. The Blackfoot first met Fidler in 1792–93 when Fidler, equipped with surveying equipment, wintered with the Peigan band led by prominent headman, Sakatow, in what is now southern Alberta. During that winter, Fidler met many Peigan, Kainah, and Siksika, established amicable relations with them, and learned much of their language and way of life.[7]

Among the Blackfoot, Old Swan's Siksika bands had a particularly close relationship with fur traders. When Old Swan drew his 1801 map, his bands benefited from trade at the HBC, North West Company, and XY Company trading posts at Chesterfield House, all of which had been established only a few months earlier. The short-lived Chesterfield House was the first Euroamerican trading complex built well inside Blackfoot wintering grounds. Before the traders could have built there they must have been confident of the advice, support, and assistance of Old Swan and his band. During the few years that the trading centre was in operation, the band provided the traders at Chesterfield House with an impressive return in wolf and fox furs, and kept them very well supplied with meat, and supported them with important services. In sum, the symbiotic relationship between the Euroamerican traders and the Siksika bands became more thorough-going at Chesterfield House than it had been anywhere else. Given the military might of the Blackfoot, and the mutually beneficial relationship that existed between the Siksika cartographers and Peter Fidler and the traders he represented, the cartographers must have felt little fear in providing the Fidler with valuable geographic knowledge.

Notwithstanding Old Swan's apparent intentions to provide Fidler with accurate information, his map evidently confused the inquisitive trader. Thanks to Fidler's travels with the Peigan in the winter of 1792–93, and the travels of other traders and surveyors like David Thompson, Euroamericans had accumulated considerable knowledge of the landscape as far south as "Nin nase tok que" (Chief Mountain).[8] But Fidler must have understood instantly that Old Swan's cartographic portrayal of the region varied significantly from those of western Europeans, and seemed to vary from his own first hand knowledge. How then could he make sense of Old Swan's portrayal of the Europeans' *terra incognito*? Perhaps he intentionally collected more maps hoping that they could enable him to decipher the enigmatic cartographic style of the first map. If so, Fidler evidently never did feel comfortable enough with the results to produce his own synthesis of the maps.

The fact that Fidler collected more Native maps may not have solved the riddle for him, but it certainly enhances our ability to understand Old Swan's map today. Our attention is focussed on Old Swan's map of 1801, but the interpretation presented here is based on an analysis of five maps.[9] The Ak Ko Mok Ki map of 1802 depicts a smaller area than Old Swan's original 1801 map.[10] Ak ko wee ak's map is a detailed map of the Bow and Oldman River basins.[11] Little Bear's map is a perplexing map that covers the region from the North Saskatchewan River to the Yellowstone River. Its cartographic style departs somewhat from the other Blackfoot maps, perhaps because of Peter Fidler's coaching.[12] Finally, a map drawn by an unidentified Gros Ventre man portrays the western plains from the Bow River to New Mexico.[13] Given the combination of remarkable similarities and important differences among the maps, it would be unwise for anyone to attempt to understand one without also studying the others.[14] Maps are products of societies, not just of individuals. Similarities among the maps, and the fact that Old Swan's map depicts areas Old Swan had never seen, suggest that the maps represent the accumulated knowledge of a community, not merely of individuals. Moreover, the Blackfoot and Gros Ventre evidently shared knowledge and perceptions of the landscape and of cartographic conventions.[15] Finally, the distinctive cartographic style of the Blackfoot maps provides compelling evidence that mapping was a longstanding tradition in Blackfoot society that predated the arrival of Europeans.

The Old Swan map is deceptively simple. Its simplicity can be deceiving because it is easy to equate simplicity with lack of sophistication. If we assume that the unadorned map represents vague or simplistic knowledge of the territory being depicted, or crude, inexact map-making skills, we also expect that aspects of the maps will be "inaccurate." This would be a serious error. The key to understanding the content of the Old Swan map, and the key to using it as a historical source, is an *assumption* that this map, and the accompanying maps, are accurate, and that any perceptions of their inaccuracy are probably rooted in our inability to understand the cartographic conventions they employ.

As simple as the Blackfoot mapping system may appear, it is complex and sophisticated. Old Swan's map illustrates the very essence of successful cartography: selectivity. Geographer Mark Monmonier has noted that "to avoid hiding critical information in a fog of detail, the map must offer a selective, incomplete view of reality."[16] Denis Wood has similarly argued that "the map's *effectiveness* is a consequence of the *selectivity* which it brings the past to bear on the present."[17] In this way good cartography is like any other effective communication; the intended audience will find it clear and direct. Good prose is concisely written. Poetry is language distilled. If most Western maps are analogous to prose, Old Swan's is akin to poetry. Blackfoot maps resided in the minds of their authors, only occasionally assuming concrete form in the form of sketch maps committed to sand, snow, or leather. They had to be easily recalled. The straight-line cartographic style of these Blackfoot maps is perfectly suited to convey all the information necessary to navigate the northwestern plains, in a very simple, easily memorized, format. One must not be fooled by the apparent crudeness of these maps; simplicity was a goal, not a mere characteristic of Blackfoot cartography.

An ideal way to appreciate the way Old Swan's map conveys its meaning is to examine point "F" on the map. Old Swan identified the place as *Ki oo pee kis* which Fidler translated as "Bear's Tooth." The map places it on the left bank of the Missouri River where it meets the Rocky Mountains.[18] Apparently, the mountain was important to Blackfoot maps. Except for Ak ko wee ak's map, which does not depict the upper Missouri River, every Native map that Fidler collected portrays the mountain. Evidently, the straight lines representing the "Rocky Mountains" and the Missouri River, form the core of Old Swan's map. They were probably the first two lines drawn on each map. The Missouri River system is depicted in a way that resembles the veins of a leaf until each river meets the Rocky Mountains at roughly a right angle. Bear's Tooth, point "F" was prominently located at the intersection of these two important lines.

What did Aaron Arrowsmith make of Bear's Tooth? His 1802 map shows that he assumed that Old Swan's line of the "Rocky Mountains" represented the continental divide, and that the end of the Missouri River corresponded to the ultimate source of the Missouri River (See Figure 10–3). To make his map plausible to his Western audience, Arrowsmith merely made the mountains more serpentine, but he ignored Fidler's note on the Ac Ko Mok Ki map that "the Mountain to the South of the Mis sis soury river inclines almost East—or between E & SE & is considerably lower & not so far across as in Lat. 53° to 49°." On Arrowsmith's map, Bear's Tooth became a prominent mountain along the continental divide overlooking the source of the Missouri River. In short, Arrowsmith assumed that Old Swan adhered to Western mapping standards.

In 1977, historical geographers Wayne Moodie and Barry Kaye apparently made the same assumption Arrowsmith made. Now possessed with Western maps of the same area, however, they also apparently further concluded that the map was only a crude drawing, for they argued that the "Bear's Tooth" corresponded to the Beartooth Mountains of Wyoming.[19] This interpretation, like many others, implies an assumption that the Blackfoot were either very confused about the region, or were unsophisticated mappers. In fact, *Ki oo pee kis* does not represent a mountain at the headwaters of the Missouri, or the Beartooth Range in Wyoming. The Blackfoot did, however, place it very precisely and accurately on their maps. In order to appreciate this fact, one must understand how the Blackfoot perceived the "Rocky Mountains."

The "Rocky Mountains" of Old Swan's map have been central to misinterpretations of the map. They are "false friends." In language translation a false friend is a word that is liable to be misunderstood because it resembles a nonsynonymous word in another language. In many contexts it would be incorrect to translate the French words *parent*, *face*, or *rapport* by using English words of the same spelling. These words can be "false friends." Those who have interpreted the Old Swan's map have simply assumed that the "Rocky Mountains" of the Plains Native bands were the same as the Rocky Mountains depicted on today's maps. More specifically, they assumed that if the Rocky Mountains are reduced to a single line, that line must correspond to the continental divide. This cannot be correct.

The Blackfoot "Rocky Mountains" varied from modern Euroamerican perceptions of those mountains in several ways. As early as 1792 Fidler recorded a description of the Rocky Mountains that differs considerably from the present understanding of the Rocky Mountains. Fidler wrote that

> the [Peigan] Inds say, who have been at war, a great distance to the Southwards that inclining still more Easterly, [the mountain] becomes lower—& that there it is divided into 4 or 5 parallel ridges—with fine plains betwixt them & a small river running thru each of these Vallies—where yew becomes plenty—& 2 or 3 other kinds of wood they describe which I have never seen.[20]

This description represents the *mistakis* ("backbone")[21] which Fidler translated as the "Rocky Mountains," but the *mistakis* does not correspond to the Rocky Mountains as we know them today. It shows that the *mistakis* ran east and then south-east along the Big Belt, Little Belt, Big Snowy, Pryor, and Crazy mountains. These mountains are much lower than the Rocky Mountains and are separated by broad grassy valleys.

Nowhere does the line of the *mistakis* on Old Swan's map represent the continental divide. Blackfoot maps were maps designed by a plains people, and they truly represent a view of the plains from the plains. Accordingly, the *mistakis* does not represent the great divide as Arrowsmith assumed, or even a geological formation, but the panorama that the mountains present to the northwestern plains. Between the Bow and Missouri rivers, the front ranges of the Rocky Mountains, rise abruptly above the adjoining plains. Therefore, between those two rivers they are visible from a great distance on the plains. North of the Bow River a wedge of forests and substantial foothills separate the Rocky Mountains from the plains. South of the Missouri, substantial mountains obscure any view of the Rocky Mountains from the plains. The *mistakis* then, roughly corresponds to the front ranges of the Rocky Mountains from the Bow River to the Missouri, and beyond the Missouri River it corresponds to the edge of other mountains that dominate the skyline.

The cartographic and oral evidence that Fidler collected confirms that the Blackfoot knew that the *mistakis* swung eastward south of the Missouri River, notwithstanding the depiction on Old Swan's map. The practice of representing with straight lines what are obviously irregular topographical features was practical. The *mistakis* could serve the same function as cardinal directions do on modern Western maps. Cardinal directions serve as abstract reference lines that allow map readers to determine their position and chart a desired course. The Siksika, like many human societies, had no convenient means to determine cardinal directions. Instead, topographical features served as concrete reference lines. Rather than charting a course east or north, for example, a Blackfoot might travel parallel to, or away from, or towards a river or line of mountains. In 1905, Brings-Down-the-Sun, a Peigan, described the Old North Trail in a way that reveals that the Blackfoot used the *mistakis* as such a reference line:

> There is a well known trail we call the Old North Trail. It runs north and south along the Rocky Mountains. No one knows how long it has been used by the Indians.... It forked where the city of Calgary now stands. The right fork ran north into the Barren Lands as far as people live. The main trail ran south along the eastern side of the Rockies, at a uniform distance from the mountains, keeping clear of the forest, and outside of the foothills. It ran close to where the city of Helena now stands, and extended south into the country, inhabited by a people with dark skins, and long hair falling over their faces (Mexico).[22]

The *mistakis* was the backbone of the Blackfoot world, and the spine of Old Swan's map. Any Blackfoot traveller, educated in straight-line cartographic conventions, could ignore the sinuosity of the feature without danger of becoming disoriented. Indeed, the straight lines on Siksika maps do not reflect a weakness, but a strength of Siksika maps.

Old Swan's map contains all the information necessary to navigate the northwestern plains, in a form that is readily committed to memory. Clouding a map with unnecessary detail would help neither people familiar with the terrain (because they would recognize places by sight), nor a people unfamiliar with the terrain, since they would be more likely to forget vital details of the map, if not the entire map. The use of topographical features such as rivers, mountain ranges, and coastlines as concrete reference lines or points and the related use of the straight-line cartographic style is neither unnatural nor uncommon.[23]

Aside from Bear's Tooth, Old Swan identified twelve places along the *mistakis*. Scrutiny of the map suggests that he included them because of their visual impact when viewed from the plains. Fidler explained to the HBC officials in 1802 that on the map he was sending them, "The places marked the Devil's Head, Pyramid, King, Heart &c &c are parts of the mountain that considerably overtop the rest."[24] Fidler, was wrong. Most of the mountains included on the maps were not particularly tall, but they do appear to be the tallest when seen from the plains. A mountain was especially worthy of inclusion if it served as an ideal reference point, capable of guiding travellers towards a specific place, whether it be a certain entry point into the mountains, or a culturally or religiously significant place. Thus, the Blackfoot might easily overlook tall mountains included on modern maps but include smaller but more culturally important, neighbouring mountains. One of these mountains is point "F" on Old Swan's map, *Ki oo pee kis*.

If the *mistakis* of the Blackfoot maps are the front ranges of the Rocky Mountains, *Ki oo pee kis* must be at the place where these mountains meet the Missouri River. On 19 July 1805, when the Lewis and Clark expedition reached what Meriwether Lewis dubbed "the gates of the Rocky Mountains," Lewis remarked on the "vast collumns of rocks mountains high."[25] Reuben Gold Thwaites noted that "at the entrance to the Gate of the Mountains is a curious elevation, now called the Bear's Teeth, from several peaks of rock which form a fanciful resemblance to those articles."[26] Beartooth Mountain (elevation 6792') is still identified by that name on modern topographical maps, but it is omitted from all but the most detailed modern topographical maps because by Western cartographic standards it is of little significance. There are several taller mountains even within a 20-mile radius.[27] Why would a mountain that is rarely included on Euroamerican maps be so prominent on Native maps? Reuben Thwaites's and Brings-Down-the-Sun's remarks offer clues. Beartooth Mountain, like many of the other landforms identified on Old Swan's map, is a valuable navigational marker. When knowledgeable travellers approach the mountains from the northeast, as the Blackfoot did on the war expedition of November 1800, they can easily make out the distinctive shape of Beartooth Mountain from up to a hundred miles away. After passing through the Gates of the Mountains, they can still see the mountain from the south as they travel towards the Three Forks. Similarly, the mountain labelled "A" on Old Swan's map, known to the Blackfoot as *Omok kow wat che mooks as sis*, is now better known as Devil's Head Mountain near Calgary, Alberta.[28] It is a small mountain that is remarkable for its shape and visibility from the plains. Devil's Head Mountain is particularly visible during the winter when chinook winds bare its steep sides. Then it forms a dark silhouette in front of the taller snow-clad mountains behind it. The mountain labelled "B" on Old Swan's map is known to the Blackfoot as *Nin nase tok que* (Chief Mountain).[29] Just south of today's Canada-US border, Chief Mountain is an unmistakable landmark, visible far onto the plains, even beyond present-day Lethbridge, Alberta. From there it is the most conspicuous mountain even though nearby mountains are taller.

Not only their appearance, but also their location help explain why certain landforms were included on these maps. Beartooth Mountain's location at the exact location where the Missouri River enters the plains must help explain its inclusion on the map. Beartooth Mountain was not only a marker, but also a destination. Just as Devil's Head Mountain led the Blackfoot towards the upper Bow Valley, and Haystack Butte[30] *Is se cut to yis*, ("D") led them to Lewis and Clark Pass, Beartooth Mountain led the Blackfoot to and from the upper reaches of the Missouri River. Its location explains why it was such an important landmark for the Blackfoot.

The Blackfoot did not travel by canoe, but rivers were very important to them nonetheless. Water sources were scarce on the northwestern plains, especially in the late summer. Therefore, knowledge of the location of water, and the approximate distance between rivers was important to those planning Blackfoot travel schedules.[31] In the winter, river valleys were essential sources of firewood, shelter, and usable water. At any time of the year then, river valleys were destinations for the Blackfoot. Rivers were also important to Old Swan's map but he portrayed rivers differently than westerners did. He drew the Missouri River as a straight line. Its tributaries join it after travelling in a broad arc from the *mistakis*. We shall see that the rivers as Old Swan depicted them posed a particular interpretive challenge for Arrowsmith, but in one respect, Arrowsmith seems to have found Old Swan's depiction of rivers straightforward.

Western maps show major rivers all the way from their mouths to their sources, even though they are only small streams at their headwaters. Assuming that the Blackfoot did the same, Arrowsmith found this aspect of Old Swan's map easily comprehensible. If he had understood that the *mistakis* represents that apparent wall of mountains that adjoins the plains, he would have understood that Old Swan's map could not show any rivers to their sources. The *mistakis* crosses several rivers; the continental divide, by definition, never does. The *mistakis* crosses the Missouri River and its southern tributaries well downstream from the continental divide. For example, the intersection of the *mistakis* and the Missouri River at Beartooth Mountain is several hundred miles downstream from that river's source.

Arrowsmith clearly was perplexed about how to render Old Swan's portrayal of the rivers on the plains. Simply transcribing the obviously foreign method of representing river systems would have made the map implausible to any Western audience. So, he gave each river a meandering route and replaced the leaf-vein pattern of river systems with the tree-branch pattern that his audience was familiar with. His goal, however, must have been plausibility rather than accuracy, for his interpretations were based on pure fantasy. For instance, Arrowsmith decided to have three join to become a major southern tributary of the Little [Milk] River that debouched into the Missouri River near the Hidatsa Villages. Ironically, in his effort to make his map scientifically credible in Europe, Arrowsmith became an imaginative artist, reinventing the American landscape.

On western maps, main streams tend to be drawn wider than tributaries since they usually carry more water than tributaries. The leaf-vein convention employed on Blackfoot maps provided a simpler alternative way of indicating which stream the community understood to be the main stream and which were its tributaries. The leaf-vein style demanded that maps not depict rivers' changes in direction. For the Blackfoot any resulting loss of detail was inconsequential. As pedestrian/equestrian peoples, the Blackfoot need not have been bothered with the turns of a river, or the shapes of lakes just as, as plains people, they did not need to portray the changes in direction of mountain chains. The straight-line conventions may seem flawed to modern readers but Native map readers would well have understood what was and what was not implied by them.

The Blackfoot maps suggest that the Blackfoot had flexible ways of naming rivers. Its seems that according to Blackfoot conventions a river could assume the name of any of its tributaries. For example, Old Swan's 1802 map depicts the *Ki oo sis sa ta* ("Bear River"), which corresponds to the present-day Marias River. It also shows the Teton River flowing into the Marias River just before its confluence with the Missouri. This is entirely consistent with modern Western cartographic conventions. On his 1801 map, however, Old Swan did not depict the Marias River at all. Instead, he included a river called *Na too too kase*. This is the Two Medicine River, a tributary of the Marias River. Old Swan, however, showed the Two Medicine River flowing directly into the Missouri. Clearly, then, the name *Na too too kase* was being applied to part of the *Ki oo sis sa ta*. By Western standards, any map that portrayed the Two Medicine River ought also to show the Marias River to its headwaters. Thus, the cartographer would have to draw two rivers even if only one was of interest. Siksika convention clearly did not require, although it did allow for, this portrayal. Circumstances might dictate which portrayal was most appropriate and oral communication would have avoided confusion. It is impossible to account conclusively for these flexible conventions but it is worth noting that their flexibility would have allowed the Blackfoot to draw simple area maps that avoided presenting unnecessary information.

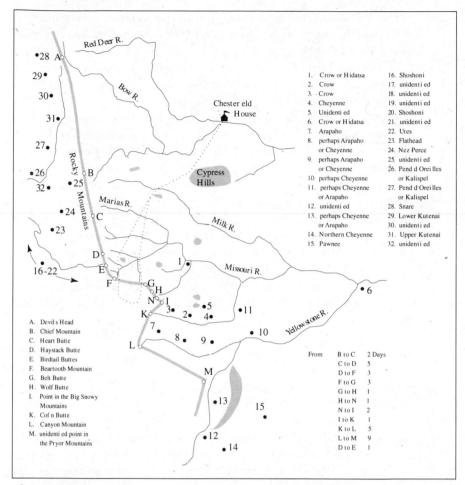

Map labels within the figure:

Red Deer R.

•28 A

29•

Bow R.

30•

Chester eld House

31•

Cypress Hills

27•

Rocky Mountains

•26 B

32•   •25

Marias R.

•24   C

•23

Milk R.

D

16-22   E

F   Missouri R.

G

H

N   I

•6

K   3•   •5

7   2•   4•   •11

8•   9•   •10

Yellowstone R.

L

A. Devil s Head
B. Chief Mountain
C. Heart Butte
D. Haystack Butte
E. Birdtail Buttes
F. Beartooth Mountain
G. Belt Butte
H. Wolf Butte
I. Point in the Big Snowy
    Mountains
K. Cof n Butte
L. Canyon Mountain
M. unidenti ed point in
    the Pryor Mountains

M

•13   15
        •

•12

•14

1. Crow or Hidatsa
2. Crow
3. Crow
4. Cheyenne
5. Unidenti ed
6. Crow or Hidatsa
7. Arapaho
8. perhaps Arapaho
   or Cheyenne
9. perhaps Arapaho
   or Cheyenne
10. perhaps Cheyenne
11. perhaps Cheyenne
    or Arapaho
12. unidenti ed
13. perhaps Cheyenne
    or Arapaho
14. Northern Cheyenne
15. Pawnee

16. Shoshoni
17. unidenti ed
18. unidenti ed
19. unidenti ed
20. Shoshoni
21. unidenti ed
22. Utes
23. Flathead
24. Nez Perce
25. unidenti ed
26. Pend d Orei lles
    or Kalispel
27. Pend d Orei lles
    or Kalispel
28. Snare
29. Lower Kutenai
30. unidenti ed
31. Upper Kutenai
32. unidenti ed

From   B to C   2 Days
        C to D   5
        D to F   3
        F to G   3
        G to H   1
        H to N   1
        N to I   2
        I to K   1
        K to L   5
        L to M   9
        D to E   1

〜 *FIGURE 10–4*

A Translation of Old Swan's Map of 1801. Old Swan's map depicts the northwestern
plains at the height of Blackfoot power in the region. The map, which shows the
approximate locations of bands that were not closely associated with the Blackfoot,
shows that the enemies of the Blackfoot were restricted to the margins of the region.
Adapted from Theodore Binnema, "Indian Maps as Ethnohistorical Sources," and D.W. Moodie and Barry
Kaye, "The Ac Ko Mok Ki Map," The Beaver 307, no. 4(1977): 4-15.

Different segments of the same river could also have different names.[32]
A river might have several names, each that was an apt description of only
part of its course. If this was so, a cartographer could draw an entire river,
mention one of the names, and his reader would understand that a portion
of the river was being emphasized. While these naming conventions might

seem very confusing to modern readers, and the explanation given here is only tentative, the conventions would have served admirably the goal of producing effective but simple maps.[33]

The *mistakis* and rivers formed the basic framework of Blackfoot maps, conveniently dividing a vast region into segments, but other symbols provided the additional essential information necessary to navigate the entire region. What is instantly obvious is how few other features Old Swan selected for his map. The sparseness of the map is a attributable to effective use of cartographic selection and to the topography of the region. The northwestern plains are not flat, but uneven, dotted with low mountains and cut by deep river valleys. Except in these river valleys, the landscape would have been almost completely devoid of trees. The land falls off gradually but steadily northeast or southeast from the Hudson Bay/Gulf of Mexico divide. Even small hills can afford a traveller expansive views that might include the *mistakis* or other distant highlands like the Cypress Hills, Sweetgrass Hills, Bearspaw Mountains, or Judith Mountains. The tops of these highlands offer even more expansive views. For example, under normal atmospheric conditions the Sweetgrass Hills and the Bearspaw Mountains are easily visible from the Cypress Hills.

Once the particular style of Old Swan's map is understood, it becomes clear that the map provides a simple, but very sophisticated portrayal of a vast region. Old Swan provided enough information for a person to travel from the Bow River to the Yellowstone River and beyond, confidently. Once we understand how Old Swan's map communicates its information, it becomes easy to surmise the location of most of the landforms. Figure 10–4 translates Old Swan's map from the Blackfoot cartographic language of the early nineteenth century to the conventional Western style. Not all of the landforms on Old Swan's map are identified precisely, but the approximate locations of all of them are indicated.

Any exploration of *how* a map means, helps alert us how cartographic conventions are not universal but specific to a particular community, time, and place. Peter Fidler and Aaron Arrowsmith's inability to understand Old Swan's map cannot be attributed to that map's inferior or inaccurate portrayal of the landscape. They were confused by the map because they did not grasp the syntax of the map. Western maps are no more objective, accurate, or transparent. Non-Westerners can be as baffled by Western maps as Arrowsmith was by Old Swan's. David Pentland has explained that

> the overwhelming detail of a topographic map causes more confusion
> than enlightenment for a Cree guide. He will become disoriented even
> in areas he has known since childhood, attempting to get his bearings
> by counting off the creeks along the course of a river, not realizing

that the cartographer may have omitted his favorite landmarks while including others he has never given any attention to.[34]

Curiously, Pentland concluded that, far from being universally understandable, the modern Western cartographic tradition is unique. He argued that "the Eskimo, the tribesmen of Siberia and central Africa, and the Cree Indian all have agreed on a set of conventions for map making—it is the modern cartographer with his satellite photographs and computers who is out of touch with the rest of the world."[35] Western cartographers, like Old Swan, could not avoid producing maps embedded with culturally specific information.

Our primary concern here has been to understand how this map communicates its information. This attempt has also incidentally uncovered ways in which the map has preserved information about the Blackfoot at the turn of the nineteenth century, but this has not been the purpose of this study. Nevertheless, it is appropriate briefly to examine some of the potential for Old Swan's map to become a valuable primary source for historians.

Historians have access to very few documents generated by the indigenous peoples of the northern plains. Old Swan's map, therefore, is a rare treasure. It can tell us a great deal about the Blackfoot history and culture in 1801 that is not otherwise available.

The Blackfoot maps provide the earliest information regarding the names the Blackfoot (actually the Siksika specifically) attached to certain rivers and landforms between the North Saskatchewan and Yellowstone Rivers. Blackfoot nomenclature may be very revealing. Blackfoot names tended to serve a utilitarian purpose. Descriptive names are the most common, although many places were named after animals or resources that seem to have been associated with the feature. Some features, like Beartooth Mountain and Swan's Bill, evidently acquired their names because they reminded the Blackfoot of specific animal parts. Only a few names are obviously related to Blackfoot culture and history. The common Western practice of naming features to commemorate specific individuals is nowhere evident. A few places relate to specific events in Blackfoot history (like Shield River) although these events are not likely major turning points in Blackfoot history as a western historian might conceive them. A number of place names are related to Blackfoot religion and mythology (Oldman River, Chief Mountain, "Gods" Lake). These places tended to be well north of the Missouri River, supporting the view that the Blackfoot, in 1800 already had a long history in the Oldman River basin. They were very familiar with the resources of that region and appear to have held a strong attachment to it.

It would be potentially very fruitful to study how the names of certain landforms and rivers changed over time. The fact that Old Swan's map gives

Gros Ventre names rather than Blackfoot names for the rivers south of the Missouri suggests that the Blackfoot were not yet as familiar with that region as they would be later in the century. By the end of the nineteenth century the Blackfoot were very familiar with the region south of the Missouri River.

Old Swan's map also sheds light on the military history of the northwestern plains. Specifically, the Chesterfield House journals show that a party of 175 Blackfoot left Chesterfield House on 30 November 1800 and arrived back at Chesterfield House on 10 January 1801 after failing to find any enemy bands.[36] It would be impossible to know where this party travelled without Old Swan's map of 1801. Old Swan traced the route of the Blackfoot 41-day war excursion of 1800–01 on the 1801 map. It shows that the warriors' route included several important landmarks depicted on the maps. They travelled first to the Cypress Hills, and then to the Sweetgrass Hills. From there they travelled almost directly to Beartooth Mountain, travelling west of the *ow wan nax* hills. Once in the mountains they apparently travelled up the Missouri valley in search of enemies, perhaps following Sixteenmile Creek or the Gallatin River/Bozeman Pass/Shields River route to find the Smith River which they followed to return to the plains. From there they travelled north to the Sweetgrass Hills, Cypress Hills, and back to Chesterfield House. Not only does the map shed light on the specific war party of 1801, but it also hints at the state of military relations more broadly. Evidently, by 1800 the military dominance of the Blackfoot had forced most of their enemies to retreat well south of the Missouri River, or west of the Rocky Mountains. This map apparently offers a snapshot of the Blackfoot world when the Blackfoot were at the height of their military power. Less than a decade later, the political geography of the region would begin its dramatic change. Cordial relations between the Blackfoot and Cree bands would collapse in July of 1806, forcing the Blackfoot to face enemies to the north and the south. In the same month, members of the Lewis and Clark expedition would meet Peigan warriors in the upper reaches of the Marias basin. Thirty years of hostility between the Blackfoot and the traders and trappers from the United States would follow. Meanwhile, increasingly well armed after 1806, the Crow, Shoshoni, and Flatheads would no longer be easy victims of the Blackfoot. Now translated, the Old Swan map can be used to greater advantage to extract the valuable evidence it holds concerning the Blackfoot at their height of influence.

Notes

1. The Blackfoot consist of the Siksika, Kainah, and Peigan bands.
2. D.W. Moodie and Barry Kaye, "The Ac Ko Mok Ki Map," *The Beaver* 307, no. 4 (Spring 1977): 10–11. For more information on Aaron Arrowsmith, see Coolie Verner, "The Arrowsmith Firm and the Cartography of Canada," in Barbara Farrell and Aileen Desbarats, eds., *Explorations in the History of Canadian Mapping: A Collection of Essays* (Ottawa: Association of Canadian Map Libraries and Archives, 1988), 47–54.
3. Barbara Belyea, "Mapping the Marias: The Interface of Native and Scientific Cartographies," *Great Plains Quarterly* 17 (1997): 168–69.
4. The only detailed study of any of these maps is contained in Moodie and Kaye, "The Ac Ko Mok Ki Map," 4–15. This article's analysis is limited to the "Ac Ko Mok Ki map." The Ac Ko Mok Ki map is also discussed in D.W. Moodie, "Indian Map-Making: Two Examples From the Fur Trade West," in Graeme Wynn, ed., *People Places Patterns Processes: Geographical Perspectives on the Canadian Past* (Toronto: Copp Clark Pitman, 1990), 56–67. A brief study of this map is found in three pages of Alice B. Kehoe, "How the Ancient Peigans Lived," *Research in Economic Anthropology* 14 (1993): 87–105. All of the maps being discussed in this study have been described in Judith Beattie, "Indian Maps in the Hudson's Bay Company Archives: A Comparison of Five Area Maps Recorded by Peter Fidler, 1801–1802," *Archivaria* 21 (1985–86): 166–75; and "The Indian Maps Recorded by Peter Fidler, 1801–1810," paper presented at the International Conference on the History of Cartography, Ottawa, 8–12 July 1985. The present study focusses on the Old Swan map rather than the Ac Ko Mok Ki map. Although the two maps are nearly identical, the Old Swan map has a few details not included in the redraft.
5. For example, Lesley Cormack has argued that the belief that medieval cartographers assumed the world was flat stems from a misinterpretation of medieval T-O maps, Lesley B. Cormack, "Flat Earth or Round Sphere: Misconceptions of the Shape of the Earth and the Fifteenth-Century Transformation of the World," *Ecumene* 1 (1994): 364–85. For a discussion of the subjectivity of maps see J.B. Harley, "Maps, Knowledge, and Power," in Denis Cosgrove and Stephen Daniels, eds., *The Iconography of Landscape: Essays on the Symbolic Representation, Design and Use of Past Environments* (Cambridge: Cambridge University Press, 1988), 277–312; and J.B. Harley, "Deconstructing the Map," *Cartographica* 26, no. 2 (1989): 1–19. That maps must be translated rather than transliterated is also discussed in J.B. Harley and David Woodward, eds., *Cartography in Prehistoric, Ancient, and Medieval Europe and the Mediterranean,* Vol. 1 of *The History of Cartography* (Chicago: University of Chicago Press, 1987), 3. The scholarship on Native North American mapping has grown very large. For a discussion of the historiography of Native mapping, including the Ac Ko Mok Ki Map, see Barbara Belyea, "Amerindian Maps: The Explorer as Translator," *Journal of Historical Geography* 18, no. 3 (1992): 267–77. Also see David Woodward and G. Malcolm Lewis, eds., *Cartography in the Traditional African, American, Arctic, Australian, and Pacific Societies*, Vol. 2.3 of *The History of Cartography* (Chicago: University of Chicago Press, 1998).
6. Mark Monmonier, *How to Lie with Maps* (Chicago: University of Chicago Press, 1991), 2. Therefore, as Monmonier argues *all* maps "must distort reality," "must offer a selective, incomplete view of reality"; all maps must lie (p. 1).

7. Fidler sent to London a map of the region he saw on this trip. The original map has not survived although it was incorporated into A. Arrowsmith's map of North America, 1795 (a copy of which is found in HBCA, G. 4/26).

8. Chief Mountain is "B" on Old Swan's map (Figure 10–1). Arrowsmith's map of 1802 (Figure 10–3) synthesizes the Euroamerican knowledge of the river systems north of the Missouri River at the time.

9. HBCA, E.3/2 fos. 106d–107. *Ak ko makki* means "Old Swan" in the Blackfoot language. The HBC traders tended to call Old Swan "Feathers," and the North West Company traders called him "Painted Feathers." See Theodore Binnema, "Old Swan, Big Man, and the Siksika Bands, 1794–1815," *Canadian Historical Review* 77 (1996): 1–32.

10. The rough copy of this map is found in HBCA, B.39/a/2 fo. 93. A redrafted version can be found in HBCA, E.3/2 fo. 104.

11. The rough copy is found at HBCA, B.39/a/2 fo. 92d and Fidler's redrafted version in E.3/2 fo. 103d.

12. HBCA, E.3/2 fos. 104d–105. A rough copy is in B.39/a/2 fos. 85d–86.

13. HBCA, E.3/2 fos. 105d–106.

14. Information about all the known authors of these maps is summarized from Theodore Binnema, "Old Swan, Big Man, and the Siksika Bands." Also see Theodore Binnema, "Conflict or Cooperation?: Blackfoot Trade Strategies, 1794–1815" (MA thesis, University of Alberta, 1992). Old Swan is discussed throughout; Little Bear on pp. 65–69, 71; and Ak ko we ak on pp. 67–68, 71. Also see Hugh A. Dempsey, "A ca oo mah ca ye," *Dictionary of Canadian Biography*, Frances G. Halpenny, ed., Vol. 8 (Toronto: University of Toronto Press, 1985).

15. The map which differs the most from the others is Little Bear's map, although its differences, it will be argued later, probably stem from Fidler's prompting rather than from a different perception of the region.

16. Monmonier, *How to Lie with Maps*, 1.

17. Denis Wood, *The Power of Maps* (New York: Guilford Press, 1992), 1. Emphasis in the original.

18. The 1801 map does not explicitly identify the double line as the "Rocky Mountains," but the Ac Ko Mok Ki Map does.

19. Moodie and Kaye, "The Ac Ko Mok Ki Map," 9.

20. HBCA, E.3/2 "Journal of a Journey," 30 December 1792. A similar passage appears in Fidler's note to the Company published in Moodie and Kaye, "The Ac Ko Mok Ki Map," 14.

21. See Brian Reeves, "Ninaistákis—the Nitsitapii's Sacred Mountain: Traditional Native Religious Activities and Land Use/Tourism Conflicts" in David L. Carmichael, Jane Hubert, Brian Reeves, and Audhild Schanche, eds., *Sacred Sites, Sacred Places* (New York: Routledge, 1994), 265; James Willard Schultz, *Blackfeet and Buffalo: Memories of Life Among the Indians* (Norman: University of Oklahoma Press, 1962), 34; and George Dawson, "Report on the Region in the Vicinity of the Bow and Belly Rivers, North-West Territory," Geological Survey of Canada, *Report of Progress, 1882–84,* 159C (where the word is rendered *mis-tokis*).

22. Walter McClintock, *The Old North Trail* (London: Macmillan, 1910), 434–35.

23. According to G.R. Crone, many early Western maps also show little concern with the absolute representation of direction. Depiction of conspicuous landmarks was more important, *Maps and Their Makers: An Introduction to the History of Cartography*

(London: Hutchinson University Library, 1966), xi. For similar comments on non-Western maps see Clara Egli Le Gear, "Map Making by Primitive Peoples," *Special Libraries* 35, no. 3 (1944): 82; and H. de Hutorowicz, "Maps of Primitive Peoples," *Bulletin of the American Geographical Society* 43 (1911): 672–73. For an example of a map that uses a coastline as a reference line see June Helm, "Matonabee's Map," *Arctic Anthropology* 26, no. 2 (1989): 28–47. According to David H. Pentland, fifteenth-century European maps, eighteenth-century Chipewyan maps, and twentieth-century Cree maps all show rivers as "straight or curved lines, lakes as ovals." He has also noted that contemporary Cree can use stars for navigation but they "prefer to rely on topographical clues rather than the stars"; David H. Pentland, "Cartographic Concepts of the Northern Algonquians," *Canadian Cartographer* 12 (1975): 149, 157.

24. Moodie and Kaye, "The Ac Ko Mok Ki Map," 13.

25. Reuben Gold Thwaites, ed., *Original Journals of the Lewis and Clark Expedition, 1804–1806* (New York: Antiquarian Press, 1959), 2: 248.

26. Thwaites, ed., *Original Journals of the Lewis and Clark Expedition*, 2: 248. Many locals today will recognize Beartooth Mountain (elevation 6792') as the nose of the Sleeping Giant. It is the most remarkable mountain looming over Helena, Montana, about 50 kilometres to the south.

27. These include Sheep Mountain (7368'), Hogback Mountain (7813'), and Rock Slide Mountain (7093').

28. When Fidler was with the Peigan in 1792 he described *O mock cow ate che mooks as sis* as "a sharp cliff" that was "conspicuous" and "remarkable," E.3/2 "Journal of a Journey," 29 November 1792. The name appears to mean "Big Swans Bill." The name "Devil's Head" is apparently derived from the Cree name of the mountain. Devil's Head Mountain (9174') is just north of the Ghost River and north of Lake Minnewanka, near the present-day Ghost River Wilderness area.

29. This mountain is the subject of Reeves, "Ninaistákis."

30. Captain Meriwether Lewis followed a distinct trail eastward up the "River of the Road to the Buffalo" (Blackfoot River), over Lewis and Clark Pass, and to the upper Sun River valley in July 1806. He noted passing the "Shishequaw Mountain" (Haystack Butte), a conical eminence lying east of the eastern range of the Rocky Mountains, Thwaites, *Original Journals of the Lewis and Clark Expedition*, 5: 195–96.

31. In 1792 Fidler noted that the length of a day's journey was dependent on the distance between water sources, HBCA, E.3/2 "Journal of a Journey," 4 December 1792.

32. Barb Tilander-Mack, ed. & comp., *Native Mapping Project: Treaty Seven Maps and Names* (n.p.: Friends of Geographical Names of Alberta Society, n.d.), 14, found that the upper Highwood River had its own name. Schultz (374) gave different names for the Milk River, and for its north and south forks.

33. If one should think this unfamiliar convention unnatural one should consider that on modern maps one will find that both the Bow and Oldman Rivers "end" where they join. At the same point the South Saskatchewan "begins." The "headwaters" of the Missouri River are considered to be at the confluence of the Gallatin, Madison, and Jefferson Rivers. The Cree of the Hudson's Bay region also had interesting naming conventions, conventions which fur traders adopted. Thus, early HBC company traders had separate names for different portions of the Hayes River. Meanwhile, two rivers flowing in opposite directions but separated by only a short

portage might share the same name. A fascinating account of Cree naming conventions is given in Pentland, "Cartographic Concepts," 157–58.

34. Pentland, "Cartographic Concepts," 158–59.
35. Pentland, "Cartographic Concepts," 159.
36. See Beattie, "Indian Maps Recorded by Peter Fidler," 6.

11 Paul Kane and the Authorship of *Wanderings of an Artist*

I.S. MACLAREN

PAUL KANE (1810–1871), a Canadian artist, travelled with fur-trade brigades from Toronto to Vancouver Island and back more than 150 years ago. These travels afforded him observations of fur-trade and Native lifeways during the height of the Hudson's Bay Company's monopoly in the North-West and on the Pacific Slope. Kane is probably best known by his oil-on-canvas paintings of people and places encountered on his travels, and almost as well for a book, *Wanderings of an Artist among the Indians of North America*, which was published in London, England in 1859, about a decade after he returned from his travels in October 1848.[1]

How the hinterland of North America was represented, invented, and produced by Paul Kane during his travels, as well as subsequently, during the century and a half since he enjoyed Christmas dinner at Fort Edmonton in 1847, has much to do with cultural developments elsewhere. In the age before there were professional travel writers, the change of roles that occurred in order for an explorer or even a traveller to become an author, is an area of research that richly repays enquiry. And the need for it arises out of a concern for the reliability of published narratives as the record of the eyewitness traveller. In terms of the exploration of what is now western Canada, this concern began arising as early as 1778, the year when Captain James Cook's third voyage to the Pacific Ocean arrived on the west coast of Vancouver Island while in search of a northeast passage around the top of or through the continent of North America. A good example of the concern can be found in the disclaimer that prefaces Alexander Mackenzie's *Voyages* (1801):

...when, at length, the opportunity [to publish my journals] arrived, the apprehension of presenting myself to the Public in the character of an Author, for which the course and occupations of my life have by no means qualified me, made me hesitate in committing my papers to the Press; being much better calculated to perform the voyages, arduous as they might be, than to write an account of them. However, they are now offered to the Public with the submission that becomes me.[2]

Despite the fact that *diminutio* is a standard rhetorical figure in the prefaces of exploration and travel writing, the disclaimer, "being much better calculated to perform the voyages...than to write an account of them," also serves to alert readers of this genre to the curious fact that the role of explorer/traveller does not have much in common with the role of published author adept in literary expression worthy of publication and worthy of notice by well-educated readers. It is true that some older scholarly judgements do not worry about the gap between these two roles; for example, the view of the *Literary History of Canada* is that Samuel Hearne's *Journey* (1795) was "one of the most sophisticated early journals and narratives" of exploration.[3] But such judgements tended to arise from an appreciation of explorers and early travellers as heroes, and, in the USAmerican tradition, even as nation-makers. Meanwhile, other studies on the genre of exploration and travel writing, including Percy Adams's memorable *Travelers and Travel Liars*, only deepen one's anxiety about whether or not the verbal descriptions and visual depictions in these narratives are the explorers' or travellers' own, and not the product of some English ghost-writer who had never sailed across the Atlantic.[4]

What is needed for further study of this genre's dependability as an authoritative historical document is more than a passing understanding of a few aspects of bibliography. These include not only the strict physical bibliography, "the study of the signs which constitute texts and the materials on which they are recorded," which, all the same, is bibliography's "starting point," but also the study of the "processes, the technical and social dynamics, of transmission and reception whether by one reader or a whole market of them."[5]

That concern for process over product, of the transmission of narrative over the simple material thing of a book itself quickly takes one to John Mandeville's *Travels*, a highly fraught narrative written in about 1356 by, it is now thought, an armchair traveller. Even if it is generally agreed now that it marks the first important example of a combination of travel and fiction — Jonathan Swift's *Gulliver's Travels* (1726) is perhaps the best known example in English — one needs to remember that, 250 years after it first appeared, Richard Hakluyt included it in the first edition of his authoritative anthology of exploration writing, *Principal Navigations* (1598). Its steady refrain is "I John Mandeville saw it with my own eyes." The reader hears it frequently as the pilgrim passes through the lands of Tartars, Bedouins, Saracens, Malaccans and other 'reprehensible sub-humans' on his way to Cairo and back again by way of India and China—so frequently that the reader's "awareness of the narrator's presence" elicits a niggling concern for the authority and reliability of the eyewitness throughout exploration and travel writing.[6] Readers want, even desire to believe that the narrative is authoritative and reliable. The first-person testimony, coupled with emotional responses, beguiles us readers into that belief. The putative first-person traveller, returning from the lands beyond knowledge, surrounds himself with tropes and other rhetorical devices, and from them he creates an irresistible narrative, whether or not he is "much better calculated to perform the voyages...than to write an account of them." And, knowing as much, the author of Mandeville's *Travels* toys with his gullible reader as he closes the narrative:

> There are many other countries and other marvels which I have not seen, and so I cannot speak of them properly; and also in the countries I have been to there are many marvels which I have not spoken of, for it would be too long to tell of them all....and so I shall cease telling of the different things I saw in those countries, so that those who desire to visit those countries may find enough new things to speak of for the solace and recreation of those whom it pleases to hear them.[7]

Travel literature must instruct and it must entertain. And if the traveller proves incapable of meeting either of these requirements, readying his journals for the press will necessarily involve alteration. Such was certainly the case with Paul Kane's *Wanderings*.

Estimating the circumstances of Kane's book benefits from understanding the facts that surround the editing of publications not only from much earlier in the written record but also, as the example of *diminutio* in Mackenzie's suggests, from the generations preceding and contemporary with Kane's. A key case can be found in the books of Captain James Cook, the British Royal Naval explorer of the Pacific Ocean, who was cast in the role of institutional, corporate, and/or imperial agent. Appearing in the last third of the eighteenth century, when the literature of exploration and travel was selling better than novels or any other writing in the English language, the narratives of Cook's voyages featured the theme of manifest destiny, a theme that systematically deprecated Native peoples in order to render null their apparent right to lands that European empires wanted to arrogate.

Bishop John Douglas, who edited Cook's journals from his second and third voyages, deployed a series of rhetorical shifts to emphasize this theme. The narrative of the third voyage was published posthumously in 1784, Captain Cook having met his demise in Kealakekua Bay, Sandwich (Hawaiian) Islands, on Valentine's Day, 1779. The "edition" by Douglas, a sedentary man of the Cloth in the editorial tradition of Hakluyt and Samuel Purchas, bears the title *A Voyage to the Pacific Ocean. Undertaken, By Command of His Majesty... Written by Captain James Cook...*. It can be read as the official account of the British nation's then latest explorations; it can be read as a sensational and eagerly acquired adventure story about a gentleman killed in Hawaii by blood-thirsty cannibals, the account selling out its print run in "three days, at four and a half guineas...eager purchasers offer[ing] ten guineas for a copy."[8] Alternatively, it can be read as the work of a canon of the Church of England whose Christianity is spelled out through its pages and can be traced to such other writings as *Miracles Examined With a View to Expose the Pretensions of Pagans and Papists* (1751), and the forward to *A Sermon Preached before the Incorporated Society for the Propagation of the Gospel in Foreign Parts* (1793).[9] Finally, it can be read as an exercise in hero-making by Douglas on behalf of his nation. But it cannot be read as the explorer's account of his explorations. What did Mr. Cook see with his own eyes? Apparently, not what his own book states.

Read as the official account—indeed, for nearly two hundred years it remained the sole account "Written by Captain James Cook"—it proclaims what publication intended to signify. As far as European nations were concerned, publication of the narrative of an explorer appointed by his monarch was an act that laid imperial claim to knowledge of the lands, coastlines, and peoples discovered. The form of the official account thereby effected a weighty symbolic significance well beyond the sum of its contents. For this reason, the purpose of Douglas's edition differed from that of the unofficial and unsanctioned accounts that had already been published by various of Cook's officers and sailors.[10] Douglas's official if unacknowledged role amounted to nothing less than the declaration of a Pax Britannica on a major portion of the world.

When he prepared Cook's *Voyage Towards the South Pole* for publication in 1777, Douglas had found that "Cook agreed to most of [his] suggestions even when they entailed changes of substance, urging that the text be made," as Cook put it in a letter to Douglas, "'unexeptionable [*sic*] to the nicest readers.'"[11] The nicest readers, such custodians of Enlightenment English thought as the Reverend John Wesley and Elizabeth Montagu, both of whom had responded with alarm to John Hawkesworth's edition of Cook's journals from his first voyage to the Pacific,[12] subscribed to, among others, the four-stages theory. It advanced a developmental and hierarchical structuring of civilization, by which nomadic hunters occupied the lowest stage and mercantile societies the highest, pastoral and agricultural societies assuming the middle two stages.[13] Far more deep-seated in English thought than the competing and comparatively notional concept of the Noble Savage, this theory, whether formally or informally advanced, frequently precluded any idea but the one that "primitive cultures should have inhuman attributes."[14]

When Cook was still alive, after his second voyage, the Canon of Windsor and St. Paul's tactfully protected nice readers by making the captain's plain text "unexceptionable" by means of euphemisms and circumlocutions: "Tho little appears to be done by me," wrote Douglas, "the Journal, if printed as the Captain put it into my Hands would have been thought too incorrect, & have disgusted the Reader."[15] Subsequently, the "great detector of impostures," as writer James Boswell dubbed Douglas, imposed himself much more in introducing and editing the deceased Cook's third journal. In his "Autobiography," Douglas described how he used Cook's journal as only his "Ground work," but he later deleted that description and substituted the following:

> The Public never knew, how much they owe to me in this work. The Capt's M.S.S. was [sic] indeed attended to accurately, but I took more Liberties than I had done with his Acct of the second Voyage; and while I faithfully represented the facts, I was less scrupulous in cloathing them with better Stile than fell to the usual Share of the Capt....[16]

Although it is clear from this retrospective statement that Douglas strove to represent Cook's discoveries in ways that would entertain and inform the English public, the editor's wording will yield different degrees of significance to researchers in different fields of study. Must style concern an ethnographer or historian, for example, if facts remain "faithfully represented"? What Cook himself reported as having seen and how he shaped his journal are not the same thing as what the Admiralty and a clandestine editor who was also an officer of the Church of England—the national church, it goes almost without saying—thought that the British public should see, and how it ought to be shown. How they are not is discernible in a study of the two versions of Cook's four weeks' stay (30 Mar.-26 Apr. 1778) in Nootka Sound, Vancouver Island. For now, a very brief illustration will have to suffice.

On one occasion when Cook goes ashore, one can hear the elevation of Cook's social status. The trip occasioned a negotiation over the cutting of grass for the domesticated animals aboard Cook's ships. The journal's description of that negotiation (first passage) is less formal, more candid, and briefer than the book's (second passage); coincidentally, Cook is plain-spoken and unexaggerated in his journal, unlike Douglas's published persona of Cook:

> The Inhabitants of this village received us in the same friendly manner they had d[o]ne before, and the Moment we landed I sent some to cut grass not thinking that the Natives could or would have the least objection, but it proved otherways....[17]

> The inhabitants received us with the same demonstrations of friendship which I had experienced before; and the moment we landed, I ordered some of my people to begin their operation of cutting. I had not the least imagination, that the natives could make any objection to our furnishing ourselves with what seemed to be of no use to them, but was necessary for us. However, I was mistaken....[18]

Readers of the official, published narrative see Cook prominently; they see a masterly captain, if not quite a monarch, giving orders to his people. Most significantly, the repetition of the first-person pronoun in the published account emphasizes the explorer's power. The focus thus sharply on Cook, Douglas keeps it there, watching him mount a self-justification that observes the strictest decorum and is governed by the rhetorical confines of *isocolon* (repetition of a grammatical structure): "no use to them,...necessary for us." Butter *might* melt in this Cook's mouth, but only just, for the editor manages to make the explorer appear both mistaken and, yet, innocent. In terms of the style, part of that innocence derives from the way in which *isocolon* reverses meaning in the guise of repeating it. Another part of the innocence comes from the choice of a passive construction—"I was mistaken"—rather than the plainer form of an admission in the active voice—I made a mistake. Underlying the style, another claim of innocence is the unspoken assumption of the four-stages theory, that the representative of a culture where agriculture and animal husbandry are practised has a more legitimate claim to grass than does the representative of only a hunter/fisher culture, who makes no systematic use of vegetation or the soil that grows it. As in most such confrontations as recorded in the narratives of imperial European nations, the ostensibly innocent party appears to be the injured one. In light, however, of every officer's complaint, including Cook's, that the Nootka (Nuu-chah-nulth) were prone to thievery, the implicit reversal of blame in this instance, where the English are made to pay for what they came to steal, is ironical, if not to editor Douglas. One can hear a Nootkan reasoning that he or she could put to better use than a sailor a piece of metal that the latter was using only as a button: "no use to them,...necessary for us."

Just as the visitors found themselves being tolerant with Nootkans who helped themselves to everything on board ship that could be traded or pocketed, the Nootkans found themselves tolerant of their visitors, permitting them water and wood free of charge while charging for the grass. In fact, the Nootkans struck the pre-published Cook not just as the preeminent Pacific traders and property owners, but also as people who regarded themselves in every way the Europeans' equals. As one ethno-historian has written, "neither group asserted a dominance, neither perceived the other as superior and, therefore, neither responded with submission."[19] Such an assessment could not be inferred from Douglas's book alone, and, remembering that the world had only it for 189 years following Cook's stay at Nootka Sound until the Hakluyt Society published his journals a few decades ago, one must allow that many generations of British and other readers perceived matters in an unbalanced perspective.

Guarding Cook as "unexceptionable" usually involved a variety of rhetorical devices, including *euphemism* (the replacement of a blunt and straightforward word or expression with a mild and roundabout one) and various figures of *amplification* (expansion), but Douglas also had to avoid an occasional *faux pas* that betrayed Cook's humble, north-of-England origins. Departing Nootka Sound, Cook was involved in an elaborate ceremony of gift exchange with a prominent Nootkan whose name no officer recorded but who might have been the father of Maquinna.[20] This ceremony, "carried out according to the practice of the Nootkan chief rather than the British captain," involved several exchanges, each more valuable than the last.[21] When he ended by giving his host "a New Broad Sword with a brass hilt," Cook wrote that the gift made the Nootkan "as happy as a prince."[22] This vernacular English captures the spirit of the moment genuinely: Cook had received what he knew to be the much valued "Beaver skin Cloak" straight off the man's back, and he responded with the sword, the symbolic significance of which rendered it much more valuable than any other of the metal goods ("toys" Douglas dismissively calls them[23]) exchanged during the previous four weeks. "Happy as a prince," however, hardly rises to the stately level required for the public persona of the captain (Douglas thought, after all, that Cook's unvarnished journal from the second voyage to the Pacific would have "disgusted" its reader). It amounts to an inappropriate *tapinosis* (undignified language) in a book "Published by Order Of the Lords Commissioners of the Admiralty" about a voyage undertaken "by the Command of His Majesty."

Douglas's refinement of the captain's *faux pas* does more than correct, however; it unbalances the equality of this spontaneous ceremony of gift giving. It preserves the substance of the exchange but effectively alters the essence of it. The alteration, which occurs by means of *hyperbole* (exaggeration), introduces a muted yet unmistakably patronizing tone: "I presented to him a new broad-sword, with a brass hilt; the possession of which made him completely happy."[24] Up to this point, the reader of Douglas's edition has already received an unbalanced impression of the exchanges because, where Cook's journal uses verbs that signify plain giving and receiving—"present[ed]," "gave me," "made him a present"—Douglas has changed the first verb to the more consciously ceremonial "bestowed," and entirely altered the sense of the journal's "gave me": "he insisted upon my acceptance of the beaver-skin cloak which he then wore."[25] The formality and refinement of "bestowed" implicitly go unmatched by the Nootkan's improprieties of insisting and of his undressing before the captain in order to give him his cloak. As well, it keeps the published Cook from showing any genuine interest in an equal exchange, keeps him from situating himself on the same level as the Nootkan; for, if one can give and receive all manner of items from equals, one bestows gifts on inferiors and juniors (and did in the English of Douglas's time). Through the apparently minor edition of these two altered verbs, the idea of English domination of the Nootkans seeps into the published account. It would seem that Douglas is keen to keep his reader aware of the inequality of the people involved in this published version of the scene, which effectively displays the power of his and his empire's magnanimity. It is little wonder, then, that in introducing the volume, Douglas is found capable of congratulating his countrymen on "our having, as it were, brought them [all Native peoples of the Pacific Rim] into existence by our extensive researches."[26]

With the end of the exchange, the book's chapter has drawn nearly to a close, but Douglas chooses this moment to lend the exchange more significance than it possesses in the journal. In an effective use of *climax* the editor proceeds to estimate the rewards to be reaped from Cook's consummate performance, which will smooth the waters for future trade (an idea unvoiced in Cook's own journal): "I make no doubt, that whoever comes after me to this place, will find the natives prepared accordingly, with no inconsiderable supply of an article of trade, which, they could observe, we were eager to possess; and which we found could be purchased to great advantage."[27] Thus, Douglas's insistence in the ceremony of exchange on imbalance and, by means of it, on a hierarchical distinction among peoples, sets up the published chapter's close in which Cook gains material "advantage" (trade imbalance) over the savage.

This has been a long introduction to the figure of Paul Kane and his travels, but it provides a context in which to understand the genre of exploration and travel writing into which *Wanderings* entered in 1859. The late eighteenth- and early nineteenth-century cases of Cook, Alexander Mackenzie, and arctic explorers Samuel Hearne, John Franklin, and George Back all show how systemic and substantive alterations in order to emphasize manifest destiny turn up in comparisons between published and unpublished versions of travels, whether it was the traveller himself or an unacknowledged editor who made the changes.

Paul Kane was no Captain Cook, but, as we have seen, then neither was the published persona of Captain Cook. Both were of lowly origin. Kane was of mixed blood, Irish and English. His father, Michael Kane, was born in Preston, Lancashire and joined the Royal Horse Artillery at age eighteen. Owing apparently to what was termed "an unfortunate circumstance," he married Frances Loach, from Mallow, County Cork, while on a tour of duty in Ireland. His service record states that he was able to "read and write."[28] By the time that the family emigrated to the town of York, Upper Canada in about 1819, four sons and two daughters had been born; their son Paul was nine years old. Despite his and others' efforts later in life to claim that Paul had been born in York, Russell Harper has satisfactorily and impressively put paid to that ruse.

York had a population of 700 in 1815, 2,235 in 1828, and more than 9,000 by 1834, when its name changed to Toronto.[29] There was no universal public education in Upper Canada before the 1840s and it remains unclear if Kane benefitted from much schooling. In 1877, six years after the painter died, Nicholas Flood Davin published *The Irishman in Canada*. In it he claimed that Kane had attended York District Grammar School, but, as Russell Harper notes, he gives no source.[30] This claim is dubious, both because this was John Strachan's school for the children of the élite of Upper Canadian society, and because the Grammar School Act of 1819 "failed to provide for free education; the most that was thought to be financially feasible was free tuition for ten poor students in each district" of the colony.[31]

Certainly Kane was not fluent as a writer; few letters have survived in his hand but there is more than one indication that people despaired of receiving correspondence from him.[32] In his early manhood, he was not illiterate but it might not be far from the truth to think of him as only a step or two above the social level of a bum. One can say with assurance no more about him as a painter than as a journalist. Certainly, he attended no military or naval academy the likes of Woolwich or Sandhurst, where the midshipmen-artist members of the Admiralty's search for a Northwest passage or the officers *cum* topographical landscape artists in the garrisons of British North America in the years following the defeat of Napoleon learned all about the picturesque and the sublime in art. If Kane was not wholly self-taught, he doubtless had but a few lessons from anyone knowledgeable about landscape aesthetics and landscape tastes.

At the age of 23, he had himself listed in the *York Commercial Directory… 1833–4* as a "Coach, Sign and House-painter, 158 King-street."[33] Even though it might not have merited inclusion in a *commercial* directory, the fact that he also painted pictures at that time is known from his contribution of nine—one an original—to the exhibition in July 1834 of the Society of Artists & Amateurs in Toronto,[34] an exhibition organized by Irishman Charles Daly (1808–1864), who would become city clerk for Toronto the next year. York had no self-conscious labour force because it had little industry; rather, it featured self-employed tradesmen and artisans.[35] Perhaps Kane could not eke out a living there because of "the lack of an established bourgeoisie, which would have required portraits as well as lessons in drawing and painting."[36] Perhaps he caught the travel bug early in his twenties. In any case, he moved to Cobourg, Upper Canada, then to Detroit and later to Mobile, Alabama in the 1830s. In Cobourg, he worked for F.S. Clench, a furniture maker. Was he a bohemian? A drifter? Russell Harper wrote with good reason in 1971 that "mystery shrouds certain aspects of Paul Kane's life"; certainly, the intervening quarter-century has uncovered few other facts about the man, but it is probably fair to suggest that Kane knew as many of the rough as of the smooth sides to life. It could be that a lack of schooling either at home or elsewhere disinclined him to write, that his father's social position did not merit positive attention from anyone in York with social power, and even that his mixed-blood ethnicity, English and Irish, was held against him in a York that would later promote universal education as one way to keep tabs on the Irish youth.

It might be fair to say, as was said of Alexander Mackenzie in his book, that Kane was better calculated to perform his travels than to write an account of them. However, Kane also made his travels in calculated fashion. Although no one has ever managed to prove satisfactorily that, when he sailed to Italy in June 1841 and continued a year later to England, he saw the USAmerican painter George Catlin's exhibition of Indian life in London, it is generally understood that he did so and that it "made a profound impression" on him.[37]

It seems that he then determined to become a sort of Canadian Catlin, although anticipating a better financial result than Catlin ever realized. However, sailing for North America in the spring of 1843, he must have been nearly broke; although, later in life, he took pains to conceal as much by stating repeatedly that he spent four years in Europe, in fact he went back to Alabama to paint portraits, and to discharge debts or amass savings in order to make his famous trip.[38]

"Rare laurels" is what one *Canadien*, in 1833, thought awaited the painter who would "really use the Indian's world."[39] This is accurate in several ways. Kane, whom society seemed in no hurry to promote, must have realized that he could make himself a more handsome life by, first, sketching Native North Americans, who would charge little or nothing for the opportunity, and, second, selling oil-on-canvas portraits of these people to wealthy Euro-North Americans. Indians were all the rage, partly thanks to the great popularity of Fenimore Cooper's novels and the novels of backlash against them, such as James Montgomery Bird's *Nick of the Woods* (1837), partly thanks to the widespread belief that Indians were vanishing and that they would be unavailable as subject matter within decades if not within a matter of years. Kane would dine off them for the rest of his days. They were, as one critic of "late imperial" anthropology has put it, "'available' for representation."[40]

And if the representation did not suit the society consuming it, if the writer risked disgusting his readers, it could be "readied," as the saying went, in order to entertain and instruct them. No book of travels was published to lose money. That process of readying narratives for publication is basic to what USAmerican Peter Whiteley calls the "metropolitan aesthetic gaze." I want to call it the "metropolitan imperial aesthetic gaze" because London remained the centre for British North American publishing during Kane's lifetime and because Canada had manifest destiny on its mind regarding the West during the middle of the nineteenth century. Publishing was a way of commodifying colonial, fur-trade, or Native life that did not necessarily involve much in the way of informing readers. To consume the representation of another culture does not require that a reader of travels commit to learning, only to taking pleasure. Clifford Geertz's term, "ethnocentric sentimentalism,"[41] refers to what can displace the effort to learn in order to understand another culture *from the other culture's basis of understanding*. Yes, it might be impossible for us to understand from another basis of understanding than our own culture's, but conceding that impossibility hardly justifies the consuming, the cannibalising of another culture's self-expressions.

Thus, in moving to consider what Kane wrote and painted while travelling from 1845 to 1848, as distinct from what appeared in book form under his name in London in 1859 and the oil-on-canvas paintings he produced, sometimes in multiple copies, back in Toronto during the decade following his western travels, I do not mean to shift the responsibility for what happened entirely from Kane himself. The juggernaut of corporation (Hudson's Bay Company), empire, and nation-in-the-making required a willing accomplice. Kane needed to make a living and he did it by exploiting cultures and then selling his work to the segment of the populace that could afford to exploit *his* own labour. Still, it may well be that he alienated himself *from himself* in creating this role, for he died an alcoholic from cirrhosis of the liver at the age of sixty, a recluse whom Canadian nation-making had to re-fashion into respectability.[42]

Paul Kane's field notes from his trip to lakes Huron and Michigan in 1845 as well as his western trip in 1846-1848 are owned by the Stark Museum of

Art in Orange, the easternmost town in the state of Texas.[43] There, too, are many of Kane's finished field sketches from his travels.[44] Because Kane spelled phonetically and usually wrote with graphite rather than ink, these documents are difficult to read. As one transcribes them, it grows clear that they contain no basis for sections of the published book, *Wanderings*, expressing harsh judgements of Natives; indeed, in a manner not unlike the relation between Captain Cook's own journals and Canon John Douglas's published edition of Cook's third voyage, Kane's field notes contain no overt and few implicit pejorative comments about Native North Americans, in distinct contrast to the representation of Natives in *Wanderings*.

The first chapter of *Wanderings* offers a good illustration of the pattern and effect of the alterations deployed to represent Natives to the reading public. It features a story that the published persona of Paul Kane claims to have heard at Manitowaning, on Manitoulin Island, Lake Huron. Its plot of tragic love begins with the introduction of Shawwanossoway, "One with his Face towards the West," an Ojibwa warrior who turned skilled medicine-man as the result of "a romantic incident." This incident prompted him to abandon "the tomahawk and scalping knife for the peaceable profession of the medicine-man, or, in common parlance, the necromancer or conjuror, in which he has obtained great repute among his people. There dwelt many years before...."[45] Hereafter follows the legend for which the field notes provide no basis whatsoever. It features Shawwanossoway and his rival Mucketickenow, also named "Black Eagle." The object of their affection is Awhmidway, "or, 'There is music in her footsteps'" who, it goes almost without saying, but the book says it anyhow, "exceeded in beauty the rest of the tribe, and was eagerly sought in marriage by all the young warriors of her nation."[46]

The draft manuscript of *Wanderings* also exists. Not written in Kane's hand, it contains the first version of this tale.[47] In it, the heroine is accorded the name of "Connahwahbum (or one who looks at the stars)." This name has been borrowed from elsewhere in the narrative (all the way over at Fort Edmonton, in fact), although it does not exist anywhere in Kane's field notes. Incidentally, the translation, "There is music in her footsteps," for Awhmidway is probably nonsense, and, because "Shawan" means *south* in Ojibwa, the translation, "One with his Face towards the West," for Shawwanossoway inspires little confidence. As well, Mucketickenow is not a warrior "of her nation," that is, Ojibwa; rather, he is Menomini: Kane sketched him in September 1845 when he met him on the Fox River, west of Lake Michigan. This fact leaves the reader of *Wanderings* who also knows Kane's field notes wondering, on the one hand, at the earnest attempt at accuracy made by Kane while he travelled, and, on the other, at the flagrant undoing of it by those responsible for assembling the publication that appeared under his name.

Wanderings does not even bother mentioning that Kane had met and sketched Mucketickenow, only that he had heard this "romantic incident" in which he figured. Small wonder that the book is silent on this connection, for the published version of the tale relates that Shawwanossoway, "rage and jealousy [having taken] full possession of his heart, and plans of vengeance rapidly succeed[ing] each other," murders Mucketickenow,[48] many years *before* Kane met him over in Green Bay. This is all by way of saying that the various stages of Kane's writing amount to a bibliographical mess, and certainly do not add up to a verifiable, reliable travel narrative. *Wanderings* begins to wander even in its first chapter.

Meanwhile, what are the repercussions for the real people who figure so dramatically in this published purple patch, which, nevertheless, lacks any originality? The tale, inserted into the book, exemplifies the genre known as the "lover's leap" legend, in which a noble savage dies, often at the hand of an ignoble savage, for a noble cause, such as pure love. "What the creators of these legends have done," writes Francis de Caro,

> is to play upon the [white US]American ambivalence towards the Indian, utilising the negative stereotype to explain the disappearance of the embodiment of the positive one to which they are sympathetic. Each legend presents noble savages who are destroyed,...Ignoble Indians, deplorable customs, natural disasters are at fault,[49]

but Euro-North Americans are not; thereby, their ambivalence towards Natives is resolved quite tidily. In this example of a lover's leap legend, Shawwanossoway destroys Mucketickenow out of pure rage because of pure love. We know that they were both real people; we are less sure about the identity of Awhmidway. The character by that name knows nothing of her lover's death, despairs of his ever returning, and fears the heightened resolve of her parents that she should marry Shawwanossoway, an apparently spotless suitor. She flees on the appointed wedding night, paddling off in the bridal canoe into a tempest of thunder and lightning. When he finally catches up to her, Shawwanossoway and her brother encounter a consummate natural disaster in the form of

> a troop of wolves, and their horror may well be conceived on discovering the remains of the being they loved almost wholly devoured, and only to be recognised by her torn and scattered garments.
>
> With aching hearts, they carefully gathered her cherished remains, and, placing them in the canoe, returned to the camp, where she was wept and mourned over for many weeks by her disconsolate relatives and friends, and buried with all the ceremonies of her tribe. ...

Shawwanossoway was so much grieved at the misery which his ungovernable passions had brought upon the object of his warmest love, that he formed the plan of abandoning his warlike pursuits; and lifting up the tomahawk to the Great Spirit, that it might be employed only as an instrument of justice, he took in its stead the rattle of the medicine-man; nor did he ever after act inconsistently with his altered character.

Six miles from Manetouawning is another village....[50]

So the interjected tale ends and the travelogue resumes with an absurd abruptness. The gratuitous nature of the tale is glaring. The reader does not learn who related it to the persona of Kane. It makes a mockery of Shawwanossoway, a real person whom Kane did meet, not just a character in a tale. By its silence on the matter, it denies Kane's ever having met, let alone sketched, Mucketickenow. And it renders Awhmidway a prisoner of her own despair and a victim of misfortune. All three pay dearly for their passions, two of them mortally, one of them criminally. To the white man, who closes the tale without comment, the fate of all three implicitly signals that Indians are on the wane, that they deserve this fate, and that there is little to be done to reverse the trend.

This is the view of the mid-nineteenth century, and so it is incumbent upon us to see this bibliographical development of the text as a revision for that era's political correctness. In published form, it aligns with, say, the official account produced by Bishop Douglas under the name of Captain Cook. Similarly, *Wanderings* arrogates to itself the authority of the eyewitness:

The following pages are the notes of my daily journey, with little alteration from the original wording, as I jotted them down in pencil at the time; and although without any claim to public approbation as a literary production, still I trust they will possess not only an interest for the curious, but also an intrinsic value to the historian..., as they relate...to those wild scenes amongst which I strayed almost alone, and scarcely meeting a white man or hearing the sound of my own language.[51]

The wording is original, all right, but putting it in the pen of the traveller is nothing new for the genre. Bishop Douglas's remark, "our having, as it were, brought them into existence by our extensive researches," haunts many subsequent publications of travels in western North America, including *Wanderings*.

It can begin to be seen from this example how Paul Kane the traveller artist is displaced in his own book. After his triumphant exhibition of field sketches at the Toronto City Hall in November 1848,[52] Kane begins to fade out of the scene, replaced by his society's construction of him as a gentleman who paints portraits of noble savages, has essays read before the illustrious membership of the Canadian Institute, and, eventually, becomes an historic Canadian on whom a dream of dignified nation is foisted. The Kane who aimed to "rite thare portraits (the way they express them selfs)," as his field notes put it, ends up contributing to the discourses that enable the dispossession of Native North Americans. One of his field notes complains that the HBC brigade with which he is travelling fails to consult him about its travel plans. He feels himself "nothing but a pasenger." After returning to Toronto, whether he thought so or not, he was reduced to little more than a passenger as he metamorphosed into a public persona and his narrative was drawn up to conform to the tastes of his age and dreams of nation.

The draft manuscript of *Wanderings* is held by the Stark Museum in Orange. It is written in four hard-back, bound notebooks. Two of these provide a straightforward account of Kane's long western trip, while another begins in 1845 and carries forward into the western trip as far as the Metis buffalo hunt on the prairies southwest of the Red River Settlement. The fourth is titled "Pictorial Sketches with Historical notices" and does not relate chronologically to the other three, for it contains entries about individuals whom Kane painted during either trip, and these entries sometimes differ from, sometimes match information in the other notebooks, while also occasionally providing new information.

At this stage, the narrative has not yet been divided into chapters and much of the material in the book does not appear in it. That Kane's hand can be identified in some interlineations and corrections shows that he proofread at least portions of the four books, but he did not write the draft manuscript. Two different hands can be identified, and both are versions of the copperplate style taught to clerks in Kane's day. Exhaustive studies have been undertaken to try to identify either of the two hands but with only indifferent results. Neither of them is Kane's; neither of them is that of Harriet Peek Clench Kane, Kane's wife from September 1853 onward, or of anyone else close to Kane in those years after his return to Toronto. It is clear from the new addition of details, such as the names of all the portages on the Winnipeg River from Lake of the Woods to Lake Winnipeg, that information was gathered from at least one individual who knew the fur trade route well. However, as Jack Warwick has argued, many of these narratives were assembled by committee.[53] Clearly, Kane was not in control of the process that was metamorphosing him from traveller into author, and it may be that he had little say in the matter. Perhaps like Captain Cook, Kane was preeminently concerned that "the text be made 'unexeptionable to the nicest readers.'" Obviously, Shawwanossoway, Mucketickenow, and Awhmidway did not number among them.

Who had a say in the matter? The question remains open to speculation, but one must attend to the pressure exerted on narratives of travel and exploration by manifest destiny. In this case, both the Hudson's Bay Company and Canada West (soon to become Ontario) held interests in the way in which the North-West was represented to the reading public, and England remained imperially connected. By mid-century, Canada West had built up an abiding curiosity in the North-West. Arable land in Canada had gradually been all bought up, cleared, and farmed. Indians in what is now southern Ontario were being dispossessed and either "invited" to move up onto the Canadian Shield or parcelled off into small reservations. They were being made to disappear or, as an early Canadian poem by the Canadian Oliver Goldsmith puts it, they "went some other way." Thoughts of manifest destiny began to be entertained as one competitive response both to the USAmerican expression of it, and to an unappealing union with Canada East that had issued from Lord Durham's *Report* of February 1839 and the subsequent Act of Union of July 1840. When those in Canada West looked to the North-West, they saw only a corporate monopoly, the Hudson's Bay Company, which, being British, seemed a prelude, not an obstacle, to the process of expansion. More than this they did not see, for two reasons. One was that the HBC had carefully controlled information about its territory, seldom permitting the publication of a book that did not cast the monopoly in a favourable light, and seldom permitting travel through its territories except on its terms and with its brigades. This was the case with Paul Kane. Second, because information about the North-West was not widely available in the 1840s and 1850s, a certain reliance had to be placed on information obtainable from the United States. There, as Richard White has written,

> western North America was represented conventionally on maps as largely empty and unknown. ...[E]arlier maps, those of the sixteenth and seventeenth centuries, for example, had portrayed a densely occupied continent teeming with people. ...
>
> [However, b]y the nineteenth century all this had changed. In illustrated maps, as in contemporary prints depicting the progress of pioneers, only a few scattered Indians appeared. They were either retreating or quietly observing the coming of whites.[54]

Kane travelled a full decade before the survey expeditions of John Palliser and Henry Youle Hind were commissioned by the British and Canadian parliaments, respectively. Until their reports were made available at the end of the 1850s, it was generally presumed that the British North American North-West was equally vacant.

Then there is the fact that Toronto was burgeoning. From fewer than 2,000 in 1825, it had grown to 30,000 a quarter-century later.[55] Torontonians were beginning to desire cultural expression of their own to match the creation of railways and banks—their priorities. Here was a Canadian painter who had seized the opportunity to paint his native land (the fact of Kane's Irish birth was dropped, even by him, as were all references to his mother). Earlier paintings by him were being exhibited on his behalf even while he was in the West, and now he returned with subject matter that could feed the curiosity of English Canada.[56] Both the bourgeoisie and the academic world were interested in his notes and sketches. Suddenly, a portrait painter who had lived by the seat of his pants was cast into a bit of limelight.

The exhibition in Toronto, which, it appears, Harriet Peek Clench helped him prepare,[57] was by far the largest in the history of the city by a "son of the soil." Eighty-five of Kane's sketches in oil on paper and 155 water-colours on paper were put on exhibition beginning 9 November in Toronto's "Old" City Hall on Front Street. The exhibition met with universal acclaim. In particular, the immediacy of the sketch-portraits and, by contrast to Catlin's romantic stylization, their unexaggerated use of colour were admired by the reviewers.[58]

Kane soon garnered a commission of twelve paintings from the Legislative Assembly of the Province of Canada, who paid him £500 for the work. Earlier and more importantly, he had found himself a patron, in the person of George William Allan (1822–1901). Allan was a prominent Torontonian and only son to survive and inherit the fortune of William Allan (c.1770—1853), the first president of the Toronto Board of Trade, and "doyen of Upper Canadian Business" through the 1830s and 1840s.[59] Widowed in 1852 by the death of Louise, one of the daughters of Chief Justice John Beverly Robinson, the younger Allan served as the mayor of Toronto in 1855, as a legislative councillor for the Province of Canada from 1858 until Confederation, and as a senator from 1867 on.

Allan conferred distinction on Kane, taking an interest in him partly because he himself had been a traveller and a collector of Native artifacts, and partly because he took an abiding interest in fostering the arts in early Toronto—he made a gift to the city of the land on which the Canadian Institute was built.[60] This combination of his patron's interests and distinctions sufficed to permit Kane, 22 years after being listed as a coach, sign, and house-painter, to appear as a "professional" in *Brown's Toronto General Directory* for 1856; here his name numbers among the "Artists."[61] And through the efforts of Allan, at the time the Canadian Institute's second vice-president, Kane was nominated for membership at its meeting of 6 January 1855, and elected him a week later.[62]

By 1856, Kane's work had garnered international approval. Several works from Allan's collection of Kane's oils-on-canvas had been loaned to Canada in order to be displayed in the Canadian exhibit at the Paris Exhibition of 1855.[63] This was a crucial first exhibition for Canada at a world's fair, and certainly an important complement to the nation-making instincts that the 1850s had brought about. Within a decade of his return to Toronto, then, Kane thus had achieved recognition from his own legislative assembly and from European art critics for his oil-on-canvas studio works, but there was even more at stake. George Brown, editor of the Toronto *Globe*, editorialized on 1 February 1855 that the West, the scene of so many of Kane's canvasses, must possess the coal that could not be found in eastern British North America. Coal was vital for the development of railways, the era's technological solution to all man's woes and one of the perceived bases on which nations were built. Brown argued, in a voice that many Westerners have since identified with Toronto, that the North-West "must ultimately be incorporated into the province."[64]

The national urges of Canada West were not the only ones exerting themselves on *Wanderings*, however. This book was published in England, not Canada West. Little is known about its publication or the final stages of its composition. When it appeared in March 1859, three editors were paid for their work. Because nearly all the papers of the Longman publishing house were destroyed during the bombing of London in the Second World War, little can be gleaned from what remains. An entry under 2 March in one Divide Ledger states that six copies had been sent to the "author," and a notable number, 18, had been sent to the "editors," perhaps as many as three of them.[65] That it was published in London can be explained by the fact that it was still very much a coup for a colonial to publish at the imperial centre, and not a great many general books had yet been published in Toronto (this was not the case for Montreal).

It was the Hudson's Bay Company that could exert its editorial power in London and could benefit from the book's appearance, despite—*or perhaps particularly because of*—the decade-old age of its contents. Although the company's power was on the wane, the HBC was by no means finished with the North-West: it controlled more than one-quarter of the continent in the mid-1850s. It stood to benefit from the expression of favourable views of its operations by a gentleman. Some of these are apparent in chapters five through seven, which pertain to the Red River Settlement and the Metis buffalo hunt. It is not surprising that the persona of Kane in the published book is made into a gentleman; speaking eloquently and positively on behalf of the HBC's humane treatment of Native peoples, this gentleman, much like the re-fashioned Captain Cook in John Douglas's edition, commands authority, not the belittled stature of Kane who wrote in his field notes that he felt himself "nothing but a pasenger."

Our understanding of the metamorphosis of Paul Kane from a bohemian traveller with fur trade brigades into a gentleman author continues. Meanwhile, it seems clear that when one studies an early narrative of exploration or travel, the sorts of ideological and political pressures that come to bear on the author and his record of wilderness experience must be carefully assembled and evaluated. No-one, least of all individuals in their own age, writes history in a vacuum. And if the pressures exerted on or the demands made of the traveller prove too much for his abilities as a writer, the publishing industry could move swiftly and efficiently to produce a saleable commodity that pandered to the tastes and vested interests of the age. The case of Paul Kane is representative of this process. Knowing as much behooves students of fur trade history to approach with greater circumspection those texts that have come down to us bearing the stamp of the authoritative eye-witness. Whether it is Kane's *Wanderings*, or, in the generations and decades before it, Hearne's *Journey* (1795), Mackenzie's *Voyages* (1801), Daniel Harmon's *Journal of Voyages* (1820), George Simpson's *Narrative of a Journey round the World* (1847), or Peter Skene Ogden's *Traits of North-American Indian Life and Character* (1853), the careful evaluation of the texts as authoritative is richly repaid.[66]

Notes

1. [Paul Kane], *Wanderings of an Artist among the Indians of North America from Canada to Vancouver's Island and Oregon through the Hudson's Bay Company's Territory and back again* (London: Longman, Brown, Green, Longmans, and Roberts, 1859).

2. Alexander Mackenzie, *The Journals and Letters of Sir Alexander Mackenzie*, W. Kaye Lamb, ed., Hakluyt Society Extra Series, no. 41 (Cambridge: Cambridge University Press for the Hakluyt Society, 1970), 57.

3. Victor G. Hopwood, "Explorers by Land (to 1867)," *Literary History of Canada: Canadian Literature in English*, Carl F. Klinck, gen. ed. (1965), 2nd ed., 3 vols. (Toronto: University of Toronto Press, 1966) I: 27.

4. Percy G. Adams, *Travelers and Travel Liars* (Berkeley: University of California Press, 1962).

5. D.F. McKenzie, *Bibliography and the Sociology of Texts*, The Panizzi Lectures 1985 (London: British Library, 1986), 8.

6. Qtd. in Percy G. Adams, *Travel Literature and the Evolution of the Novel* (Lexington: University Press of Kentucky, 1983), 168.

7. [John Mandeville], *The Travels of Sir John Mandeville* (c1356), transl. and introd. C.W.R.D. Moseley (Harmondsworth: Penguin, 1983), 188.

8. J.C. Beaglehole, ed., *The Journals of Captain James Cook on His Voyages of Discovery*, III vols. in IV (London: Hakluyt Society, 1955-1974), IV: 692.

9. John Douglas, *The Criterion; Or, Miracles Examined with a View to Expose the Pretensions of and Papists...* (London, 1751); The Right Reverend John Lord Bishop of Salisbury, *A Sermon Preached before the Incorporated Society for the Propagation of the Gospel in Foreign Parts...February 15, 1793* (London, 1793).

10. W[illiam] Ellis, *An Authentic Narrative of a Voyage...In Search of a North-West Passage...*, 2 vols. (London, 1782); John Ledyard, *A Journal of Captain Cook's Last Voyage to the Pacific Ocean...* (Hartford, Conn., 1783); [John Rickman], *Journal of Captain Cook's Last Voyage to the Pacific Ocean...Faithfully Narrated from the Original MS* (London, 1781); Heinrich Zimmermann, *Reise um die Welt, mit Capitain Cook* (Mannheim, 1781).

11. Qtd. in Lynne Withey, *Voyages of Discovery: Captain Cook and the Exploration of the Pacific* (New York: William Morrow, 1987), 311; John Douglas, ed., *A Voyage towards the South Pole, and Round the World...Written by James Cook...*, 2 vols. (London, 1777).

12. See John L. Abbott, *John Hawkesworth: Eighteenth-Century Man of Letters* (Madison, Wisconsin: University of Wisconsin Press, 1982), chpt. vii.

13. Ronald L. Meek, *Social Science and the Ignoble Savage*, Cambridge Studies in the History and Theory of Politics (Cambridge: Cambridge University Press, 1976).

14. Christon I. Archer, "Cannibalism in the Early History of the Northwest Coast: Enduring Myths and Neglected Realities," *Canadian Historical Review* 61 (1980): 478.

15. John Douglas, "Autobiography" (1776–1796). British Library, Egerton MS 2181, f.42v; qtd. in Beaglehole, ed., *The Journals of Captain James Cook*, II: cxliv.

16. Ibid., ff.48-49v; qtd. in Beaglehole, ed., *The Journals of Captain James Cook*, III.1: cxcix.

17. Beaglehole, ed., *The Journals of Captain James Cook*, III.1: 306.

18. John Douglas, ed., *A Voyage to the Pacific Ocean. Undertaken, By the Command of His Majesty, for Making Discoveries in the Northern Hemisphere...Written by Captain James Cook...*, 3 vols. and Atlas (London, 1784), II: 283–84.

19. Robin Fisher, "Cook and the Nootka," in *Captain James Cook and his Times*, ed. Robin Fisher and Hugh Johnston (Seattle: University of Washington Press, 1979), 84.

20. Robin Fisher and J.M. Bumsted, eds., *An Account of a Voyage to the North West Coast of America in 1785 & 1786 by Alexander Walker* (Vancouver and Toronto: Douglas and McIntyre; Seattle: University of Washington Press, 1982), 17, 62–63.

21. Robin Fisher, "Cook and the Nootka," 89.

22. Beaglehole, ed., *The Journals of Captain James Cook* III.1: 308.

23. Douglas, ed., *A Voyage to the Pacific Ocean*, II: 279.

24. Ibid., II: 286.

25. Ibid., II: 286.

26. Ibid., I: lxxvi, lxxvii.

27. Ibid., II: 287.

28. J. Russell Harper, ed. and introd., with a *cat. raisonné*, *Paul Kane's Frontier* (Toronto: University of Toronto Press, for the Amon Carter Museum and the National Gallery of Canada, 1971), 6.

29. Edith G. Firth, ed. and introd., *The Town of York 1815–1834: A Further Collection of Documents of Early Toronto*. Publications of the Champlain Society, Ontario Series, Vol. VIII (Toronto: Champlain Society, 1966), xvii, xxvi.

30. Nicholas Flood Davin, *The Irishman in Canada* (London, 1877), 611; Harper, *Paul Kane's Frontier*, 6.

31. G.M. Craig, "Strachan, John," *Dictionary of Canadian Biography*, Vol. IX (1861–1870), George W. Brown, David M. Hayne, and Francess G. Halpenny, gen. eds. (Toronto and Buffalo: University of Toronto Press, 1976), 756.

32. Harper, *Paul Kane's Frontier*, 326, 330.

33. George Walton, com, *York Commercial Directory, Street Guide and Register, 1833–4* (York, U.C.: pr. by Thomas Dalton, 1834); qtd. in Carol D. Lowrey, "The Society of Artists & Amateurs, 1834: Toronto's First Art Exhibition and Its Antecedents," *RACAR: Revue d'art canadienne/Canadian Art Review* VIII.2 (1981): 101.

34. *Catalogue of the First Exhibition of the Society of Artist & Amateurs of Toronto. 1834* (Toronto: pr. at the Office of *The Patriot* by T. Dalton, 1834).

35. Firth, ed., and introd., *The Town of York*, 345n, xxxii.

36. Lowrey, "The Society of Artists & Amateurs, 1834," 100.

37. Harper, *Paul Kane's Frontier*, 13. Catlin might have left a small exhibition in London, but from early June 1842 until May 1843, the time when Kane is thought to have been in England, Catlin was touring the provincial cities of Great Britain, lecturing and exhibiting *tableaux vivants* of costumed Indians. See William H. Truettner, *The Natural Man Observed: A Study of Catlin's Indian Gallery* (Washington, D.C.: Smithsonian Institution Press, 1979), 44; and George Catlin, *Catlin's Notes of Eight Years' Travels and Residence in Europe, with His North American Indian Collection*, 2 vols. (London: G. Catlin, 1848), I: 100.

38. Harper, *Paul Kane's Frontier*, 14.

39. Ibid., 8.

40. Bea Medicine, "The Anthropologist as the Indian's Image Maker," *The American Indian Reader: Anthropology*, Jeannette Henry, ed. (San Francisco: Indian Historian Press, 1972), 25; qtd. in Thomas Biolsi, and Larry J. Zimmerman, eds., *Indians and Anthropologists: Vine Deloria, Jr., and the Critique of Anthropology* (Tucson: University of Arizona Press, 1997), 9.

41. Qtd. in Peter Whiteley, "The End of Anthropology (at Hopi)?", in Biolsi and Zimmerman, eds., *Indians and Anthropologists*, 185.

42. "Liver Complaint" is the cause of death given in the Census for the Province of Ontario, 1871, Archives of Ontario, C–9972.

43. Paul Kane, Field Notes 1846–48, Stark Museum of Art, Orange, Texas, 11.85/5; Landscape and Portrait Log 1846–48, and Field Notes 1845, 11.85/4. An edition of the first of these is in I.S. MacLaren, "'I came to rite thare portraits': Paul Kane's Journal of his Western Travels, 1846-1848," *The American Art Journal* 21.2 (Spring 1989): 6–88.

44. Why they are there and not somewhere in Canada is an interesting question, but one that lies beyond the scope of this paper. See I.S. MacLaren, "Paul Kane goes South: The Sale of the Family's Collection of Field Sketches," *Journal of Canadian Studies* 32.2 (Summer 1997): 22–47.

45. *Wanderings*, 16.

46. Ibid., 17.

47. [Paul Kane], Draft Manuscript, Stark Museum of Art, Orange, Texas: 17 June 1845-July 1846, 11.85/2A; 9 May 1846-6 September 1848, 11.85/2B; 6 October 1846-12 September 1848, 11.85/2C; and 17 June 1845-30 November 1845, followed by "Pictorial Sketches with Historical Notices," 11.85/3.

48. *Wanderings*, 19.

49. Francis A. de Caro, "Vanishing the Red Man: Cultural Guilt and Legend Formation," *International Folklore Review* 4 (1986): 77.

50. *Wanderings*, 22-23.

51. Ibid., viii-ix.

52. *Catalogue of Sketches of Indians, and Indian Chiefs, Landscapes, Dances, Costumes, &c. &c. by Paul Kane* (Toronto: pr. for Scobie and Balfour, Adelaide Buildings, King Street. November, 1848).

53. Jack Warwick, "Discovery: Reference and Fable," unpublished paper, presented at "De-Centring the Renaissance/Dé-centrer la Renaissance: Canada and Europe in Multi-Disciplinary Perspective, 1350–1700," Victoria College, University of Toronto, 7–10 March 1996.

54. Richard White, "Frederick Jackson Turner and Buffalo Bill," in *The Frontier in American Culture: An Exhibition at the Newberry Library, August 26, 1994-January 7, 1995*, James R. Grossman, ed. (Chicago: The Newberry Library; Berkeley, Los Angeles, London: University of California Press, 1994), 17.

55. Brian S. Osborne, Jean-Claude Robert, and David A. Sutherland, "Population in the Canadas and the Maritimes to 1851," *Historical Atlas of Canada. Vol. II: The Land Transformed 1800–1891*, R. Louis Gentilcore, ed. (Toronto, Buffalo, London: University of Toronto Press, 1993), Plate 10.

56. Carol D. Lowrey, "The Toronto Society of Arts, 1847–48: Patriotism and the Pursuit of Culture in Canada West," *RACAR: Revue d'art canadienne/Canadian Art Review* XII.1 (1985): 21–22, 34, 37.

57. Harriet Peek Clench, "Catalogue of Sketches of Indians, and Indian Chiefs, Landscapes, Dances, Costumes, &c. &c. By Paul Kane. Toronto, November, 1848," MS, 9 p, Royal Ontario Museum, ROM 92 ETH 42–50.

58. See Harper, *Paul Kane's Frontier*, 17.

59. "Allan, William," *Dictionary of Canadian Biography*, Vol. VIII (1851–1860), Francess G. Halpenny, gen. ed. (Toronto: University of Toronto Press, 1985), 10.

60. Henry J. Morgan, ed., *The Canadian Men and Women of the Time: A Hand-book of Canadian Biography* (Toronto: W. Briggs, 1898).

61. Qtd. in Carol D. Lowrey, "The Society of Artists & Amateurs, 1834," 101.

62. Royal Canadian Institute, Minutes 1849–1863, Thomas Fisher Rare Book Library, University of Toronto, MS Coll 193, Box 36; cited in Conrad E. Heidenreich, "Report to the Royal Canadian Institute on the Identification of the Paul Kane Picture owned by the R.C.I.," unpublished report, 11 May 1995.

63. Harper, *Paul Kane's Frontier*, 34.

64. Qtd. in Suzanne Zeller, *Inventing Canada: Early Victorian Canada and the Idea of a Transcontinental Nation* (Toronto: University of Toronto Press, 1987), 97.

65. Longman Archives, University of Reading, Divide Ledgers D7 (p. 193), D5 (p. 689).

66. [Alexander Mackenzie], *Voyages from Montreal on the River St. Laurence, through the Continent of North America, to the Frozen and Pacific Oceans; in the years 1789 and 1793...* (London: T. Cadell, 1801), facs. rpt. (Edmonton: Hurtig, 1971); [Samuel Hearne], *A Journey from Prince of Wales's Fort in Hudson's Bay to the Northern Ocean 1769, 1770, 1771, 1772. 1795* (London: for A. Strahan and T. Cadell, 1795.), Richard Glover, ed. (Toronto: Macmillan, 1958); [Sir George Simpson], *Narrative of a Journey round the World during the Years 1841 and 1842*, 2 vols. (London: Henry Colburn, 1847); Daniel Haskel, ed., *A Journal of Voyages and Travels in the Interiour of North America,...By Daniel Harmon* (Andover, Vermont: T. Flagg and Gould, 1820), W. Kaye Lamb, ed., *Sixteen Years in the*

Indian Country: The Journal of Daniel Williams Harmon (Toronto: Macmillan, 1957); [Peter Skene Ogden], *Traits of American-Indian Life and Character. By a Fur Trader* (London: Smith, Elder, 1853), rpt. (San Francisco: Grabhorn, 1933), facs. rpt. (New York: AMS, 1972).

12

Natives, Newspapers and Crime Rates in the North-West Territories, 1878–1885

R.C. MACLEOD &

HEATHER ROLLASON DRISCOLL

A FRESH LOOK at relations between
Native people and the Canadian state in the North-West Territories (NWT)
can be taken by re-evaluating the newspapers of the period. Re-interpreta-
tion of the past is what historians have always done, although in the wake of
post-modernism we are probably more conscious of the cultural context of
documents than we once were. "The Imagined West" is a category that
traditionally suggests retrospective fictional accounts of the prairie experience and that is certainly an important area of study. Imagining, however, is
very much a contemporary activity and a vital part of how behaviour is
shaped. As this study will make clear, newspaper accounts of Native peoples'
encounters with the criminal justice system were strongly influenced by the
writers' cultural filters; that is by what they imagined their society was and
what it was becoming. The Cree and Blackfoot must have been influenced
by a parallel imaginative process but that is much more difficult to study,
although there are a few tantalizing hints in the documents.

Attempts to explain current high rates of Native incarceration have
tended to assume a connection between the contemporary situation and
historical attitudes and actions associated with the courts and other legal
institutions such as the North-West Mounted Police (NWMP). Guided by

such hypotheses, scholars have searched historical documents for evidence to support assumed causal associations between past and present situations. Many of these studies rely heavily on descriptions of Native criminal activity reported in newspapers. The validity of any claims about a simple connection between past circumstances and present behaviour in the Canadian West can be contested. The basis of our challenge stems from a re-examination of newspapers as sources of information about crime. The newspapers used by scholars were often located in communities where relations between Natives and whites were characterized by unusually high stress levels. In the NWT in the last quarter of the nineteenth century, those stresses were caused by a combination of economic, social and political factors. There was an important difference in the nature of those circumstances between the northern and southern parts of the Territories. Each of the four communities that were studied had its own specific characteristics. All the newspapers portrayed Native crime at higher levels than the court case returns show.[1] It was also apparent that the communities with the strongest ethnic tensions had newspapers that produced perceptions of crime rates furthest from actual rates.

In one of the early historical studies of Native crime in Canada, Tom Thorner used the *Calgary Herald*, full of vitriolic descriptions of Native people, as the basis for an assessment of crime rates in and around Calgary during the late nineteenth century.[2] From the newspaper accounts he concluded that Natives did most of the horse stealing and cattle killing in the region. Thorner's study is interesting not only for the content, but for the methodological issues associated with it. In his introduction he notes two problems with using the newspaper to determine crime rates; it did not reveal the number of unsolved cases nor did it publish the numbers of those acquitted. Thorner does not appear to have considered issues of reliability such as whether or not the paper selectively reported cases. Nor does he consider how the attitudes of the editor and of lobby groups affected how crime was reported. Studying these factors should help to reveal how local circumstances influenced the relationship between Natives and the Canadian legal system.

Clare V. McKanna, Jr. used local newspapers as the basis for his study of Apache crime rates in Arizona between 1880 and 1912 and made similar assumptions about the reliability of this kind of source.[3] He took it as given that attitudes expressed in the newspapers were representative of local opinion. McKanna did not explain the methodology used to derive crime rates from the newspapers, making it difficult to assess the accuracy of his conclusions. Unlike Thorner, he consulted another source, state registers of criminal activity, as a way to check on the validity of crime reports in the newspapers. The essence of his claim is that, "...the Arizona territorial criminal justice system, mirroring the U.S. legal system, failed to incorporate American Indians into the non-Indian legal structure...which helps to explain the high conviction rates for Apache perpetrators."[4] Other factors he listed as contributing to the high conviction rates included the Apaches' inability to speak English and their ignorance of American law. McKanna concluded that, "...the bias illustrated by the conviction rates can be attributed to white hostility toward American Indians, particularly Apaches, poor defence counsel, all-white juries, and a system culturally insensitive to problems faced by Indians forced to adapt to new societal demands."[5] While McKanna considers some historical data, he neglects to explore the nuances of time and place. We believe that it is impossible to fully understand the developing relationship between Natives and settlers without a close examination of the social, economic and political environment in which the newspapers were produced.

Erica Pasmeny, in an article entitled "Aboriginal Offenders: Victims of Policing and Society," supports the need for in depth historical studies.[6] Without performing this kind of analysis herself, Pasmeny claims that historical scholarship will undoubtedly reveal that policing practices were responsible for the unjust treatment of Native people. She argues that in order to understand how aboriginal offenders came to be victims of discrimination by police, one must consider the historical context in which the discrimination arose. She asserts that one of the fundamental factors leading to Native over representation is the communication barrier between them and the police along with the related problem of the inability to translate abstract concepts of Canadian law into Native languages.[7] Natives therefore had a poor understanding of their legal rights according to Canadian law. From a historian's point of view, the obvious problem with Pasmeny's approach is that she decides in advance what will be found and encourages scholars to seek out evidence to support a particular thesis.

In a recent book entitled, *Aboriginal Law: Apartheid in Canada?*, Paula Mallea contends that Native peoples in western Canada had their own operational legal systems when the area came under Canadian jurisdiction.[8] After 1870, "[i]t was inevitable that conflicts should arise, not only because of tensions between ancient custom and British common law, but also because lawyers and judges across the country var[ied] greatly in their ability to show sensitivity to a different way of life."[9] While she probably overstates the degree of conflict, the point that there was a variable reaction to the situation by lawyers and judges is an important one. Our research indicates that the legal system in the North-West Territories was far from uniform and that generalizations are premature.

Sidney L. Harring provides a more balanced view of the historical interaction between Native and Canadian legal systems in nineteenth century

Ontario.[10] In many ways the research he did on Ontario could serve as a model for studies of other parts of the country. Like Pasmeny, Harring argues that the current situation of high Native jail populations is directly related to historical circumstances. Harring is one of the few scholars to follow up this assertion with a serious attempt to analyze the historical context. His study uses Ontario jail records rather than newspapers to determine arrest rates for various criminal offences. He points out that during the nineteenth century, the Canadian government believed that a legally structured frontier would prevent violent confrontations between white settlers and Natives. Consequently, he argues, the state jailed large numbers of Natives in a direct attempt to impress them with the power and authority of the law.[11] Unlike Pasmeny and McKanna, Harring argues that both tribal law and Canadian law were in operation on reserves at this time and that Native people were knowledgeable about both systems, using whichever one seemed appropriate at a given time to try to secure protection for their rights and land. In other words, Harring does not believe that barriers of language and culture provide sufficient explanation for high arrest rates. Rather, the explanation is to be found in the Canadian state's use of the law, "...to control and socialize Native people, [the law] was a powerful instrument to force assimilation."[12] Harring suggests that the pressure for assimilation took precedence over ensuring convictions and enforcing penalties. "[I]t was part of an attempt by whites to enforce their standards of behaviour on Indian people."[13] As proof that the state used arrests as a teaching mechanism, Harring provides evidence that Natives were released after arrest and jail sentences were often suspended or disregarded.

Our 1997 article, "'Restrain the Lawless Savages': Native Defendants in the Criminal Courts of the North-West Territories, 1878–1885," analyzed court case statistics for the NWT, demonstrating that crime rates among Natives were much lower than previous studies had suggested. Our evidence showed that Natives were significantly under-represented in the jails compared to whites in the population and were often treated with a degree of leniency not shown to any other group.[14] This generalization holds true for all kinds of crime from simple assaults to murder. The only partial divergence from the pattern concerns livestock theft where Native crime rates were higher than for other categories of offences, but even here the rates for Natives were lower than for the rest of the population. More exploration is needed on these rather surprising findings by looking at regional and community historical circumstances in more detail. This approach should help to reveal why the NWMP and the courts applied the law in a flexible manner and appeared to be willing to recognize the pre-existence of Native law. We also hope to find clues about why Natives sometimes actively sought the assistance of the Canadian legal authorities to resolve disputes, not merely between themselves and settlers, but within their own communities.

In the 1997 study, we used newspapers mainly as a method of checking the accuracy of the recorded NWMP court case returns.[15] While collecting this information, we noticed substantial variations between the newspapers in the opinions they expressed about the Natives and the language they used to report Native and white criminal activities. This observation led us to question the reasons for the differences. It quickly became apparent that the answer was not to be found in the nature of the papers themselves. The four earliest newspapers in the North-West Territories; the *Saskatchewan Herald* in Battleford (1878), the *Edmonton Bulletin* (1881), the *Gazette* in Fort Macleod (1882) and the *Calgary Herald* (1883), were nearly identical in most respects. They looked the same because all were printed on presses that were small enough to be hauled across the prairie on ox carts. They were fiercely partisan in their politics and equally fierce boosters in promoting and protecting community interests. All their editor-owners came from nearly identical backgrounds in Ontario; all started as printers, made the transition to reporting on large newspapers and worked their way west to found their own. The similarities among the newspapers suggest that the different portrayals of Native crime found in their pages reflects some more fundamental differences in their respective communities.

By the time of the transfer of the NWT from the Hudson's Bay Company to Canada in 1870, the Native inhabitants of the region had been experiencing significant economic change and social displacement for a decade or more. During the period covered by this study the North-West Territories was home to many peoples, but the most important groups who lived around the four communities in the study were the Métis, the Homeguard Cree, the Blackfoot Confederacy (Sarcee, Piegan, Blood, Siksika), Stoney, Crow and Sioux.[16] In 1869 the latest in a long series of smallpox epidemics spread through the western parts of the region, killing a high percentage of the Native people exposed to it.[17] Scholars have thoroughly documented the dire consequences diseases such as smallpox had for Native people. Not only was there a large initial mortality from the disease itself but there were many additional deaths due to starvation and exposure.[18] Compounding the problem of disease was the rapidly diminishing buffalo population. As the realization that their principal food source was disappearing spread among native groups in the 1850s,[19] competition increased and tensions heightened.

Changing circumstances affected the Homeguard Cree who had created an economic niche as employees of the HBC as well as the Métis who both worked with and competed against the Company. The Canadian government's plans to establish farming and ranching in this fur trade country threatened to disrupt economic patterns that had evolved over the previous two centuries. Agriculture made demands on the land and environment that were not compatible with the fur trade. Though the HBC would continue to operate under the new regime, it would lose the last vestiges of its monopoly position. The Cree were forced to renegotiate their status in the new competitive environment. The future of the Métis was similarly in question. Many of those who had left Red River since the 1840s to move west and participate in the buffalo hunt and the buffalo-robe trade had become successful independent merchants.[20] The disappearance of the buffalo affected the Métis economy as much as it did that of the plains Indians.

The most obvious series of changes resulting from the 1870 transfer of authority had to do with responsibility for law and order. The HBC had never established formal legal institutions in its territories outside Red River, but had always actively worked to resolve conflicts among Native groups out of economic self-interest. The company had no power to coerce; its ability to act as peacemaker rested instead on its monopoly control of access to European goods and the diplomatic skills of its factors. These were not always sufficient even at the height of the company's power.[21]

As their monopoly position weakened, so did their ability to intervene in Native disputes. This arguably made Native systems of law more important. William Henderson argues in his study of Native legal systems that these systems are created because "...the internal social cohesion of any societal group requires a method, or methods, of dispute resolution that does not lead directly to the disintegration of the group."[22] Native people's systems of law, "[have] deep roots in the social and economic habits and attitudes of its past and present members."[23] These statements come close to being tautological if we think about the cultures of the Native peoples as static. If, however, we recognize them as adapting under the pressure of rapidly changing circumstances, it is possible to make sense of the evidence.

What appeared on the surface to be an abrupt, almost revolutionary, change in the relations between Natives and whites on the prairies was much more gradual on the local level. The Mounted Police at no time attempted to occupy the North-West Territories and establish the authority of the Canadian state with guns drawn. In the northern part of the Territories the NWMP worked closely with the HBC and inherited their historic role as arbiters. In the south, where the ties of groups like the Blackfoot to the HBC were much more tenuous, the police adopted a strategy of personal diplomacy. James F. Macleod, Assistant Commissioner 1873–1876 and Commissioner 1876–1880, developed relationships of mutual trust and respect with leaders like Crowfoot and Red Crow.[24] Superintendent James Walsh used the same approach with Sitting Bull a few years later when the Sioux fled north across the border in the wake of the Custer battle.[25] The two distinct approaches to introducing the Native peoples to Canadian law were a reflection of the different early patterns of development of the four communities in our study. Battleford and Edmonton began as fur trade posts in the late eighteenth century; Fort Macleod and Calgary had no prior existence before their establishment as NWMP posts in the 1870s.

In 1785 William Holmes set up a HBC post where the Battle River joins the North Saskatchewan. Although the company decided to move the post further east in 1871, the original site at the confluence of the two rivers remained a popular location for stopovers by tourists, surveyors, and other travellers.[26] Knowledge about the spot spread after 1857 when the British government's Palliser expedition report on the agricultural potential of the region mentioned it. In 1872 the Canadian surveyor W.S. Gore stayed at the site of the recently moved HBC post. Three years later a new community of settlers began to emerge with the building of the telegraph line from Fort William to Edmonton between 1874 and 1878.[27] The nascent community of Telegraph Flats was chosen by Ottawa as the site for the capital of the North-West Territories in 1876, renamed Battleford and the same year the NWMP established a divisional headquarters there with 11 men under the command of Superintendent James Walker.[28] Government buildings and a substantial fort for the police were constructed over the next few years. The population by 1881 had begun to shift from being dominated by single, male labourers and former HBC employees to families as settlers arrived to farm and to take advantage of the opportunities offered by government and the expected arrival of the railway. Not surprisingly, Battleford was the first town in the North-West Territories to have its own newspaper. Published at first jointly by Patrick Gammie Laurie and Daniel Livingstone Clink, the first issue appeared 25 August 1878.[29] The partnership did not last. Clink decided, shortly after the establishment of the paper, to focus on his other job as an Indian farm instructor, leaving Laurie as sole editor and publisher.

Apart from the *Saskatchewan Herald* there are two sources describing Battleford in the early 1880s. The first is W.B. MacDougall's, *Guide to Manitoba and the North-West,* which advertised itself as, "[a] concise compendium of valuable information and constituting the latest facts and figures of importance to the emigrant, capitalist, speculator, and tourist."[30] MacDougall described Battleford as a place expected to boom and therefore a good location in which to settle or invest in a business. In addition to the government facilities, police, telegraph and newspaper, he noted that the town boasted a school, churches of three denominations and steamer service on the river.[31] The second source is the Canadian census of 1881. That Battleford has a separate listing in the decennial census is a measure of its growing importance. Although the census does not give the population of the town, it does record the presence of 214 dwellings and 230 families.[32]

Once the labourers had completed the telegraph line from Winnipeg to Battleford, they began extending it to Hay Lakes, just south of Edmonton. In the fur trade era, Fort Edmonton was an important HBC post. In the early 1870s a few retired HBC employees began to take up land in the area. The climate and soil were well suited for agriculture and there were readily accessible coal seams along the banks of the North Saskatchewan.[33] The NWMP in the form of A Division under Inspector W.D. Jarvis arrived in October of 1874. After spending the winter at the HBC fort, the police moved a few kilometers downstream and built Fort Saskatchewan in the summer of 1875, but they remained a strong presence in Edmonton. That same summer the steamer *Northcote* began regular service to Winnipeg.[34]

Alex Taylor, the first telegraph operator in Edmonton, began to distribute a weekly bulletin of world news that came in over the wire. Frank Oliver, who had started up a dry goods store and cartage business in the community, had previous journalistic experience in Ontario. He and Taylor decided to upgrade the weekly report to a regular newspaper. When the press they ordered arrived in December of 1880, the *Edmonton Bulletin* began publication. Taylor left within a few months but Oliver developed the *Bulletin* into a strong voice for the interests of Edmonton.[35]

MacDougall's *Guide* portrayed Edmonton in 1880 as a village of about 200 persons composed mainly of retired HBC employees and 'English half-breeds.' It had a grist mill, post office, hotel and, like Battleford, three churches. The neighbouring community of St. Albert just to the north had about 700 French and Métis inhabitants in an area of excellent agricultural potential.[36] The 1881 census devotes only a page to Edmonton compared to 60 for Battleford but the census taker calculated the population as 500 adult males, 300 adult females and 230 families. The census taker noted the existence of 180 houses with another 150 in the process of construction.[37]

The prospect of a rapid transition from dependence on the fur trade to an agricultural economy for Battleford and Edmonton, with the accompanying boom that MacDougall confidently predicted, was abruptly dashed by the decision of the Canadian Pacific Railway in 1881 to move its main line to the south. Inevitably the decision meant that Battleford would cease to be the territorial capital, replaced by Regina in 1883. The editors of both the *Saskatchewan Herald* and the *Bulletin* knew what the decision meant for their communities and argued in vain against it. Battleford and Edmonton would have to wait another 20 years for their transcontinental rail connections.

The other two communities in the North-West Territories with newspapers, Fort Macleod and Calgary, were affected by the CPR decision in the opposite way. In October of 1874 the main body of the newly created NWMP arrived at the reported location of American whisky trading posts on the Oldman River. The fort they constructed that fall was named after the Assistant Commissioner of the force, James F. Macleod. The police immediately established communications with the nearest American settlement, Fort Benton, Montana. This was the only source of food and other supplies available. The police made arrangements with the I.G. Baker company to ship north the goods they needed by ox train. I.G. Baker soon established a store near the post and a new community began to take shape. Ft. Macleod remained the largest single NWMP post for the next several years and the presence of about 150 police at any one time attracted those who saw an opportunity in supplying their needs. The suitability of the country around Ft. Macleod for ranching was quickly recognized by some mounted policemen. Some began ranching while still in the force, others waited until their enlistments expired. By 1877 a few Americans and a larger number of Canadians were also getting into the cattle business.[38]

Calgary was founded at the junction of the Bow and Elbow rivers as an outpost of Ft. Macleod in 1875. When the police arrived the site was occupied by a couple of gold prospectors and a small Catholic mission with one resident priest.[39] Once again the police presence acted as a magnet for settlement. I.G. Baker set up a store and, a few years later than in Ft. Macleod, ranchers began to arrive. Neither Calgary nor Ft. Macleod were deemed worthy of mention in MacDougall's book. The 1881 census likewise does not mention the two communities. The census refers to a region defined by the Bow River and Treaty Seven. The census takers separated the area into two divisions. Though the geographic boundaries of the divisions are not specified, it seems likely that Ft. Macleod and Calgary were at the centre of the two. The census refers to businesses and there were no other sizable settlements in southern Alberta at that time. Division one contained a total of 400 people, only 50 of whom were women. The census taker for the area counted five shanties, 75 built houses and 20 under construction. Division Two had 580 people and 139 dwellings.[40]

Two developments in the early 1880s brought about an abrupt change in the fortunes of Calgary and, to a lesser degree, Ft. Macleod. In 1881 the Canadian government announced a program of leasing range land designed to promote the development of large scale cattle ranching. Prospective ranchers with capital to invest could lease up to 100,000 acres at an extremely low rate of $10.00/year for every 1000 acres.[41] Senator Matthew Cochrane, a wealthy cattle raiser from Quebec, was the first to take advantage of the new system. Others quickly followed and by the end of 1882 more than four million acres were under lease. The requirement to supply cattle under Treaties Six and Seven provided an immediate local market while the construction of the CPR promised access to the outside world. The decision to move the main line of the railway south boosted the ranching industry in both Ft. Macleod and Calgary, but the fact that the latter community was on the railway meant that it soon eclipsed its older rival as the urban headquarters for the big ranchers.[42]

As had happened a few years earlier in Battleford and Edmonton, the economic growth brought the establishment of newspapers. The Macleod *Gazette*, published by two retired mounted policemen, Charles Edward Dudley Wood and E.T. Saunders, started life on 1 July 1882. Following the pattern in the northern communities, Saunders shortly dropped out, leaving Wood in sole control.[43] The *Calgary Herald* began publication in August of 1883.

The period between the Canadian takeover of the Territories in 1870 and the North-West Rebellion in the spring of 1885 was to a considerable extent defined by growing ethnic tensions created by the transition from the old economy of the buffalo hunt and the fur trade and the new economy of farming and ranching. All four of the communities in our study sought to bring in the new agricultural regime as rapidly as possible, not only because it seemed to promise immediate speculative gains and greater long-term prosperity, but also because agriculture represented important cultural values like progress, modernity and Christianity. Because of decisions made elsewhere about the location of the railway, Ft. Macleod and Calgary were more successful in making the transition than their northern neighbours. As Arthur Ray has shown, the fur trade did not disappear after 1870. Even though world prices were very low in the 1870s the local fur trade economy in Edmonton and Battleford survived the decade and rebounded strongly in the 1880s.[44] The immediate effect of the new regime in this part of the region was the increase in competition for the Hudson's Bay Company. Individuals and small companies could and did offer direct cash payments for furs. This meant that the fur trade remained an important part of the local economy at a time when agriculture was growing very slowly. From the Native perspective the competition kept up prices and offered a greater variety of trade goods.

In the south, the only significant fur trade was that in buffalo robes. The disappearance of the great herds by the early 1880s brought a sudden and final end to that business. From the point of view of ranchers and farmers this was no great loss, indeed it was a positive advantage. Cattle and other domestic livestock could not share the range with bison. The necessary consequence of the end of the bison, as whites in southern Alberta saw it, was that the Native peoples who had depended on the animals must now settle on their reserves and learn agriculture or perish. To many, it did not matter a great deal which of those alternatives happened. The main thing was that the Native population not be allowed to stand in the way of progress. For Natives in the south there was nothing like the continuation

FIGURE 12-1

Newspaper Crime Reports and Actual Crime Rates

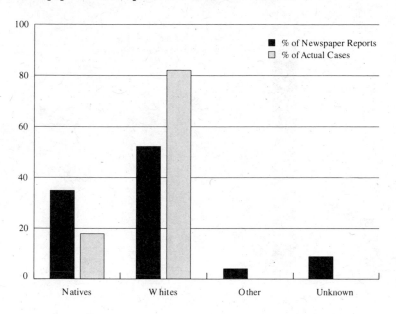

of the fur trade to ease the transition. The federal government provided farm instructors and agricultural assistance under the terms of Treaty Seven, but the fact remained that this was a total break with the traditional economy.

Because of the dominant cultural attitudes of all whites in the North-West Territories in this period there are some similarities in how the newspapers wrote about Native crime. Newspapers in all four communities exaggerated the amount of Native crime (or, if you prefer, played down the amount of white crime). We found a total of 512 reports of crime in the four newspapers between 25 August 1878 and 28 February 1885. Usually the newspapers identified the ethnicity of the defendant, making it possible to analyse the reports under the categories 'native' and 'white.' Of the 512 reports of crime, 179 referred to Natives and 268 to whites. There were 21 references to persons identified as black or Métis which we designated 'other' since neither of these would have been viewed at the time as belonging to either of our major categories. An argument could be made for including the Métis in the 'native' category but we chose not to do so since they were treated differently by the Canadian government at the time and certainly saw themselves as a distinct people. In the 44 cases for which we were unable to discern the defendant's ethnicity, the report was classified

FIGURE 12–2
Types of Crime Reports

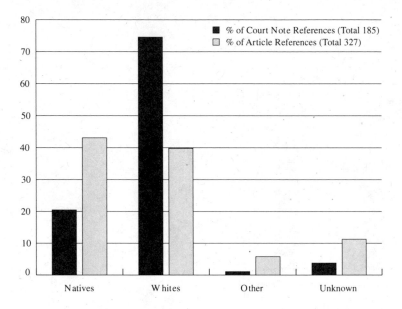

as 'unknown.' In some cases the only information the newspaper gave was a French surname. Since we could not be sure whether the individual was French-Canadian or Métis these were put into the 'unknown' category.

Our earlier study of crime rates in the North-West Territories based on court case returns showed that, with approximately equal populations, Natives were the defendants in 17.9 percent of the cases while whites accounted for 82.1 percent.[45] As Figure 12–1 demonstrates, the newspapers exaggerated the criminal activities of Natives and underestimated those of whites. Newspapers were the only public medium of the period and it seems obvious that readers would get the message from them that Native crime rates were more than double actual rates.

A closer look at how newspapers wrote about crime suggests that the perception of Native crime was even more exaggerated. The press handled crime reports in two quite distinct ways; articles ranging in length from a couple of paragraphs to several pages and brief court case notes of one to five lines. Articles attempted to include the complete history of the crime, or as much of it as the reporter could uncover. There were no legal restraints preventing the papers from identifying suspects as perpetrators and they were not hesitant to speculate about motives and character. Alleged crimi-

FIGURE 12-3
Types of Crime Reports, *Saskatchewan Herald*

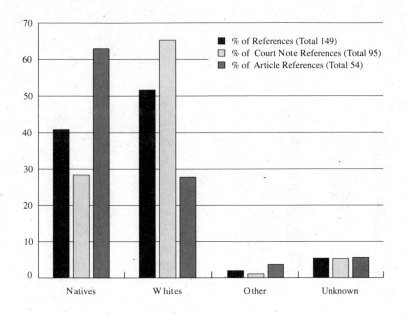

FIGURE 12-4
Types of Crime Reports, *Edmonton Bulletin*

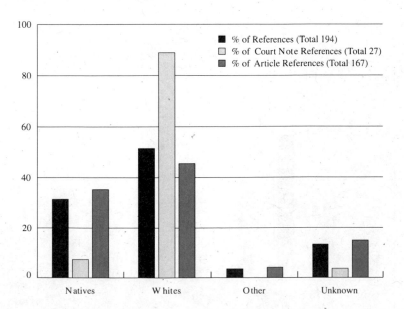

FIGURE 12-5

Types of Crime Reports, Macleod *Gazette*

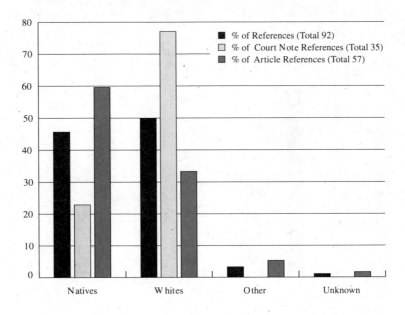

- % of References (Total 92)
- % of Court Note References (Total 35)
- % of Article References (Total 57)

FIGURE 12-6

Types of Crime Reports, *Calgary Herald*

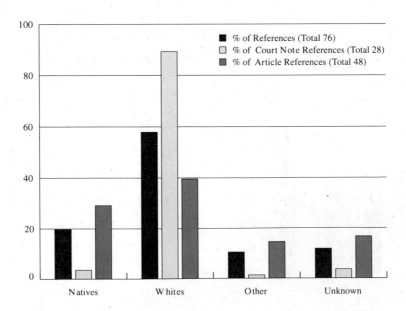

- % of References (Total 76)
- % of Court Note References (Total 28)
- % of Article References (Total 48)

FIGURE 12-7
Ethnic Population of NWT 1885

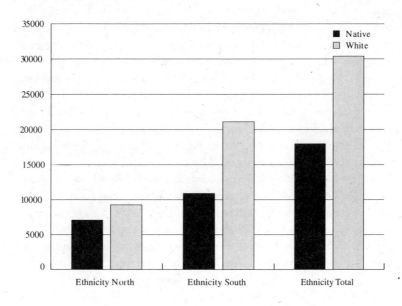

FIGURE 12-8
Crime Rates — North and South

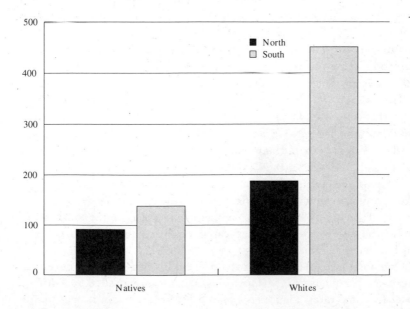

nals were often described in highly coloured and sensationalistic prose. Court case notes listed only basic details such as the date of the trial, the name of the accused, type of crime and the outcome of the hearing. The difference in impact on the reader of a full-page story and a one or two line report, usually buried in the second or third page, hardly requires comment. As Figure 12–2 indicates, the neutral medium of the court case notes presents a reasonably accurate picture of the extent of Native criminal activity. The percentage of this kind of reference was 20.5, only slightly higher than the actual figure of 17.9. In contrast 43.1 percent of the articles dealt with crimes by Natives, almost two and a half times the real rate.

When this approach is applied to the individual newspapers, local and regional patterns begin to emerge. The most prominent difference is between the northern and southern communities. While all four newspapers obviously created a higher perception of Native crime rates than was actually the case, the effect was stronger in the southern papers. In the Macleod *Gazette* and the *Calgary Herald*, between 80 and 90 percent of the references to Native crime took the form of articles while less than half the references to whites were in articles. The northern papers featured Native crime less prominently. In the *Saskatchewan Herald* just about half the total references to crime took the form of articles and a much smaller percentage of references to whites were in this form. Thus, while the proportion of articles on Natives is more than double that for whites, because this type of report occurred less often than in the southern papers, the appearance of bias would have been less pronounced. In the *Edmonton Bulletin* articles on white crime were proportionately much greater, resulting in coverage that gave a closer approximation of the real crime rates for both groups. The bias of coverage in the *Calgary Herald* is less obvious than in the Macleod *Gazette* but the Calgary figures may be unreliable due to the shorter period of publication and the smaller total numbers of reports.

There is a qualitative north-south difference in the reporting of Native crime that is less easy to quantify but is no less significant. The Battleford and Edmonton papers were more likely than their southern counterparts to take the trouble to find and report the names of Native offenders. The *Gazette* and the *Calgary Herald*, in contrast, often referred to Natives who ended up in the courts as 'bucks' or 'squaws.' The identification of individual names has an important effect on the reader. One who is named is a person, with a unique life history, family ties and a place in the community. Those who are relegated to faceless categories by contemptuous labels are much easier to marginalise.

One possible explanation for the differences in newspaper coverage between the two parts of the Territories is that it might reflect real differences in crime rates. Figure 12–8 shows that there were, in fact, quite

FIGURE 12-9
Distribution of NWMP 1878–1885

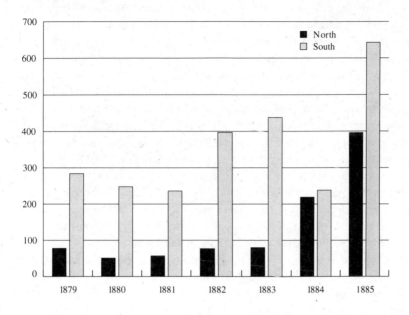

striking differences in the amount of crime per capita for both Natives and whites between north and south. Natives in the south had crime rates approximately double those in the north. Interestingly, whites in the south were convicted of crimes at a rate nearly three times that in the north. This is probably in part due to what criminologists have long recognized as the 'police effect;' larger numbers of police tend to produce higher crime statistics. As Figure 12–9 shows, there were substantially larger numbers of police in the south than the north. It would be a mistake to dismiss the entire difference on these grounds, however. The larger numbers of NWMP stationed in the south corresponded to a larger population (Figure 12–7). Indeed in 1884 and 1885, there were probably more police per capita in the north than the south.

It would thus appear that the southern area was a significantly more violent and crime-prone society than the north in this period. This is true for both the Native and white parts of the population and it is more or less what the economic and social differences between the two parts of the region would lead us to expect. For Natives the continuation of their place in the fur trade economy undoubtedly meant that their traditional institutions of dispute resolution continued to function. In the south the abrupt economic change probably began a breakdown of Native institutions of justice earlier. For whites the explanation is that economic boom areas attract disproportionate numbers of young, single males. These are the people in almost every society who commit the highest number of crimes.

The final question that needs to be addressed is how much, if any, the biases in newspaper coverage affected how the justice system treated Native people? Is there a connection between public opinion and the way laws are enforced? It is a given that people from different ethnic groups distrust each other to varying degrees. Criminologists, especially in the United States, have devoted a great deal of attention to exploring the extent to which the criminal justice system translates that distrust into the unequal treatment of minorities. The results of this research show a wide variation from apparently very pronounced bias to none; illustrating, at least, how complex the question is. Common sense would suggest that if those with discretionary power in the legal system believe that a group of people is more prone to crime and violence than others, members of that group will be treated more harshly. At one level our findings seem to support such a conclusion. The measurably harsher attitudes to natives in the south correlate to higher native crime rates. But the fact that white crime rates in the south are higher yet indicates that more fundamental influences are involved .

It is clear from the study that those people who lived on the northern prairies in this period imagined their communities differently than did their counterparts in the south. There the Cree and other First Nations inhabitants were considered part of the community, even if individuals might commit crimes. In Calgary and Fort Macleod the Native people were thought of almost exclusively as impediments to the rapid development of the country. As the Macleod *Gazette* put it in 1883,

> It has just come to this, these Indians must be kept on their reserves, else the indignant stockmen will some day catch the red rascals and make such an example of them, that the noble red man will think h—l's a poppin, besides a probable attack of kink in the back of the neck, and we can't say that we should greatly blame them either. That a lot of dirty thieving, lazy ruffians should be allowed to go where they will, carrying the latest in improved weapons, when there is no game in the country, seems absurd.[46]

The other difference that is quite striking is that the northern newspapers were prepared to try to see things from the Native point of view. In 1882 the *Edmonton Bulletin* published a lengthy interview with Peter Erasmus concerning the activities of Big Bear's Cree who had been accused of horse stealing.

In regard to horse stealing Big Bear said: "It is true our young men steal but they were not the first to commence it. Both Blackfeet and Americans from across the line were the first to take our horses and continued to do so for two years. Thinking that the white men would get our horses we kept quiet. We complained to them here as well as at other places and all the satisfaction we got was that we were told to 'Go and do the same.' When they told us that I said to them 'Do you want us to break the peace? I thought your office here was of another character, I see plainly you do not want to help us.' Our young men heard this and this is how so much stealing has been done."[47]

This kind of report was not to be found in the southern newspapers. Those who wrote and read the *Gazette* and the *Calgary Herald* imagined a society in which the Native population was invisibly ensconced on their reserves.

Notes

1. R.C. Macleod and Heather Rollason, "'Restrain the Lawless Savages': Native Defendants in the Criminal Courts of the North West Territories, 1878–1885," *Journal of Historical Sociology* 10, no. 2 (June 1997): 157–84.
2. T. Thorner, "The Not So Peaceable Kingdom: Crime and Criminal Justice in Frontier Calgary," in A.W. Rasporich and Henry Klassen, eds., *Frontier Calgary: Town, City and Region, 1875–1914* (Calgary: University of Calgary Press, 1975).
3. Clare V. McKanna, Jr., "Murderers All: The Treatment of Indian Defendants in Arizona Territory, 1880–1912," *American Indian Quarterly* 17 (Summer 1993): 359–69.
4. Ibid.
5. Ibid., 362.
6. Erica Pasmeny, "Aboriginal Offenders: Victims of Policing and Society," *Saskatchewan Law Review* 56 (1992): 403–25.
7. Ibid., 405.
8. Paula Mallea, *Aboriginal Law: Apartheid in Canada?* (Brandon: Bearpaw Publishers, 1994).
9. Ibid., 23.
10. Sidney L. Harring, "'The Liberal Treatment of Indians': Native People in Nineteenth Century Canadian Law," *Saskatchewan Law Review* 56 (1992): 297–371.
11. Ibid., 348.
12. Ibid., 324.
13. Ibid., 347.
14. Macleod and Rollason, 157–83.
15. See ibid., 161–63 for an explanation of the methodology.

16. Olive Dickason, *Canada's First Nations: A History of Founding Peoples from the Earliest Times,* 2nd ed. (Toronto: Oxford University Press, 1992), 281; B.O.K. Reeves, "'Kootsisaw': Calgary Before the Canadians," in A.W. Rasporich and Henry Klassen, eds., *Frontier Calgary: Town, City and Region, 1875–1914* (Calgary: University of Calgary Press, 1975), 20.

17. J.G. MacGregor, *Edmonton: A History* (Edmonton: Hurtig, 1967), 78.

18. Alfred Crosby, *The Columbian Exchange: Biological and Cultural Consequences of 1492* (Wesport: Greenwood Publishing, 1972); J.W. Verano and D.H. Ubelaker, eds., *Disease and Demography in the Americas* (Washington, D.C.: Smithsonian Institution Press, 1992).

19. John L. Tobias, "The Subjugation of the Plains Cree," *Canadian Historical Review* 64 (1983): 522.

20. Gerhard Ens, *Homeland to Hinterland: The Changing Worlds of the Red River Métis in the Nineteenth Century* (Toronto: University of Toronto Press, 1996), 172–73.

21. Theodore Binnema, "Old Swan, Big Man and the Siksika Bands, 1794–1815," *Canadian Historical Review* 77, 1 (March, 1996): 1–32.

22. William B. Henderson, *Native Customs and the Law* (Ottawa: Research Branch, Corporate Policy, Indian and Northern Affairs, 1985), 17.

23. Ibid., 31–32.

24. Hugh A. Dempsey, *Red Crow, Warrior Chief* (Saskatoon: Western Producer Prairie Books, 1980), 82–83; R.C. Macleod, *The North West Mounted Police and Law Enforcement, 1873–1905* (Toronto: University of Toronto Press, 1976), 21–37.

25. R.C. Macleod, "James Morrow Walsh," *Dictionary of Canadian Biography*, Vol. XII, 1071–72.

26. Arlean McPherson, *The Battlefords: A History* (Saskatoon: City of Battleford, 1967), i, 19, 22.

27. David R. Richeson, "The Telegraph and Community Formation in the North-West Territories," in John E. Foster, ed., *The Developing West: Essays on Canadian History in Honor of Lewis H. Thomas* (Edmonton: University of Alberta Press, 1983), 140.

28. John Peter Turner, *The North West Mounted Police, 1873–1893*, Vol. I (Ottawa: King's Printer, 1950), 308.

29. William L. Clink, ed., *Early Battleford: Selections from the Saskatchewan Herald, 1878–1900* (Willowdale, Ontario: William L. Clink, 1985), v.

30. W.B. MacDougall, *MacDougall's Guide to Manitoba and the North-West* (Winnipeg, 1880), 51.

31. Ibid.

32. Canada, *Census, 1881*, microform copy, marker 322. It is important to note that one of the features of the census in this period is that the kind of information recorded varied with the individual census taker. For some communities the census takers recorded only total population, for others statistics on gender, ethnicity and religion were collected.

33. Gilbert Stelter, "What Kind of City is Edmonton?" in Bob Hesketh and Frances Swyripa, eds., *Edmonton: The Life of a City* (Edmonton: NeWest Publishers, 1995), 10; Geoff Ironside, "Slopes and Shafts," in Bob Hesketh and Frances Swyripa, eds., *Edmonton: The Life of a City* (Edmonton: NeWest Publishers, 1995), 194–95.

34. MacGregor, *Edmonton*, 81–82.

35. Janne Switzer, "Edmonton's Forgotten Man—Alexander Taylor," in Bob Hesketh and Frances Swyripa, eds., *Edmonton: The Life of a City* (Edmonton: NeWest Publishers, 1995), 51.

36. *Guide*, 52.

37. *Census, 1881*, marker 324.

38. David H. Breen, *The Canadian Prairie West and the Ranching Frontier 1874–1924* (Toronto: University of Toronto Press, 1983), 8–9.

39. Grant MacEwan, "The Town-Country Background at Calgary," in A.W. Rasporich and Henry Klassen, eds., *Frontier Calgary: Town, City and Region, 1875–1914* (Calgary: University of Calgary Press, 1975), 2–3.

40. *Census, 1881*, marker 324.

41. Breen, *Ranching Frontier*, 16–19.

42. L.G. Thomas, "The Rancher and the City: Calgary and the Cattlemen, 1883–1914," in Patrick A. Dunae, ed., *Ranchers' Legacy: Alberta Essays by Lewis G. Thomas* (Edmonton: University of Alberta Press, 1986), 39–61.

43. Richard Burke, "Transportation and Communication," *Fort Macleod—Our Colourful Past: A History of the Town of Fort Macleod, from 1874–1924* (Fort Macleod: Fort Macleod Historical Book Committee, 1977), 80.

44. Arthur J. Ray, *The Canadian Fur Trade in the Industrial Age* (Toronto: University of Toronto Press, 1990), 26–29.

45. Macleod and Rollason, 164–70.

46. Macleod *Gazette*, 14 May 1883.

47. *Edmonton Bulletin*, 14 October 1882.

APPENDIX

Updating *The Collected Writings of Louis Riel*

THOMAS FLANAGAN & GLEN CAMPBELL

IN 1985, the University of Alberta Press published a historical-critical edition of *The Collected Writings of Louis Riel,* consisting of four volumes of texts plus a reference volume.[1] John Foster played a significant role as a consultant although he did not edit any of the volumes. While the Louis Riel Project was based at the University of Alberta, the volume editors all came from other institutions, so John had to assist with the important task of coordination and liaison between project personnel and the host university. He especially was involved with the Press during this time, as he was chairman of their publications committee. Thus, it is fitting that a *Festschrift* honouring John's many contributions to the writing of Canadian history should include a chapter updating Riel's *Collected Writings.*

The Riel Project was largely successful in its goal of collecting and editing all of Louis Riel's known writings. However, it was discovered shortly after publication that two letters from Riel to Donald A. Smith, Lord Strathcona, had been missed.[2] Also overlooked in the John A. Macdonald Papers was a petition from Riel to A.G. Archibald, the Lieutenant-Governor of Manitoba; the *Collected Writings* had printed only a draft found in Riel's own papers.[3] No other omissions have come to light, but two hitherto unknown letters from Riel, plus a fragment of English poetry, have also been discovered.[4] The three omissions and the three new discoveries are presented here together with editorial commentary to explain their historical significance. In the years since 1985, several other Riel holographs have also been discovered that are of less historiographic importance because their contents were already known. These are briefly discussed at the end of this appendix.

Nothing presented here will revolutionize the study of Louis Riel, but it is still worthwhile to make these documents known. History is a cumulative discipline that steadily advances through uncovering and exploiting new sources of information. With their pioneering use of documentary, oral, and archeological sources about native peoples in Canada, John Foster and his students have exemplified this aspect of the historian's craft. We are proud to be in their company in this volume.

ᑫᐤ Louis Riel to Donald A. Smith, 23 September 1870

This letter is printed in Beckles Willson's biography of Donald A. Smith.[5] Willson, a prominent journalist and author who had earlier written *The Great Company,* a history of the Hudson's Bay Company, had the cooperation of Smith's heirs, who gave him access to his papers.[6] The original cannot now be found among the Smith papers in the National Archives of Canada or the Hudson's Bay Company Archives. Probably it has been destroyed, along with the second letter to Smith also included here; Smith's heirs burned most of his papers after Willson published his book.[7]

When he wrote this letter, Riel had taken refuge with the Oblate priest J.-M.-J. Lefloch in the village of St. Joseph, Dakota Territory, in the United States. The letter gives Riel's account of why he left Fort Garry on 23 August 1870, just before the arrival of Colonel Wolseley's expeditionary force. At Wolseley's request, Smith had governed Manitoba for eight days until the official governor, Adams G. Archibald, arrived on 2 September. After Archibald took up his office, Smith remained involved in attempts to bring peace to the troubled affairs of Red River. Although earlier biographers of Riel have used Willson's book, they have not drawn attention to this letter. That Riel wrote directly to Smith at this juncture suggests that they had already developed a personal relationship.

Dakotah, U.S.,
September 23d, 1870.

Sir,—
We can never forget the gross violation of country and property in which we have been treated. Expecting something far different from an honourable British officer, I, as the chosen head of the Provisional Government, which has administered here on behalf of the Dominion of Canada since last November, expected to receive Colonel Wolseley and Governor Archibald at Fort Garry and formally deliver up to the Government. My guards were instructed to fire a salute and the enclosed address was to have been read to the appointed Governor in token of submission to the régime of Canada, with our rights and liberties guaranteed to us. The proceeding was denied to us, and we fortunately had news of the temper of injustice animating the new

coming[8] and if we are said to have fled it was to save ourselves and them from bloodshed.

You have already ascertained the truth of this from your people here, namely, that we remained at our posts until the last moment, only from a sense of the duty we owed our people.

Yours respectfully,
Louis Riel.

ᕈᕈ Petition to Adams G. Archibald, 9 December 1871

The text printed below is from the petition in Riel's own handwriting, found in the papers of Sir John A. Macdonald. Although this manuscript remained undiscovered during the work of the Riel Project, an earlier draft was found and printed in the *Collected Writings*.[9] The wording of this version is slightly improved over the rough draft but not significantly different in content. However, it includes the names of 26 signatories not found in the draft.

The invasion of Riel's home described in this petition was an attempt to execute an arrest warrant issued by a local magistrate on 23 November 1871. In February 1872, in order to avoid further attempts at arrest, Riel and Ambroise Lépine left for St. Paul, Minnesota. A translation follows the original French letter.

St Vital 9 Décembre 1871

A son excellence
    Le lieutenant gouverneur
        de Manitoba

Excellence,

Hier soir, vers 9 heures, 8 Décembre 1871, des hommes sont venus troubler la demeure de Monsieur Louis Riel à St Vital, en y entrant effrontément, et se disant porteurs d'un warrant pour l'arrêter à cause des troubles qui ont eu lieu à la Rivière Rouge pendant l'hiver 1869–70. Et après avoir constaté l'absence de Monsieur Louis Riel, ces hommes ont montré des armes à feu dont ils se sont servi pour menacer les femmes de la maison, l'un de ces hommes jurant qu'il tuerait ce soir-là Louis Riel pour satisfaire sa vengeance. Comme des warrants levés contre ceux qui ont pris part aux troubles de 1869–70 sont injustes à cause des arrangements implicites qui ont eu lieu [entre] le Canada et ce pays; et comme, à part cela, les violences que ces hommes ont faites dans la maison d'un citoyen paisible, sont, pour ne pas dire plus, tout à fait hors de place, nous prions avec beaucoup de respect votre excellence d'empêcher que de pareilles injustices ne se renouvellent contre qui que ce soit de ceux qui se sont trouvés mêlés aux troubles 1869–70. Nous les personnes avoisinant la demeure de Monsieur Louis Riel ayant été plus particulièrement témoins des violences que les hommes susdits y ont exercés, nous hâtons de communiquer respectueusement à votre excellence la présente requête; espérons que le gouvernement prendra les mesures nécessaires pour amener à punition les coupables.

Humblement
de votre excellence
les dévoués serviteurs
nous nous souscrivons

Pierre Parenteau, Père
Jos. St Germain
Louis Desrivières
Matthias Norman
Ch. Neault
Paul Proulx
Benj. Neault
François Marion
Pierre St Germain
Pierre Parenteau, fils
François Frébucher
Bapt. Boudreau

Bapt. Laderoute
Louis Dumas
Matthias Sansregret
Jos. Neault
Amable Gaudry, fils
Godefroy Neault
Maxime Lépine
André Neault
J.B. Ritchot
Pierre Sauvé
Joseph Sauvé
Louis Carrière
Damas Carrière
François Poitras[10]

TRANSLATION

St. Vital 9 December 1871

To His Excellency
    The Lieutenant Governor
        of Manitoba

Excellency,
Yesterday evening, about 9 o'clock, 8 December 1871, some men came to disturb the place of residence of Mr. Louis Riel in Saint Vital, entering brazenly, purportedly carrying a warrant for his arrest because of the public disturbances that took place in Red River during the

winter of 1869–70. And after determining the absence of Mr. Louis Riel, these men drew firearms which they used to threaten the women of the house, one of these men swearing that he would kill Louis Riel that same evening in order to seek revenge. As warrants issued against those who took part in the disturbances of 1869–70 are unjust because of the implicit arrangements made between Canada and this country; and besides that, the acts of violence committed by these men in the house of a law-abiding citizen are, to say the least, completely out of line, we respectfully ask your Excellency to make sure that similar injustices do not occur again against those who found themselves involved in the 1869–70 disturbances. We, the people neighbouring the residence of Mr. Louis Riel, having been moreover witnesses of the acts of violence committed by the above-mentioned men, respectfully expedite the present request to your Excellency, hoping that the Government will take the necessary steps to punish the guilty.

We, the devoted servants
of Your Excellency,
humbly sign our names[11]

Pierre Parenteau, Père	Bapt. Laderoute
Jos. St Germain	Louis Dumas
Louis Desrivières	Matthias Sansregret
Matthias Norman	Jos. Neault
Ch. Neault	Amable Gaudry, fils
Paul Proulx	Godefroy Neault
Benj. Neault	Maxime Lépine
François Marion	André Neault
Pierre St Germain	J.B. Ritchot
Pierre Parenteau, fils	Pierre Sauvé
François Frébucher	Joseph Sauvé
Bapt. Boudreau	Louis Carrière
	Damas Carrière
	François Poitras

❧ Louis Riel to Joseph-Eugène Antoine, 2 January 1874

This letter is located in the Archives Oblates de Montréal, dossier Manitoba et le Nord-Ouest: Affaire Louis Riel et le Soulèvement des Métis. It was discovered by the University of Lethbridge historian Raymond Huel while doing research for a biography of Archbishop A.-A. Taché. Dr. Huel was also a member of the Louis Riel project and edited the first volume of Riel's *Collected Writings*.

Riel wrote this letter from the Oblate house in Plattsburgh, New York, where he was convalescing after a period of ill health. Around the same time, he also sent New Year's greetings to Archbishop A.-A. Taché and Bishop Ignace Bourget.[12] The recipient of this letter, the Reverend Joseph-Eugène Antoine, was the provincial superior of the Oblates in Quebec. The letter shows that Riel must have stayed with the Oblates in Montreal at some point in November-December 1873. Like the other letters Riel wrote in this period, this one is *en deuil* in memory of his sister Marie, who had died 25 January 1873.

2 Janvier 1874

Mon Très Révérend Père,
   Je vous souhaite une bonne et heureuse année, à vous et à toute votre sainte communauté.
   Que Dieu, pendant cette nouvelle année, bénisse votre santé. Qu'il réjouissse votre bon coeur en favorisant d'avantage l'ordre nouveau mais déjà si prospère qui a l'honneur de vous avoir pour Provincial dans cette partie de l'Amérique.
   Mon Père, je tâche de mettre à profit les avantages de votre hospitalité. Suivant votre désir et votre généreuse invitation, je me suis mis ici comme chez moi.
   En dépit de la sollicitude des Révérends Pères, des tours de voiture que je prends très souvent avec le gentil petit cheval de la maison, et malgré les soins de la bonne Henriette, ma santé s'affaiblit.
   Il est donc à propos, mon Père, que je vous demande à ce sujet un petit souvenir devant le bon Dieu.

> Veuillez agréer l'expression de mon
> respect et de mes bons sentiments.
> Votre serviteur dévoué
> Louis Riel

TRANSLATION

2 January, 1874

Very Reverend Father,
   I wish you and your holy community a good and happy New Year.
   May God bless your health during this new year. May He gladden your good heart in looking even more kindly on the new but already prosperous order which has the honour of having you as provincial in this part of America.

Father, I'm trying to make the most of your hospitality. Following your wish and your generous invitation, I've made myself at home.

Despite the constant attention of the Reverend Fathers, of the carriage rides that I often take with the order's nice little horse, and in spite of the care offered by the good Henriette,[13] my health is weakening.

Therefore, Father, I'm asking that you pray for me.

> Yours respectfully,
> Your devoted servant,
> Louis Riel

๙ Louis Riel to Donald A. Smith, 12 February 1874

This letter is also printed in Willson's biography of Smith.[14] The abrupt opening and closing, without any of the usual formalities, suggest that the text printed by Willson was an extract from a longer letter.

Riel wrote this letter at a critical point in his career. On the following day, 13 February 1874, he would be elected for the second time as MP for Provencher.[15] On 14 February, Ambroise Lépine would appear before Judge E.B. Wood in Winnipeg on the charge of having murdered Thomas Scott; an arrest warrant for the same charge was also outstanding against Riel.

In writing to Smith, Riel was addressing a fellow member of the House of Commons. Smith was the MP for Selkirk and, like Riel, would be re-elected on 13 February. While hardly a supporter of Riel, he favoured an amnesty for all involved in the Red River uprising as a way of bringing peace to the country. Moreover, he had been involved behind the scenes with Riel and Lépine in 1872, in conveying money to them so they could leave Canada and go to St. Paul, Minnesota.[16] In writing this letter, which expresses his view of Thomas Scott's execution, Riel was trying to encourage Smith's efforts in favour of an amnesty. In fact, on 1 April 1874, Smith moved in the House of Commons that a committee of nine be appointed to investigate the amnesty question, and he became chairman of the committee.[17]

Incidentally, the letter shows that Riel was in the Dakota Territory on 12 February 1874. The existing literature places Riel in Montreal at this time, but it is not surprising that he would have made a trip to St. Joseph to be in closer touch with the attempts of his supporters to secure his re-election in Provencher.

Dakotah Territory,
February 12th, 1874.

You yourself will recall that when, on February 17th [1870], Boulton was captured with 47 men, bearing arms under the walls of Fort Garry,

Scott was amongst them, and was thus captured a second time. When imprisoned for his attempt against the authority of the Provisional Government he was distinguished by his violent conduct. On March 1st, Scott and a fellow-prisoner forced the doors of their prison and called upon the rest to attack the guards. This time he was overpowered, but the Métis, knowing how kindly Scott had been treated, were so indignant at this violence that they laid hands upon him and would have avenged themselves on the spot, but for the intervention of one of the Council. It was lastly demanded that this man should be brought before a court-martial. I intervened, he was summoned before me, when I urged him to behave himself, and to promise that he would give no more trouble, so as to justify me in clemency, and in refusing to yield to the express wishes of the Métis. Scott replied with contempt and refused to behave himself as a prisoner, so that he was seen to constitute a danger to the government and the peace of the Settlement.

Consequently, as every means had failed, the 3d of March, this man Scott was brought before the Council of War. Witnesses having been heard made oath, he was solemnly convicted of treason and sentenced to death. On the following day he paid the penalty of plotting and taking arms against the government and against public peace and order under the authority which the people had confided in us.

❧ Louis Riel to Julie Riel, 9 August 1882

This letter was acquired in 1988 by the National Archives of Canada.[18] Small excerpts printed in 1943 in the Ottawa newspaper *Le Droit* were included in Riel's *Collected Writings*,[19] but this is the first time that the whole text has been made available to scholars. Unfortunately, a large tear at one corner affects all four pages of the folded manuscript. Reconstructed readings are interpolated in square brackets.

This letter is of particular biographical interest because Riel had not written to his mother or brothers and sisters for more than two years.[20] The reason for his long silence is not known; curiously, Riel mentions and apologizes for it in his letter, but does not explain it. There were two other times in his life when he cut himself off from his family: 1866–68, after his plan to marry Marie-Julie Guernon failed; and 1876, when he was committed to mental hospitals in Quebec.[21] In both periods Riel must have felt that his family would not be proud of the situation he was in. He may have felt the same way in the years 1880–81, when he gave up his plan to marry Evelina Barnabé, the sister of a priest, and turned instead to Marguerite Monette dite Bellehumeur, the daughter of a buffalo hunter.

[Ca]rroll 9 Août 1882
Madame V[eu]ve Riel

Bien chère Maman,

Je me fais souvent le reproche de ne pas vous écrire. [Je ne] fais pas bien de vous laisser dans l'incertitude [sur mo]n compte. Pardonnez-moi d'avoir été presque [deux a]ns sans vous envoyer de mes nouvelles. Vous [ête]s sans doute inquiète à mon sujet. Et de mon côté, je suis inquiet par rapport à vous, à mes frères, à mes soeurs et à toute la famille. Et croyez-moi bien que si mon silence m'a donné l'air de vous mettre en oubli, je n'ai pas laissé écouler un seul jour cependant sans prier le bon Dieu pour vous.

Je dois vous apprendre, bien chère maman, que je suis marié depuis plus d'un an. J'ai pris une fille de la Prairie du cheval blanc, une Métisse canadienne française. Elle s'appelle Marguerite. Elle est fille aînée d'un Monsieur que vous n'avez jamais, je pense bien, ni vu ni connu: Jean Monette dit Bellehumeur est son nom.

Je n'ai fait bénir mon marriage[22] que cet [an au mois] de mars. Car par ici nous n'avons pas [l'occasion] de voir le prêtre plus qu'une fois par [an].

Ma femme m'a donné un petit garçon [qui est] bien portant, Dieu Merci. Il a trois m[ois au]jourd'hui. Il est venu au monde le neuf [mai]. Et comme les prêtres qui sont le plus p[rès se] trouvent à 150 milles d'ici, je n'ai pa[s eu] la consolation de le faire baptiser [mais il a] été ondoyé. Et en attendant la céré[monie mê]me, sa mère lui fait faire voir a[u moins le] signe de la croix, en faisant mouvoir [sa petite] main droite et en disant les paroles pour lui. Elle aimerait tant que son enfant fût chrétien de désir.

Bien chère maman, je suis toujours pauvre mais pas plus découragé qu'avant. A mon retour de Miles City, il y a deux ans, j'ai perdu d'un seul coup trois chevaux qui sont morts de la gourme. Peu de temps après, les Sioux m'en ont volé deux. Et l'été passé, la gourme m'en a encore tué deux autres de file. Dans l'hiver, j'avais été bien malade, de sorte que les profits que j'avais faits en arrivant ici, ont été bien partis.

[Dans ce] temps-ci, je bûche du bois de corde. Et je le [vends] aux bateaux à vapeur qui voyagent sur [le M]issouri.

[Mon] beau-père a passé une partie de l'été avec moi. [Il a] eu le malheur de perdre, dans le mois passé, un [de ses] enfants, un petit garçon de cinq ans. {Aprè]s cet accident, il est parti pour la prairie avec [toute s]a famille. Il est campé à vingt milles d'ici. Le [buffa]lo est tout autour de nous. On se procure de la [viande] fraîche aisément. J'ai encore un cheval. Il est bon [à la c]harette[23] et il réjouit[24] le buffalo.

Mon beau-père [l'a] emmené. Et il m'apporte de la viande de temps en temps. La semaine passée, il nous a apporté des dépouilles, des bosses et des langues. Nous en aurions eu pour en grand mois: malheureusement je n'ai pas bien salé cette viande, elle s'est gâtée. Il a fallu toute la jetter.[25] Et ces jours-ci nous sommes à la viande sèche. J'ai hâte que les chasseurs viennent nous faire une autre visite.

Il y a encore assez de buffalo pour que la chasse paye deux ou trois ans de plus. Et je pense qu'après cela, durant quelques années, il en restera tout juste pour entretenir les chasseurs, de sorte que nous espérons avoir du buffalo encore sept ou huit ans. Ces pauvres animaux essayent de se garder et se conserver en s'enfonçant dans les buttes et les mauvaises terres et c'est assez difficile de l[es trouver quand ils] y sont. Comme le Montana est un vrai [paradis] nous sommes portés à croire que les dernie[rs buffalos] devront se faire tuer dans nos environs, e[t les Métis(?), les] derniers qui goûteront leur bonne viande.

Voilà deux semaines de file que des acheteurs [de scrips] viennent me voir. Ils ont tous deux off[ert—] piastres pour celui de ma femme. Je n'ai [pas permis] qu'elle le donnât. J'ai la désignation de son [terrain. Je] serais content, si Joseph ou Alexandre avait [pu al]ler voir Monsieur Roger Goulet; et lui demandait [s'il pouvait] dire combien de piastres l'arpent, ce scrip pou[rrait se] vendre, s'il était vendu non pas aux spécul[ateurs mais] à un émigrant qui voudrait s'y établir. [On pourrait] avec le revenu de ce scrip s'acheter des b[êtes à cornes.] Il y a des gens par ici qui ont jusqu'à [——] bêtes à corne.[26] On peut avoir des jeune[s vaches avec] leurs veaux pour 15.00 quinze pia[stres. Une vache] faite coûte 25.00 vingt-cinq piastres avec un veau.[27] Ces prix [sont?] le prix des vaches farouches ou marronnes. Les vaches dompt-tées partent de vingt-cinq piastres et montent jusqu'à quarante. Il faut que j'essaye à élever des animaux domestiques. Et je serai bien content si je voyais[28] un bon jour, arriver[29] des gens de St Vital avec le plan de s'établir par ici. Nous tâcherions de nous placer proche à proche.

J'ai fait ce printemps une grosse entreprise. Je ne puis dire[30] si elle réussira. Il y a dans le Montana une compagnie riche et puissante qui a versé de la boisson aux sauvages tout l'hiver. C'est défendu par la loi. Je l'ai attaquée. J'ai de bonnes preuves en ma possession. Et si je réussis le moindrement elle pourra bien avoir à payer des mille piastres. Priez que le Bon Dieu me fasse réussir.[31]

Chère maman, je vous embrasse en vous souhaitant tout le bien qu'on peut souhaiter à une mère tendrement aimée. J'embrasse mes frères, beaux frères, soeurs et belles soeurs peut-être. J'ai écrit un petit mot à notre bien aimée Marguerite Marie, l'année passée. Ecrivez—

moi des nouvelles au loin. Mes respects à tous nos parents et amis. Votre fils, [Louis Riel].

Si vous écrivez à notre chère Soeur [Marguerite-Marie, dites-lui que je ne] l'oublie pas une seule journée [et que je l'aime] avec toute l'affection d'un frère.

Mes respects à ma tante Lacyprès, à Nanin, Charles, Paul et tous les autres. Est-ce vrai qu'Alexandre est marié? J'avais entendu dire qu'il avait pris une demoiselle Poitras. Si c'est le cas, nos femmes sont parentes.

Dites-moi ce qu'est devenue la terre de Cyrille Dumas. Comment cela a-t-il tourné? Le capitaine Alleyn, un acheteur de scrips de la montagne Cyprès va peut-être aller voir mon frère Joseph. Qu'il fasse attention aux questions de cet homme. Et surtout qu'il ne lui vende pas[32] les droits que [nous] avons [——] être s[——] sur [——] Lor[ette?] êtes [——] .

Donnez-moi des nouvelles de mon [——]

De mon oncle Romain, d'Augu[ste ——].

TRANSLATION

Carroll 9 August 1882
Madame Riel, widow

Dearest Mother,

I get upset with myself for not writing you. It's not right that I leave you in a state of uncertainty about me. Forgive me for having let almost two years pass without sending you any news. You've doubtless been worried about me. As for me, I've been worried about you, my brothers, my sisters, about all the family. And believe me, even though my silence makes it appear that I've forgotten you, I haven't let a day go by without praying to the Good Lord for you. I must tell you, dearest Mother, that I have been married for more than a year.[33] I married a girl from White Horse Plains, a French-Canadian Métisse. Her name is Marguerite. She's the eldest daughter of a man that you have never, I believe, met nor heard of: his name is Jean Monette, called Bellehumeur.

I had my marriage blessed only this year, in March.[34] Because around here, we don't see the priest more than once a year. My wife has given me a little boy who is, thank God, healthy. He is three months old today. He was born on May 9.[35] And as the nearest priests are 150 miles from here, I haven't had the consolation of having him [properly] baptised but he has been provisionally baptised. And while waiting for the ceremony, his mother lets him see the sign of the cross, moves his little right hand and says the words for him. She would like her child to be Christian by choice.

Dearest Mother, I am still poor but no more discouraged than before. Upon my return from Miles City, two years ago, I lost in one single blow, three horses who died from strangles.[36] Not long after that, the Sioux stole another two. And last summer, strangles killed another two, one right after the other. In the winter, I was very sick, so that any profits I had made, quickly disappeared.

These days, I've been cutting timber and selling it to the steam boats which travel the Missouri.

My father-in-law spent part of the summer with me. He had the misfortune of losing, last month, one of his children, a little five-year old boy. After this accident, he left for the prairie with his family. He is camped twenty miles from here. The buffalo are all around us. One can get fresh meat easily. I still have one horse. He's good pulling the wagon and he enjoys hunting buffalo. My father-in-law took him. And he brings me meat from time to time. Last week, he brought us some left-over meat, humps and tongues. We would have had enough for a whole month: unfortunately I didn't salt the meat well enough and it rotted. I had to throw it all out. These days we're eating dried meat. I can't wait for the hunters to pay us another visit.

There are enough buffalo for hunting to last another two or three years. And I think that after that, for several years, there will be just enough to sustain the hunters, so that we can expect to have buffalo for another seven or eight years.[37] These poor animals try to protect and conserve themselves by heading into the hills and badlands and it's difficult to find them when they're there. As Montana is a true paradise, we are led to believe that the last buffalo will be killed in our vicinity, and we will be the last to taste their good meat.

Two weeks in a row scrip buyers have come to see me. Both of them offered [——] dollars for my wife's.[38] I didn't allow her to give it up. I have the legal description of her land.[39] I would be happy if Joseph or Alexandre had been able to go and see Mr. Roger Goulet;[40] and had asked him to tell me how many dollars an acre this scrip would get, if it were sold not to speculators but to an immigrant who would like to settle there. With the revenue from this scrip one could buy himself some cattle. There are people around here who have up to [——] cattle. One can have young cows with their calves for fifteen dollars. A grown cow with a calf costs twenty-five dollars. These prices [are?] the price of wild or runaway cows. Domesticated cows start at twenty-five dollars and go up to forty. I have to try and raise domestic animals.

And I would be happy to see one of these days people from St. Vital arriving with the plan of settling around here. We would try to find a home nearby.

This Spring I undertook something big. I can't say if it will succeed. There is in Montana a rich and powerful company that has been selling liquor to the Indians all winter long. This is against the law. I attacked it. I have in my possession strong evidence against it. And if I'm successful in any way, it will have to pay thousands of dollars. Pray that the Good Lord allows me to succeed.[41]

Dear Mama, I embrace you wishing you all the love that one can have for one's mother. I embrace my brothers, brothers-in-law, sisters and perhaps sisters-in-law.[42] I wrote a short note to our dearly beloved Marguerite Marie last year.[43] Send me news from afar. My regards to all our relatives and friends. Your son, [Louis Riel].

If you write to our dear Sister Marguerite-Marie, tell her that not a day goes by without me thinking about her and that I love her with all my brotherly affection.

My respects to my Aunt Lacyprès, to Nanin, Charles, Paul and all the others.[44] Is it true that Alexandre is married? I had heard that he had married one of the Poitras girls. If that's the case, our wives are related.[45]

Tell me what has become of Cyrille Dumas' land.[46] How did that turn out? Captain Alleyn, a scrip buyer from Cypress Hills, is perhaps going to go and see my brother Joseph.[47] He should pay attention to this man's questions. And above all, he should not sell him the rights that we have [——] to be [——] on [——] Lor[ette?] [you] are [——].[48]

Give me news of my [——]
Of my Uncle Romain, of Auguste [——][49]

❧ Poem, November 1885

These lines, in Riel's handwriting,[50] are a variant of a verse published in *The Collected Writings of Louis Riel*.[51] Like the verse, they would have been composed by the Métis leader while he was awaiting execution in Regina jail:

The reading of the scripture
And of its Holy letter
Helps on greatly: that is sure.
But without the practice
Of its divine maxims
Such reading goes too short a piece.

The works first: then the hymns!
    Louis "David" Riel.

❧ Other Documents

A number of Riel manuscripts discovered since 1985 do not need to be included here because their contents are already known through printed or facsimile versions. They are itemized below and briefly discussed for the benefit of future researchers who may some day be interested in consulting the original manuscripts.

- In 1986, the Provincial Archives of Alberta identified a Riel holograph among a miscellaneous collection of material transferred in 1975 by the Legislative Library.[52] The document is a partial draft in Riel's hand of the autobiographical notes published in the Toronto *Globe*, 17 November 1885.[53] It was apparently saved by Laurent Legoff, an Oblate missionary stationed in Alberta at various times from 1882 to 1923. Father Legoff probably got it from fellow Oblate Alexis André, Riel's confessor at Regina, who had custody of Riel's prison papers and transmitted the autobiographical notes to the *Globe* for publication.

    This draft is very close to the published version except for differences in the dates of three events in Riel's life:

Event	GLOBE Date	Manuscript Date
Enters Grey Nuns' school	1 April 1853	1 September 1853
Enters Christian Brothers' school	1 December 1854	1 September 1854
Arrives in Montreal	1 July 1858	5 July 1858

    Probably, the dates in Riel's draft are correct and the discrepancies with the *Globe* version stem from printing errors.

- Another interesting discovery is a holograph version of Riel's last will and testament, dated 6 November 1885, acquired by the National Archives of Canada in 1991.[54] This text was published in two slightly different versions by the French-Canadian press shortly after Riel's execution, but the original remained unknown until acquired by the NAC. It matches the version published in *Le Manitoba* rather than that printed in the Quebec newspapers,[55] but there may also have been another redaction that went to Quebec. Riel was in the habit of rewriting important compositions, often several times.

- In 1991, the media reported the discovery in North Vancouver of a 26-page "poetic saga by Louis Riel."[56] It was written in a leather-bound ledger also containing minutes of meetings of L'Académie Canadienne de Québec, 1860–65. The owner, Louise Painchaud, said she had inherited the book from her family. Some of her ancestors, she also said, had been involved in operating the Beauport mental asylum, where Riel was confined from 1876 to 1878. A facsimile copy of these 26 pages turned out to be already in the possession of the National Archives of Canada because J.R. Painchaud had loaned the same ledger to the Archives for copying in 1960. The poems appear to be authentic and were thus included in the *Collected Writings*, but the pages written in the ledger are not in the hand of Riel.

- In 1995, the Provincial Archives of Manitoba paid $4000 in the auction market for the last letter of Louis Riel to his wife, 5 October 1885.[57] As with his will, the contents of the text were already in the public domain.[58] The text of the original manuscript agrees exactly with the version published in the *Collected Writings*.

Notes

1. George F.G. Stanley, gen. ed., *The Collected Writings of Louis Riel*, 5 vols. Vol. I, *1861–1875*, Raymond Huel; Vol. II, *1875–1884*, Gilles Martel; Vol. III, *1884–1885*, Thomas Flanagan, Vol. IV, *Poetry*, Glen Campbell; Vol. V, *Reference*, George F.G. Stanley, Thomas Flanagan, Claude Rocan (Edmonton: University of Alberta Press, 1985). Hereafter cited as *CW.*

2. Allen Ronaghan brought to the attention of George Stanley, general editor of the Riel Project, the existence of the letter of Riel to Smith, 23 September 1870 The letter of 12 February 1874, which is in the American but not the British edition of Beckles Willson, *The Life of Lord Strathcona and Mount Royal*, was discovered by Thomas Flanagan while double-checking Ronaghan's reference.

3. Brought to the attention of Glen Campbell by Lionel Dorge.

4. Louis Riel to Joseph-Eugène Antoine, 2 January 1874, Archives Oblates de Montréal, dossier Manitoba et le Nord-Ouest. Discovered by Raymond Huel. Louis Riel to Julie Riel, 9 August 1882. National Archives of Canada, news release, 12 September 1988. It is now in NAC, MG 27, I F3 Louis Riel, vol. 4. The fragment of poetry is printed as a photographic copy in Pierre Alfred Charlebois, *La Vie de Louis Riel* (Montréal: VLB Éditeur, 1991), 193. It is not in the earlier English version of Charlebois's book, *The Life of Louis Riel* (Toronto: NC Press, 1975).

5. Beckles Willson, *The Life of Lord Strathcona and Mount Royal* (Boston and New York: Houghton Mifflin Company, 1915; 2 vols.), 1: 392. With trivial differences of spelling and punctuation, it is also in the British edition of the same book (London: Cassell and Company, 1915), 260.

6. Ibid., 1: x-xi.

7. Donna McDonald, *Lord Strathcona: A Biography of Donald Alexander Smith* (Toronto: Dundurn, 1996), 8

8. Willson added [*sic*] at this point, but there is no obvious error in the text.

9. The printed version is in *CW*, 1–107 The manuscript version is in the Sir John A. Macdonald Papers, NAC, MG 26A, 78079–92.

10. At the top of this page, another hand has written "Pierre Parenteau AM / 9 Déc 1871," and an indecipherable word over the name of François Marion.

11. Of the 26 names, all but two can be identified in the tables in D.N. Sprague and R.P. Frye, *The Genealogy of the First Metis Nation* (Winnipeg: Pemmican Publications, 1983). Fifteen were neighbours of Riel in St. Vital; five were from one area of St. Norbert (lots 134–153); two were from St. Boniface; and two were from St. François-Xavier. Most were young men in their late teens or early twenties. December 8 is a Catholic holy day, the Feast of the Immaculate Conception. Those signatories who did not actually live in St. Vital may have been there visiting relatives or attending a celebration of some sort.

12. *CW*, 1–186, 1–187.

13. Unidentified.

14. More precisely, it is printed as n. 1 in 1: 359 of the American edition. It is not included in the British edition (it would belong on p. 237). The American and British editions are not quite identical, perhaps from having been copy-edited by different publishers.

15. Certificat d'élection à la Chambre des Communes, 13 February 1874, Riel, *CW*, A1–012

16. Willson, *The Life of Lord Strathcona*, 1: 453–56.

17. Ibid., 495–96.

18. National Archives of Canada, news release, 12 September 1988. It is now in NAC, MG 27, I F3 Louis Riel, vol. 4.

19. Riel, *CW*, 2–095 and 2–096.

20. Louis Riel to Joseph Riel, July 1880, *CW*, 2–072, is the last known preceding letter. His brother Joseph wrote to Louis on 22 May 1881 that he had heard nothing from him since August 1880. PAM, MG 3 D 2. His sister Henriette Poitras wrote in the summer of 1882 that they had not heard from Louis in more than two years. Draft reply to Evelina Barnabé, PAM, MG 3 D 2.

21. Thomas Flanagan, *Louis 'David' Riel: 'Prophet of the New World'* (Toronto: University of Toronto Press, 1979), 26, 70.

22. *Sic.*

23. *Sic.*

24. The *Dictionnaire Historique de la langue française* (Paris: Robert, 1992), 1075, notes that in Canadian French, the verb "jouir" maintained its former meaning of "to take advantage of, or pleasure in, one's company" "Réjouir le buffalo" would therefore mean that the horse enjoys being with the buffalo, i.e., he enjoys the hunt.

25. *Sic.*

26. *Sic.*

27. The words "avec un veau" were added by Riel in superscript.

28. Following "voyais," Riel has crossed out: "quelque bon quelqu'un de St Vital quelque".

29. Following "arriver," Riel has crossed out "quelques".

30. Following "dire," Riel has crossed out "s'il".

31. The paragraphs that follow have been written vertically on the left-hand sides of all four pages of the letter, beginning on the last page and ending on the first. On page 2, Riel writes also in the space at the top of the page.

32. Following "pas," Riel has crossed out "de terre".

33. Louis married Marguerite *à la mode du pays* 28 April 1881 on the Musselshell River in Montana, *CW,* 2–085, note 1.

34. Louis and Marguerite were legally married by Father Joseph Damiani, S.J., in Carroll, Montana, on 9 March 1882 The marriage certificate is in *CW,* 2–085.

35. Jean Riel was born 9 May 1882 near Carroll *CW,* 2–096, note 2.

36. Streptococcus equi, inflammation of equine respiratory tract.

37. In fact, commercial buffalo hunting ended in Montana in 1883–84. Frank Gilbert Roe, *The North American Buffalo: A Critical Study of the Species in its Wild State,* 2nd ed. (Toronto: University of Toronto Press, 1970), 461–62.

38. Riel is using the term "scrip" loosely. Marguerite, as the child of a Metis head of family, qualified for an allotment of 240 acres of land under s. 31 of the Manitoba Act, 1870. Thomas Flanagan, "Louis Riel's Land Claims," *Manitoba History* 21 (Spring 1991): 9. Scrip was a different legal instrument that could be redeemed for Dominion Lands; it was distributed to the Metis parents.

39. Riel must mean the legal description of Marguerite's allotment, which was located in Sections 10 & 15, Township 10, Range 10 West of the 5th Meridian. Ibid., 12, note 97. Allotments were more valuable once the legal description was known. See Thomas Flanagan and Gerhard Ens, "Metis Land Grants in Manitoba: A Statistical Study," *Histoire sociale/Social History* 27 (1994): 83–84.

40. Joseph and Alexandre Riel were Louis's two younger brothers Roger Goulet was a Metis surveyor from St. Boniface who at this time was working at the Dominion Lands office in Winnipeg. He would have been knowledgeable about land prices.

41. Riel tried to prosecute Simon Pepin and the C.A. Broadwater Company for liquor sales to Indians. See *CW,* 2–086. He wrote to Joseph Riel on 1 April 1884 that the legal action had failed. *CW,* 2–124.

42. Because he had been out of touch for two years, Riel could not know whether his younger brothers might have married in the meantime. Joseph, who was born in 1857, was looking for a wife as early as 1879 (Louis Riel to Julie Riel, 2 May 1879, *CW,* 2–064). He finally married Eléonore Poitras on 30 April 1884. Alexandre, who was born in 1863, married Elise Poitras 14 June 1881, so Riel did have one sister-in-law at the time of this letter.

43. Marguerite-Marie is Louis's sister Sara, a Grey Nun, whose religious name was Sister Marguerite-Marie. The letter Riel refers to has not been found.

44. "Tante Lacyprès" is Josephte Lagimodière (1810–1897), the wife of Amable Nault and the mother of André Nault. She was called "Lacyprès" because she was born in the Cypress Hills. "Nanin" was a family name for her son André Nault, who also lived in St. Vital. "Charles" is Charles Sauvé, another neighbour in St. Vital. "Paul" is Paul Proulx, a French-Canadian living in St. Vital. He was married to Angélique Nault, a cousin of Riel.

45. They would have been second cousins. François Poitras, the father of Alexandre's wife Elise Poitras, was the son of Henri Poitras and Marguerite Grant. Jean-Baptiste Monette, the father of Riel's wife Marguerite, was the son of Michel Monette and

Marguerite Grant. Marguerite Grant must have been married twice, although the details are unknown.

46. Riel refers to lot 533, which he had bought from Cyrille Dumas in the early 1870s and resold to Joseph Delorme in 1878 The paperwork was more or less completed in 1879. Maybe a few details had been left for Joseph to deal with. See Flanagan, "Louis Riel's Land Claims," 5–7.

47. This must be the same person as the Captain Allen mentioned in a batch of papers that Riel took to Winnipeg in June 1883, hoping to sell some land and scrip on behalf of Metis living in Montana. One paper states: "He [J.B. Falcon] sold his allotment to Capt. Allen." *CW*, 2–106.

48. Riel had a land claim near the village of Lorette, but little is known about it See Flanagan, "Louis Riel's Land Claims," 4, 8.

49. "Mon oncle Romain" is Romain Lagimodière, a brother of Riel's mother "Auguste" is perhaps Auguste Harrison, a cousin of Riel who lived in Ste. Anne des Chênes.

50. The poem is printed as a photographic copy in Pierre Alfred Charlebois, *La Vie de Louis Riel* (Montréal: VLB Éditeur, 1991), 193. It is not in the earlier English version of Charlebois's book, *The Life of Louis Riel* (Toronto: NC Press, 1975). Although Charlebois calls the poem "the last words written by Louis Riel," there is really no proof for that assertion.

51. The verse is addressed to Charles Slater, a 22-year old officer of the North-West Mounted Police who was stationed in Regina at the time of Riel's imprisonment:

Charles Slater
The reading
Of the scripture, and its letter
Must lead us well to practicing
Before we can expect to reap
CW, 4–156

52. PAA, 75583.

53. *CW*, 3–149, *CW*, 3–147, is another partial handwritten draft, and *CW*, 3–148 is a draft in typescript form.

54. NAC, MG 27, I F3 Louis Riel, vol 4. See Michel Wyczynski, "Louis Riel's Will," *The Archivist* 20 (1) (1993): 23–25.

55. The version from *Le Manitoba* is printed in *CW*, 3–122; the other is in *CW*, 3–123. The differences between them are purely stylistic.

56. "Poetic saga said to be the Riel thing," *Globe and Mail*, 22 October 1991.

57. "1885 Louis Riel Letter Auctioned for $4,000," *Globe and Mail*, 21 October 1995.

58. *CW*, 3–110.